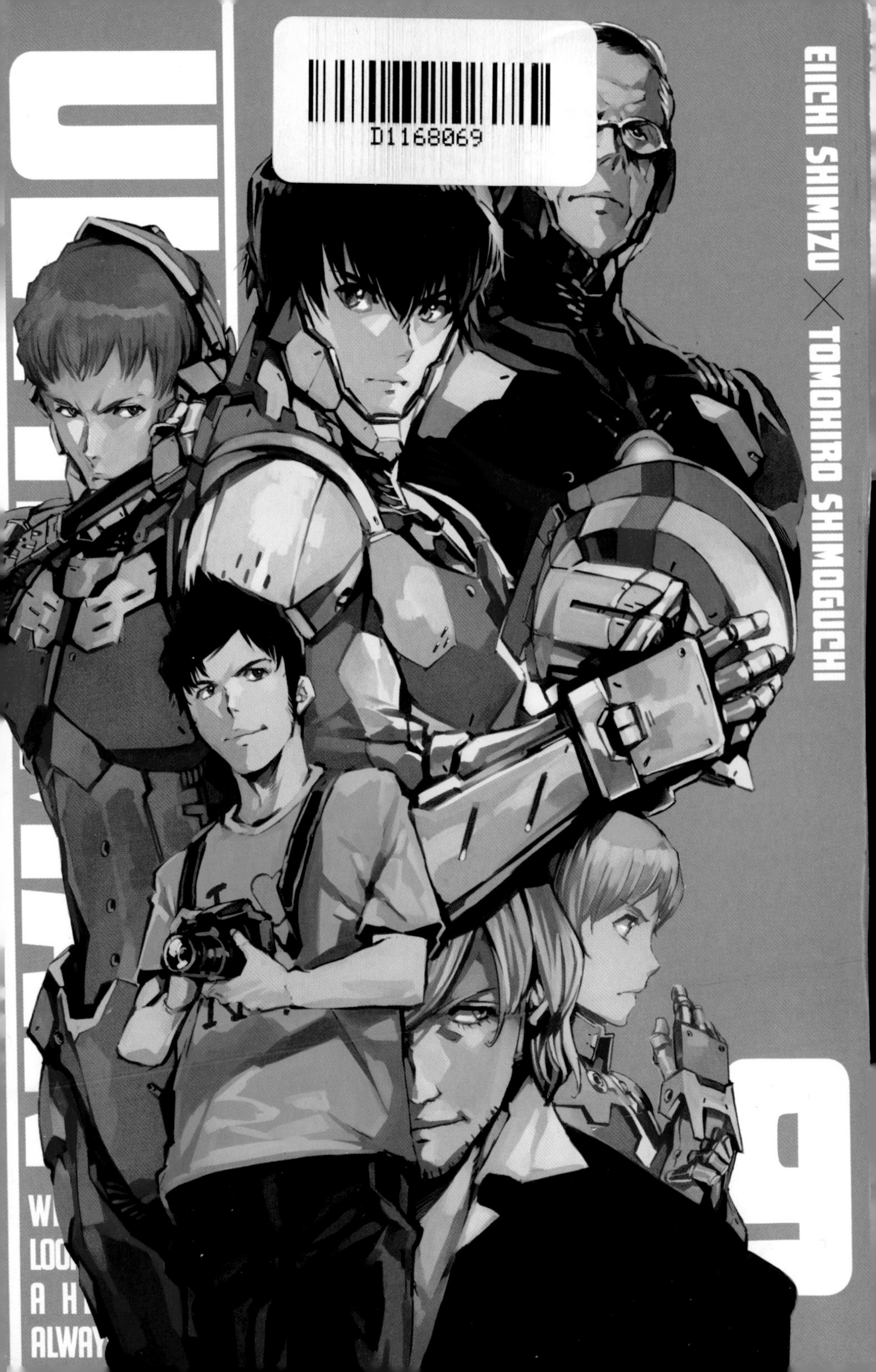
EIICHI SHIMIZU × TOMOHIRO SHIMOGUCHI
9

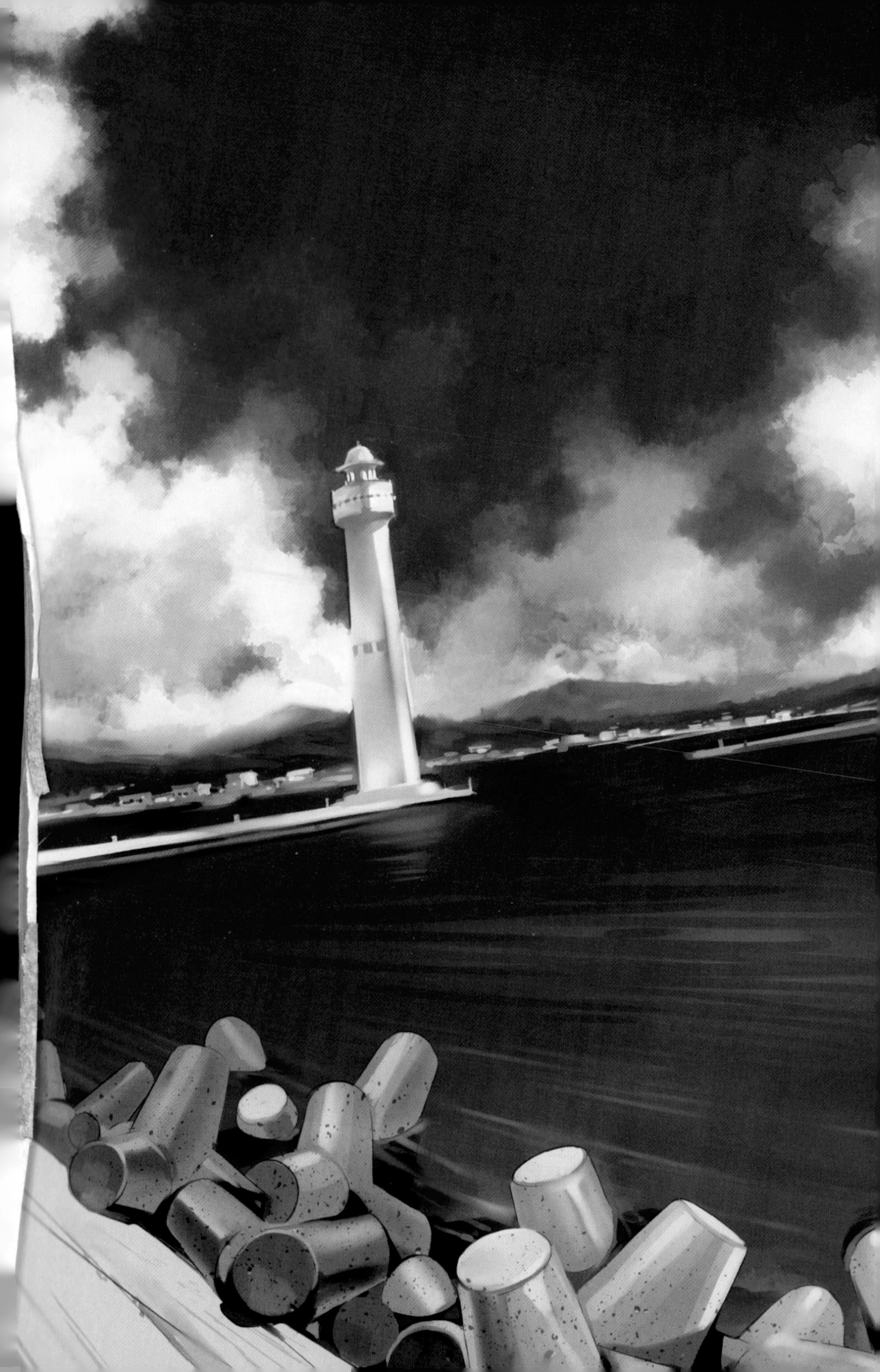

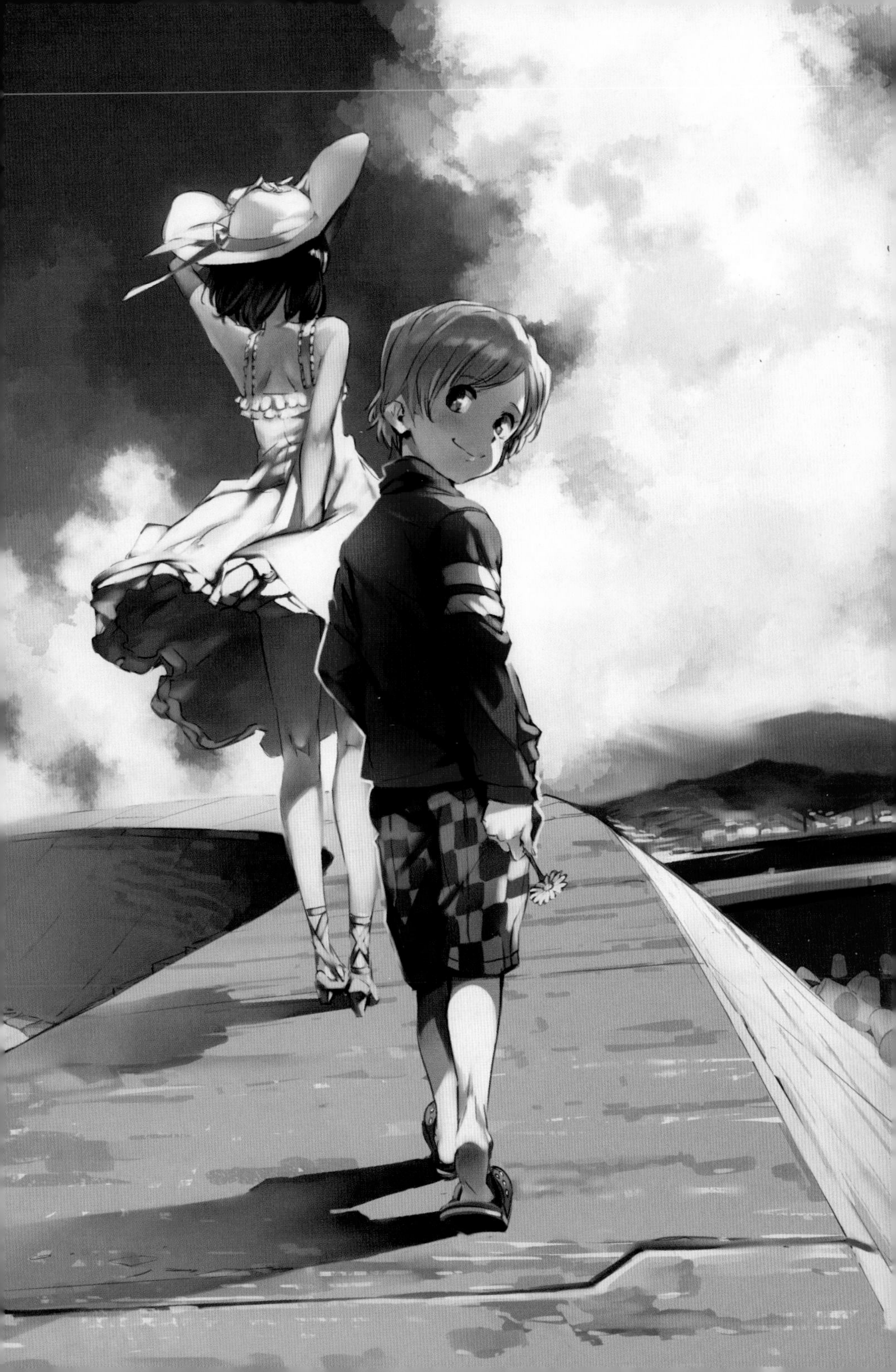

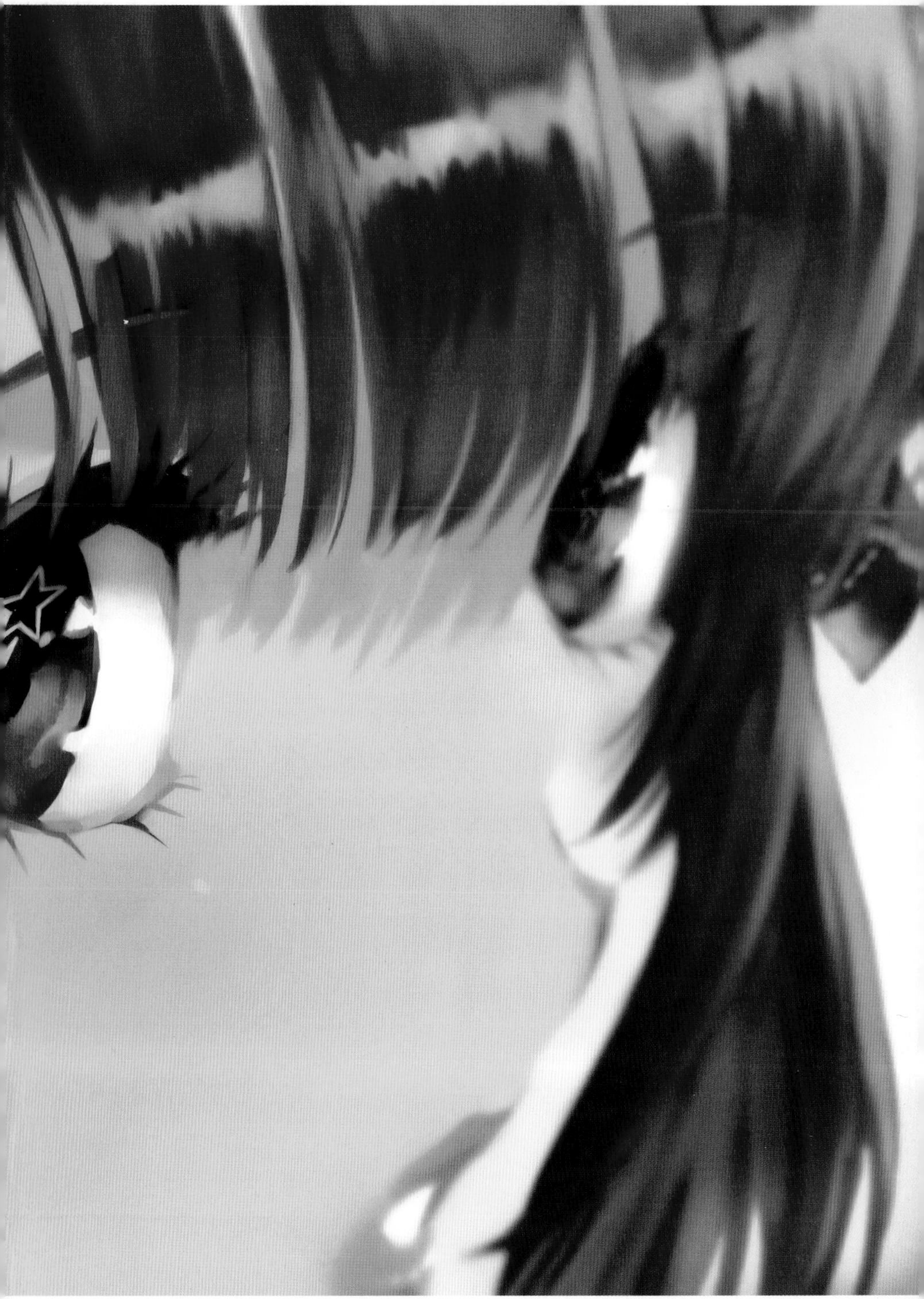

THIS IS THE BEGINNING OF A NEW AGE.

CONTENTS

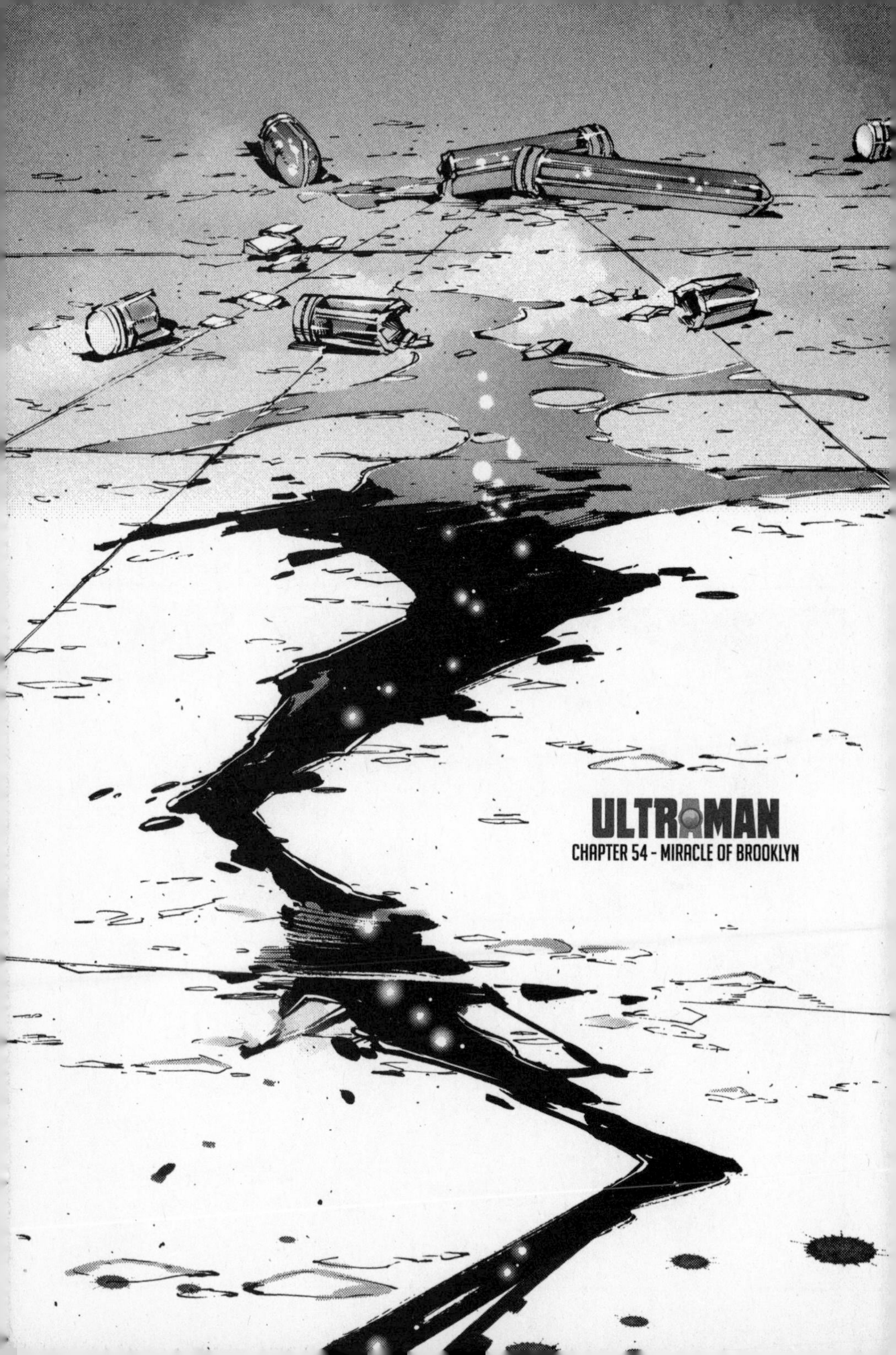
ULTRAMAN
CHAPTER 54 - MIRACLE OF BROOKLYN

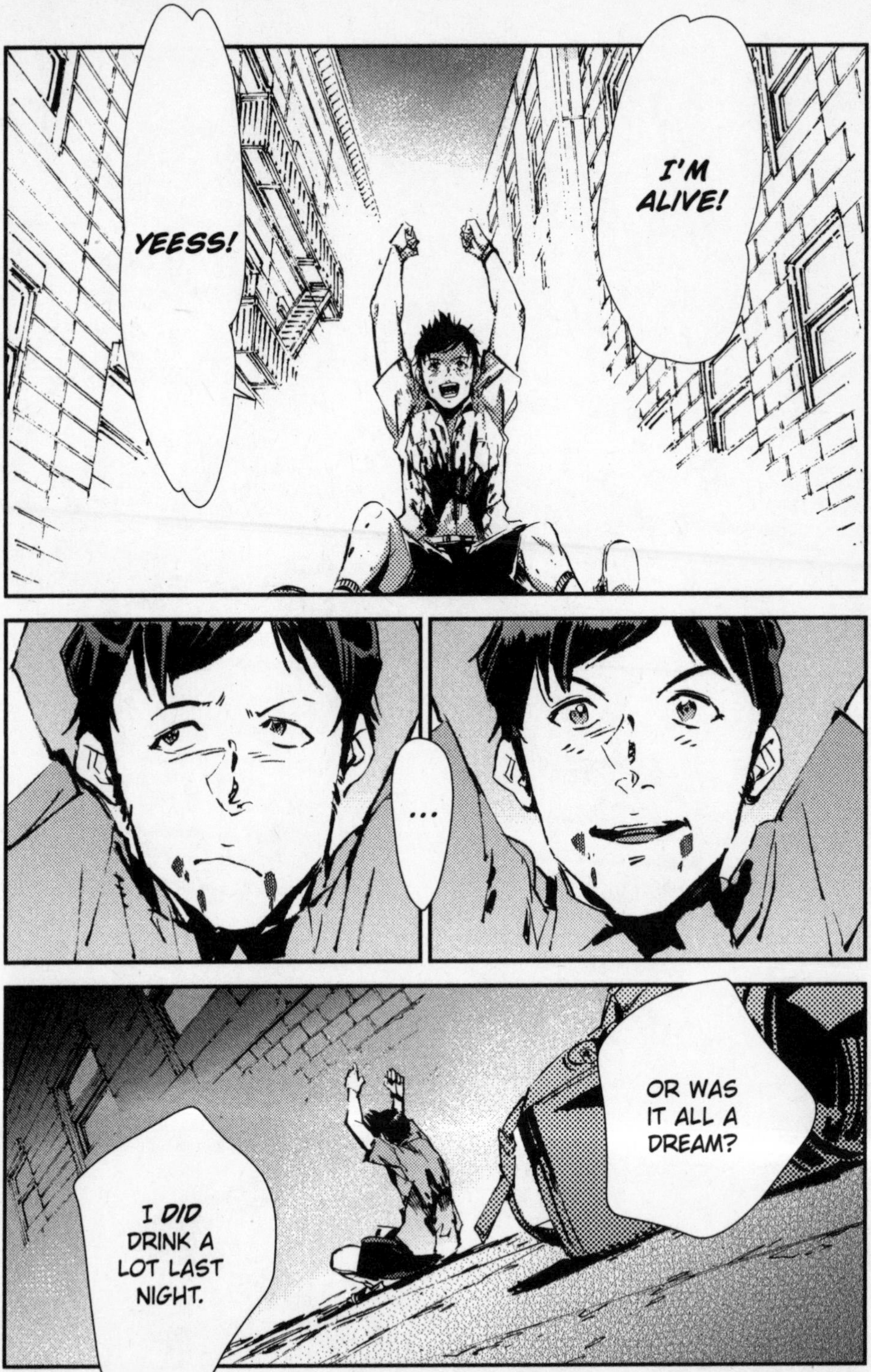
I'M ALIVE!
YEESS!
...
OR WAS IT ALL A DREAM?
I *DID* DRINK A LOT LAST NIGHT.

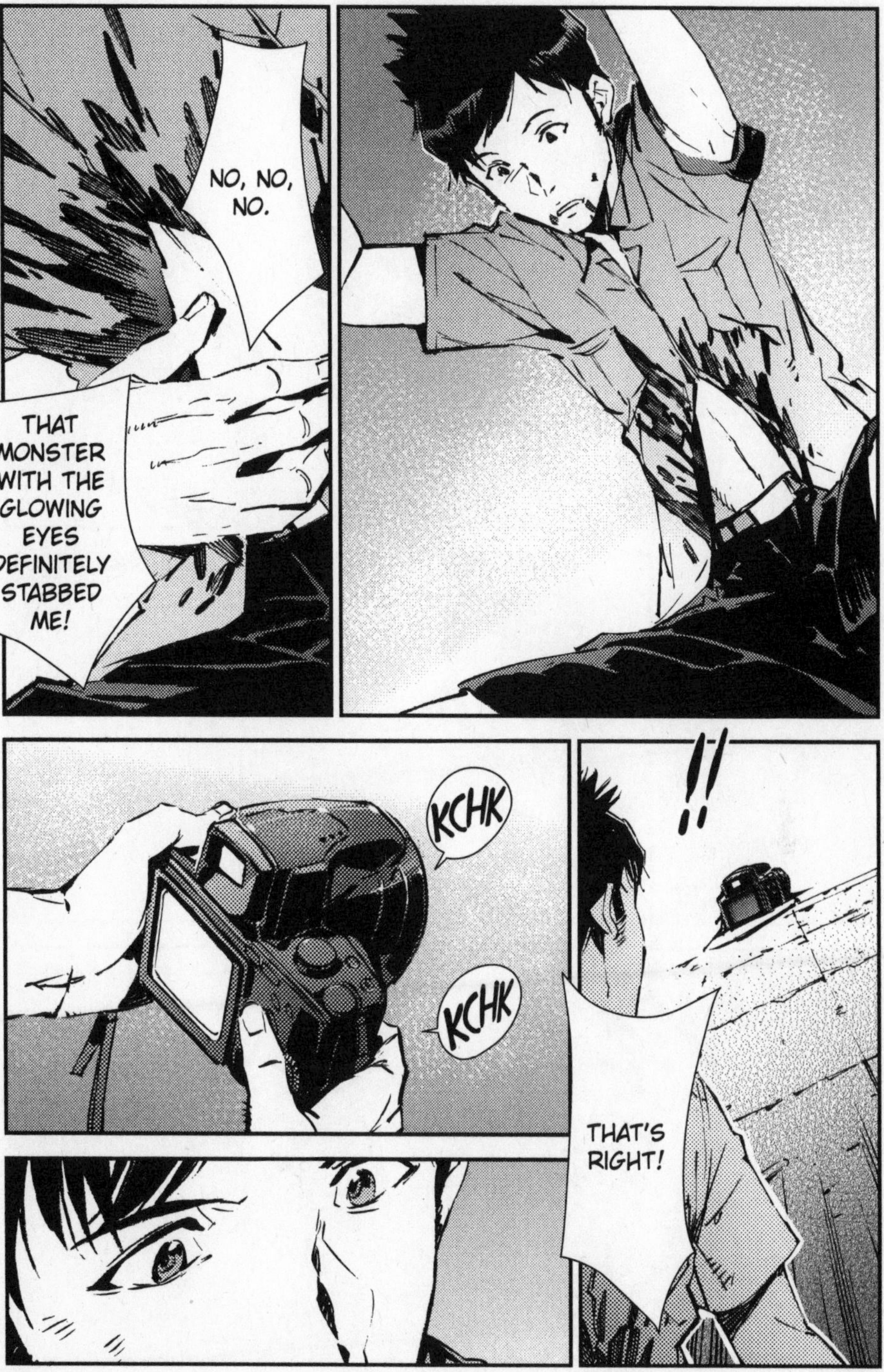
NO, NO, NO.
THAT MONSTER WITH THE GLOWING EYES DEFINITELY STABBED ME!
!!
THAT'S RIGHT!
KCHK
KCHK

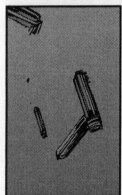

HEY, MAN, ARE YOU ALL RIGHT? I *TOLD* YOU NOT TO TAKE TOO MUCH!

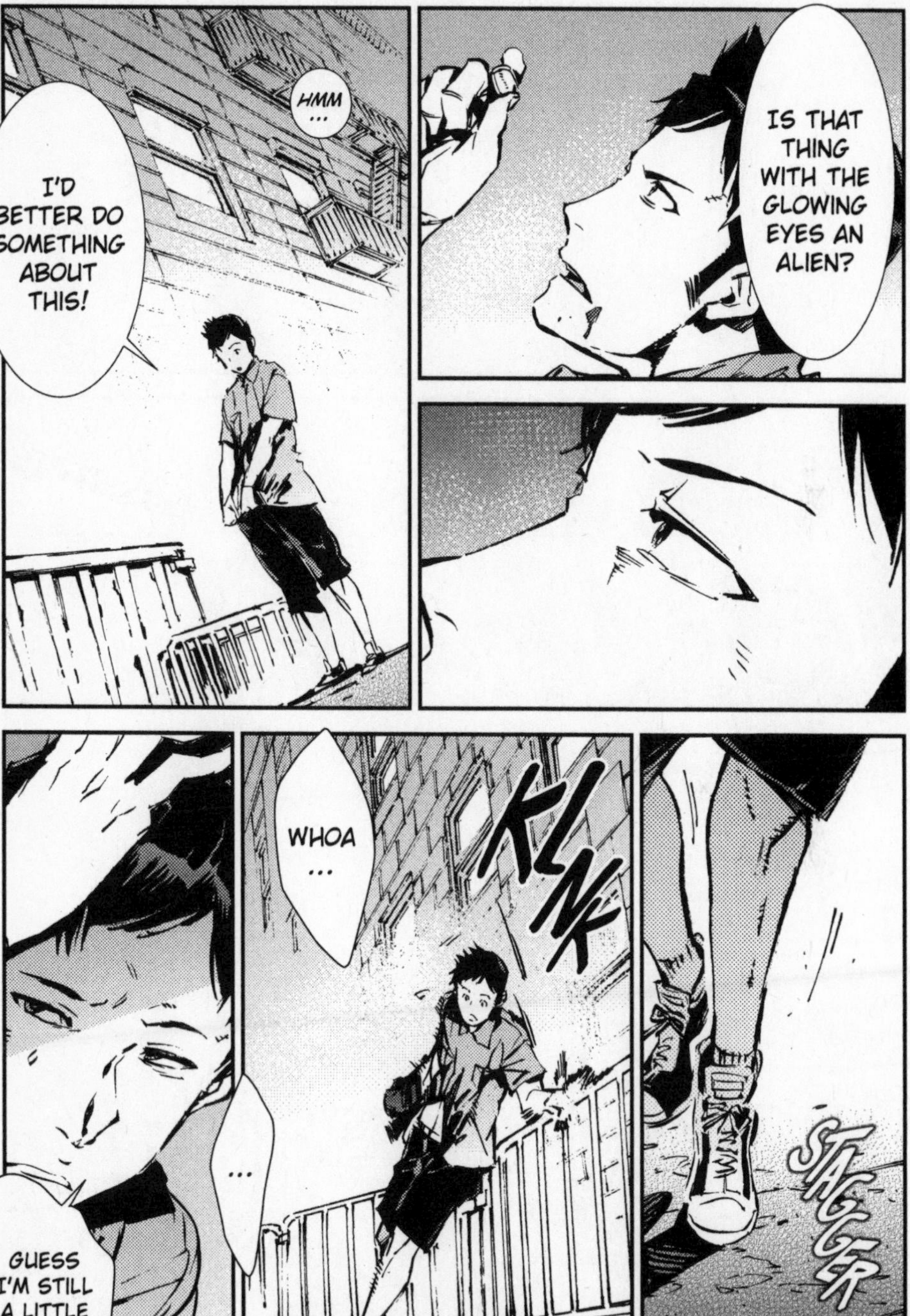
IS THAT THING WITH THE GLOWING EYES AN ALIEN?
HMM ...
I'D BETTER DO SOMETHING ABOUT THIS!
STAGGER
KLINK
WHOA ...
...
GUESS I'M STILL A LITTLE BUZZED.

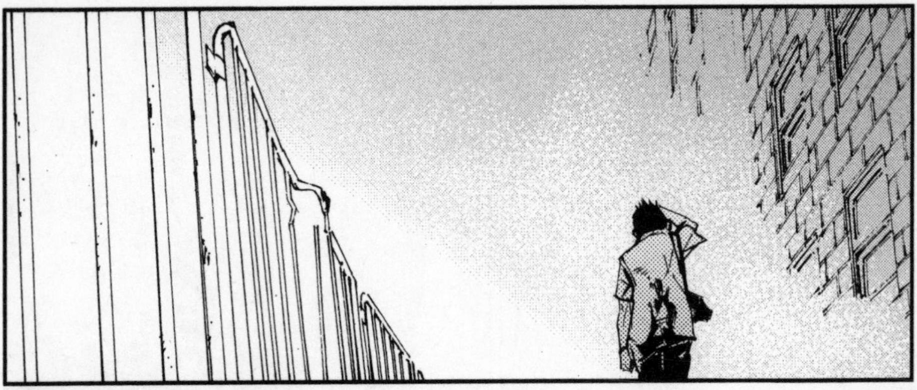
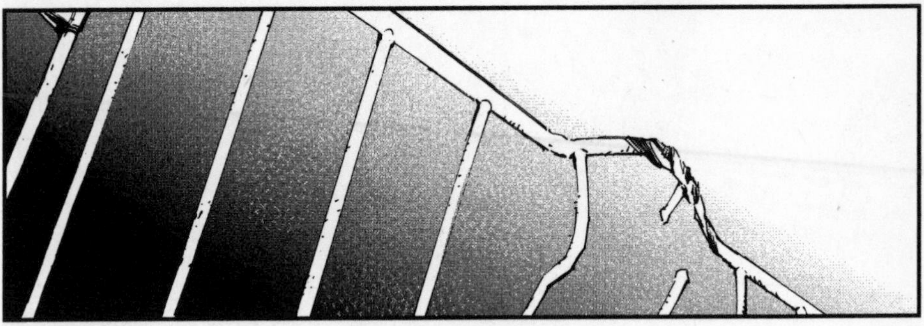
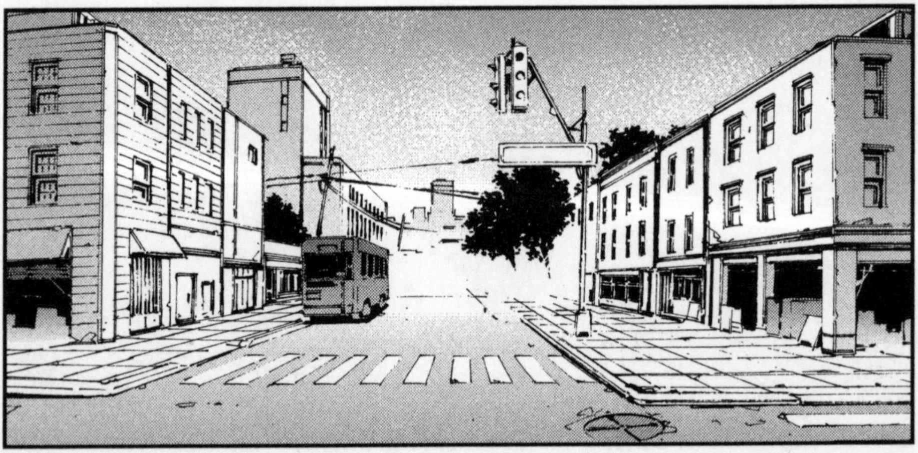

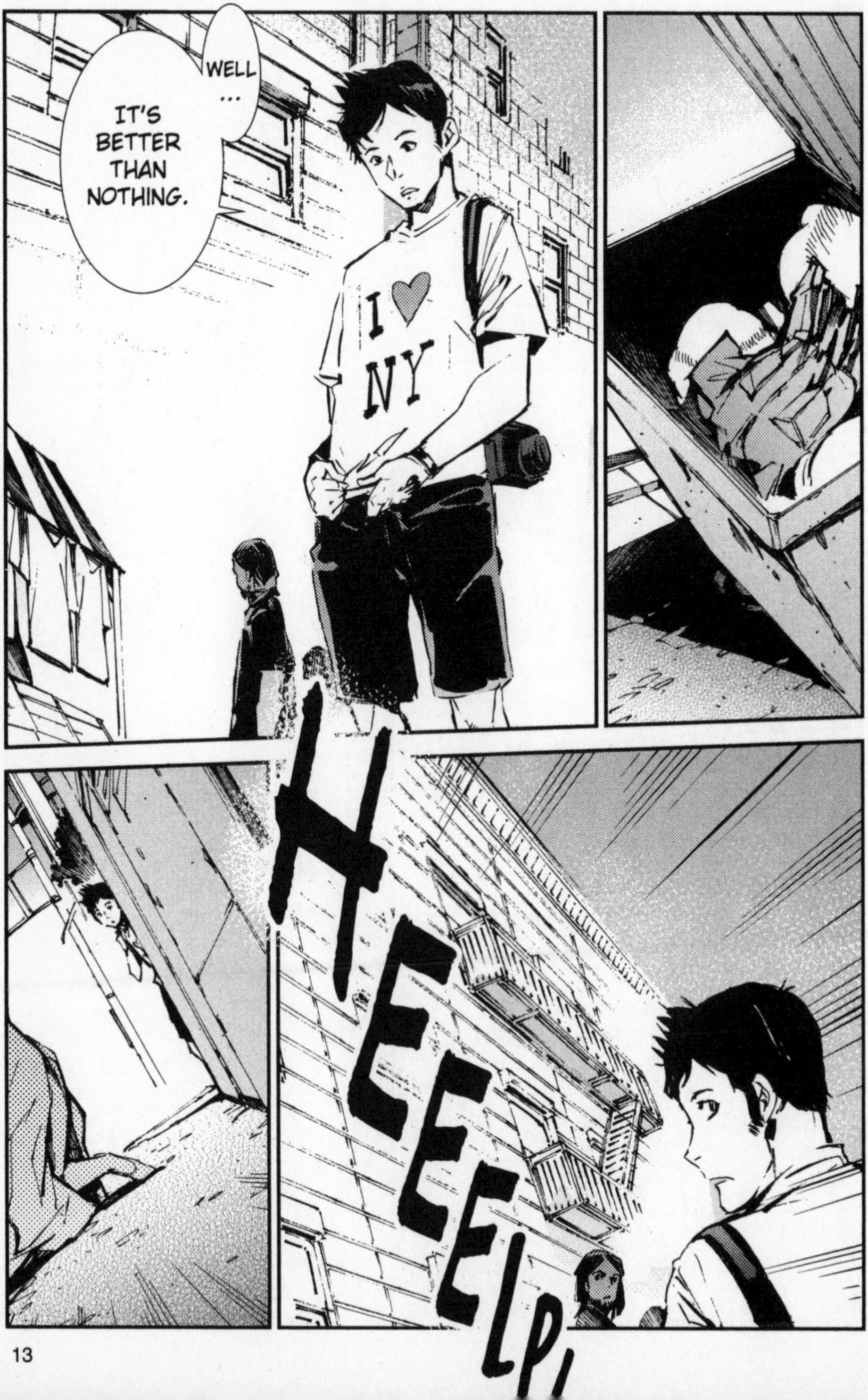
WELL ...
IT'S BETTER THAN NOTHING.
HEEELP!

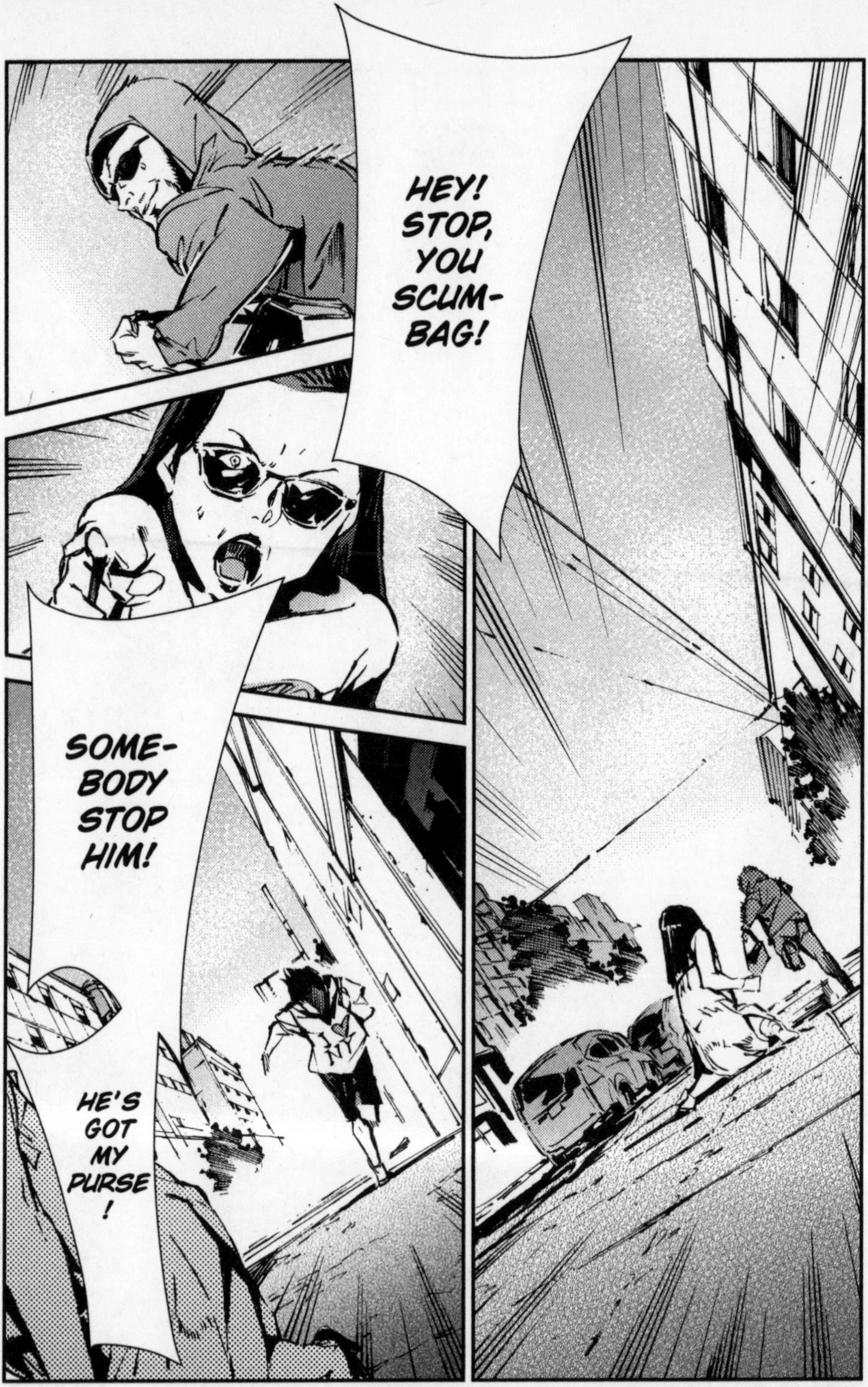
HEY! STOP, YOU SCUM-BAG!
SOME-BODY STOP HIM!
HE'S GOT MY PURSE!

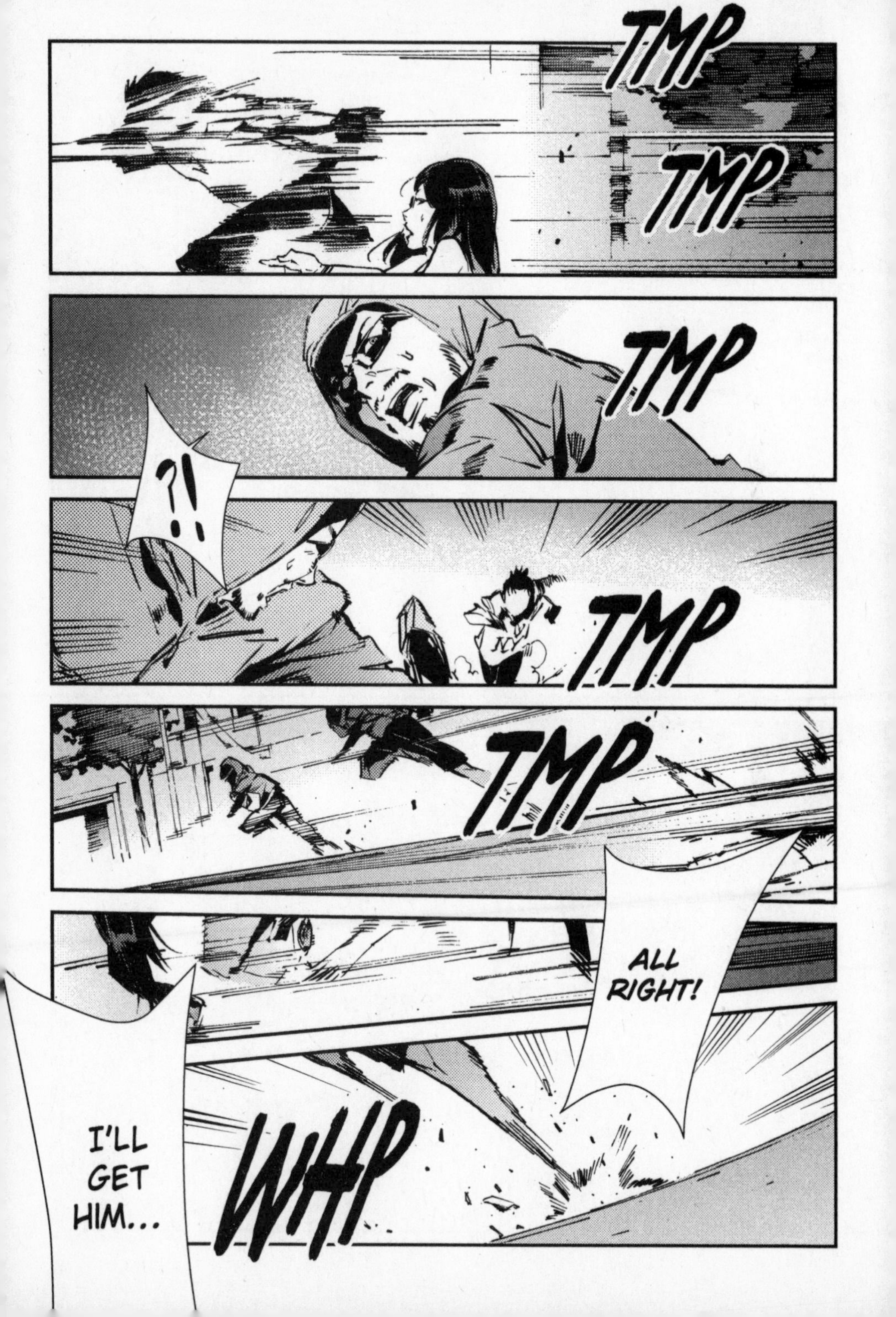
TMP
TMP
TMP
?!
TMP
TMP
ALL RIGHT!
WHP
I'LL GET HIM...

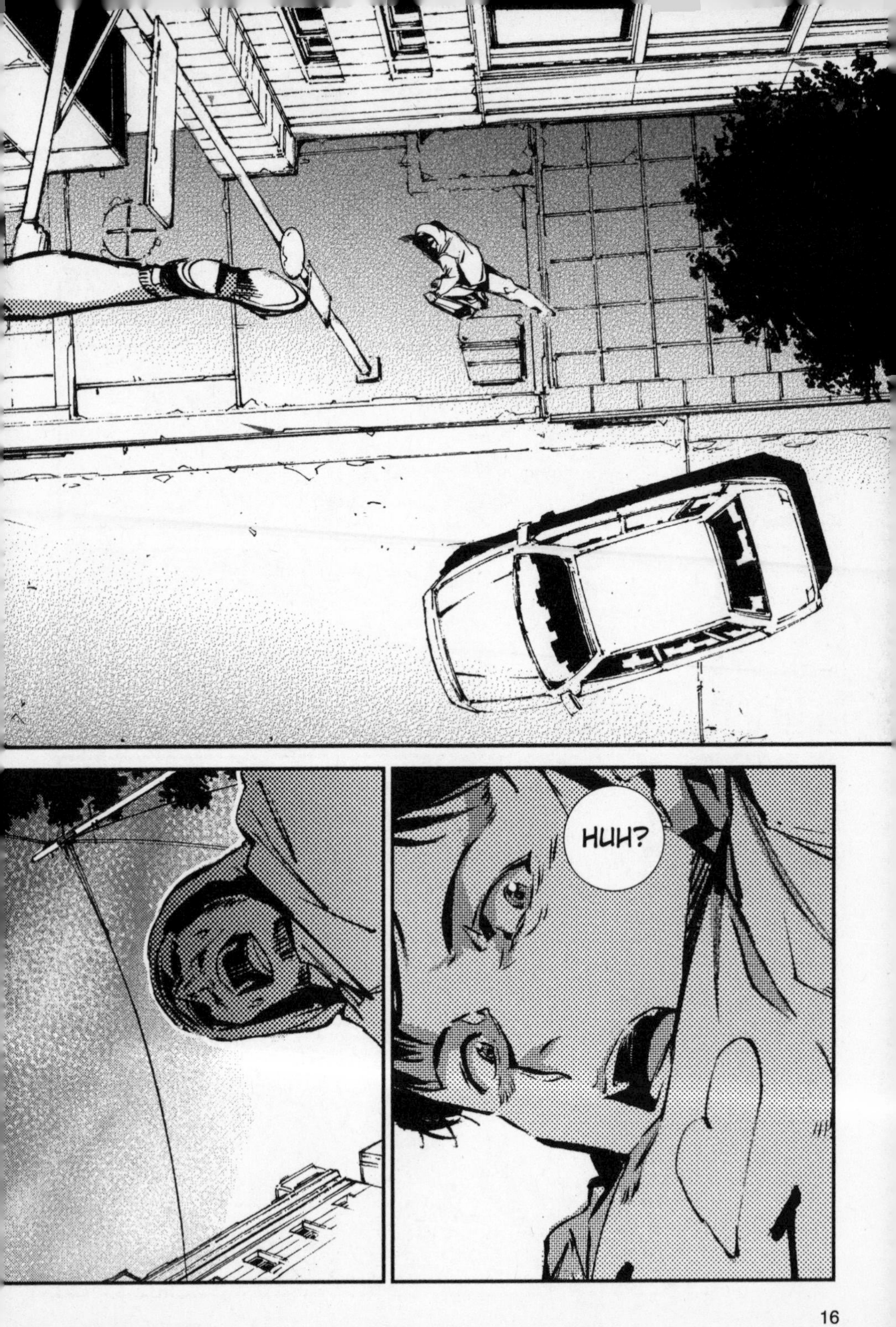
HUH?

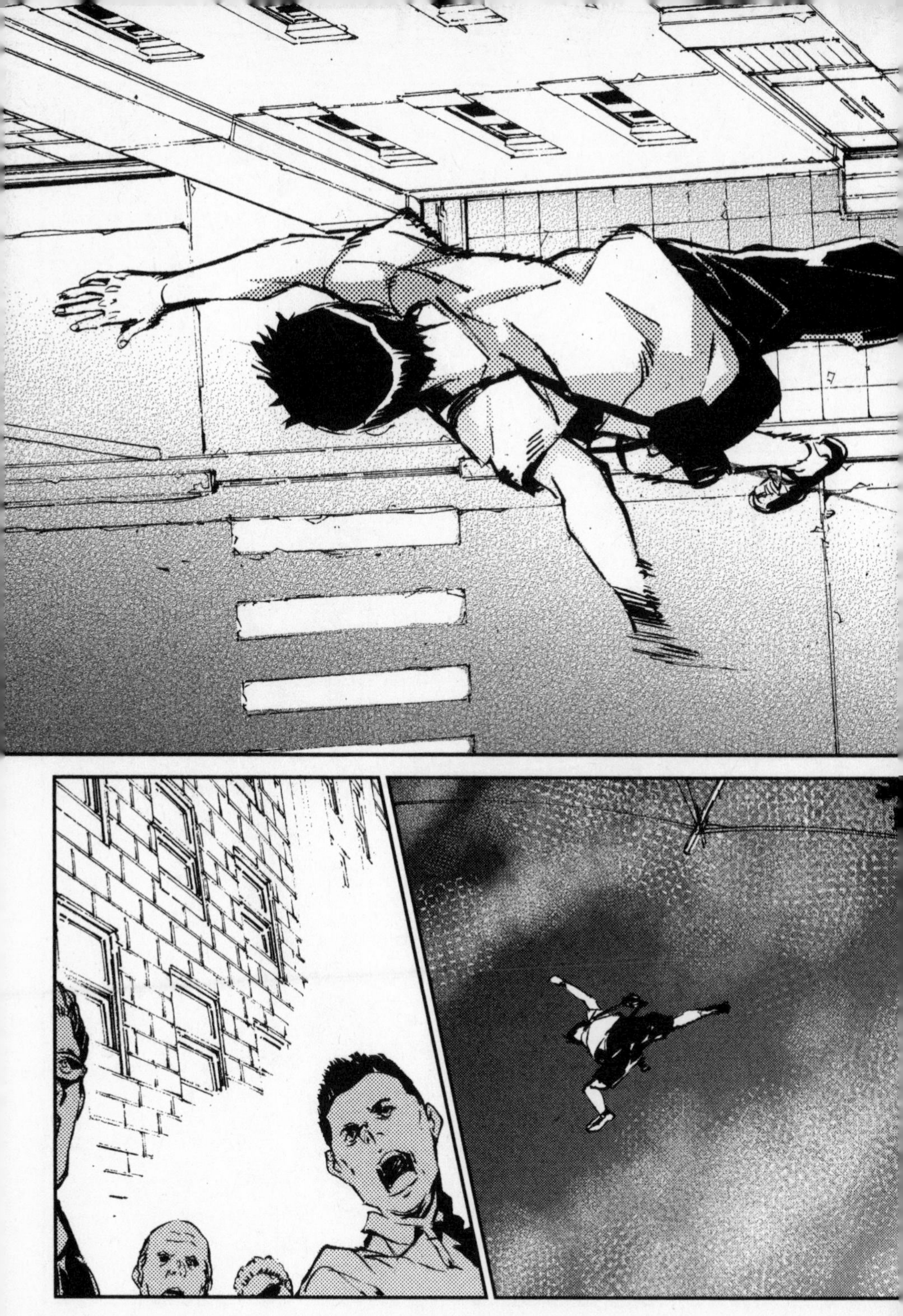

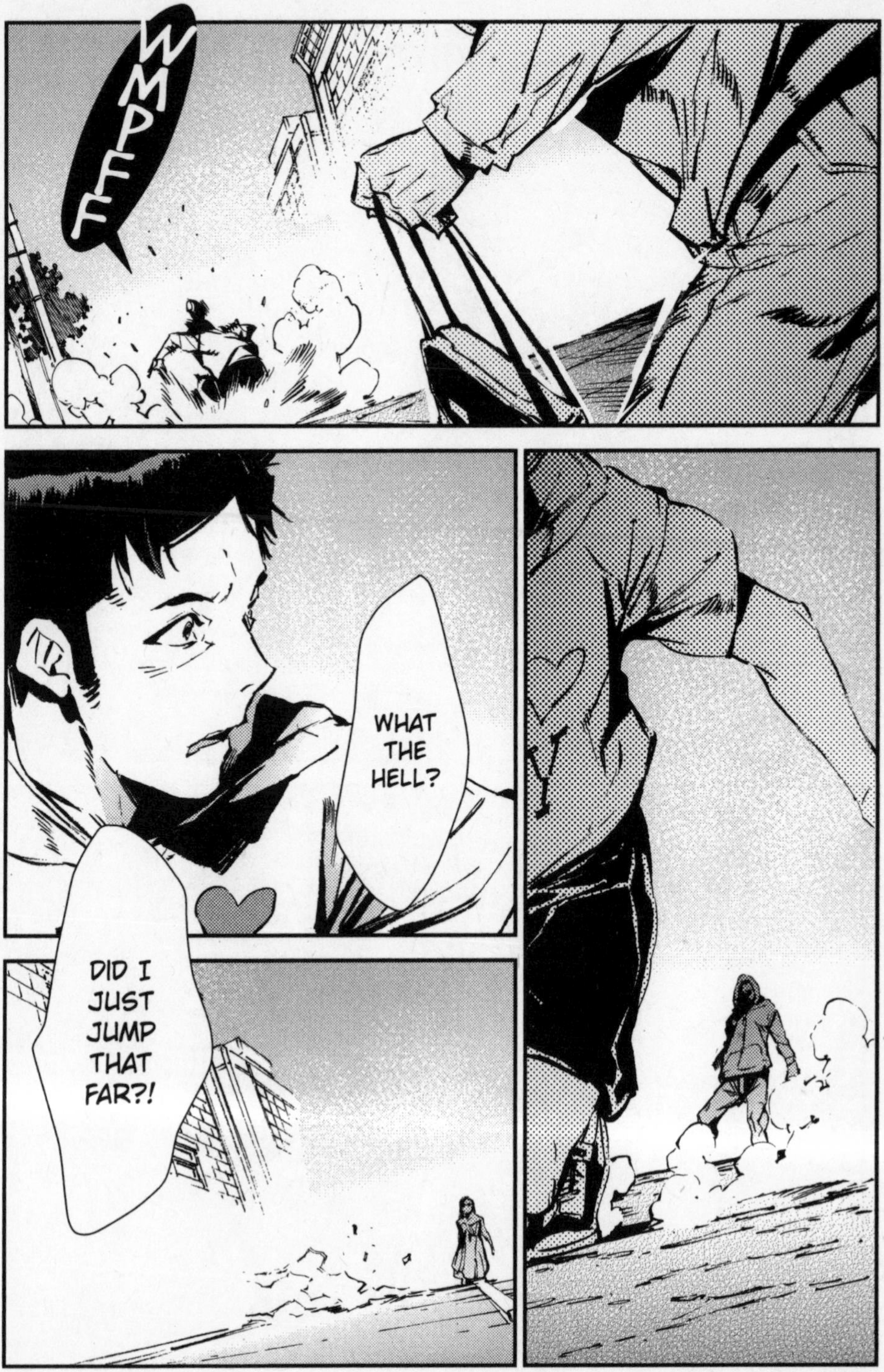
WMPFFF
WHAT THE HELL?
DID I JUST JUMP THAT FAR?!

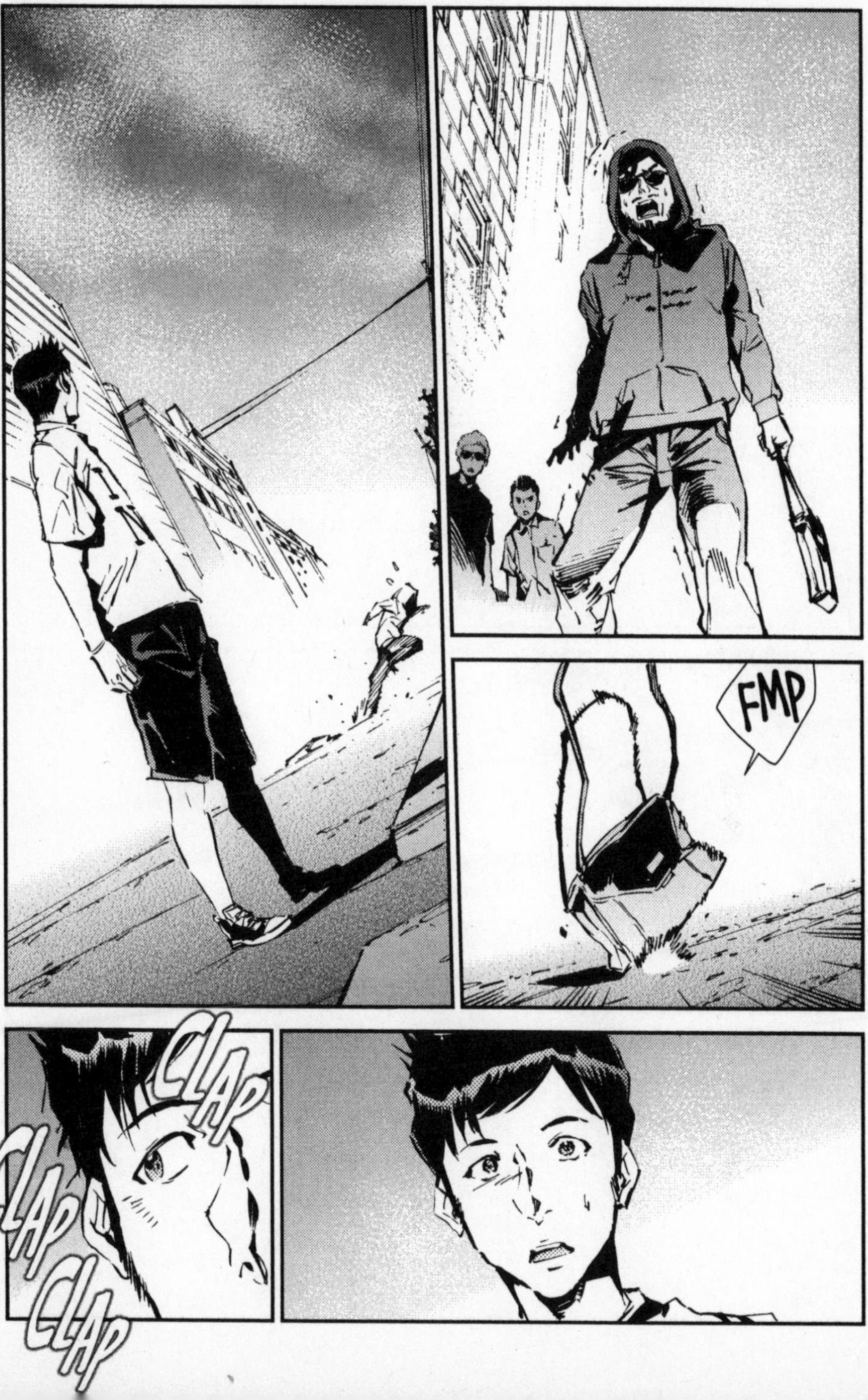
FMP
CLAP
CLAP
CLAP
CLAP

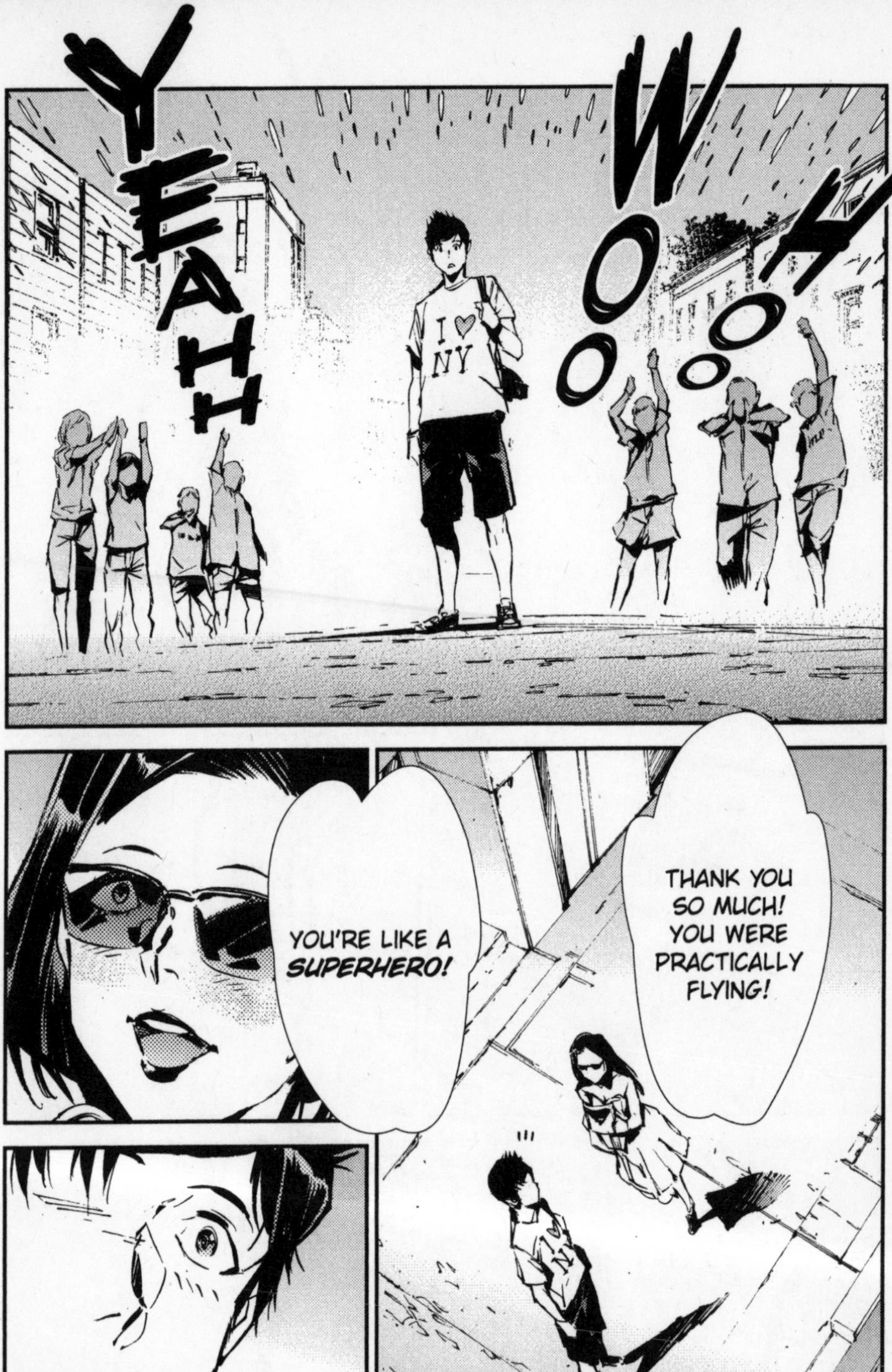
WOOOOH
YEAHH
THANK YOU SO MUCH! YOU WERE PRACTICALLY FLYING!
YOU'RE LIKE A *SUPERHERO!*

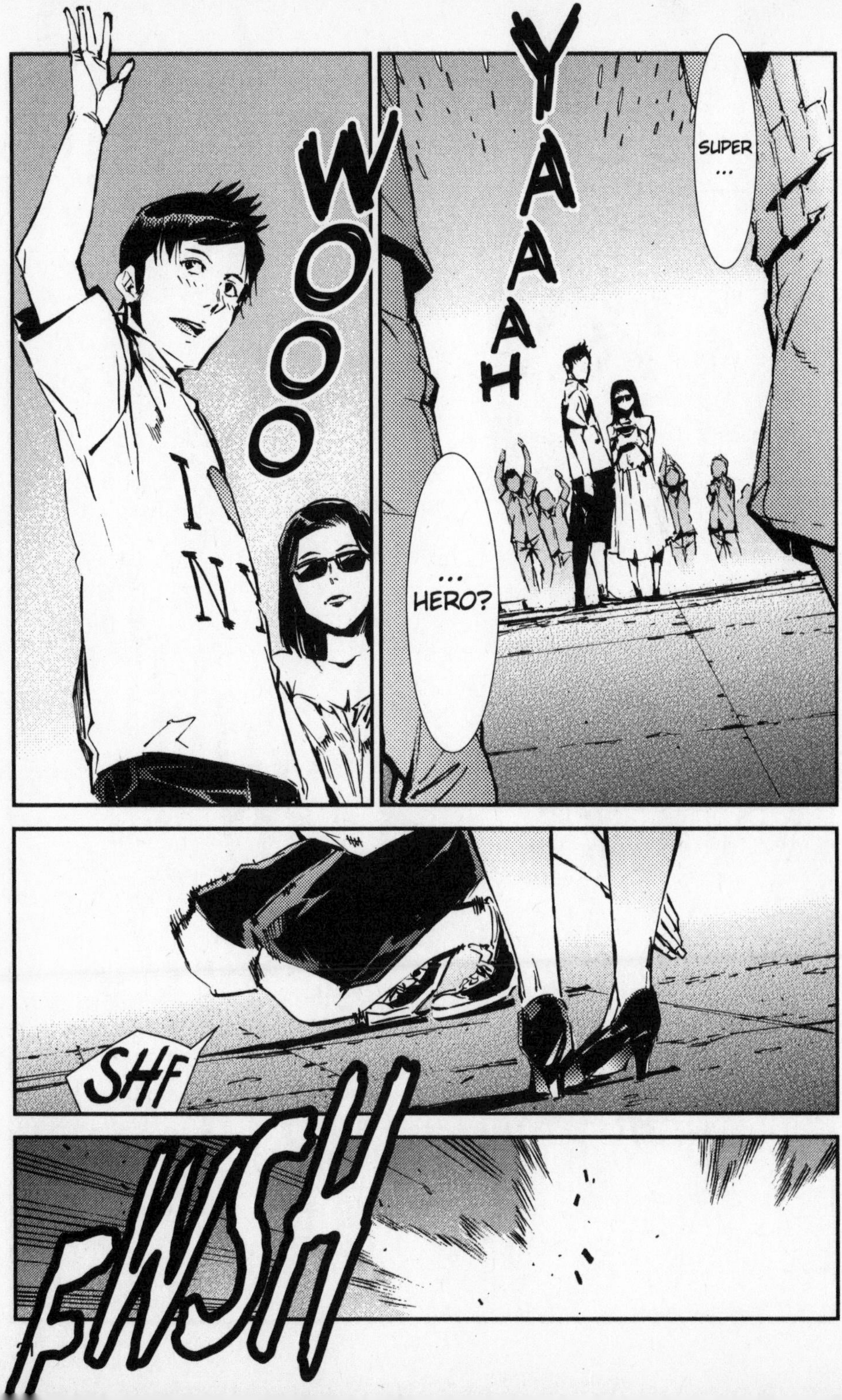
SUPER ...
YAAAH
... HERO?
WOOOO
SHF
FWSH

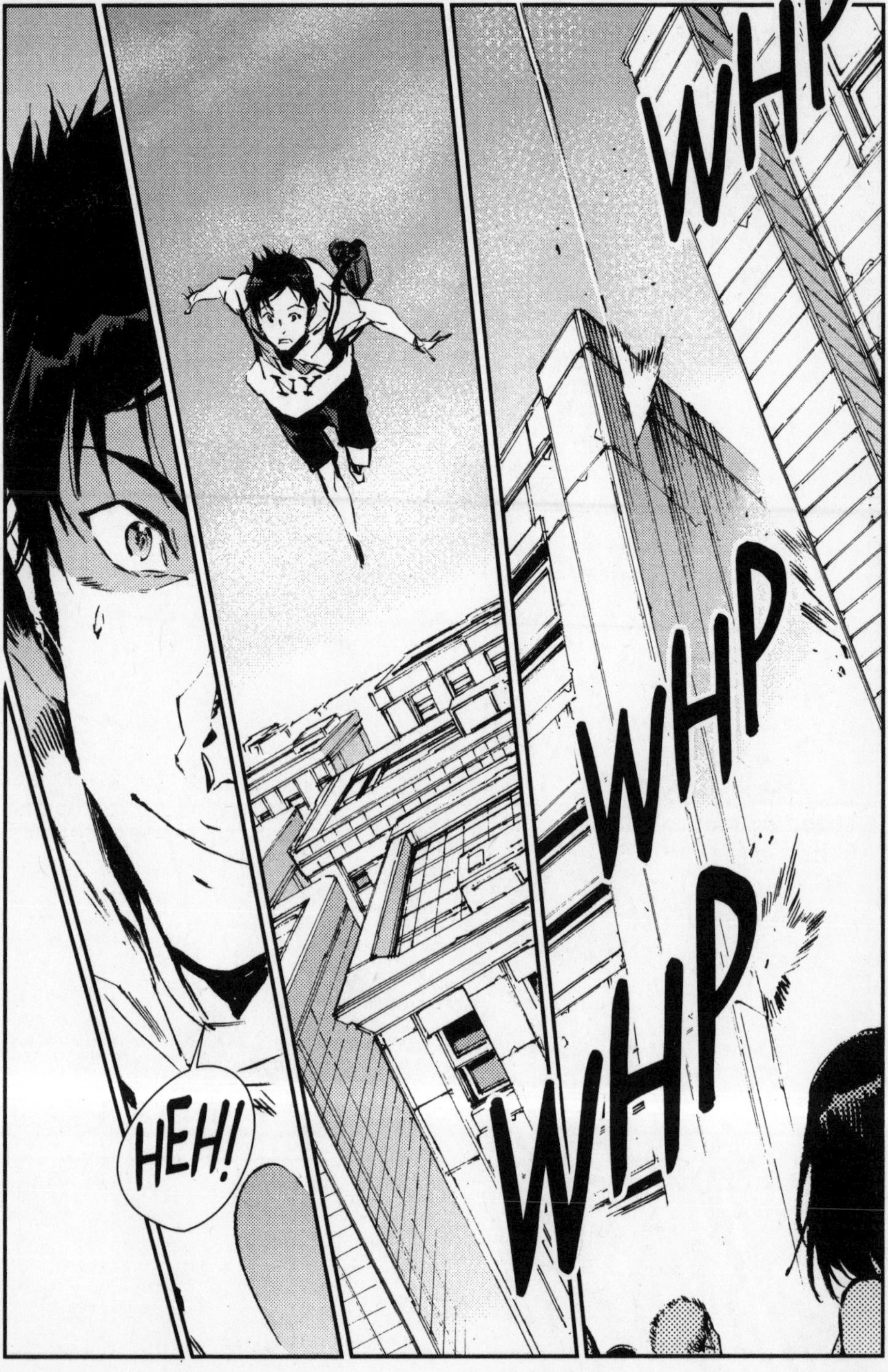
WHP
WHP
WHP
WHP
HEH!

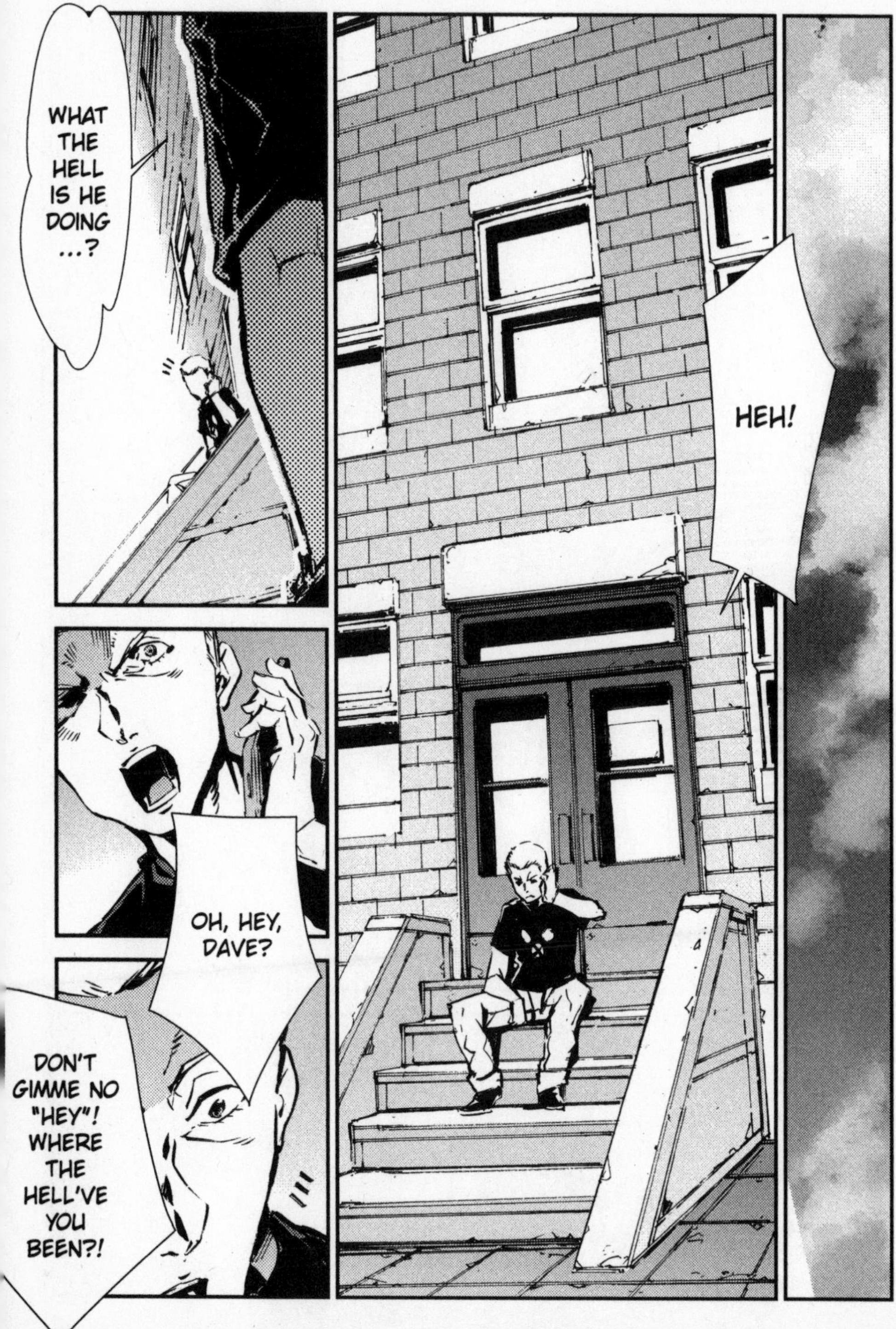
HEH!
WHAT THE HELL IS HE DOING ...?
OH, HEY, DAVE?
DON'T GIMME NO "HEY"! WHERE THE HELL'VE YOU BEEN?!

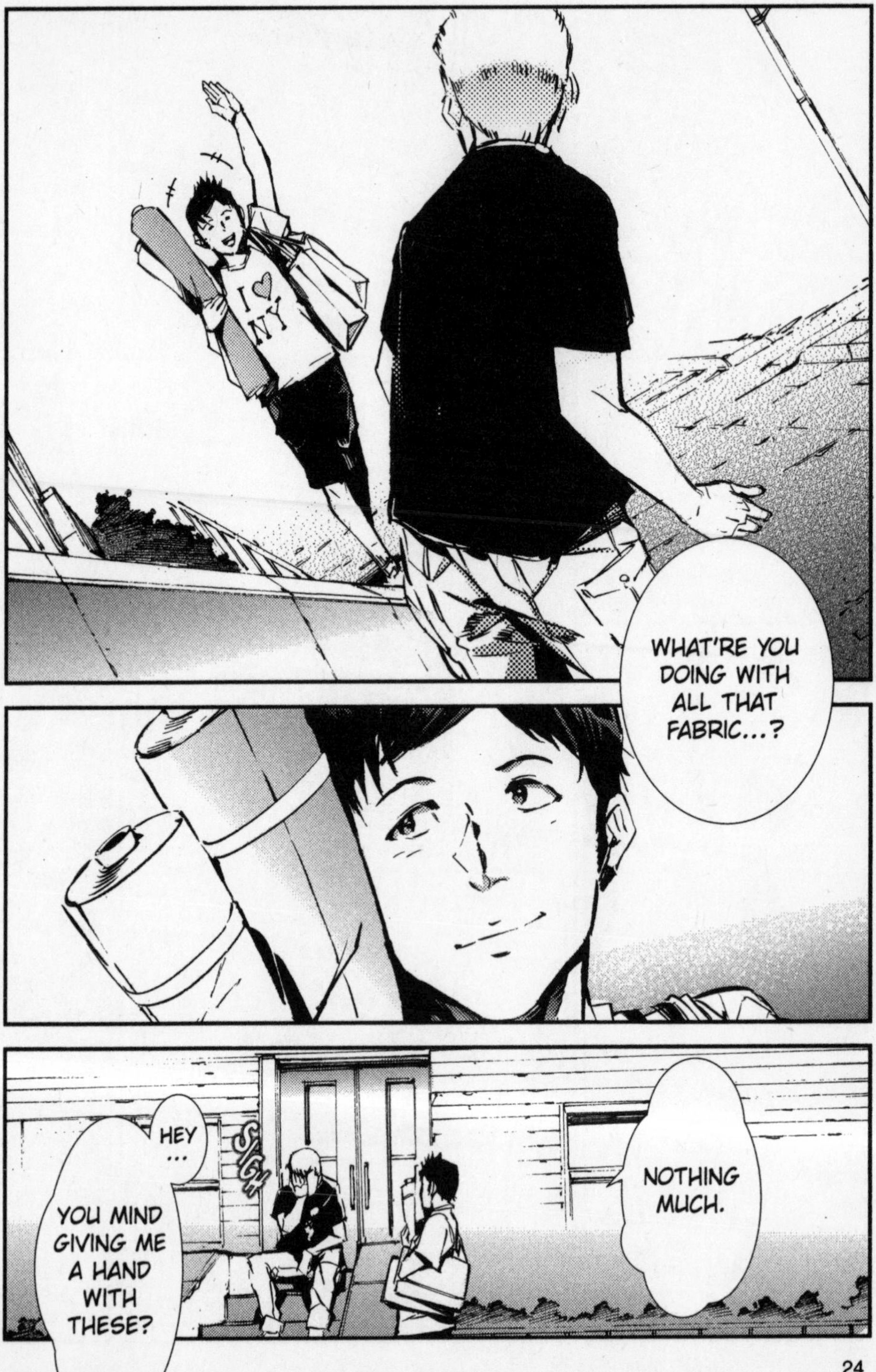
WHAT'RE YOU DOING WITH ALL THAT FABRIC...?
NOTHING MUCH.
SIGH
HEY ...
YOU MIND GIVING ME A HAND WITH THESE?

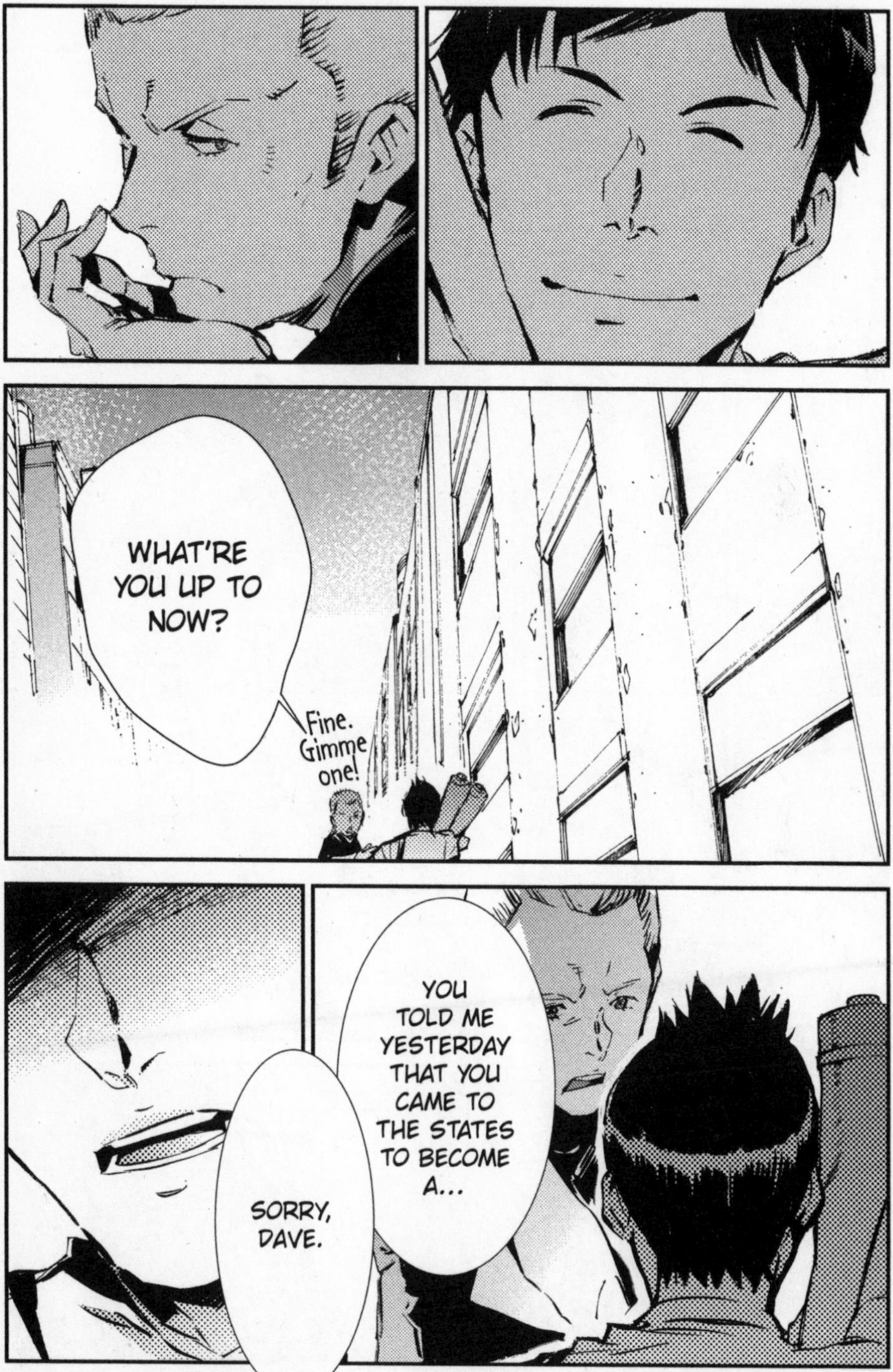
WHAT'RE YOU UP TO NOW?
Fine. Gimme one!
YOU TOLD ME YESTERDAY THAT YOU CAME TO THE STATES TO BECOME A...
SORRY, DAVE.

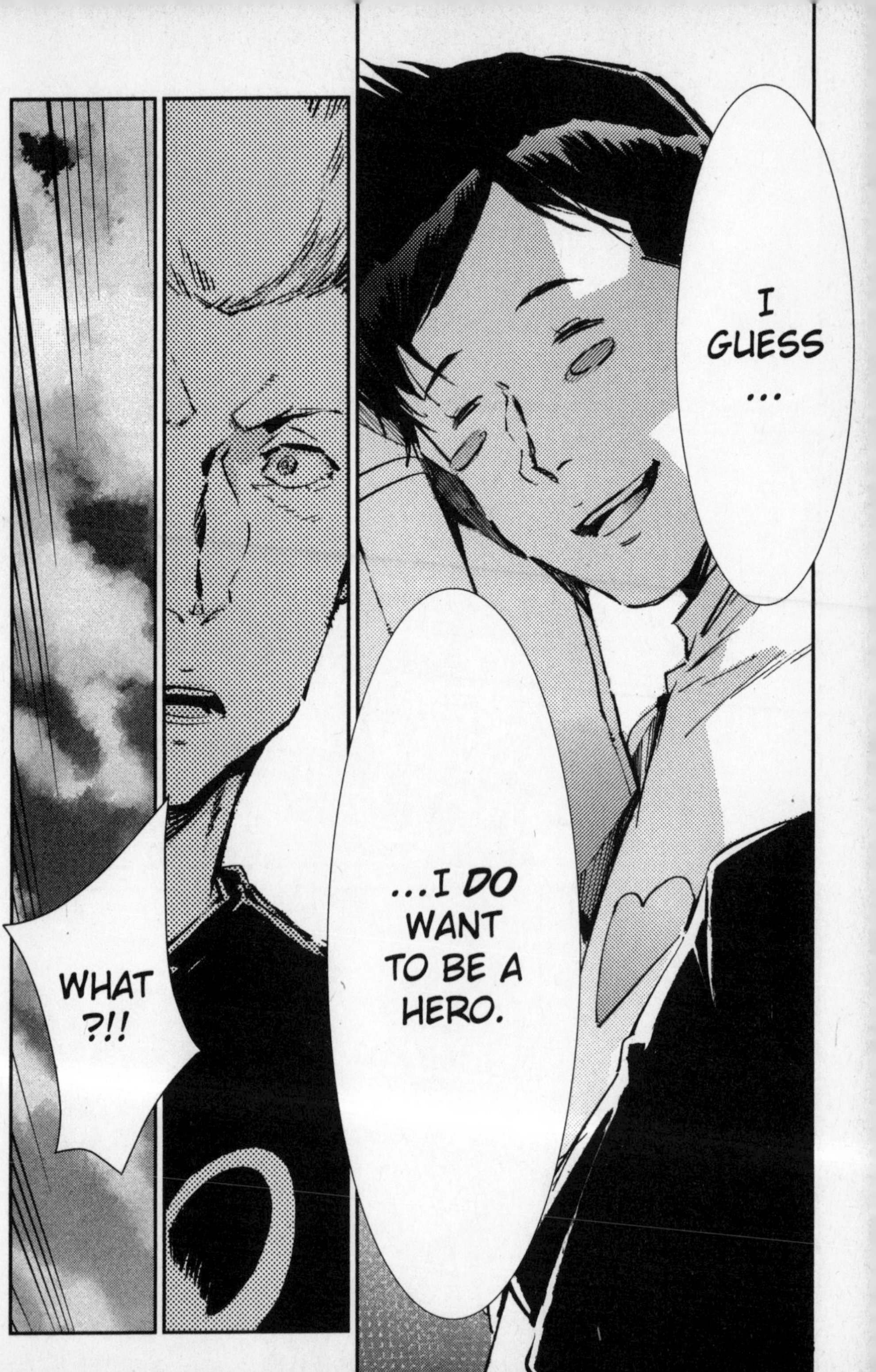
I GUESS ...
...I *DO* WANT TO BE A HERO.
WHAT ?!!

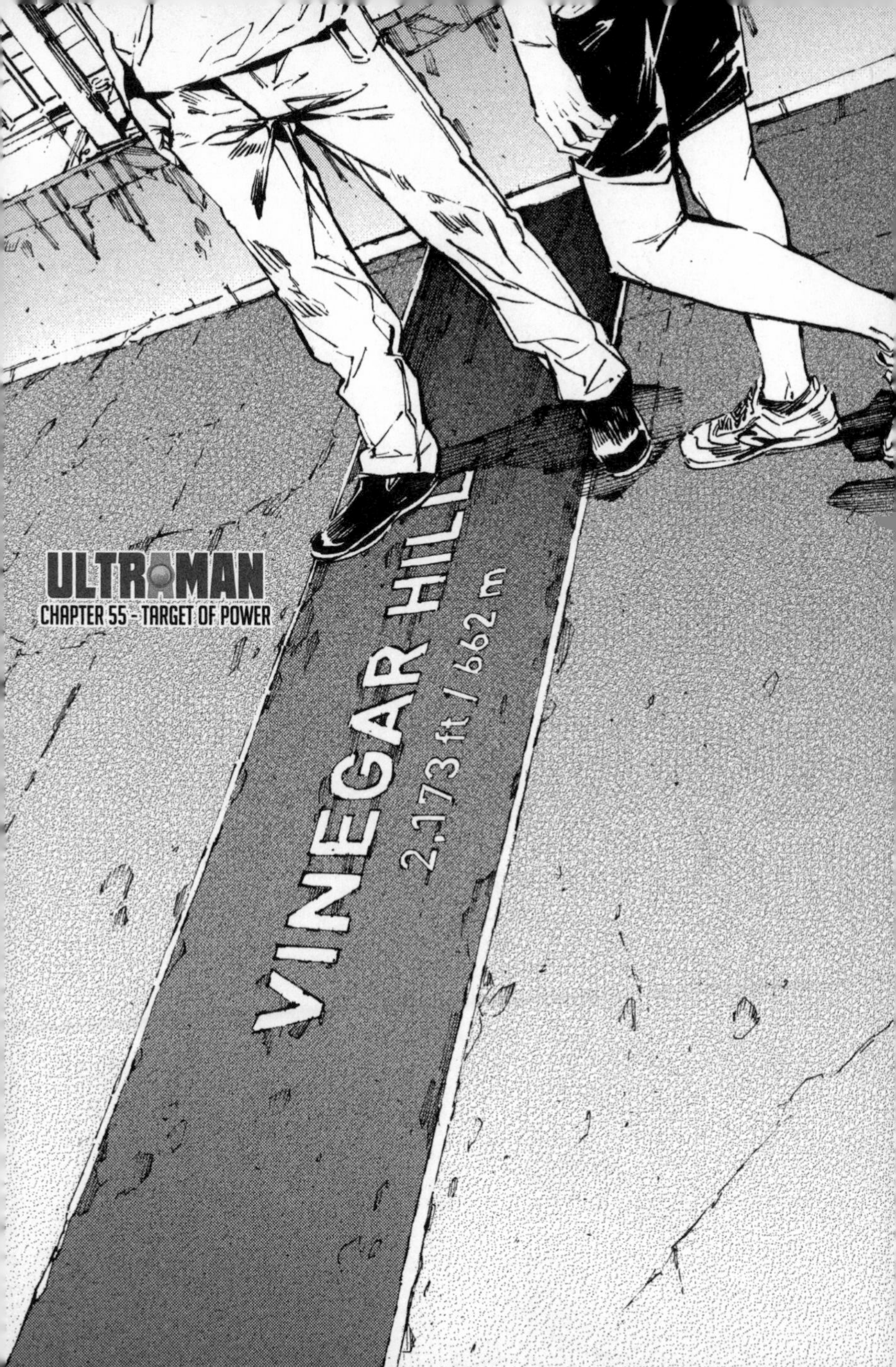
ULTRAMAN
CHAPTER 55 - TARGET OF POWER
VINEGAR HILL
2,173 ft / 662 m

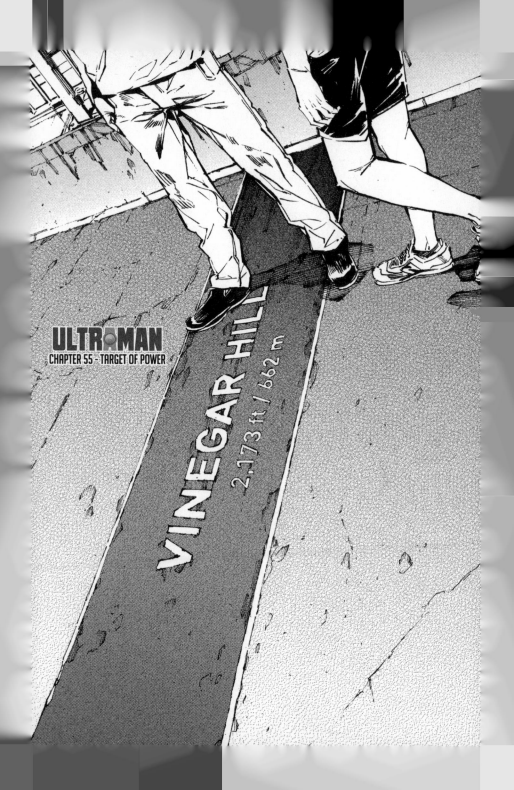

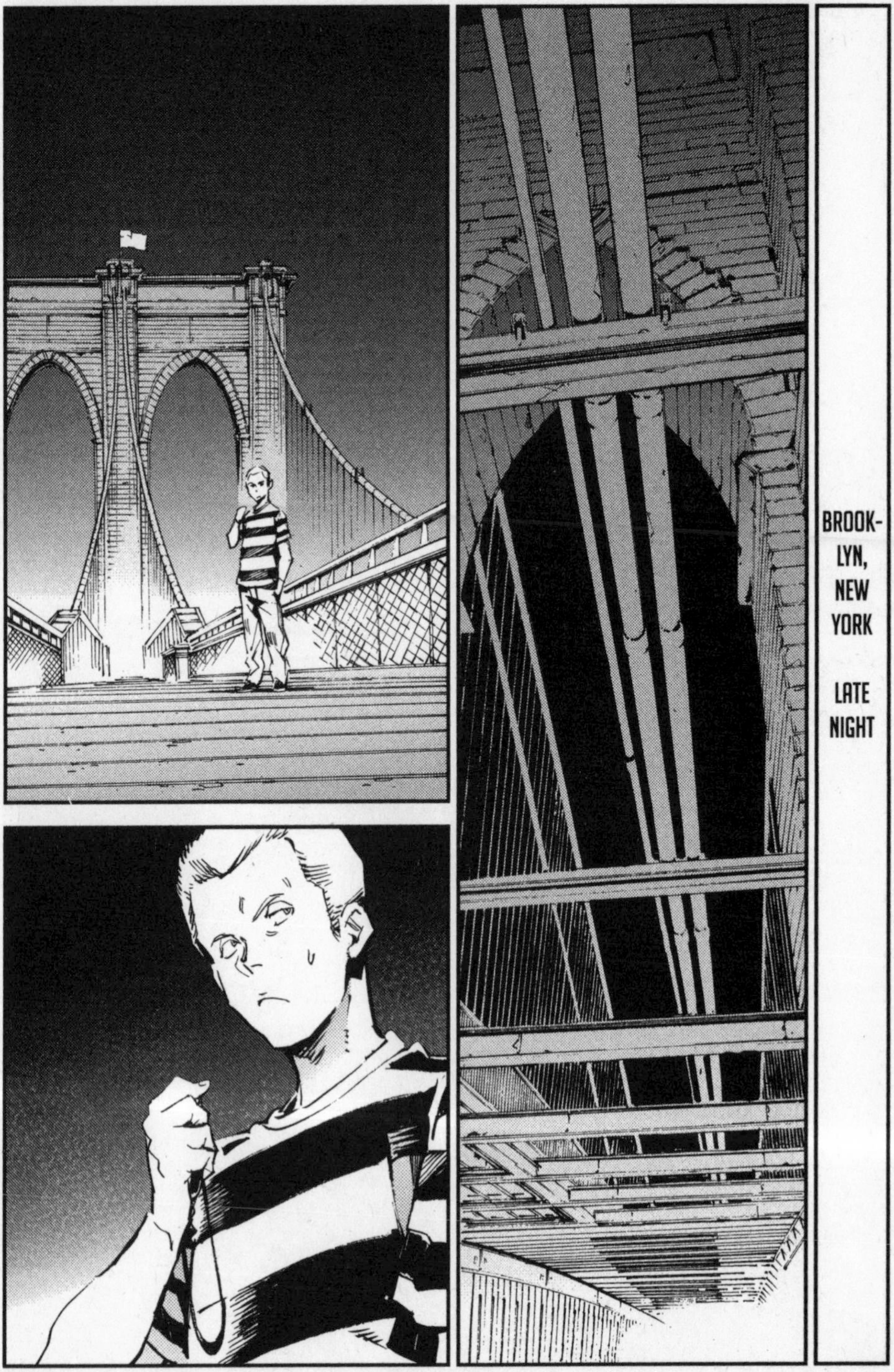
BROOK-LYN, NEW YORK
LATE NIGHT

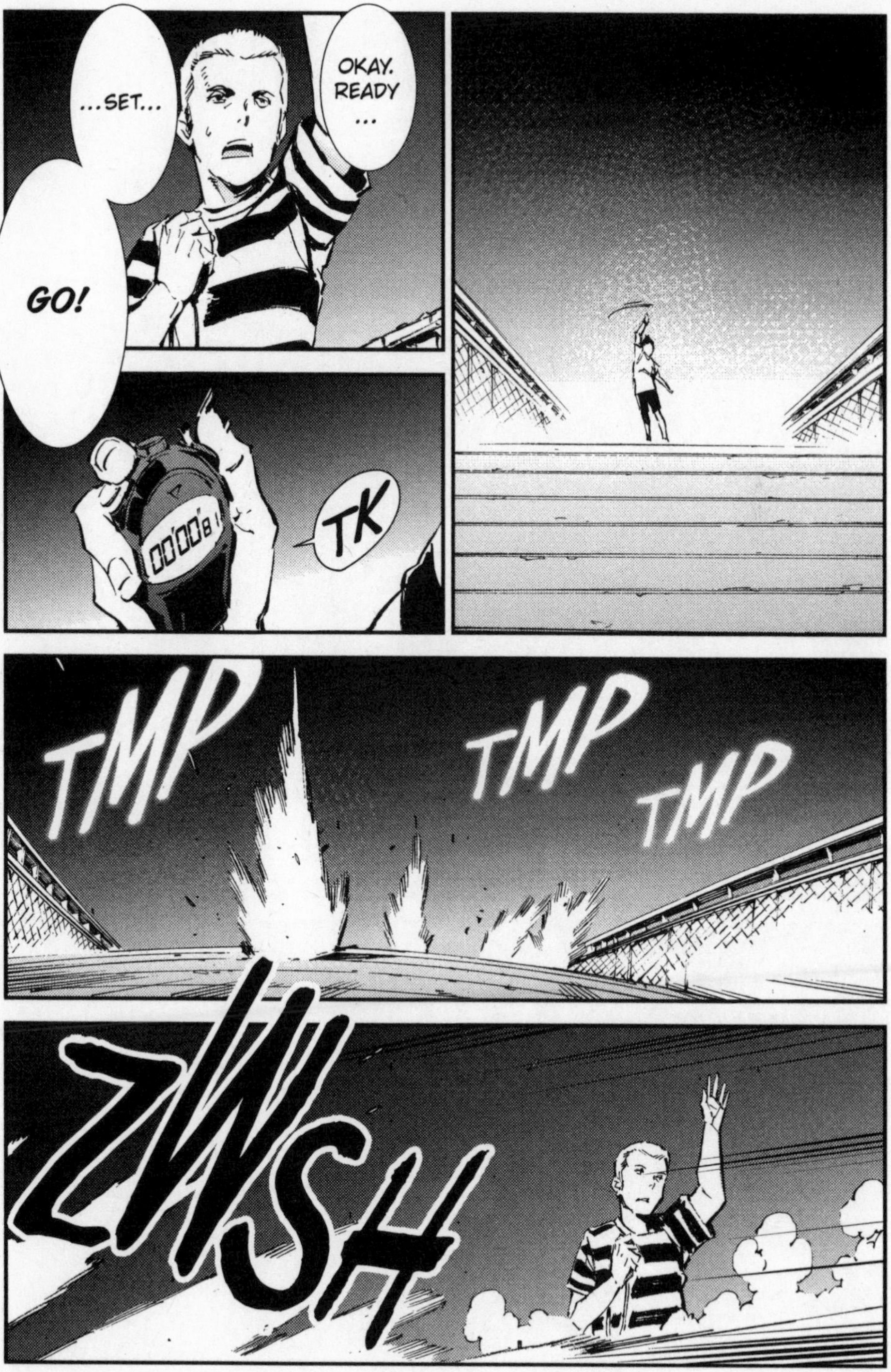

OKAY. READY ...
...SET...
GO!
TK
TMP
TMP
TMP
ZWSH

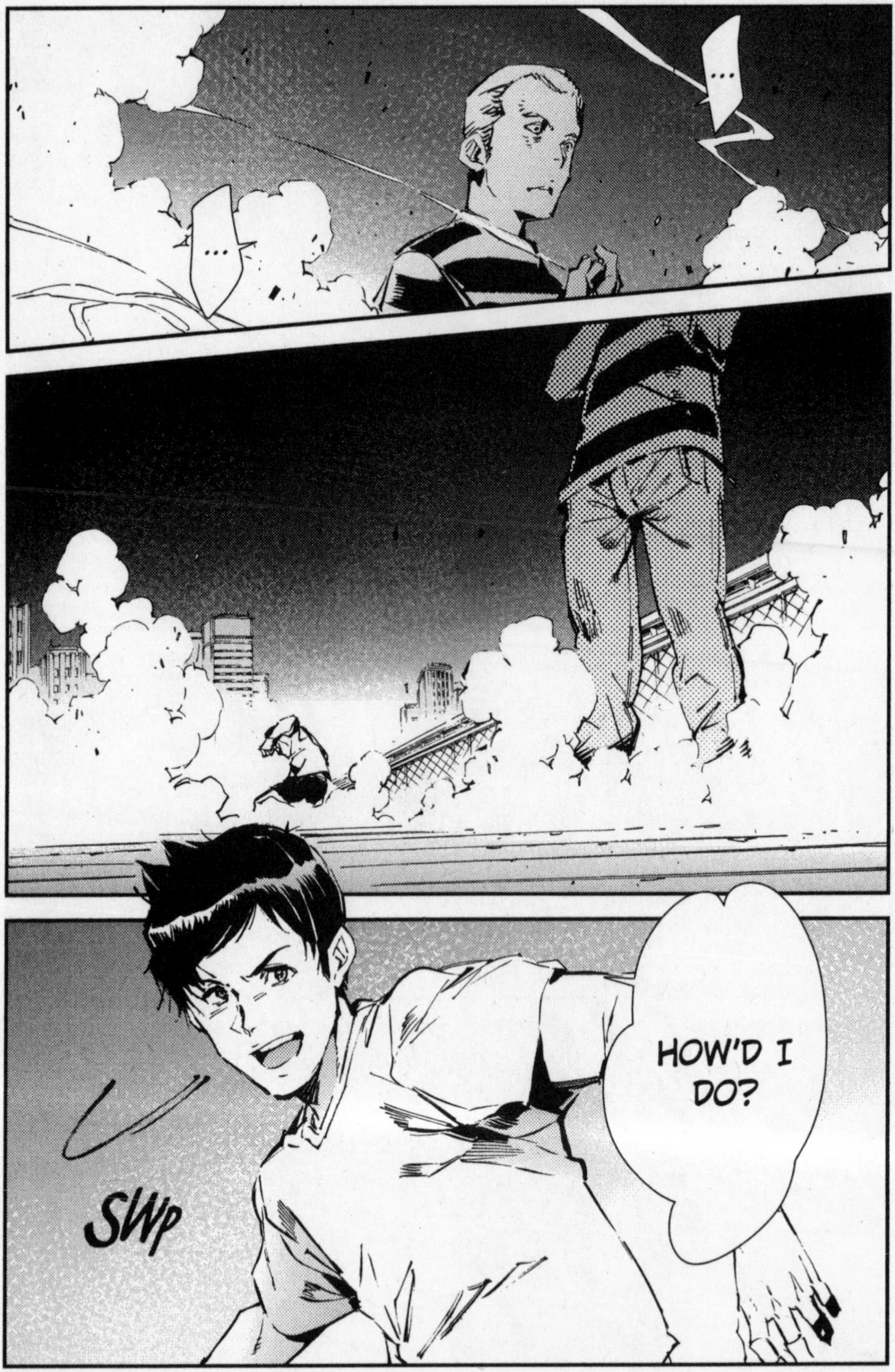
...
...
HOW'D I DO?
SWP

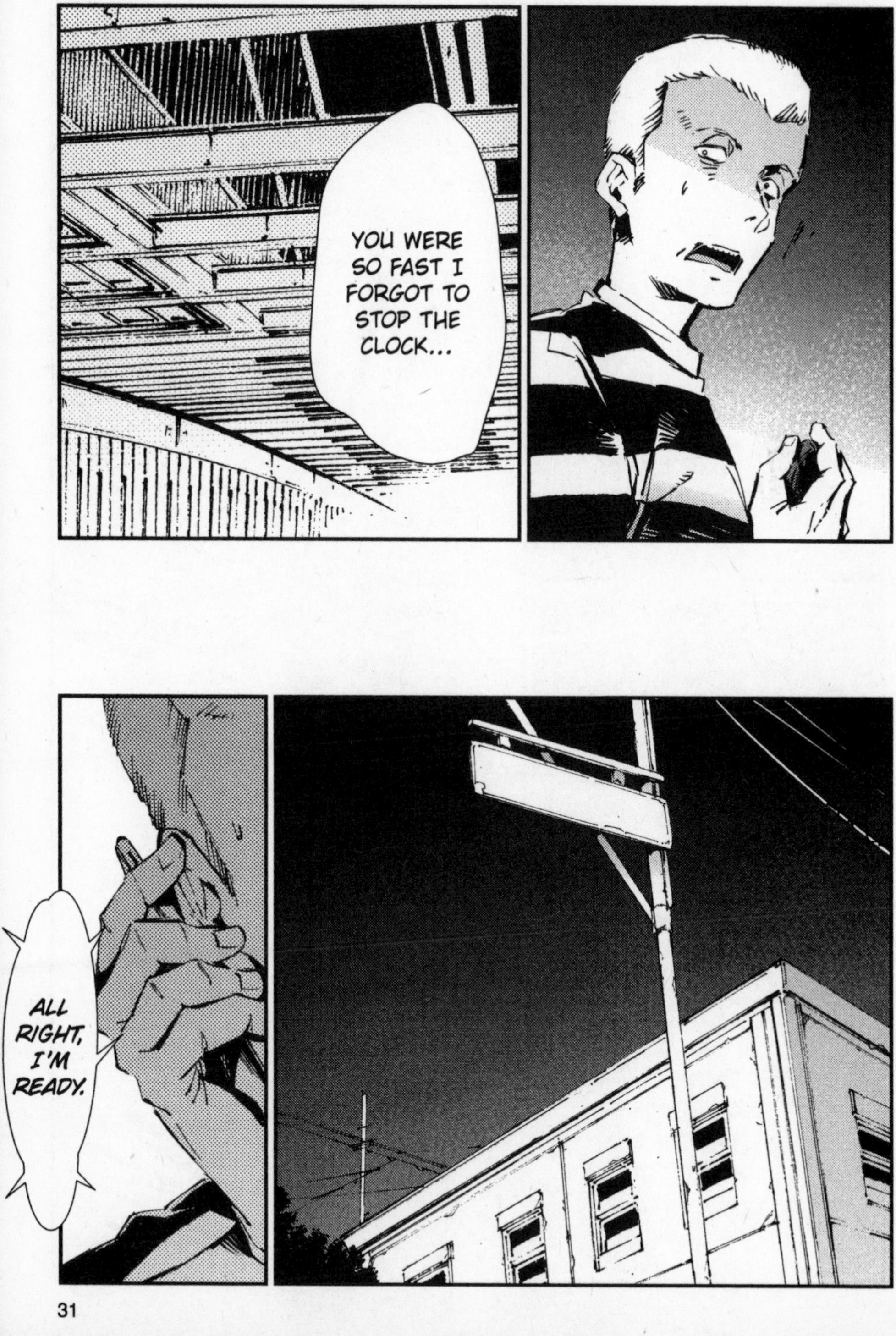
YOU WERE SO FAST I FORGOT TO STOP THE CLOCK...
ALL RIGHT, I'M READY.

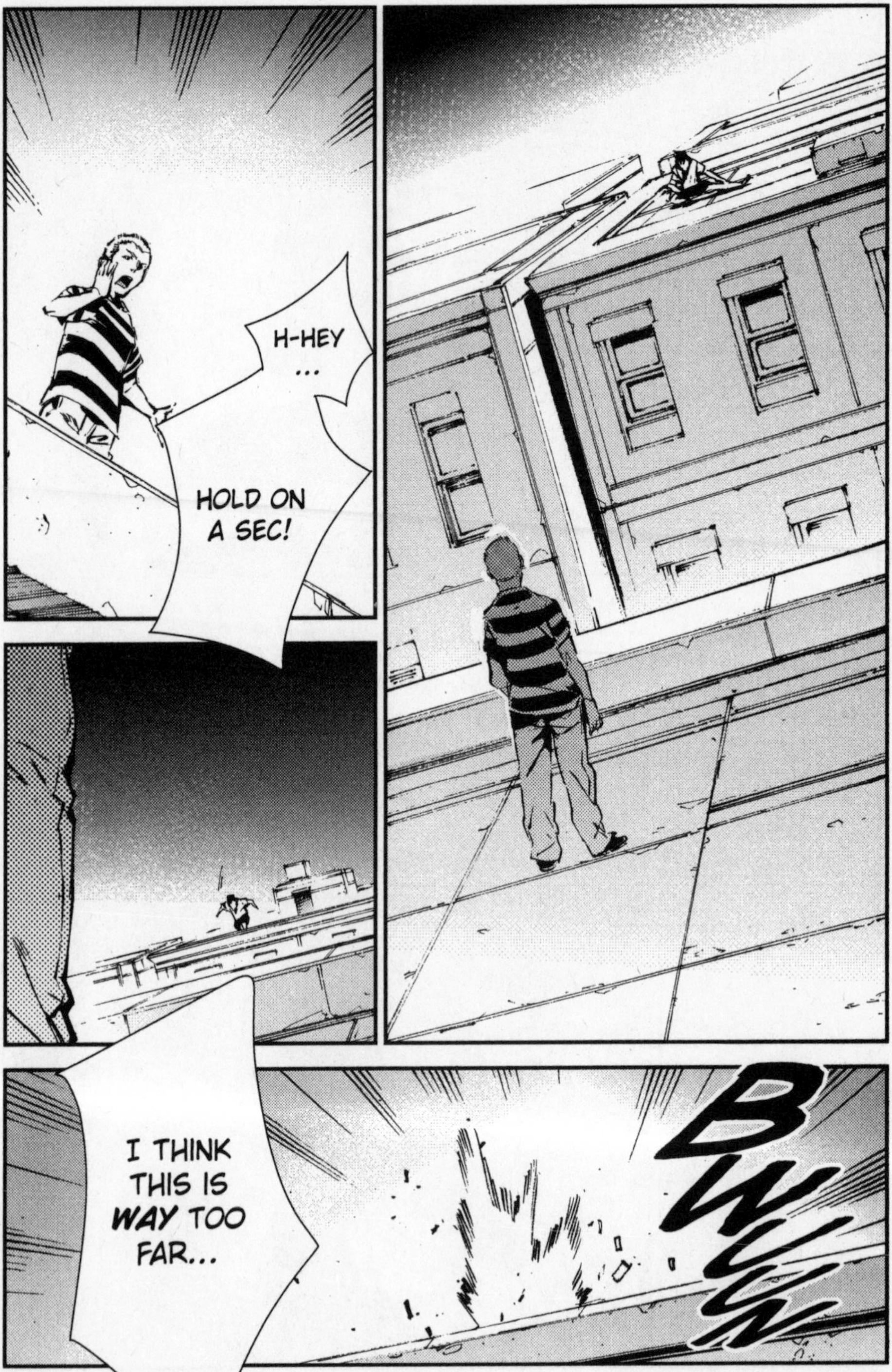
H-HEY ...
HOLD ON A SEC!
BWUN
I THINK THIS IS *WAY* TOO FAR...

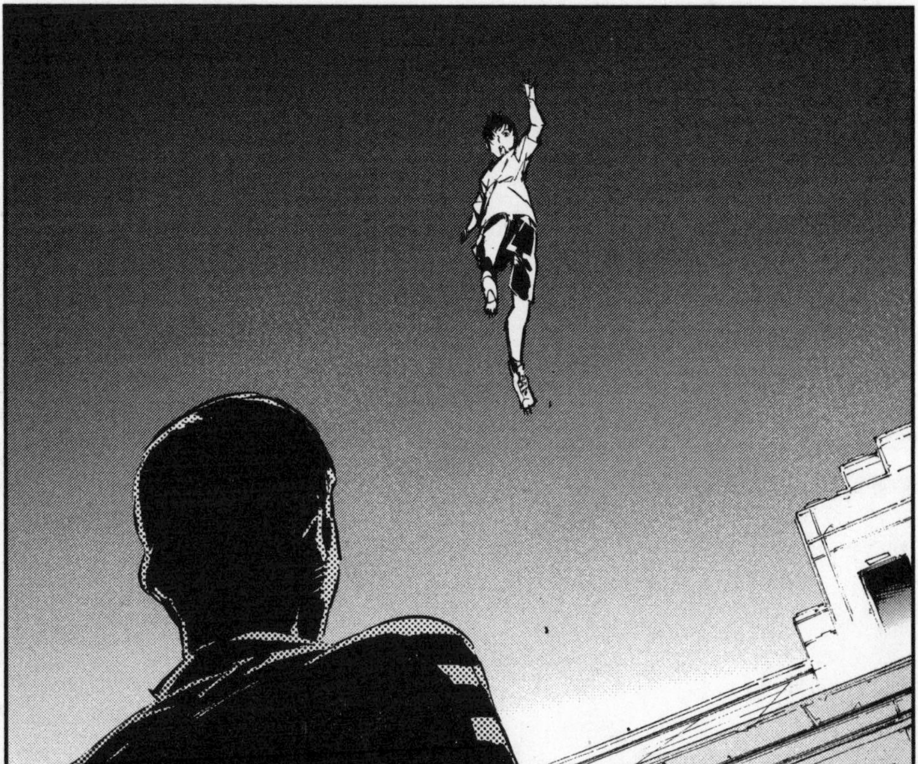

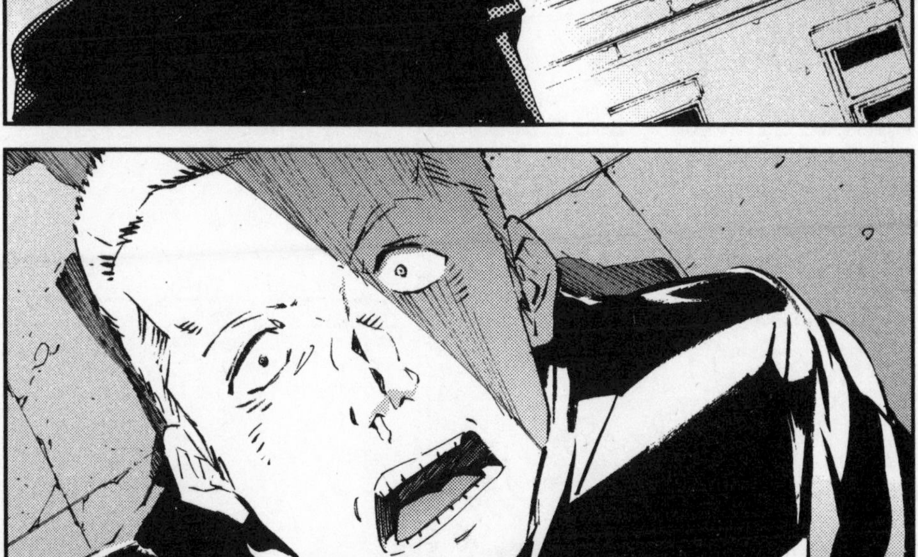

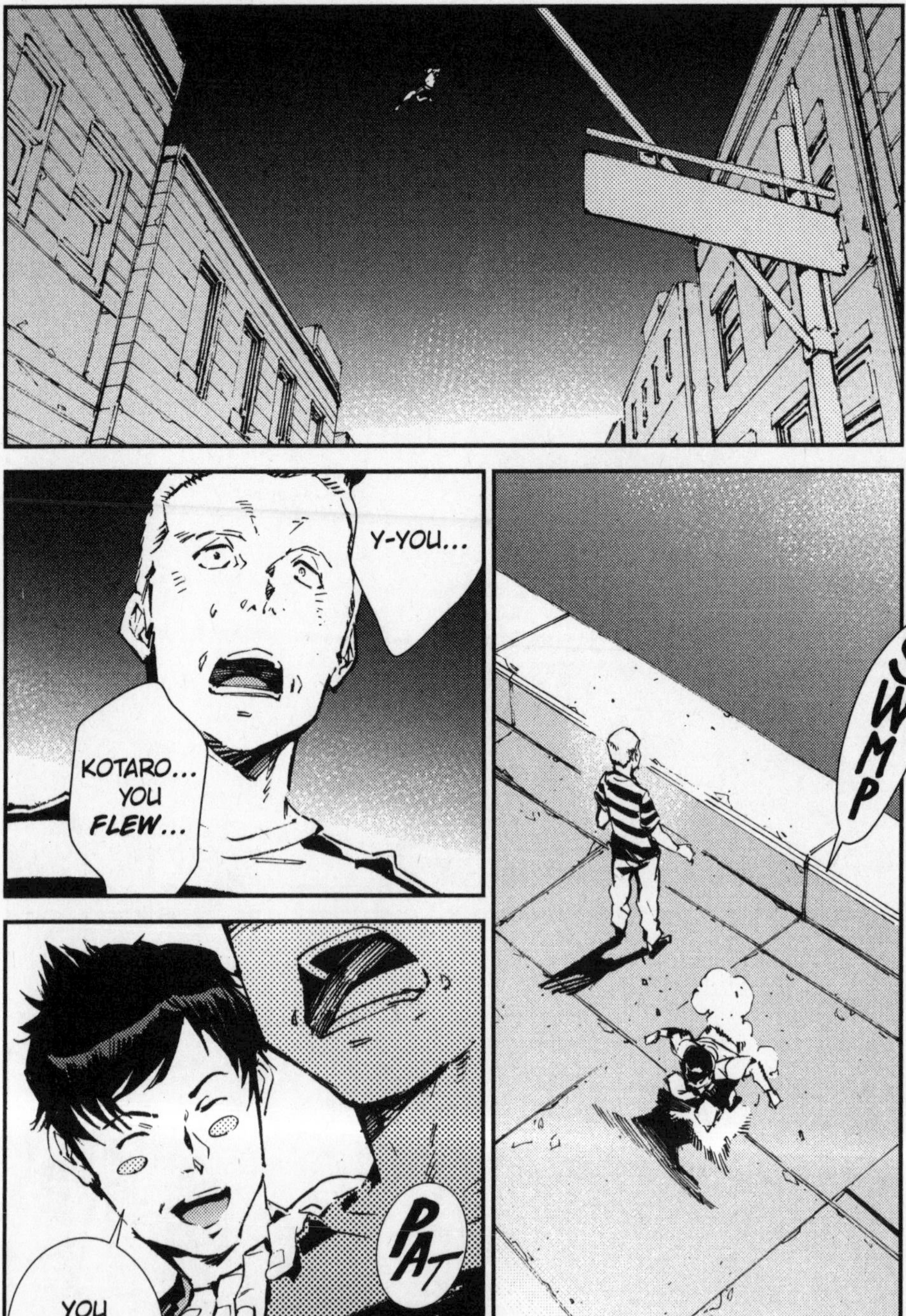
SWMP
Y-YOU...
KOTARO... YOU FLEW...
PAT
YOU BELIEVE ME NOW?

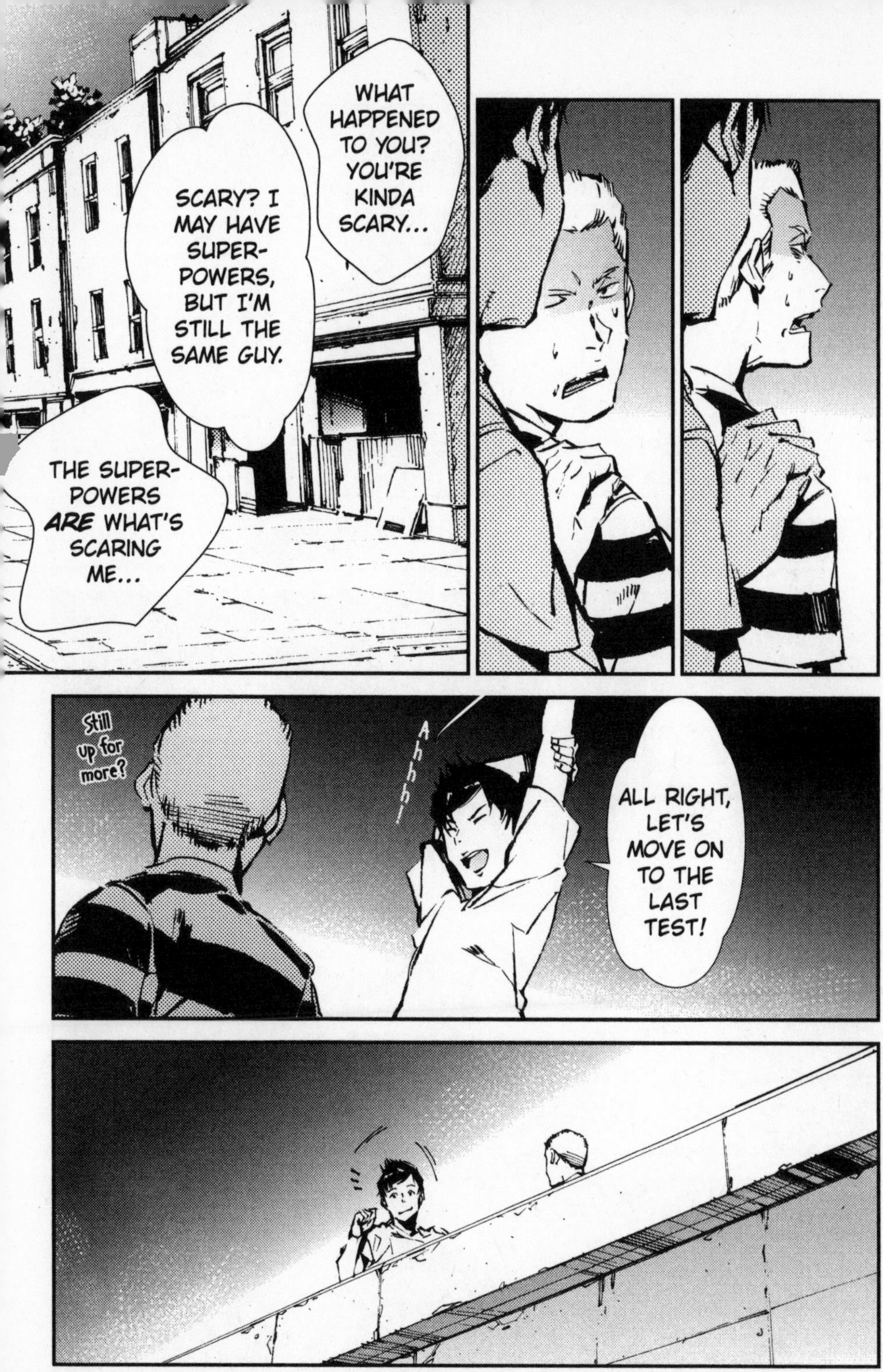
WHAT HAPPENED TO YOU? YOU'RE KINDA SCARY...
SCARY? I MAY HAVE SUPER-POWERS, BUT I'M STILL THE SAME GUY.
THE SUPER-POWERS *ARE* WHAT'S SCARING ME...
Ahhh!
ALL RIGHT, LET'S MOVE ON TO THE LAST TEST!
Still up for more?

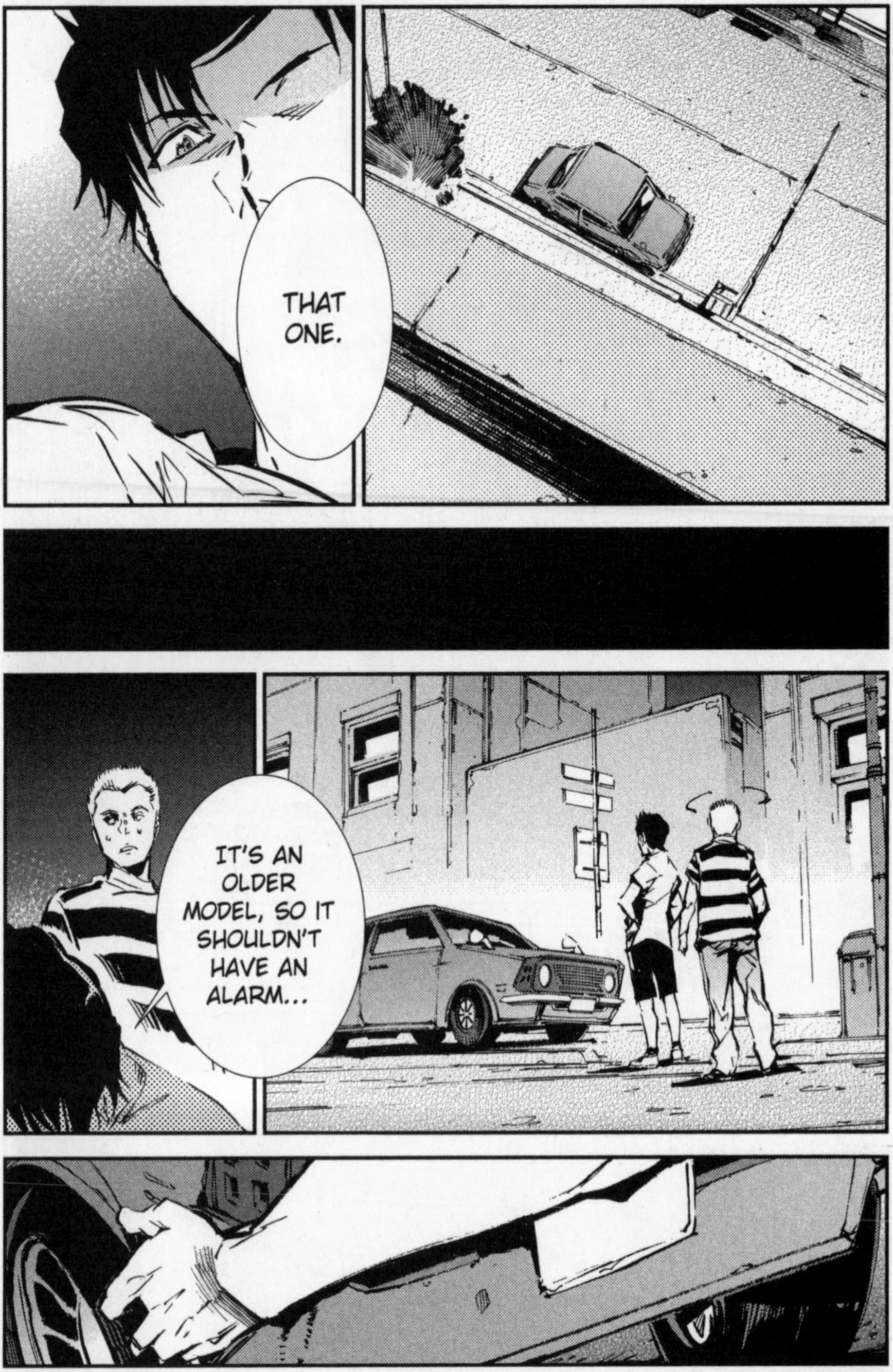
THAT ONE.
IT'S AN OLDER MODEL, SO IT SHOULDN'T HAVE AN ALARM...

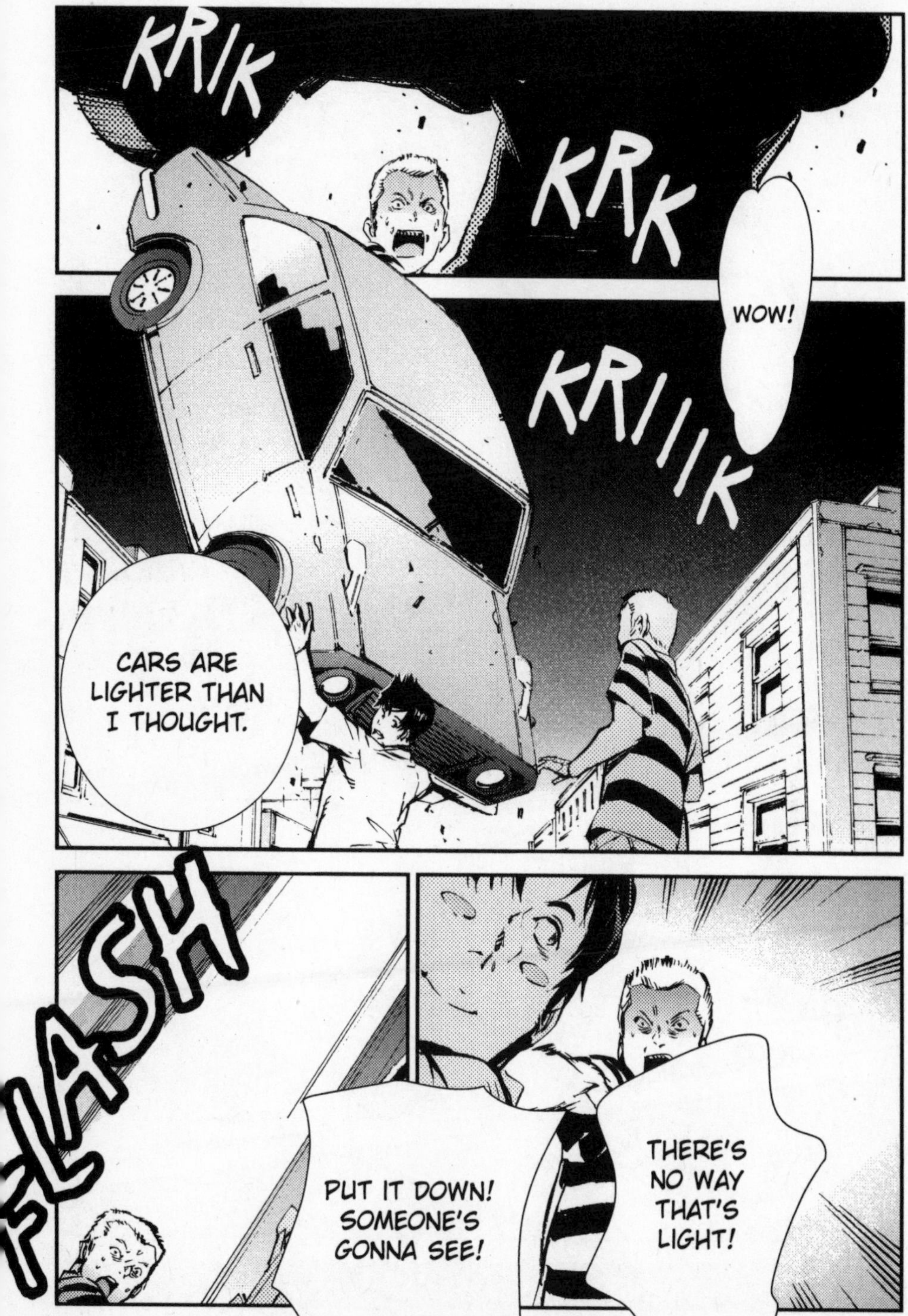
KRIK
KRK
WOW!
KRIIIK
CARS ARE LIGHTER THAN I THOUGHT.
THERE'S NO WAY THAT'S LIGHT!
PUT IT DOWN! SOMEONE'S GONNA SEE!
FLASH

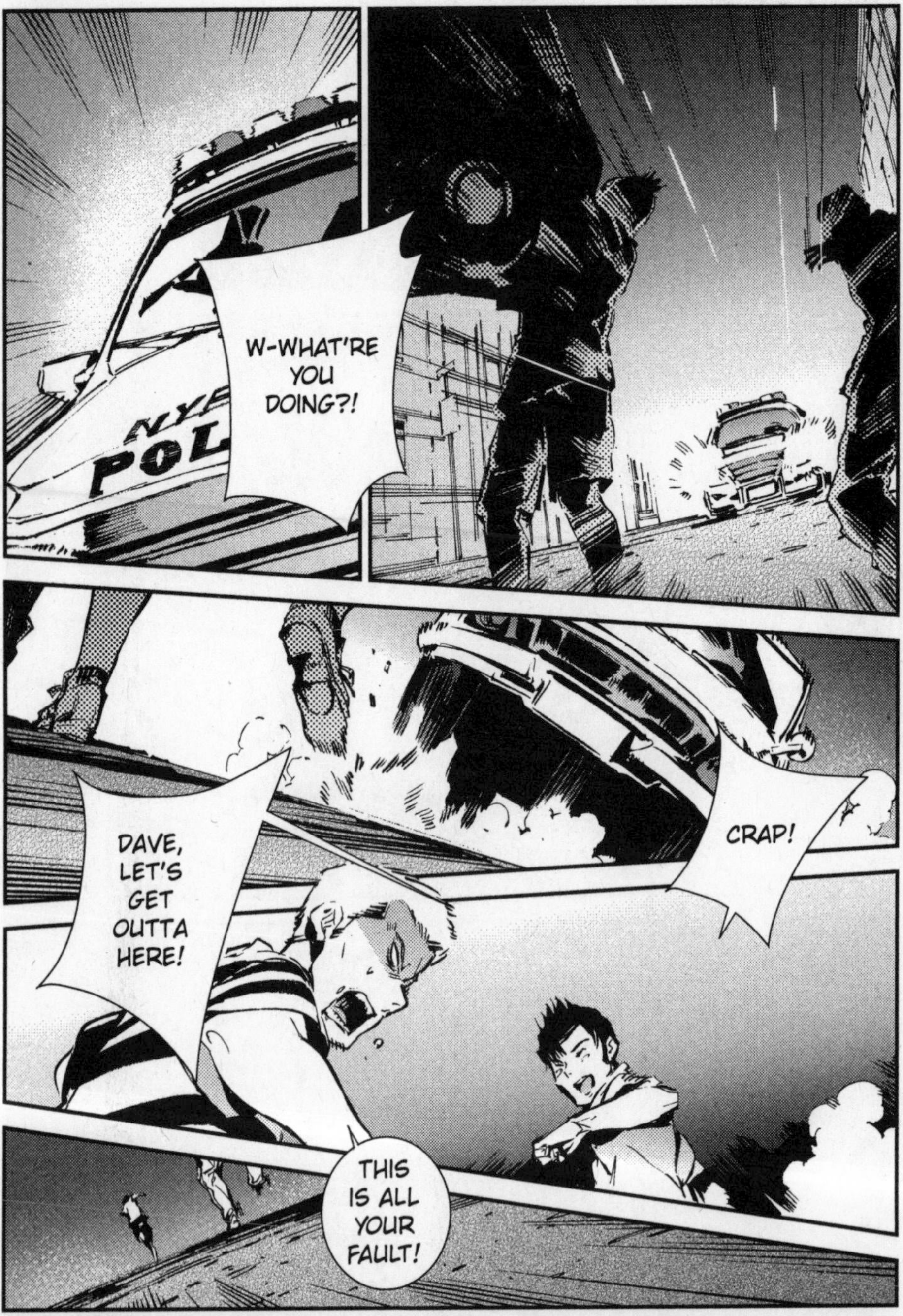
W-WHAT'RE YOU DOING?!
CRAP!
DAVE, LET'S GET OUTTA HERE!
THIS IS ALL YOUR FAULT!

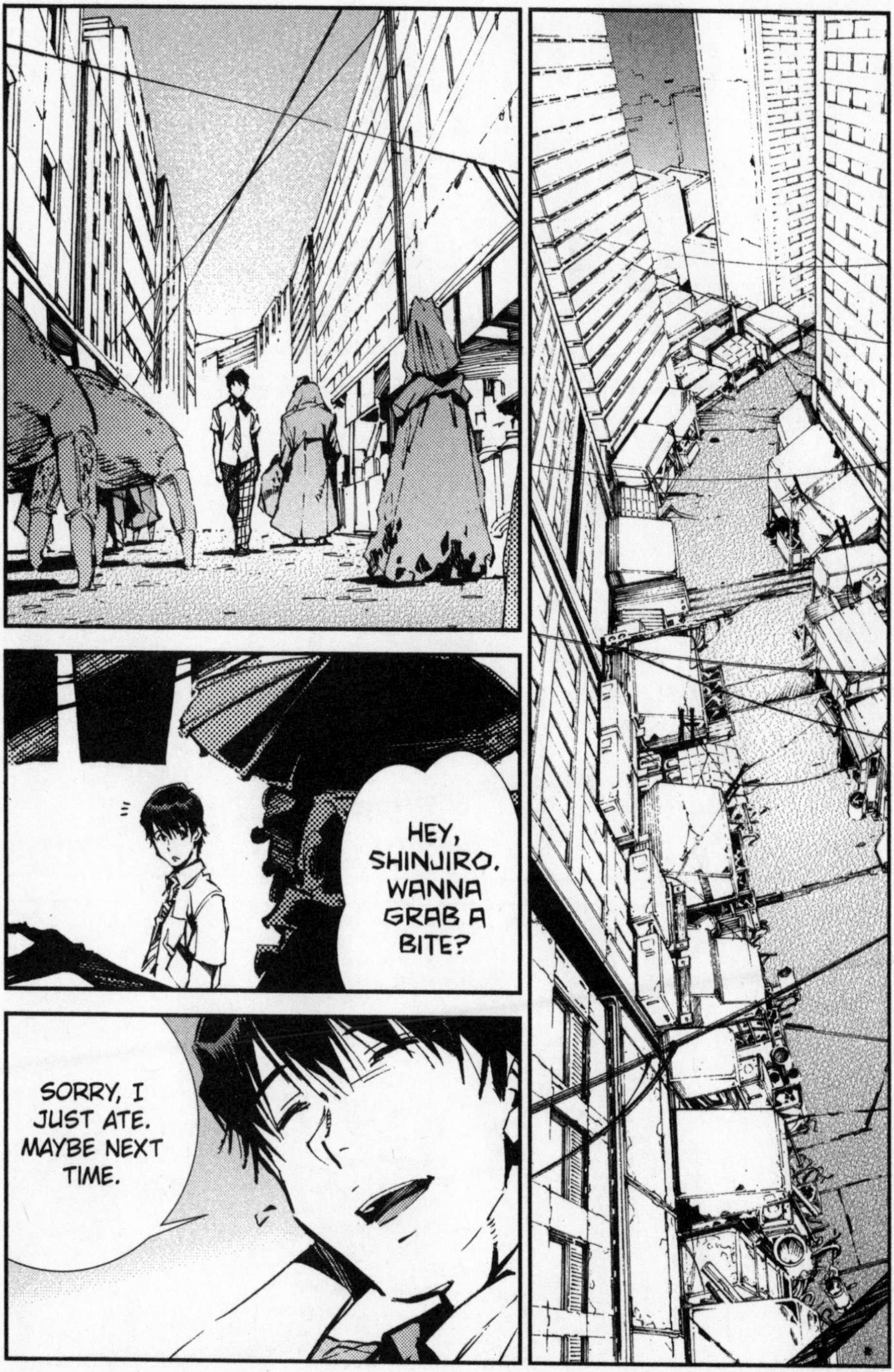
HEY, SHINJIRO. WANNA GRAB A BITE?
SORRY, I JUST ATE. MAYBE NEXT TIME.

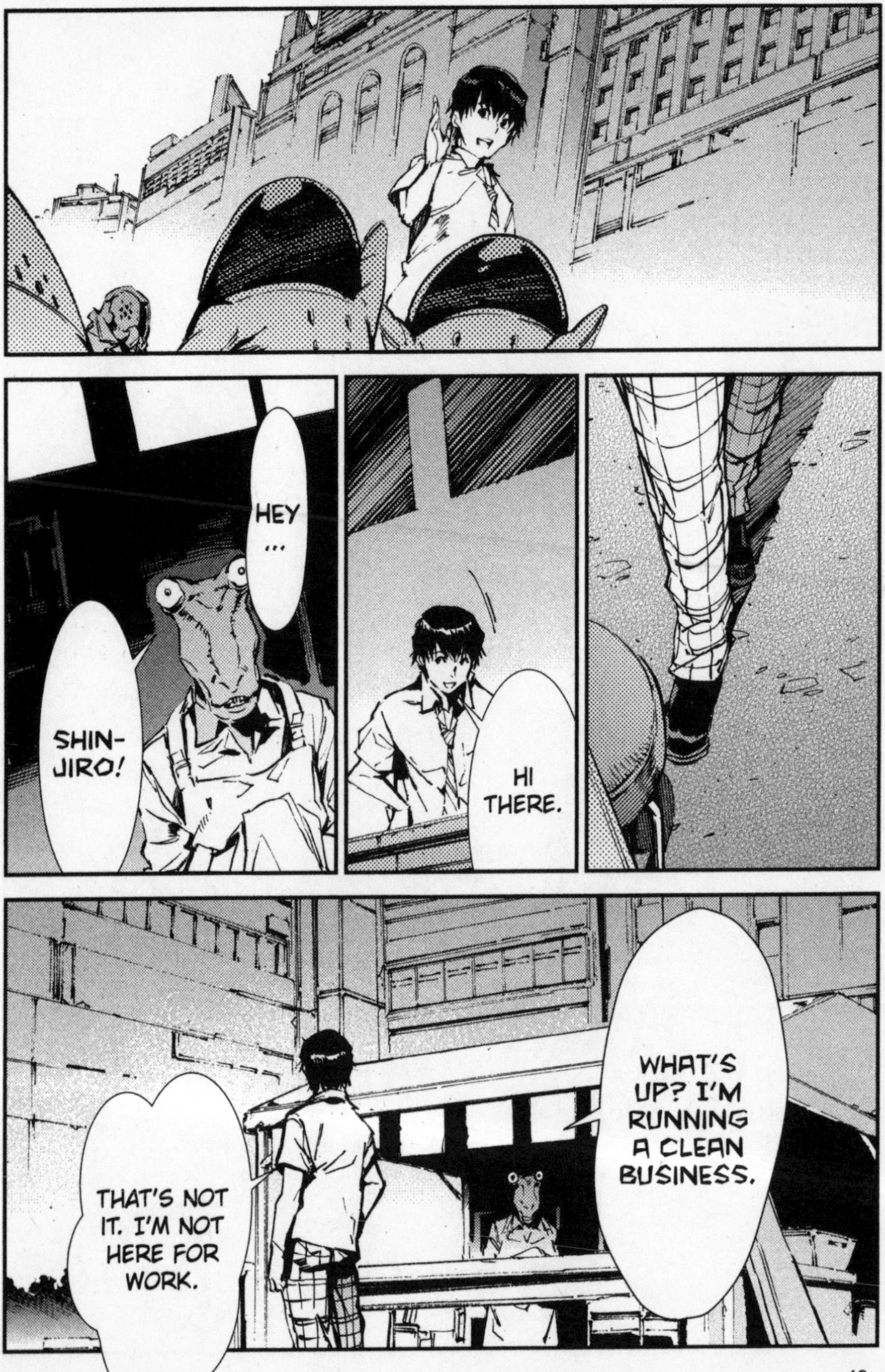
HI THERE.
HEY ...
SHIN-JIRO!
WHAT'S UP? I'M RUNNING A CLEAN BUSINESS.
THAT'S NOT IT. I'M NOT HERE FOR WORK.

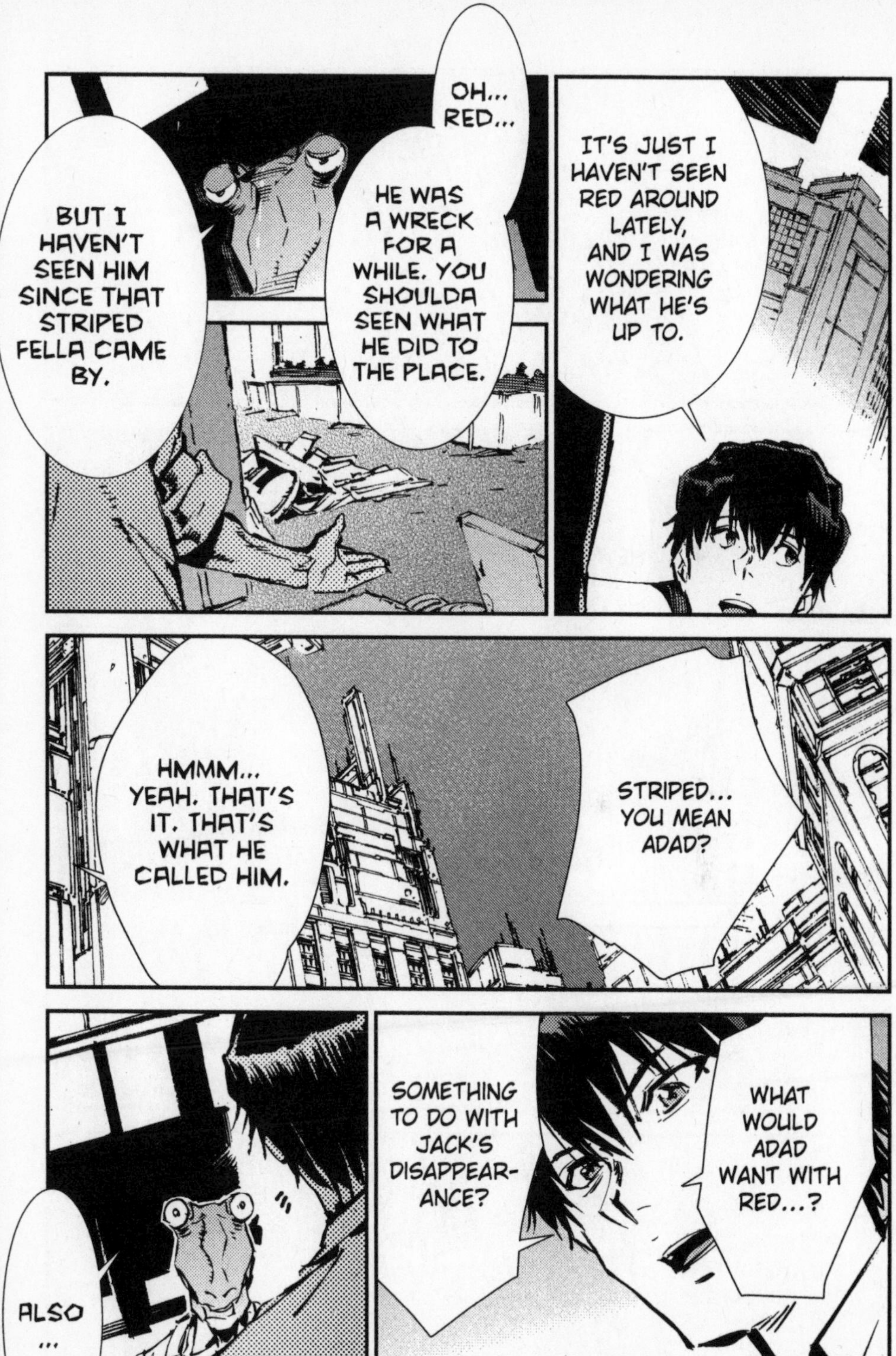
IT'S JUST I HAVEN'T SEEN RED AROUND LATELY, AND I WAS WONDERING WHAT HE'S UP TO.
OH... RED...
HE WAS A WRECK FOR A WHILE. YOU SHOULDA SEEN WHAT HE DID TO THE PLACE.
BUT I HAVEN'T SEEN HIM SINCE THAT STRIPED FELLA CAME BY.
STRIPED... YOU MEAN ADAD?
HMMM... YEAH. THAT'S IT. THAT'S WHAT HE CALLED HIM.
WHAT WOULD ADAD WANT WITH RED...?
SOMETHING TO DO WITH JACK'S DISAPPEAR-ANCE?
ALSO ...

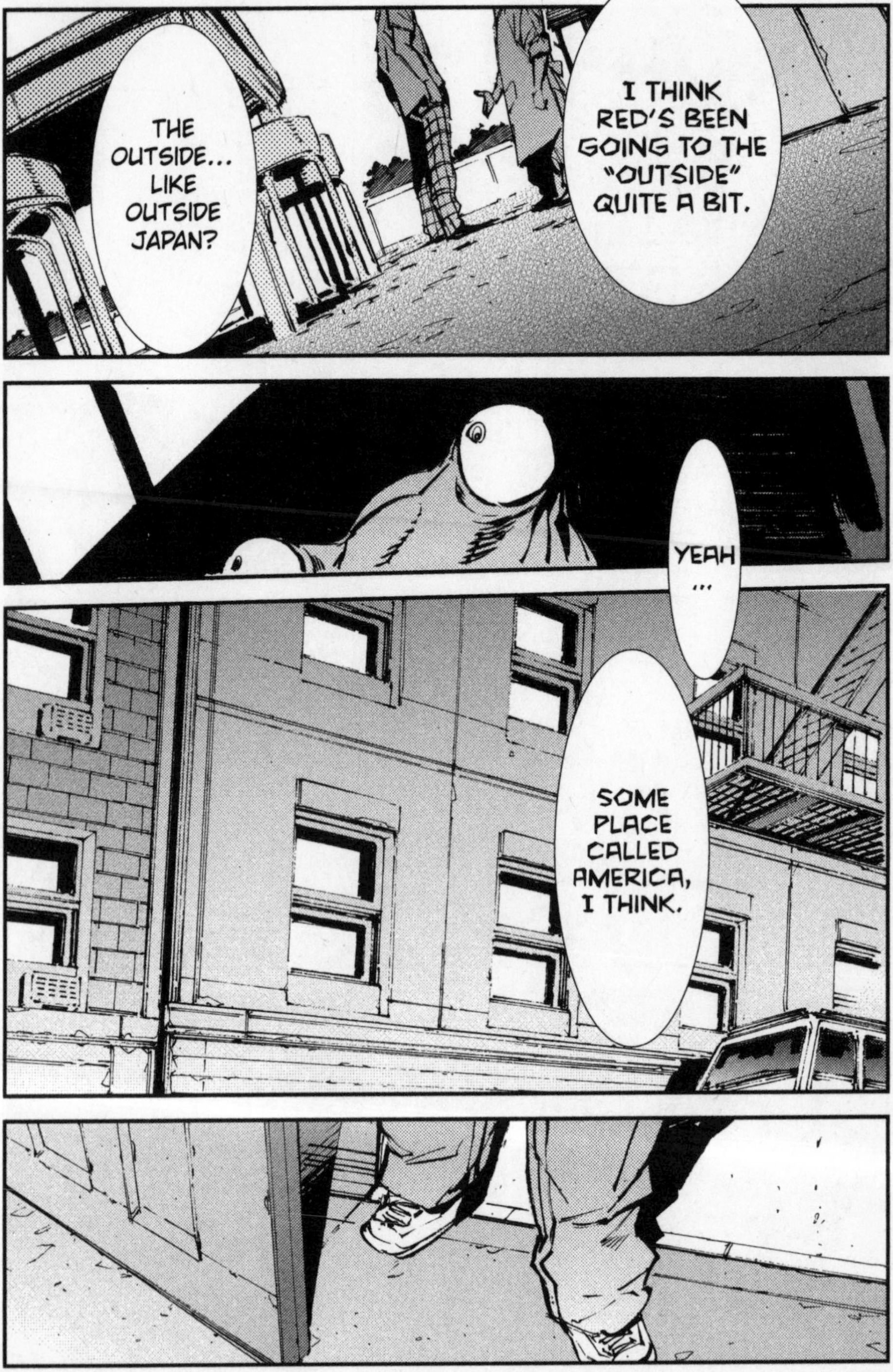
I THINK RED'S BEEN GOING TO THE "OUTSIDE" QUITE A BIT.
THE OUTSIDE... LIKE OUTSIDE JAPAN?
YEAH ...
SOME PLACE CALLED AMERICA, I THINK.

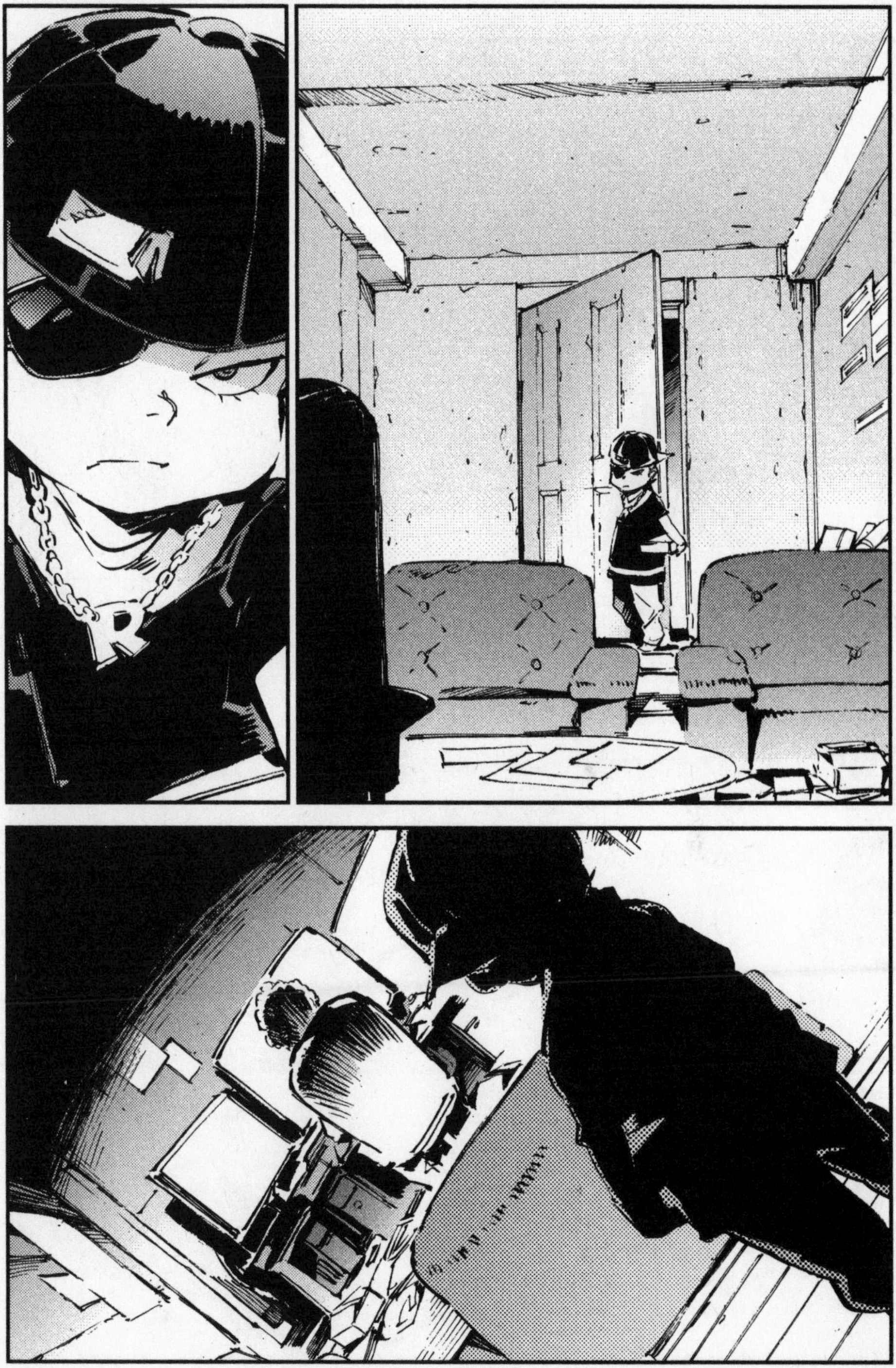

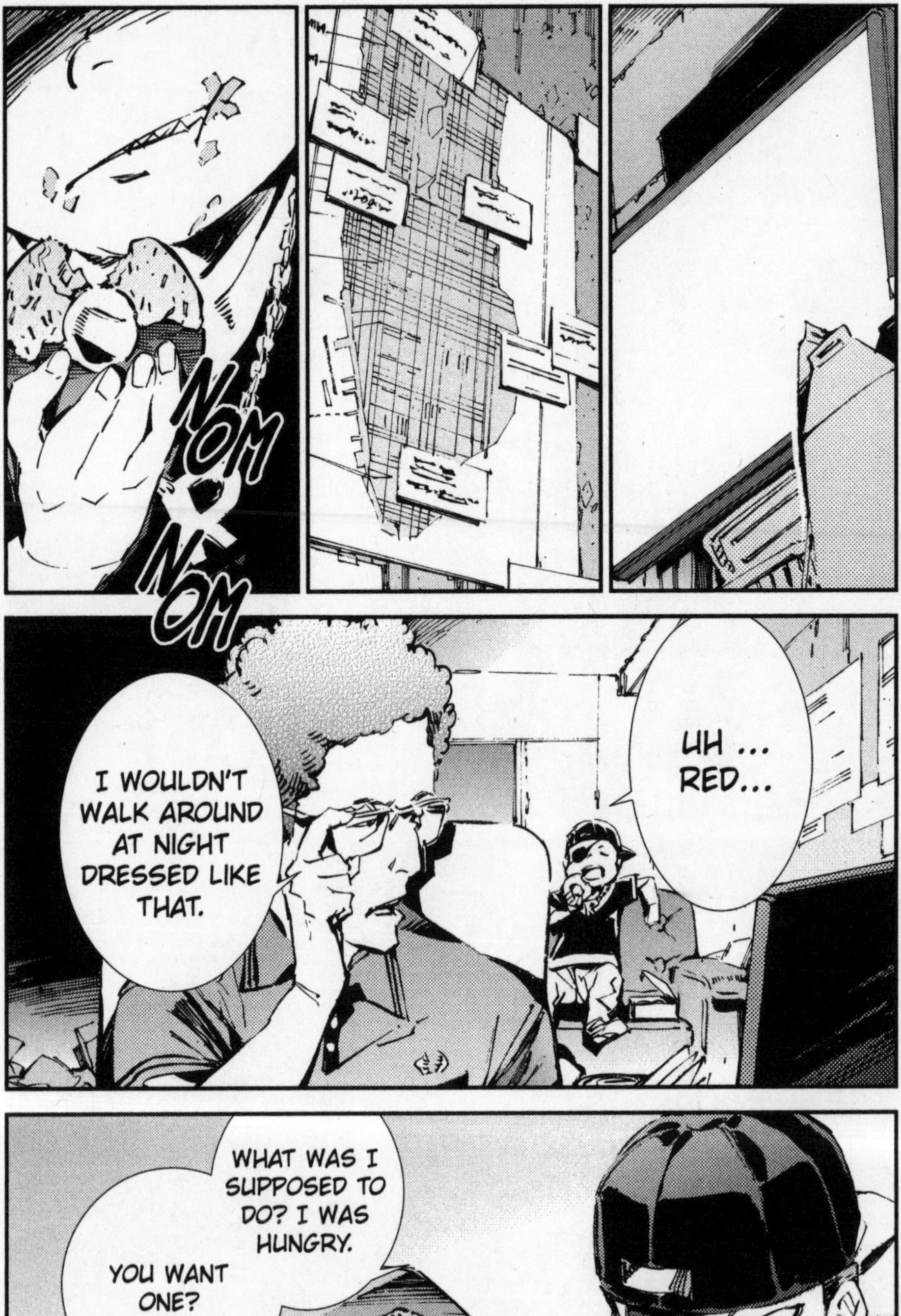
NOM NOM
UH ... RED...
I WOULDN'T WALK AROUND AT NIGHT DRESSED LIKE THAT.
WHAT WAS I SUPPOSED TO DO? I WAS HUNGRY.
YOU WANT ONE?

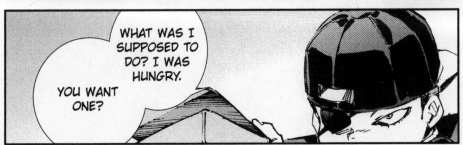

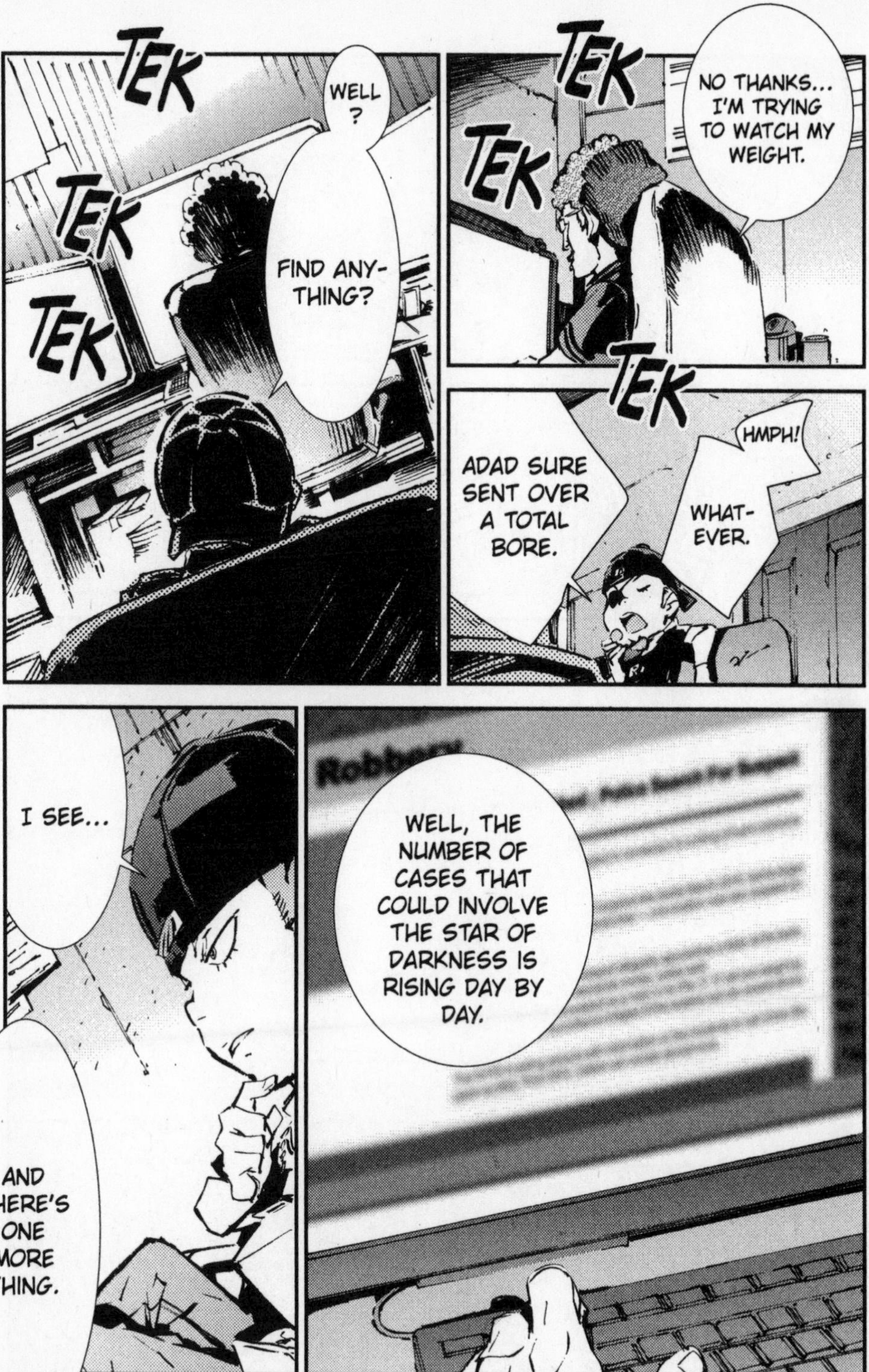
TEK
TEK
NO THANKS... I'M TRYING TO WATCH MY WEIGHT.
TEK
HMPH!
WHAT-EVER.
ADAD SURE SENT OVER A TOTAL BORE.
TEK
WELL ?
FIND ANY-THING?
TEK
TEK
WELL, THE NUMBER OF CASES THAT COULD INVOLVE THE STAR OF DARKNESS IS RISING DAY BY DAY.
I SEE...
AND THERE'S ONE MORE THING.

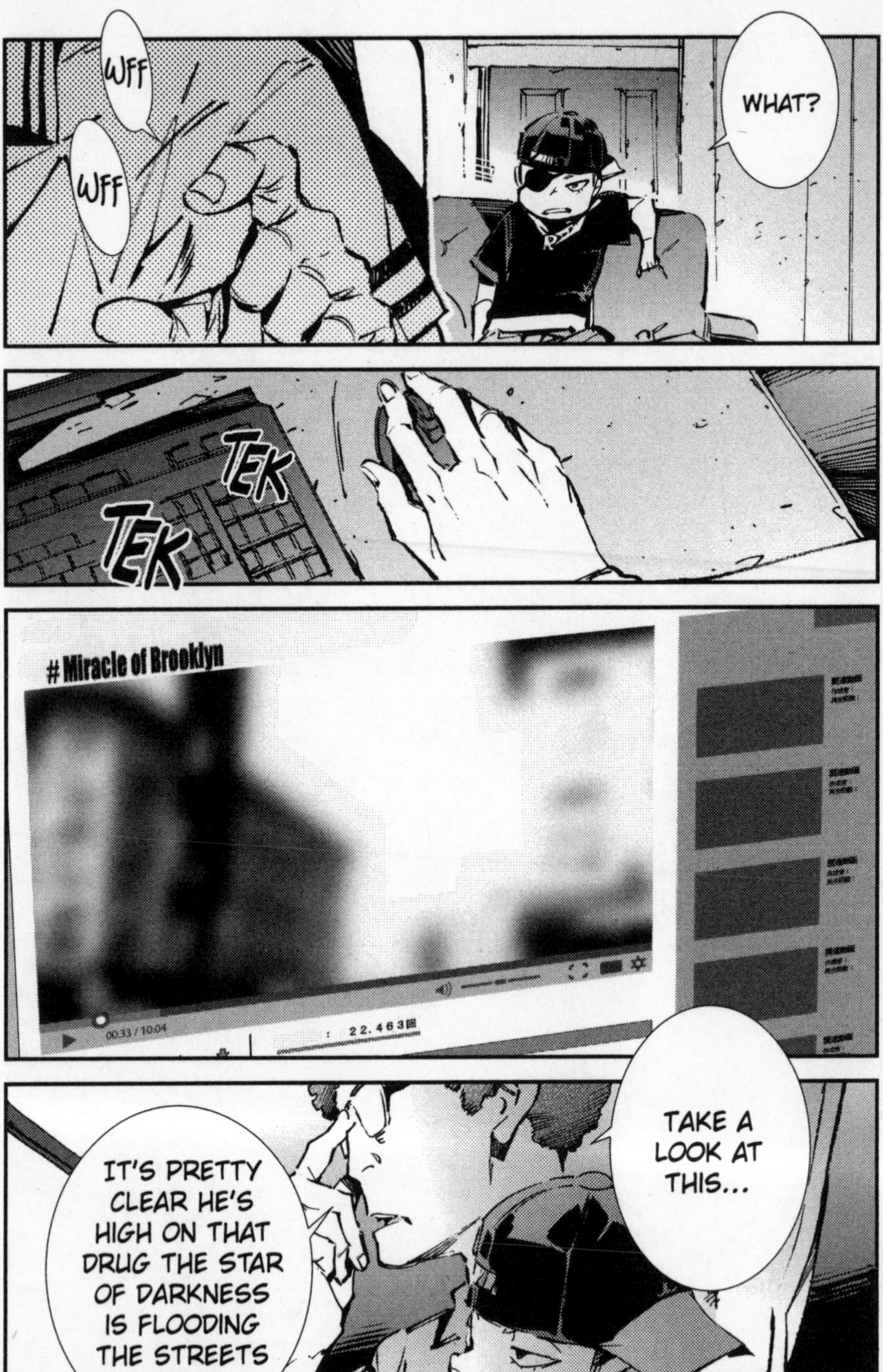
WHAT?
WFF
WFF
TEK
TEK
Miracle of Brooklyn
00:33 / 10:04
22.463回
TAKE A LOOK AT THIS...
IT'S PRETTY CLEAR HE'S HIGH ON THAT DRUG THE STAR OF DARKNESS IS FLOODING THE STREETS WITH.

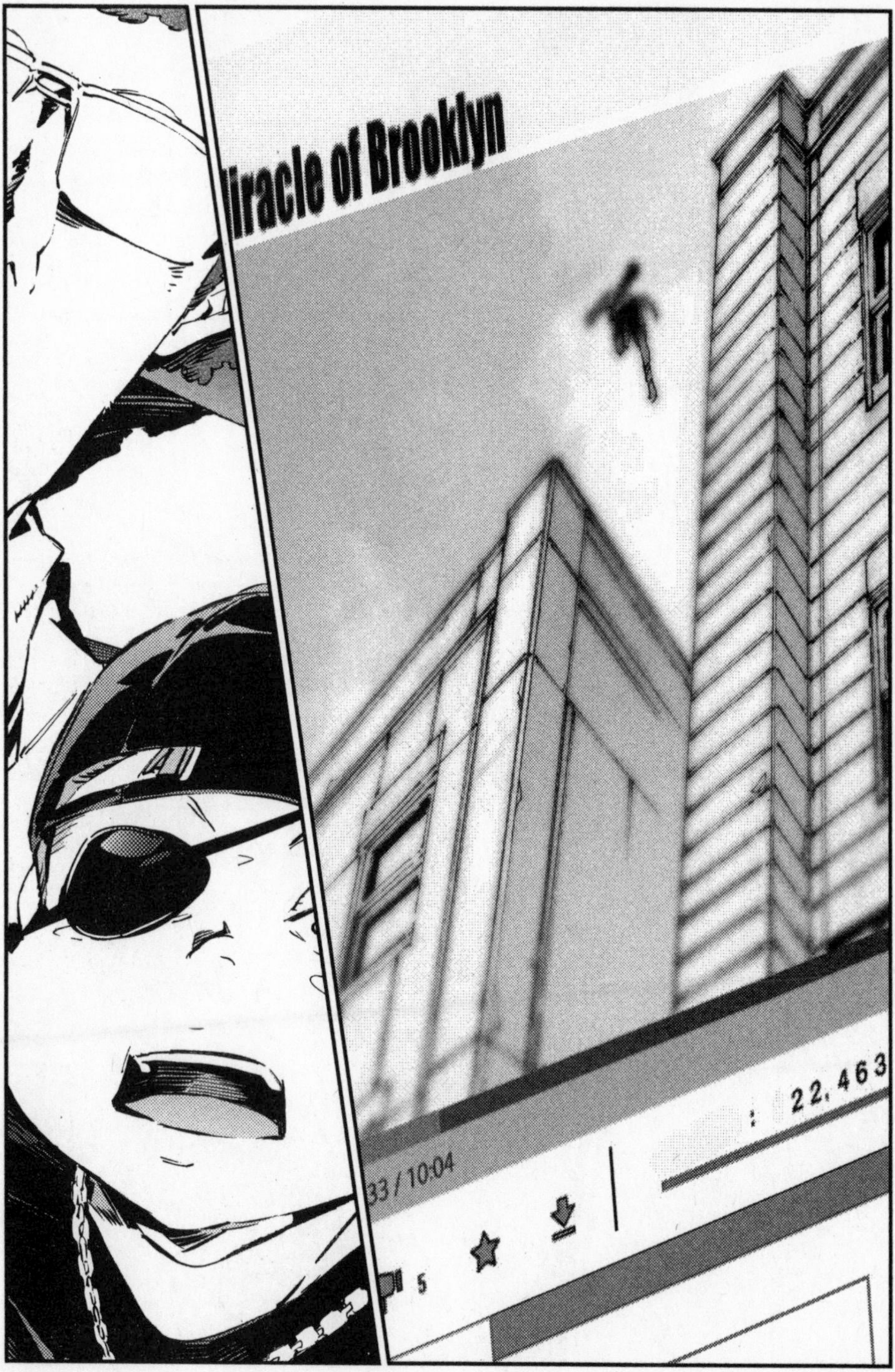
iracle of Brooklyn
22,463
33 / 10:04
5

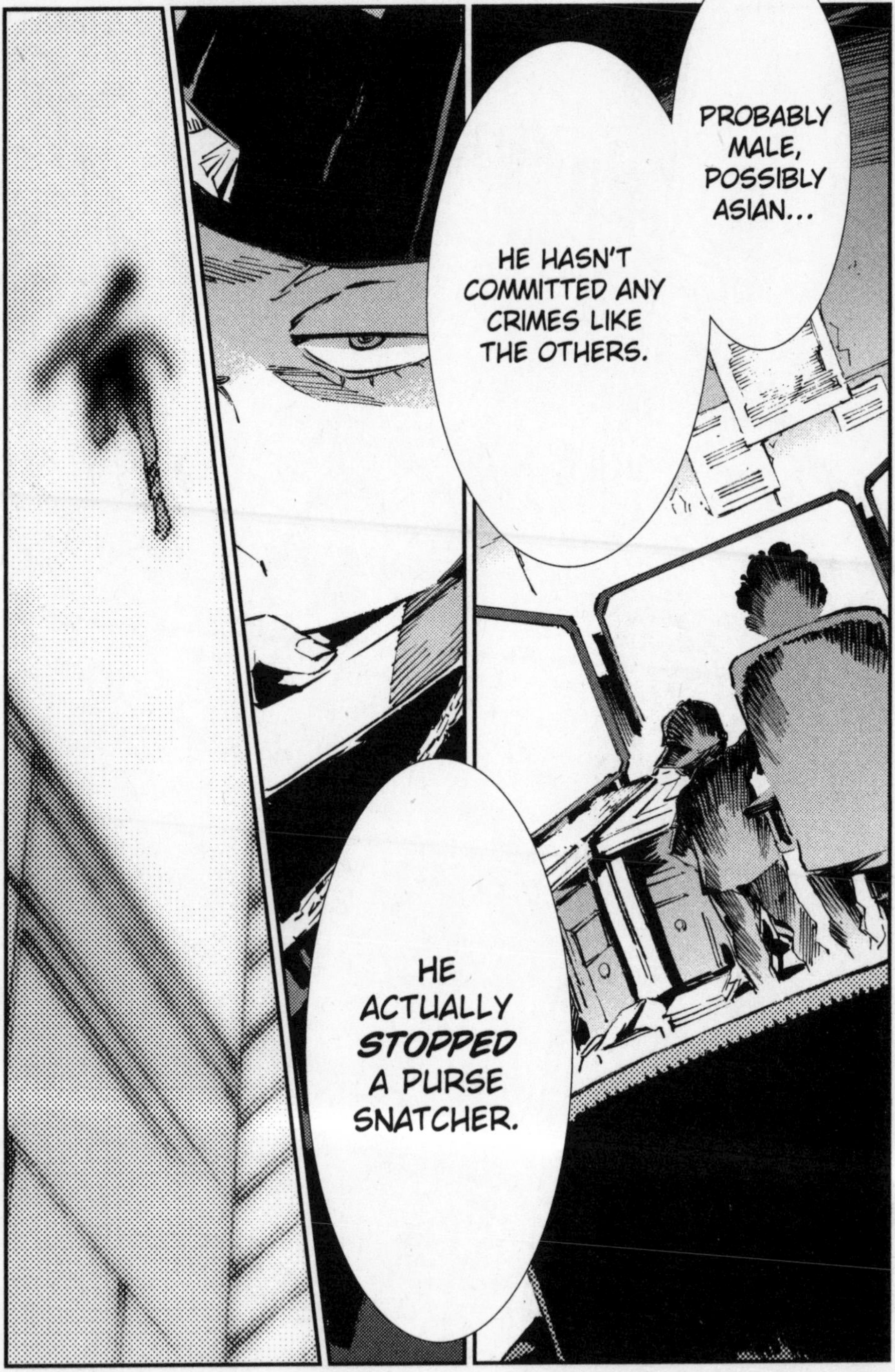
PROBABLY MALE, POSSIBLY ASIAN...
HE HASN'T COMMITTED ANY CRIMES LIKE THE OTHERS.
HE ACTUALLY STOPPED A PURSE SNATCHER.

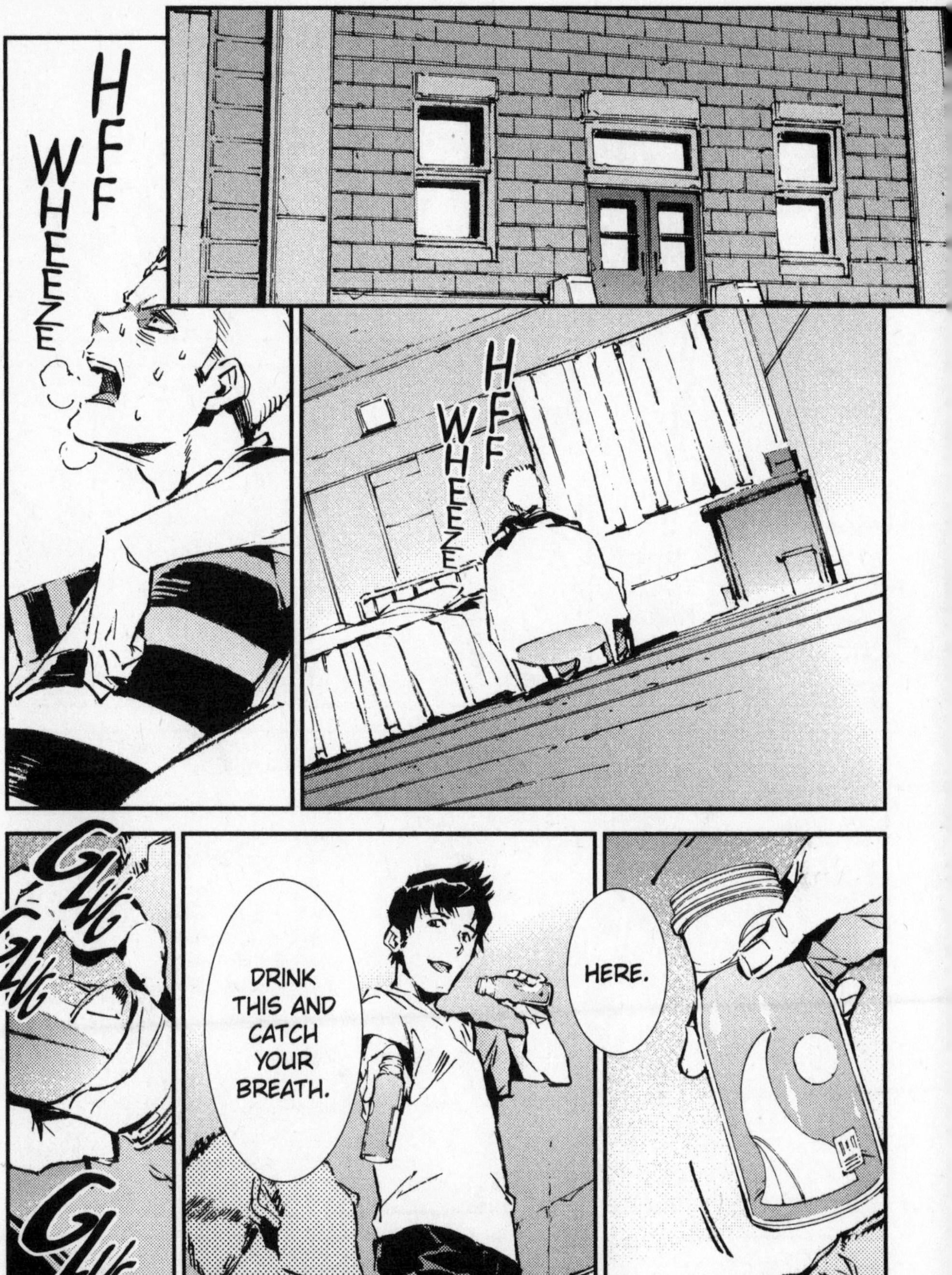
HFF
WHEEZE
HFF
WHEEZE
HERE.
DRINK THIS AND CATCH YOUR BREATH.
GLUG GLUG
GLUG

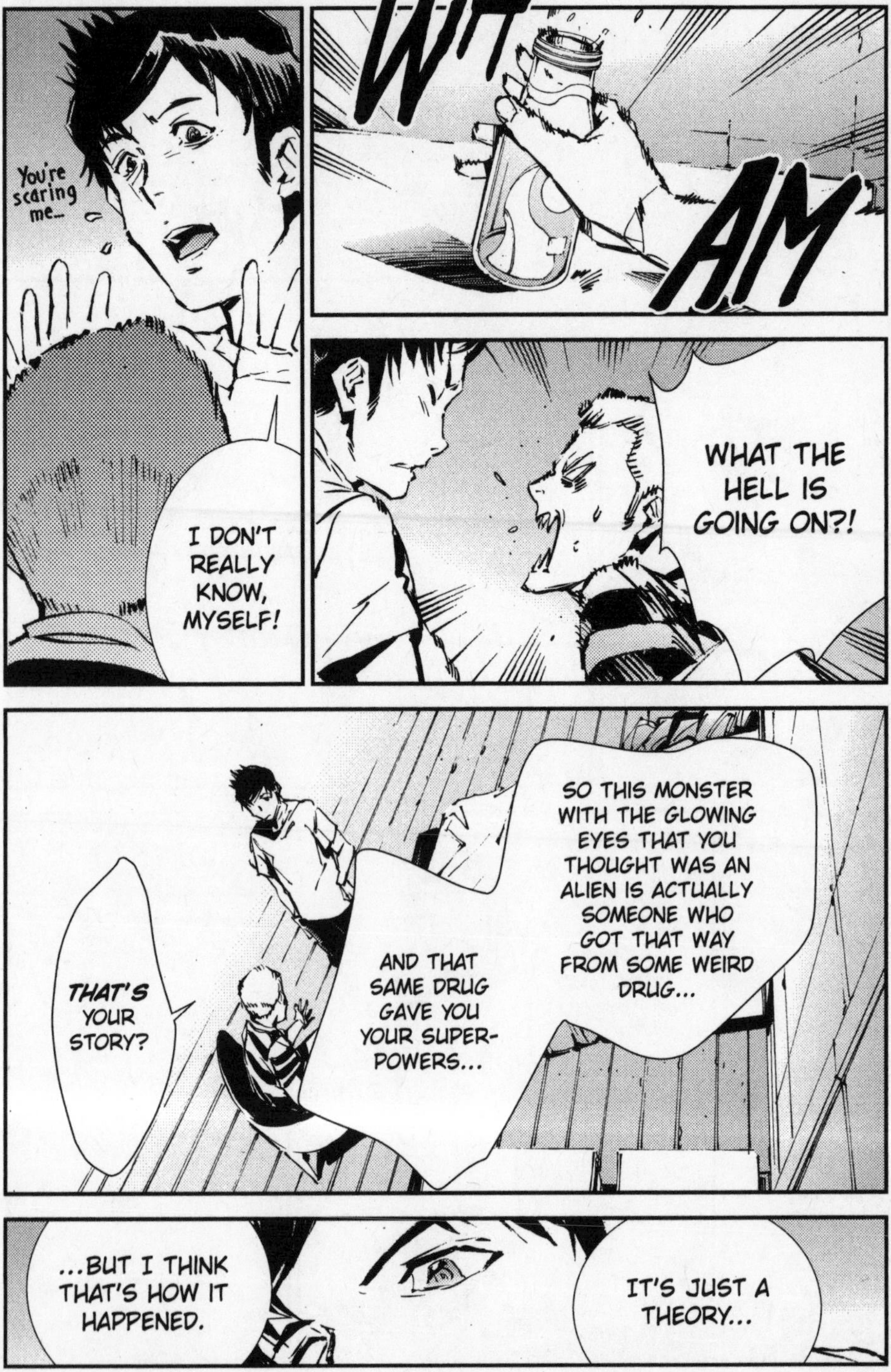
WHAM
WHAT THE HELL IS GOING ON?!
You're scaring me...
I DON'T REALLY KNOW, MYSELF!
SO THIS MONSTER WITH THE GLOWING EYES THAT YOU THOUGHT WAS AN ALIEN IS ACTUALLY SOMEONE WHO GOT THAT WAY FROM SOME WEIRD DRUG...
AND THAT SAME DRUG GAVE YOU YOUR SUPER-POWERS...
THAT'S YOUR STORY?
IT'S JUST A THEORY...
...BUT I THINK THAT'S HOW IT HAPPENED.

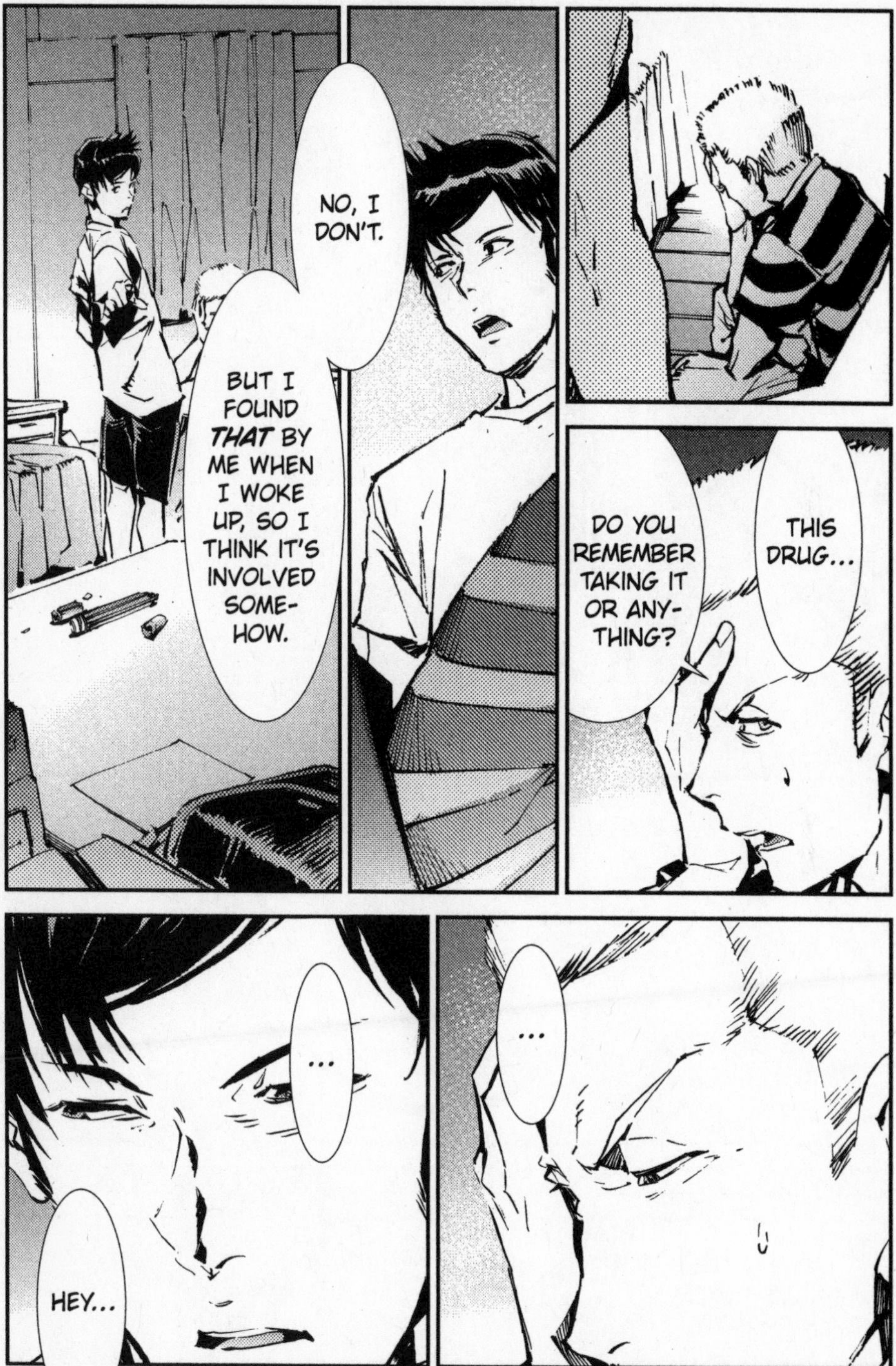

THIS DRUG...
DO YOU REMEMBER TAKING IT OR ANY-THING?
NO, I DON'T.
BUT I FOUND *THAT* BY ME WHEN I WOKE UP, SO I THINK IT'S INVOLVED SOME-HOW.
...
...
HEY...

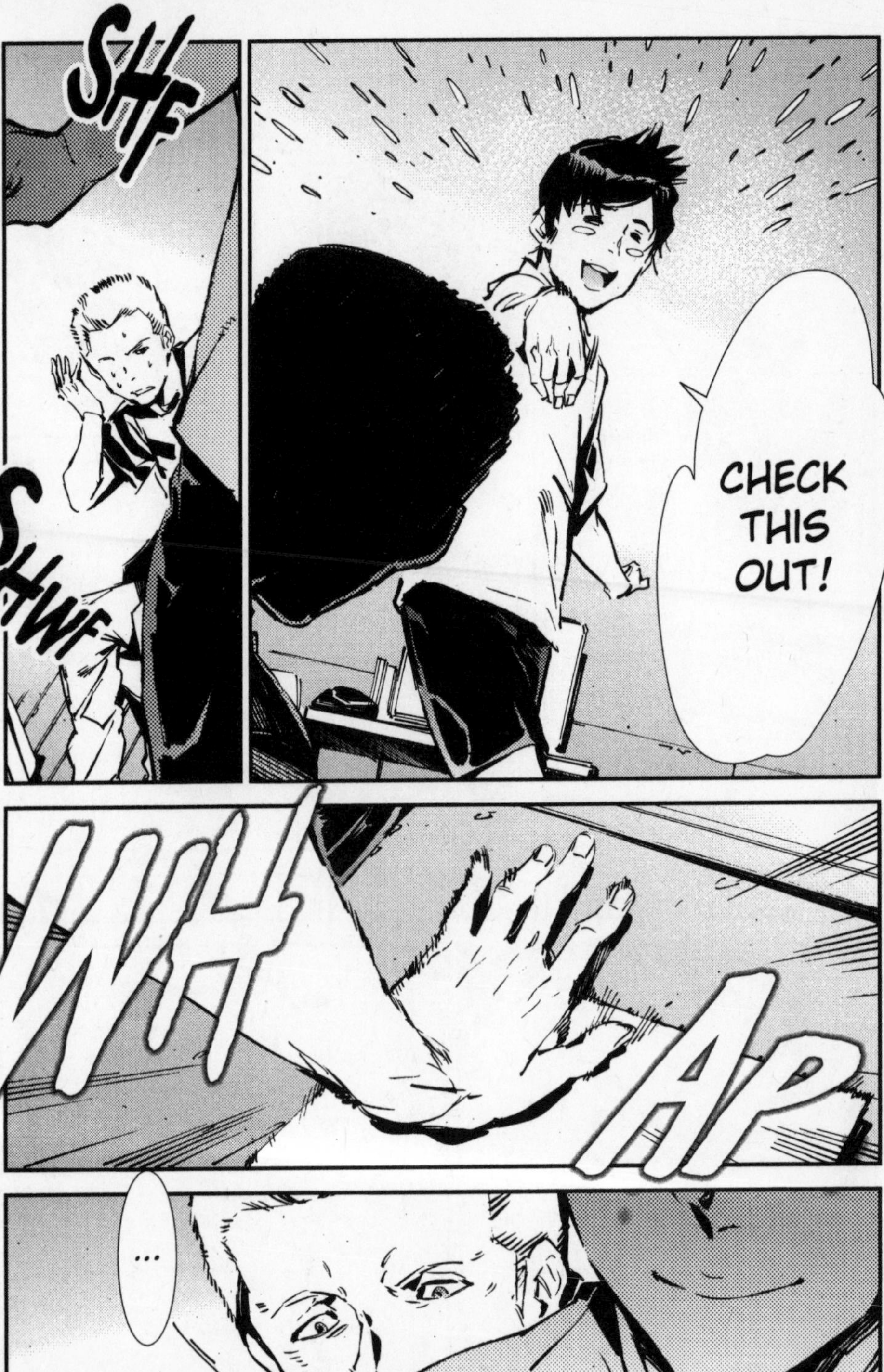
CHECK THIS OUT!
SHF
SHWF
WHAP
...

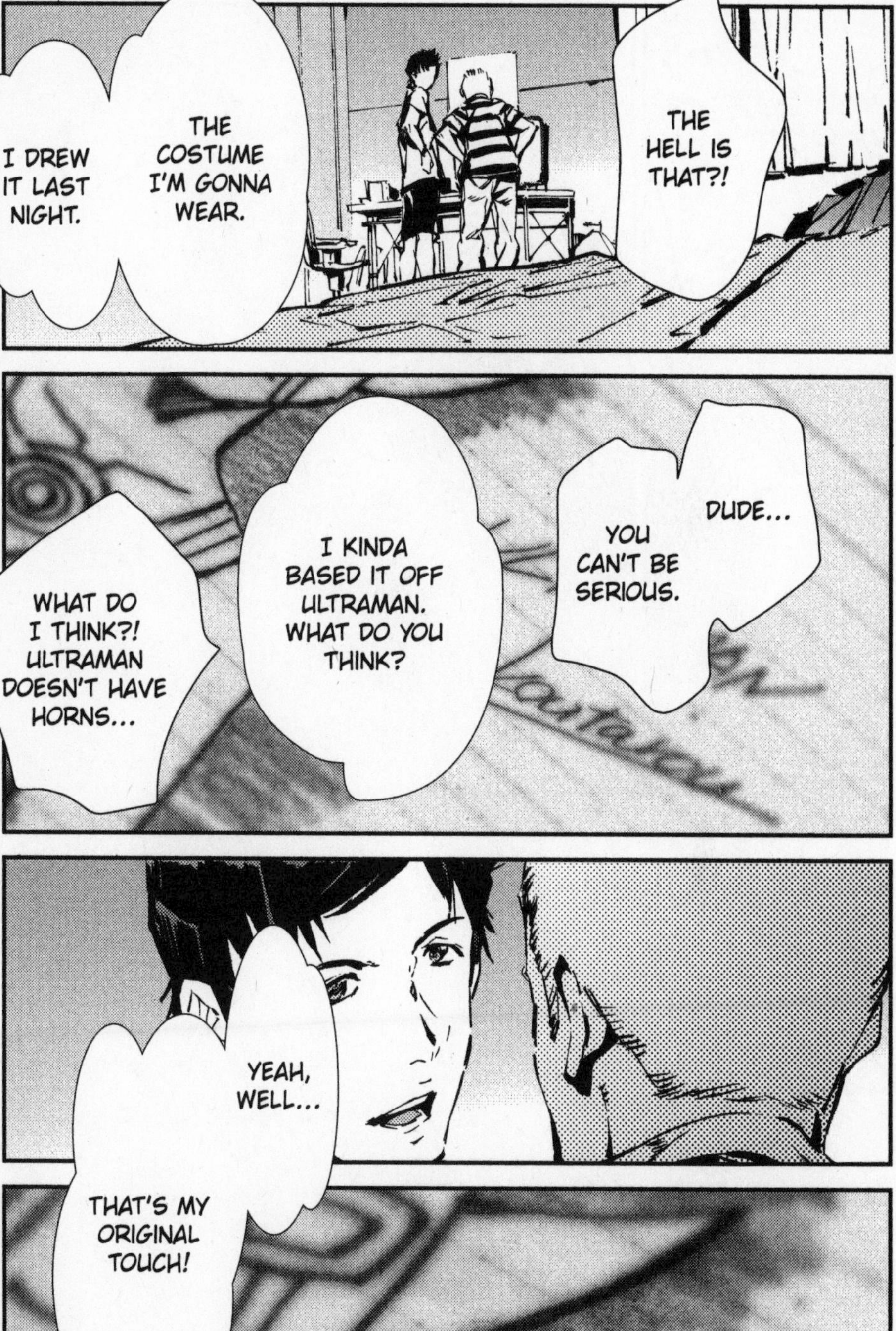
THE HELL IS THAT?!
THE COSTUME I'M GONNA WEAR.
I DREW IT LAST NIGHT.
DUDE... YOU CAN'T BE SERIOUS.
I KINDA BASED IT OFF ULTRAMAN. WHAT DO YOU THINK?
WHAT DO I THINK?! ULTRAMAN DOESN'T HAVE HORNS...
YEAH, WELL...
THAT'S MY ORIGINAL TOUCH!

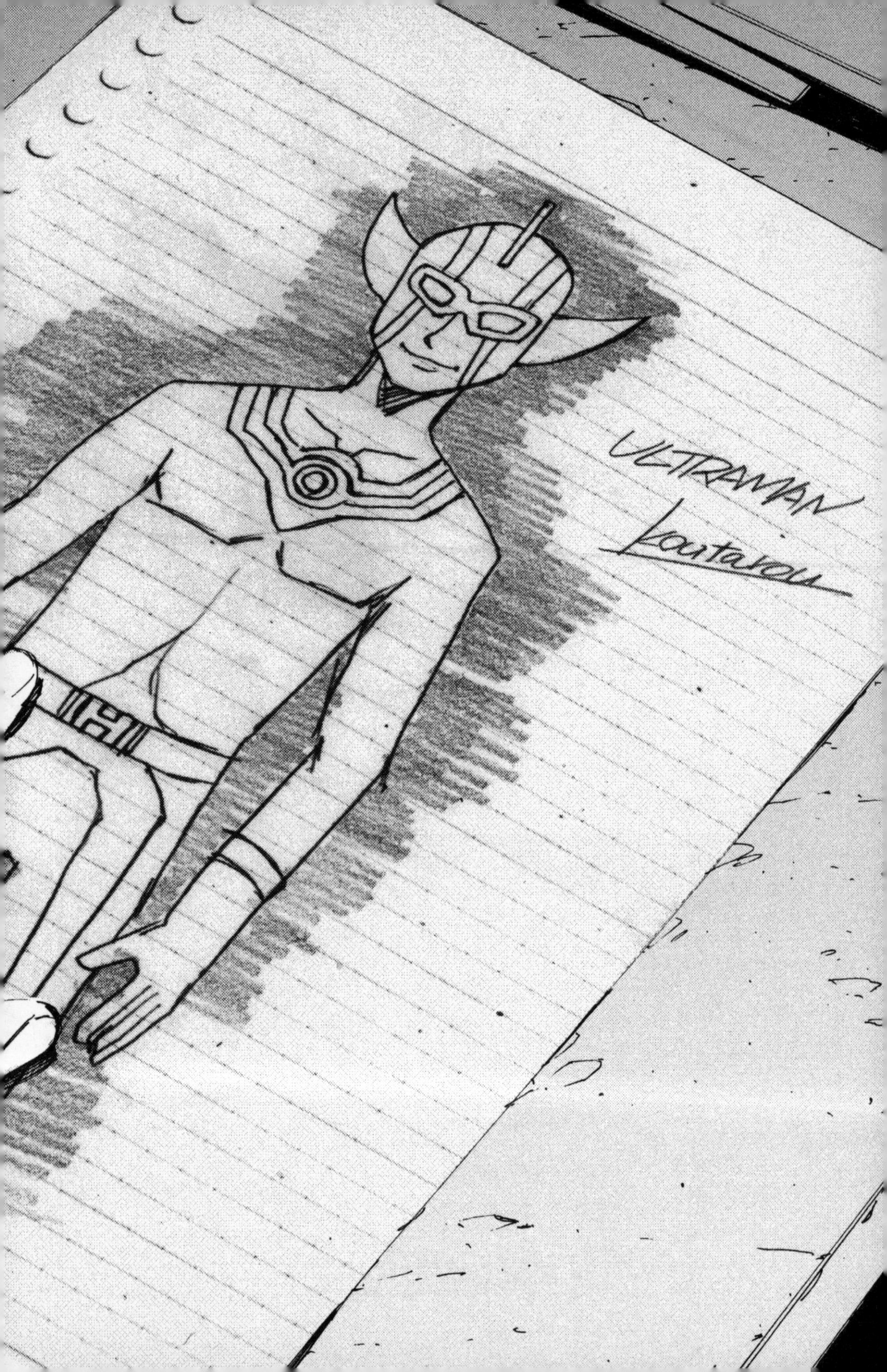
ULTRAMAN
Koutarou

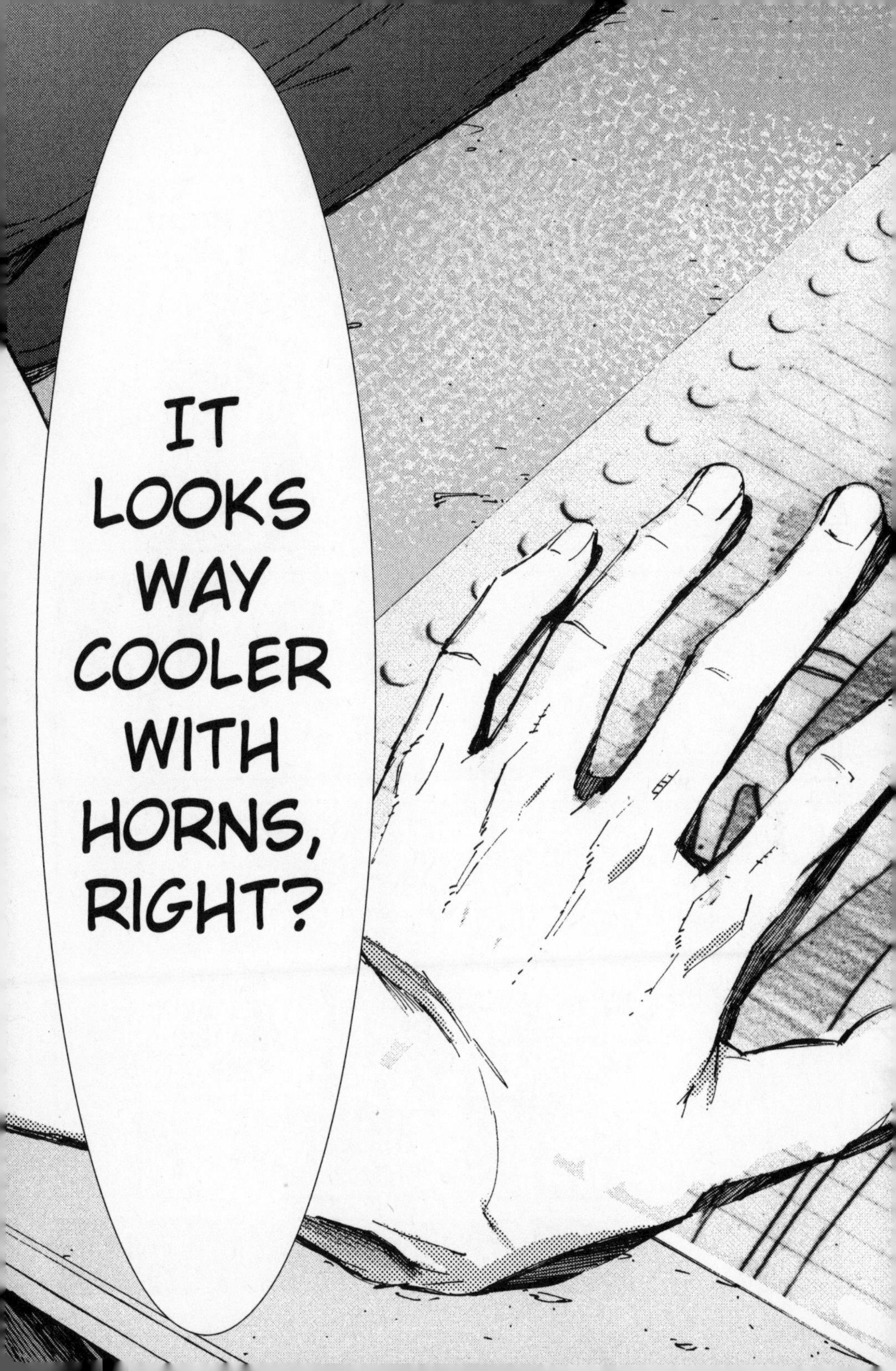
IT LOOKS WAY COOLER WITH HORNS, RIGHT?

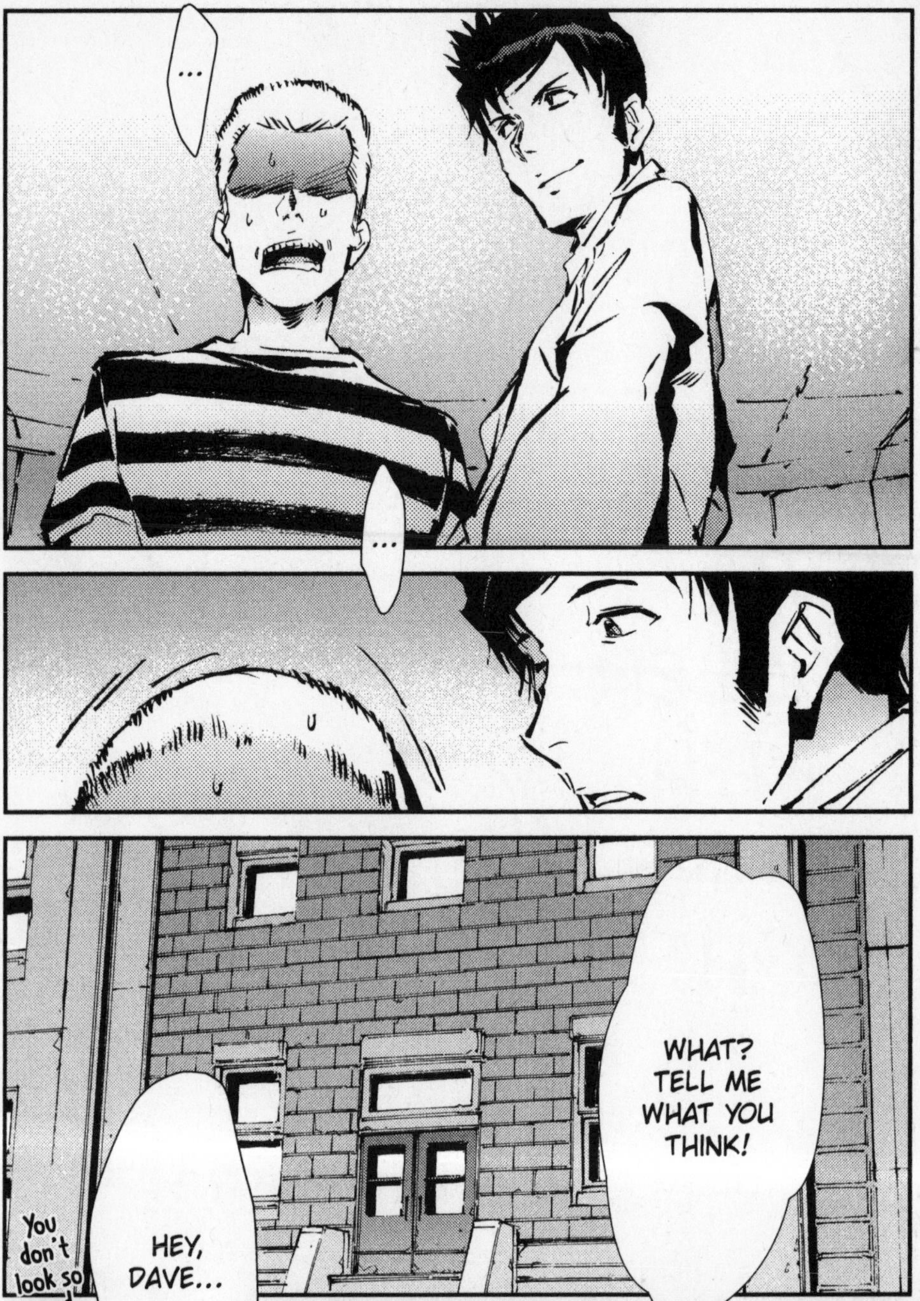
...
...
WHAT? TELL ME WHAT YOU THINK!
HEY, DAVE...
You don't look so good.

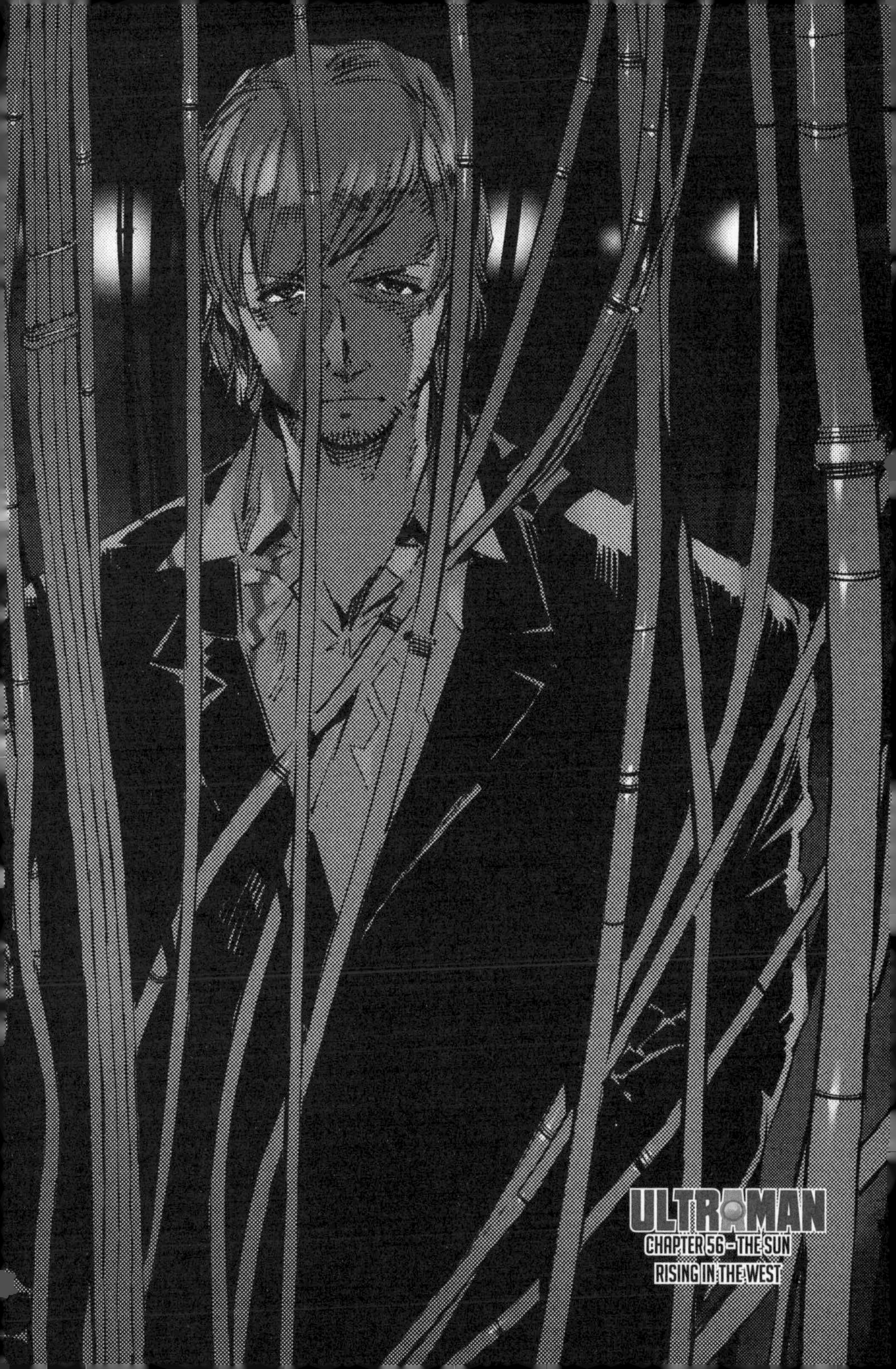
ULTRAMAN
CHAPTER 56 - THE SUN RISING IN THE WEST

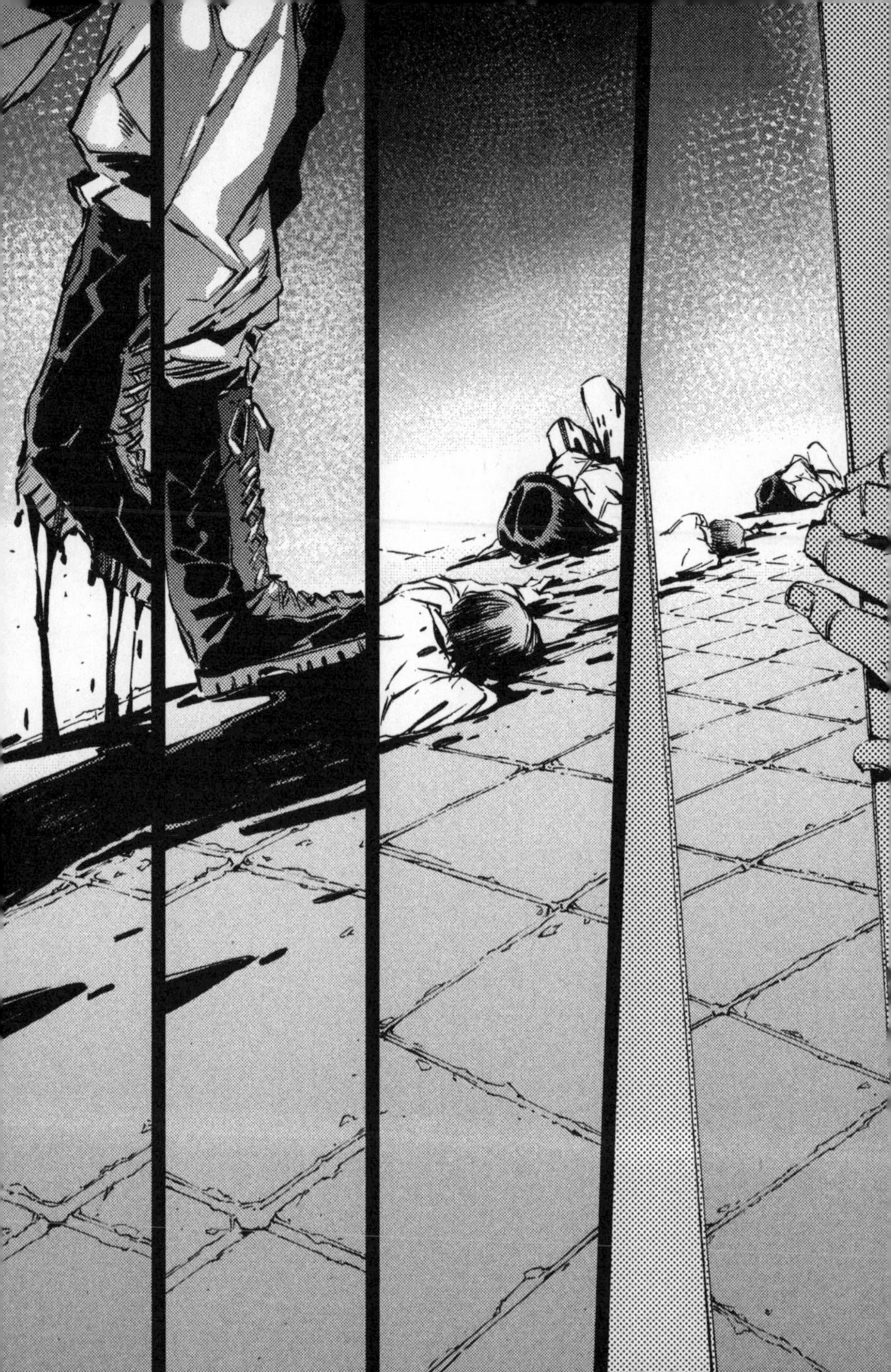

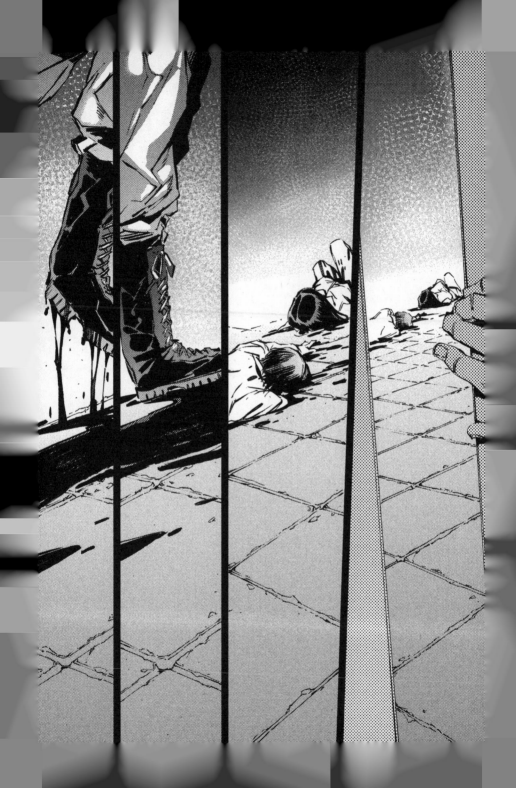

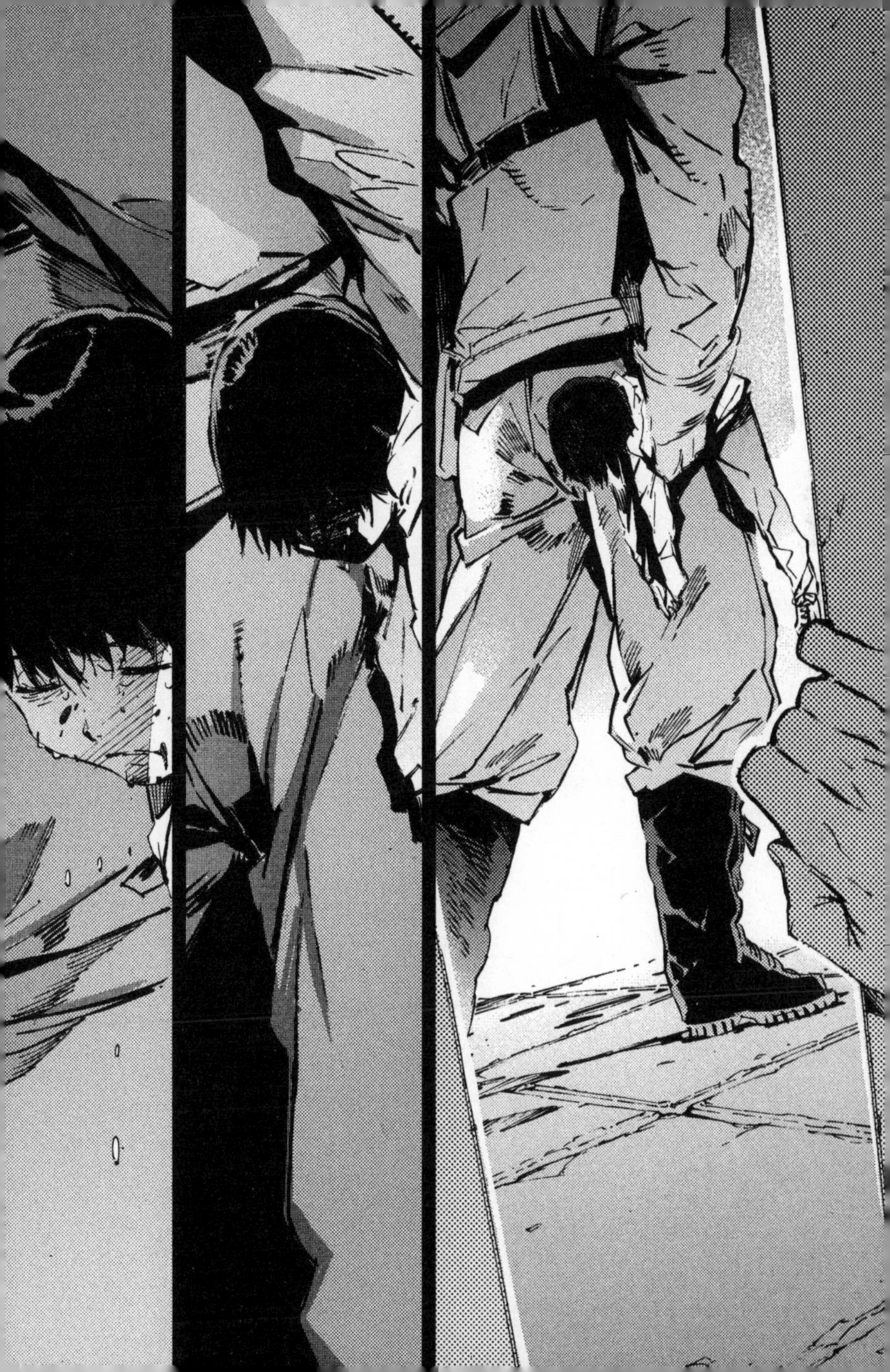

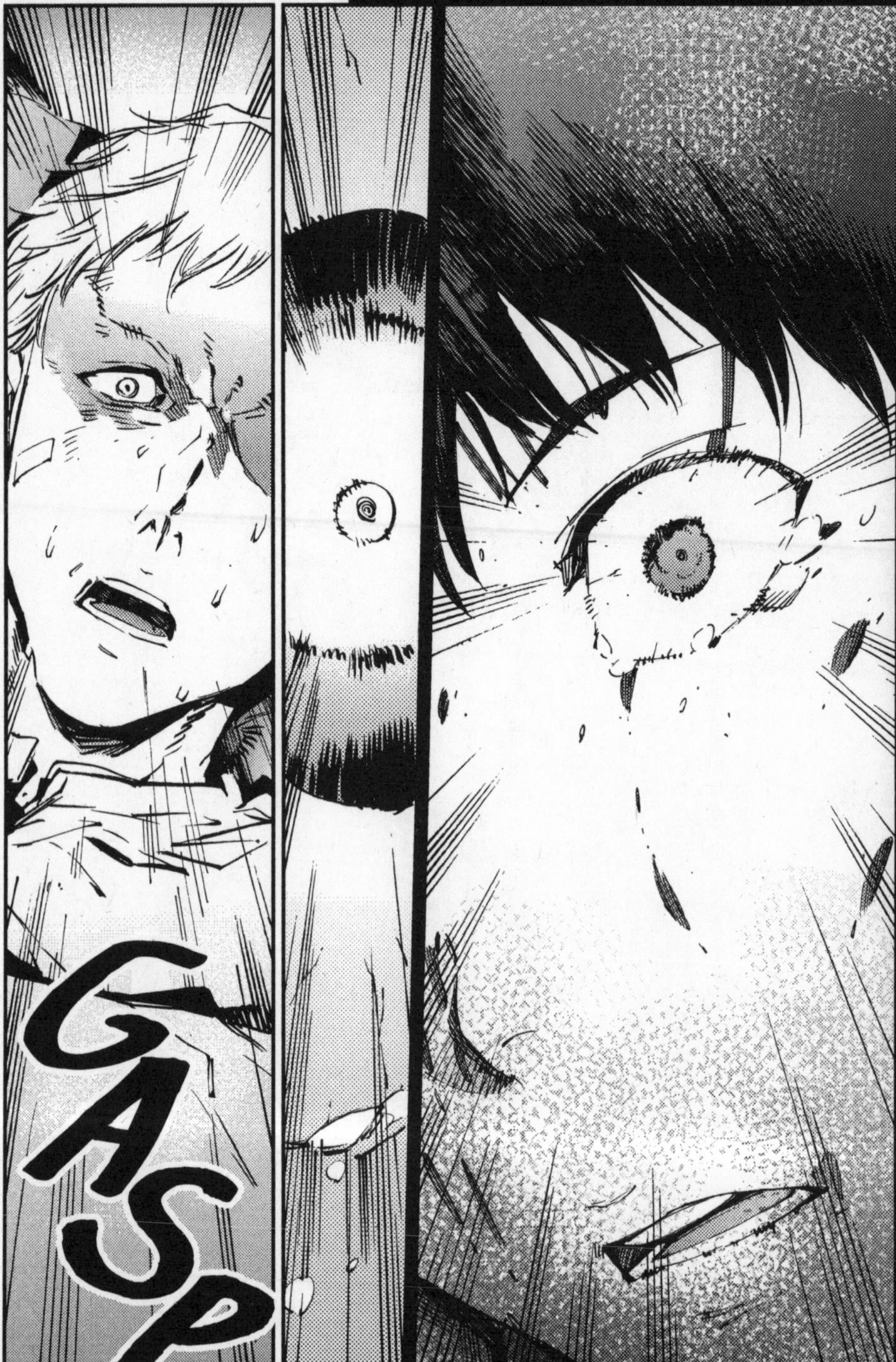
GASP

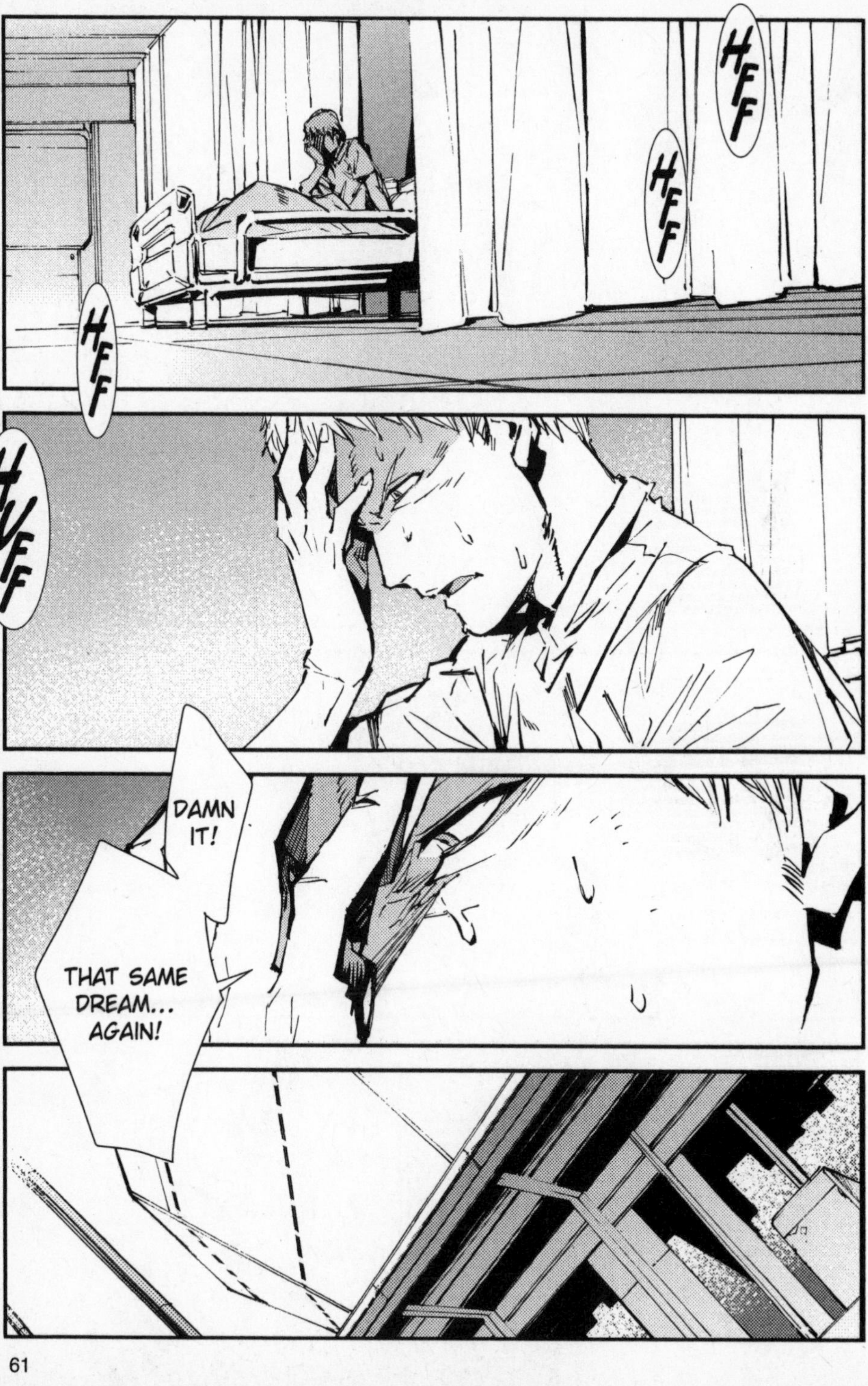
HFF
HFF
HFF
HUFF
DAMN IT!
THAT SAME DREAM... AGAIN!

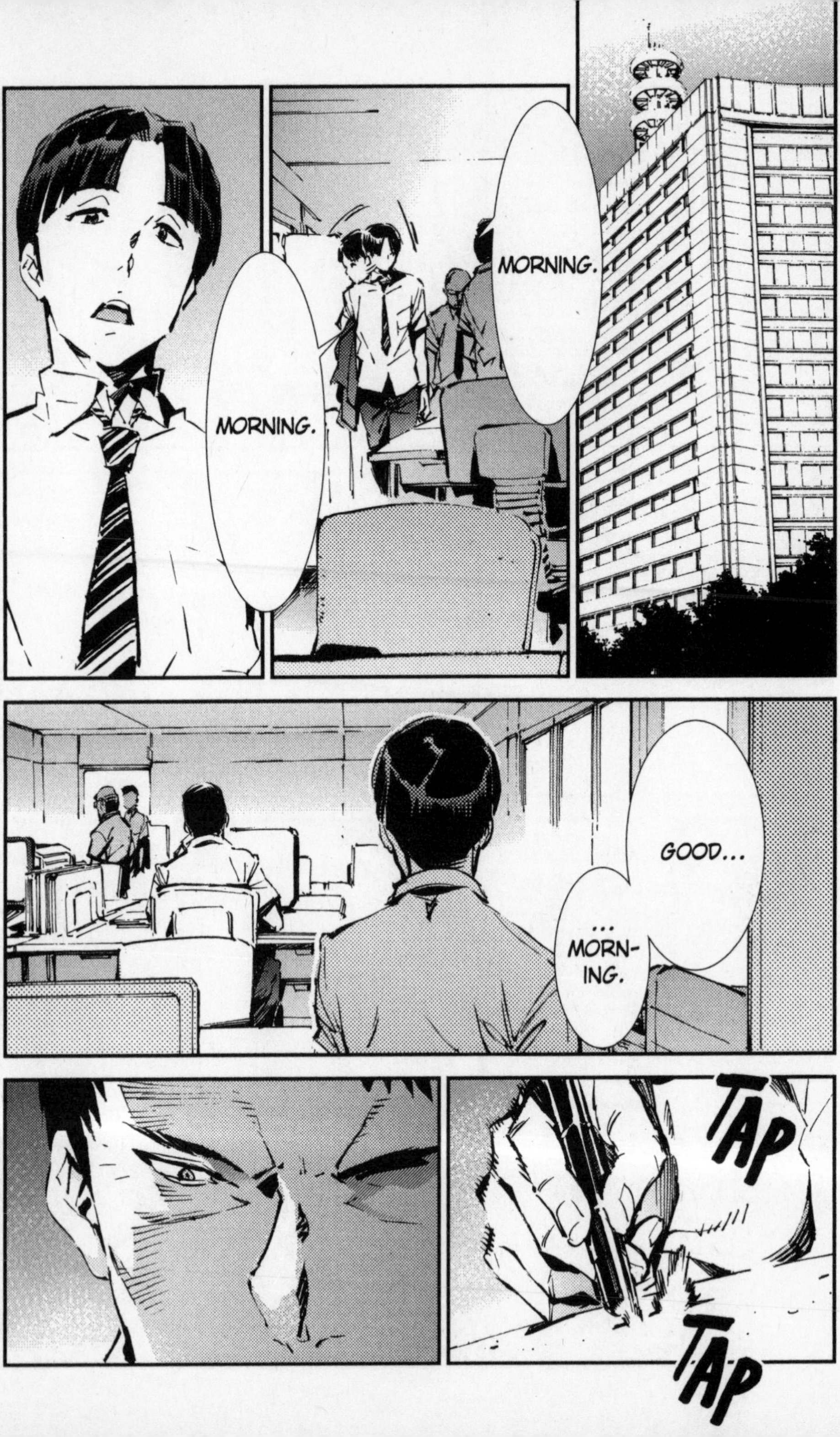
MORNING.
MORNING.
GOOD...
... MORN-ING.
TAP
TAP

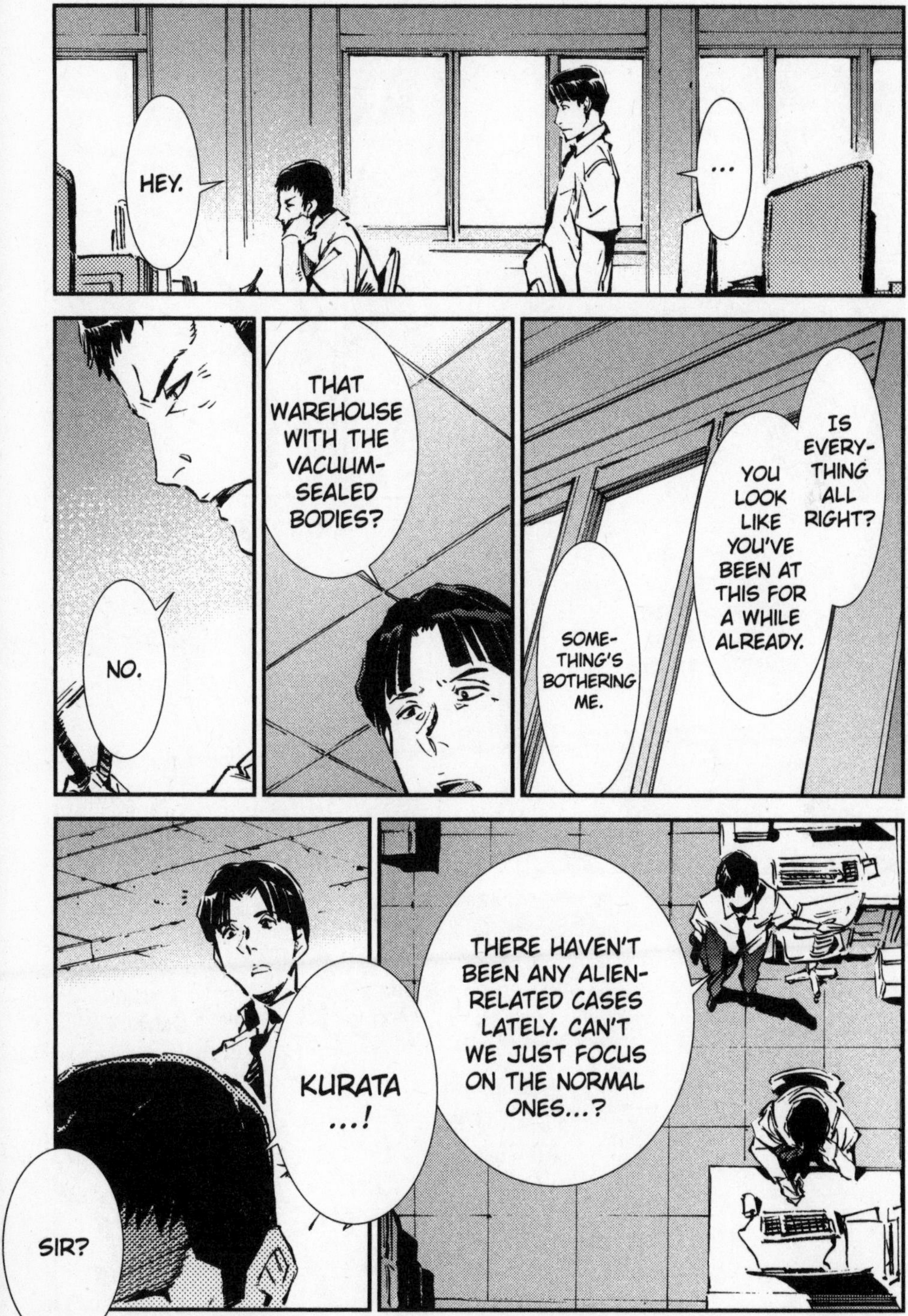
...
HEY.
IS EVERYTHING ALL RIGHT?
YOU LOOK LIKE YOU'VE BEEN AT THIS FOR A WHILE ALREADY.
SOMETHING'S BOTHERING ME.
THAT WAREHOUSE WITH THE VACUUM-SEALED BODIES?
NO.
THERE HAVEN'T BEEN ANY ALIEN-RELATED CASES LATELY. CAN'T WE JUST FOCUS ON THE NORMAL ONES...?
KURATA ...!
SIR?

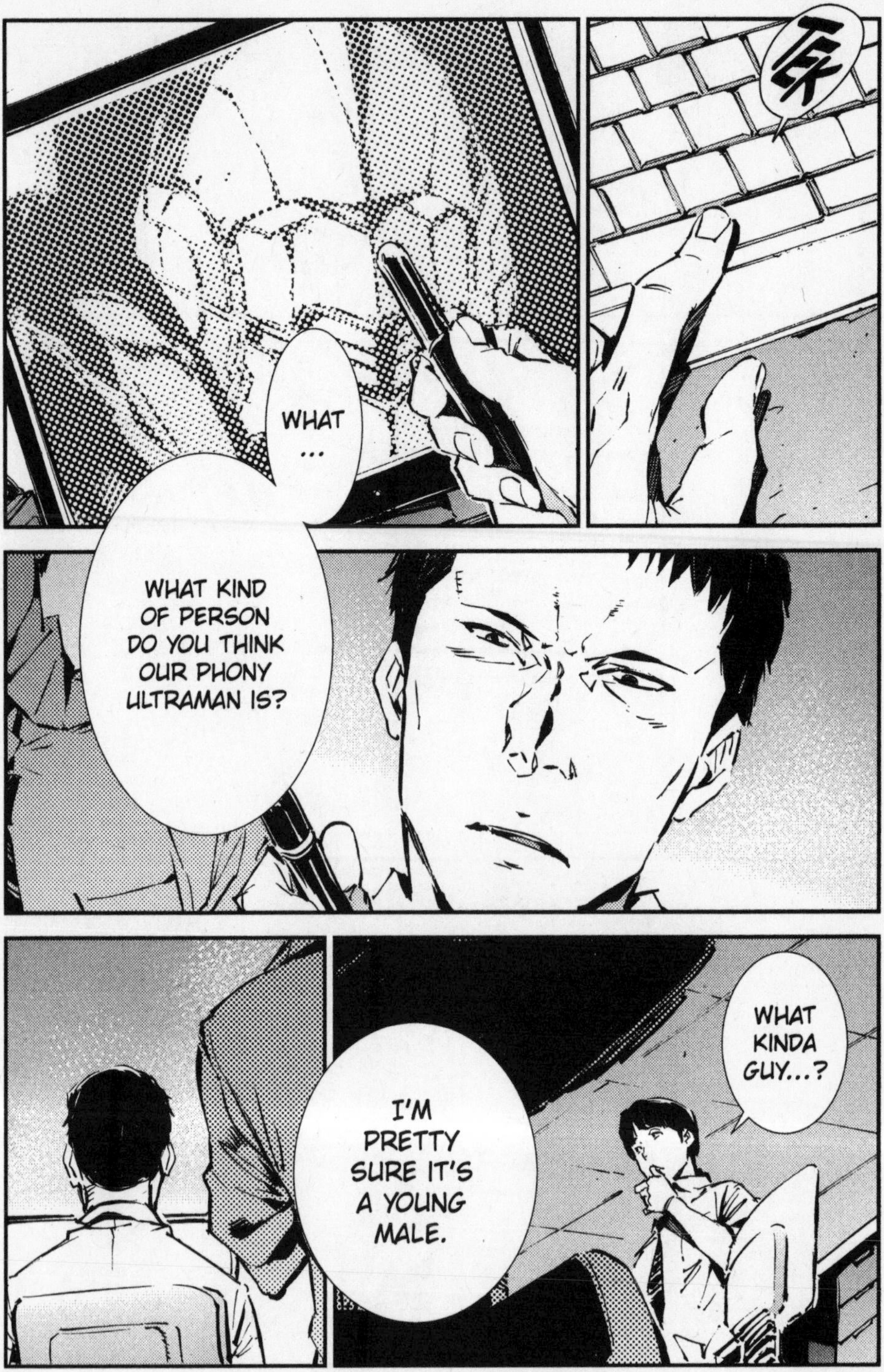
TEK
WHAT ...
WHAT KIND OF PERSON DO YOU THINK OUR PHONY ULTRAMAN IS?
WHAT KINDA GUY...?
I'M PRETTY SURE IT'S A YOUNG MALE.

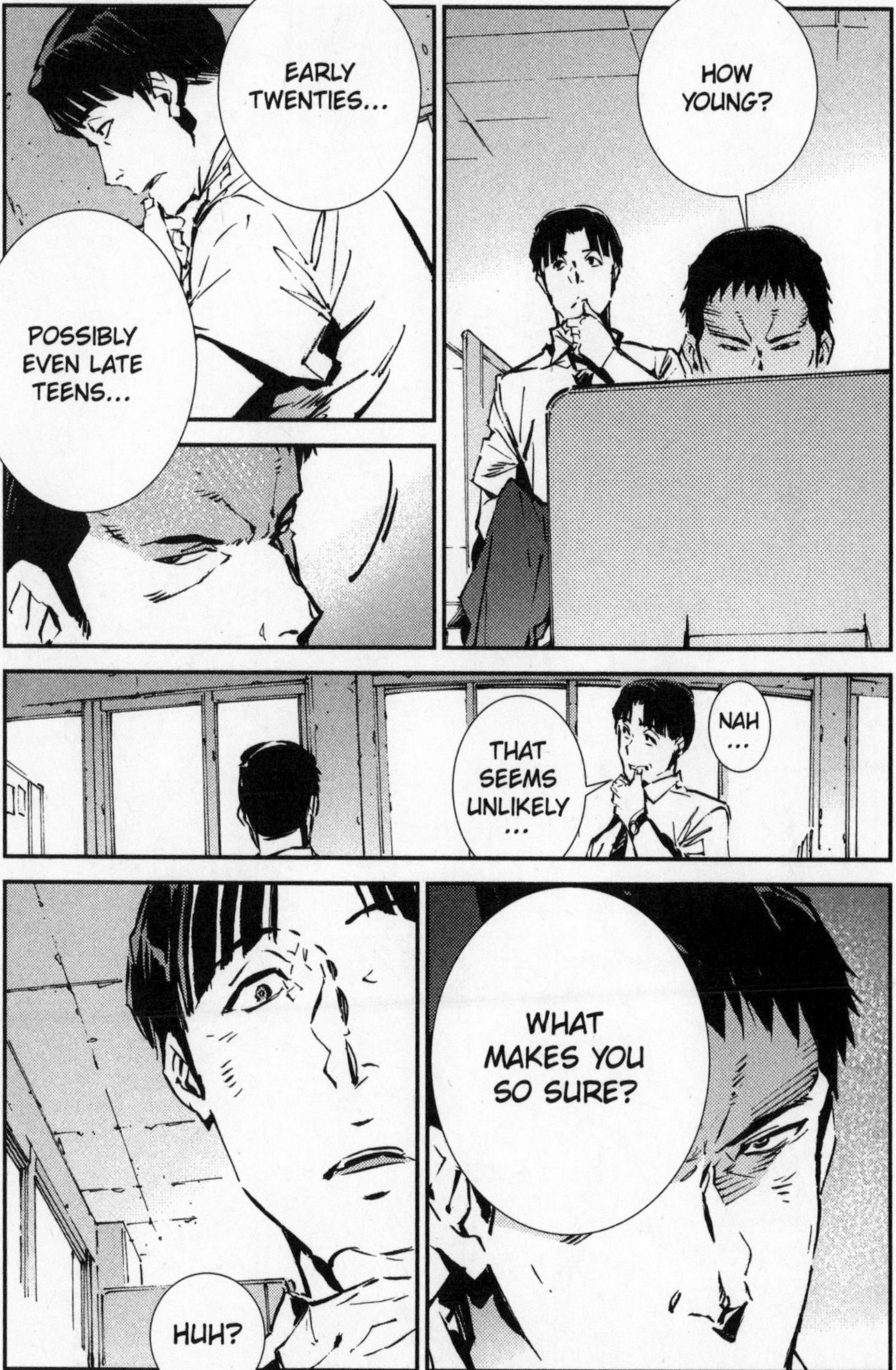
HOW YOUNG?
EARLY TWENTIES...
POSSIBLY EVEN LATE TEENS...
NAH...
THAT SEEMS UNLIKELY...
WHAT MAKES YOU SO SURE?
HUH?

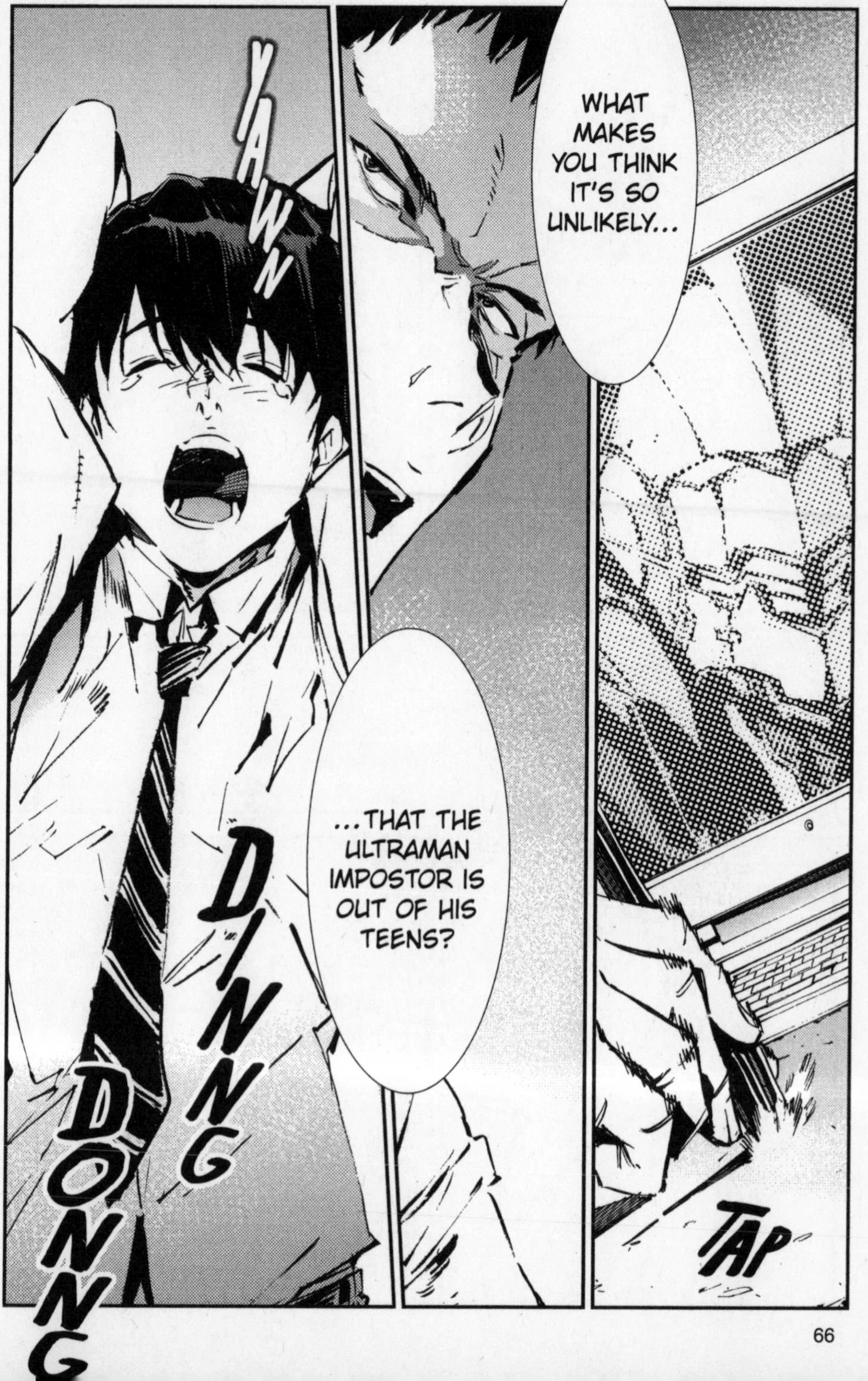
WHAT MAKES YOU THINK IT'S SO UNLIKELY...
...THAT THE ULTRAMAN IMPOSTOR IS OUT OF HIS TEENS?
TAP
YAWN
DINNG
DONNG

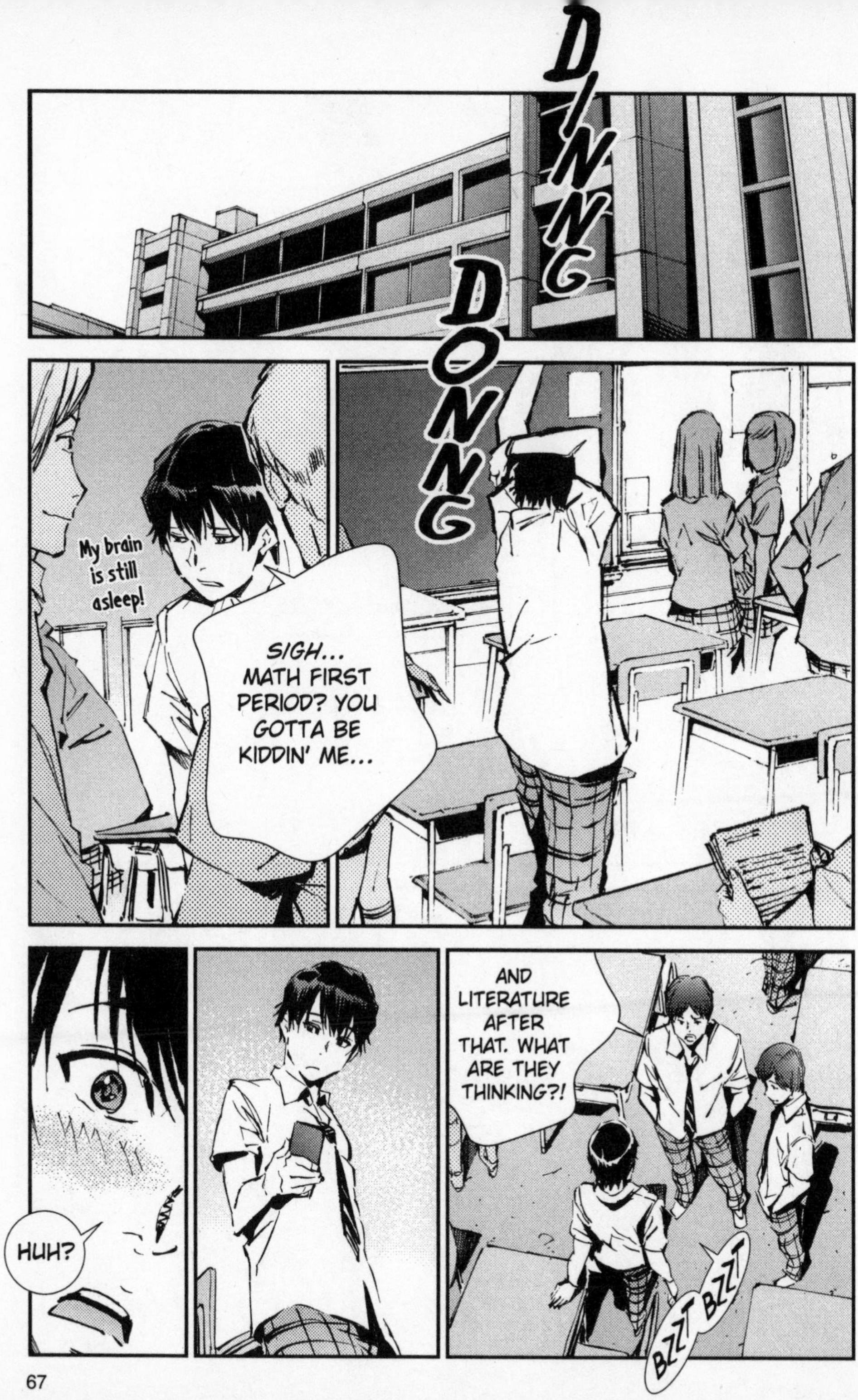
DINNG
DONNG
SIGH... MATH FIRST PERIOD? YOU GOTTA BE KIDDIN' ME...
My brain is still asleep!
AND LITERATURE AFTER THAT. WHAT ARE THEY THINKING?!
BZZT BZZT
HUH?

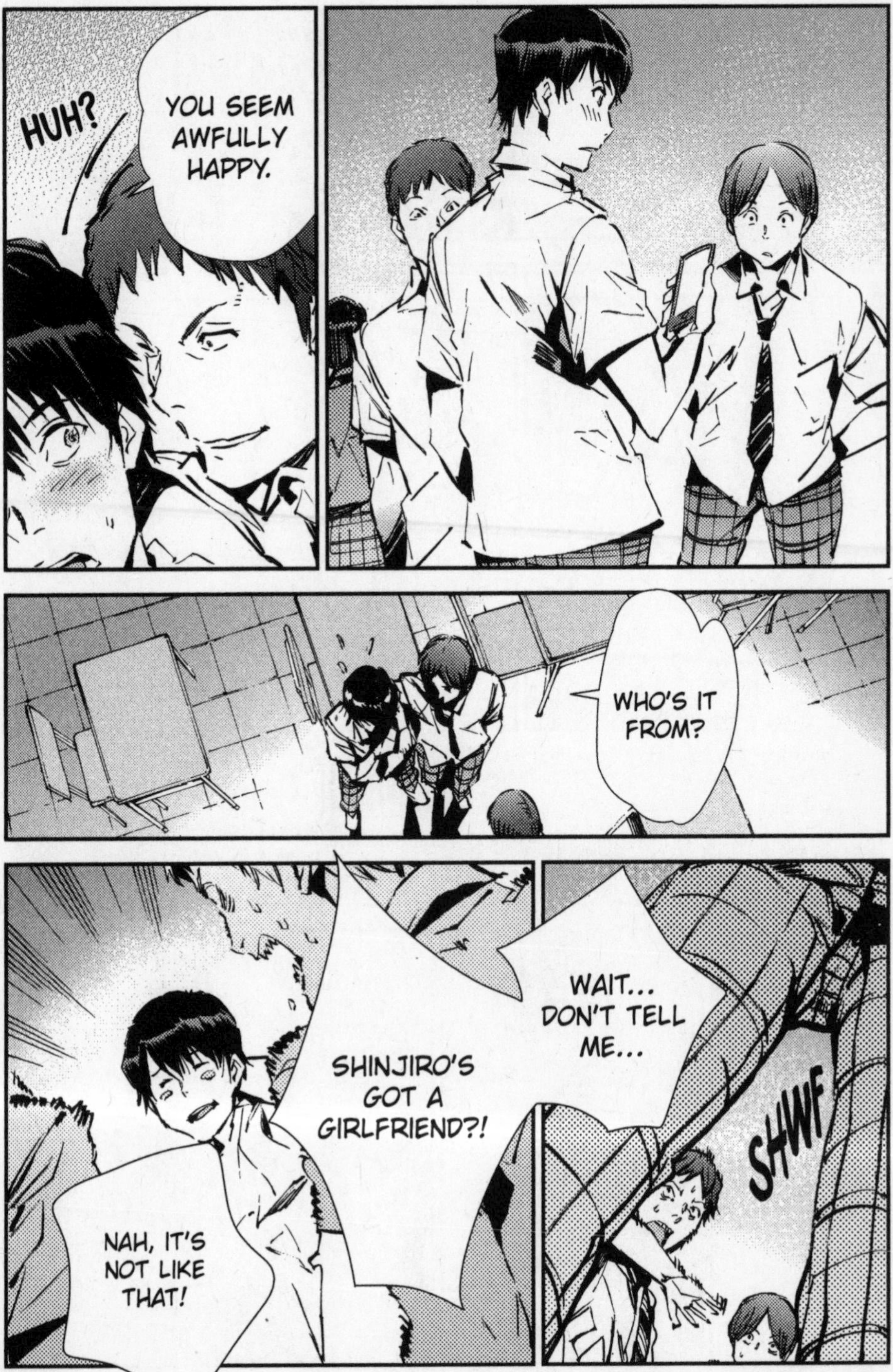
YOU SEEM AWFULLY HAPPY.
HUH?
WHO'S IT FROM?
WAIT... DON'T TELL ME...
SHWF
SHINJIRO'S GOT A GIRLFRIEND?!
NAH, IT'S NOT LIKE THAT!

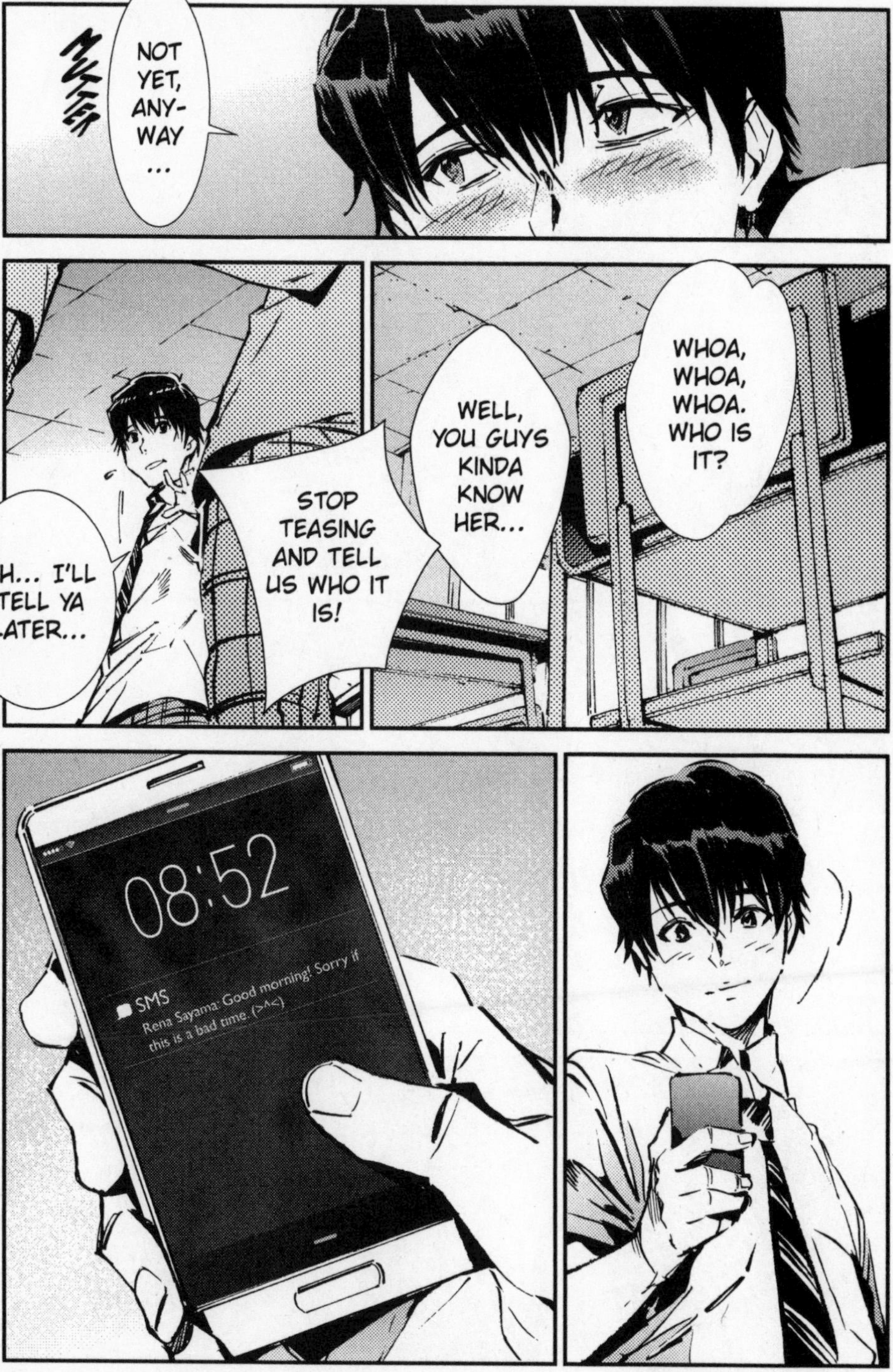
NOT YET, ANY-WAY...
WHOA, WHOA, WHOA. WHO IS IT?
WELL, YOU GUYS KINDA KNOW HER...
STOP TEASING AND TELL US WHO IT IS!
UH... I'LL TELL YA LATER...
08:52
SMS
Rena Sayama: Good morning! Sorry if this is a bad time. (>^<)

70

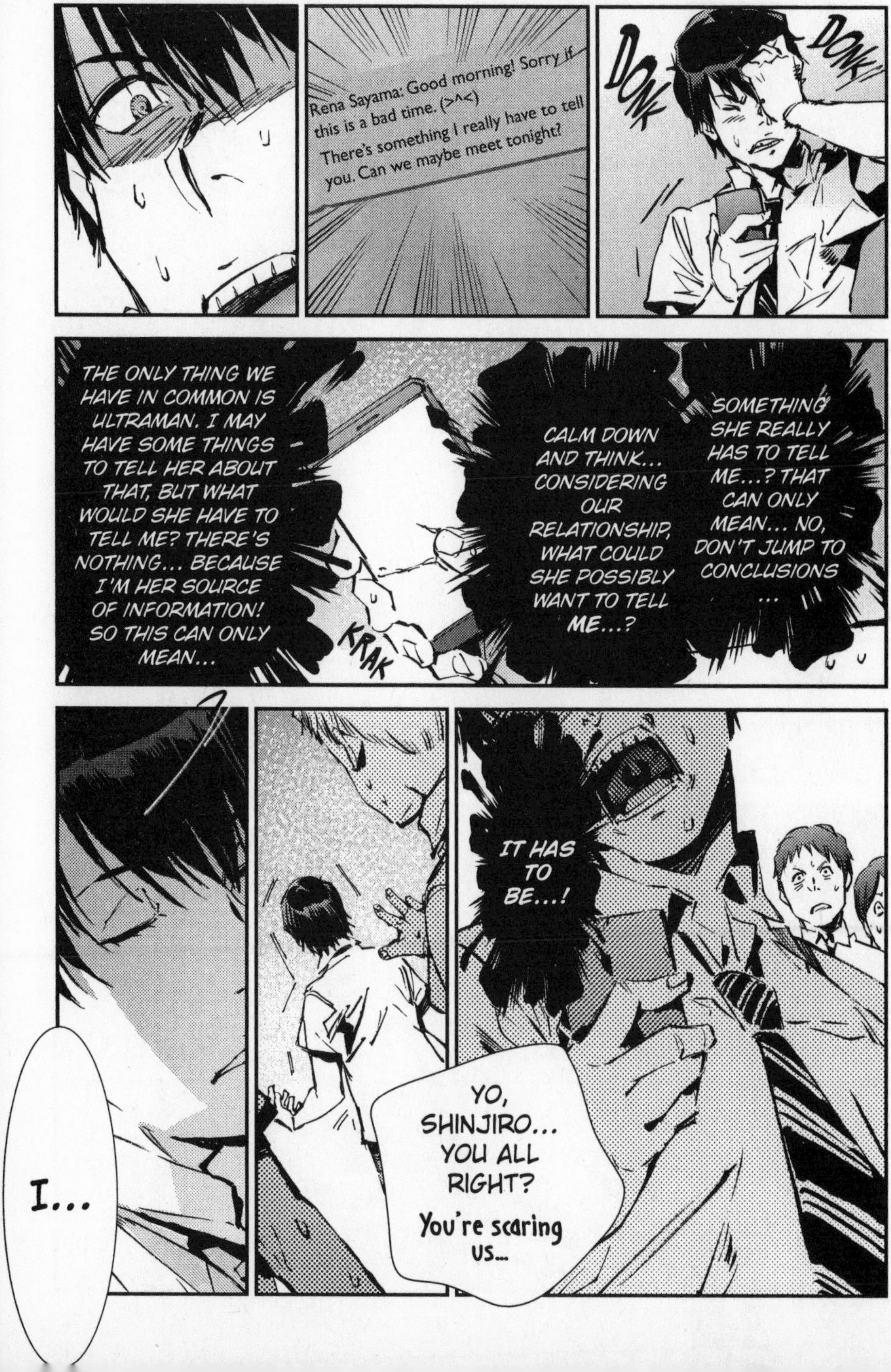
DONK
DONK
Rena Sayama: Good morning! Sorry if this is a bad time. (>^<) There's something I really have to tell you. Can we maybe meet tonight?
SOMETHING SHE REALLY HAS TO TELL ME...? THAT CAN ONLY MEAN... NO, DON'T JUMP TO CONCLUSIONS...
CALM DOWN AND THINK... CONSIDERING OUR RELATIONSHIP, WHAT COULD SHE POSSIBLY WANT TO TELL ME...?
KRAK
THE ONLY THING WE HAVE IN COMMON IS ULTRAMAN. I MAY HAVE SOME THINGS TO TELL HER ABOUT THAT, BUT WHAT WOULD SHE HAVE TO TELL ME? THERE'S NOTHING... BECAUSE I'M HER SOURCE OF INFORMATION! SO THIS CAN ONLY MEAN...
IT HAS TO BE...!
YO, SHINJIRO... YOU ALL RIGHT?
You're scaring us...
I...

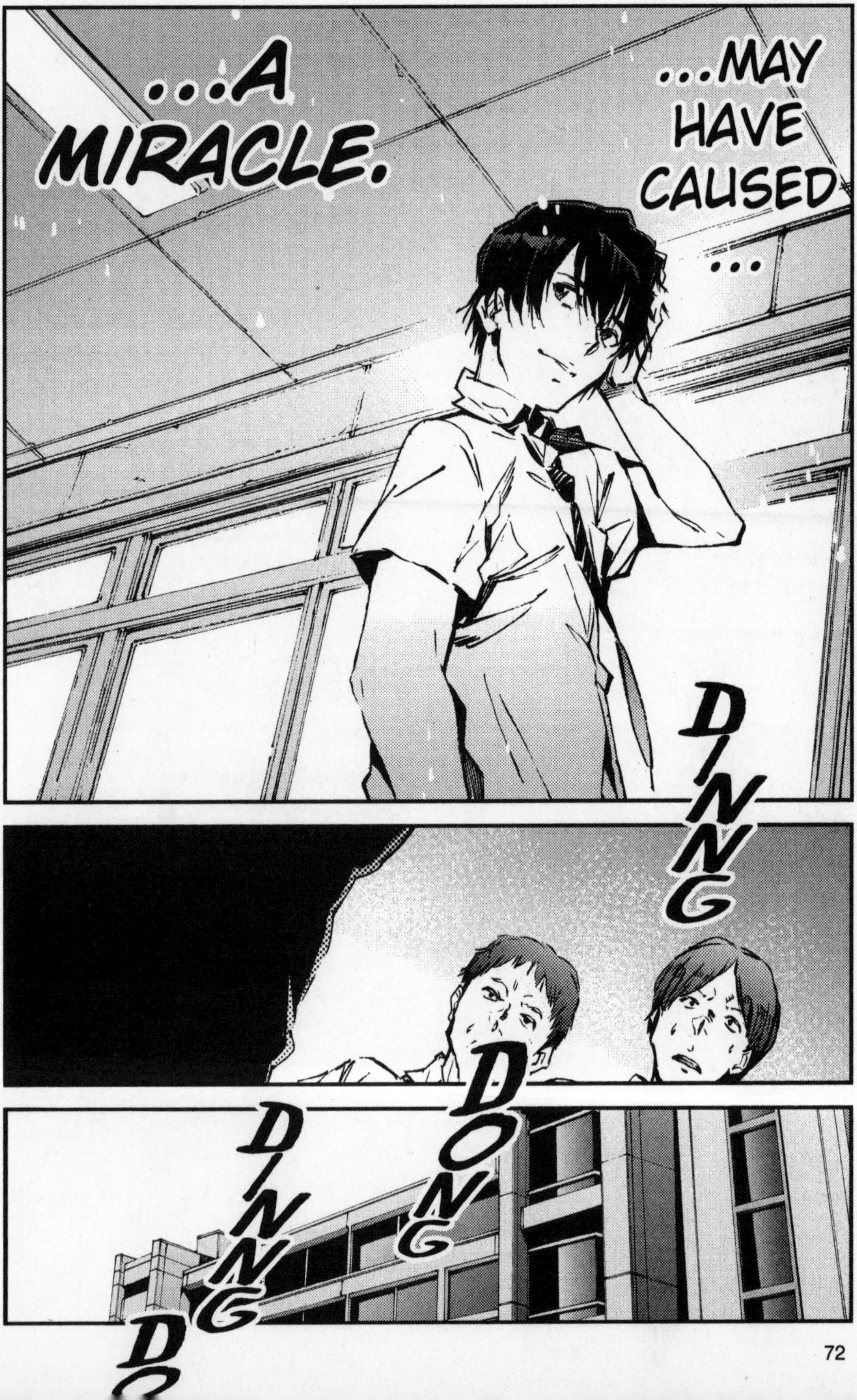
...MAY HAVE CAUSED...
...A MIRACLE.
DINNG
DONG
DINNG

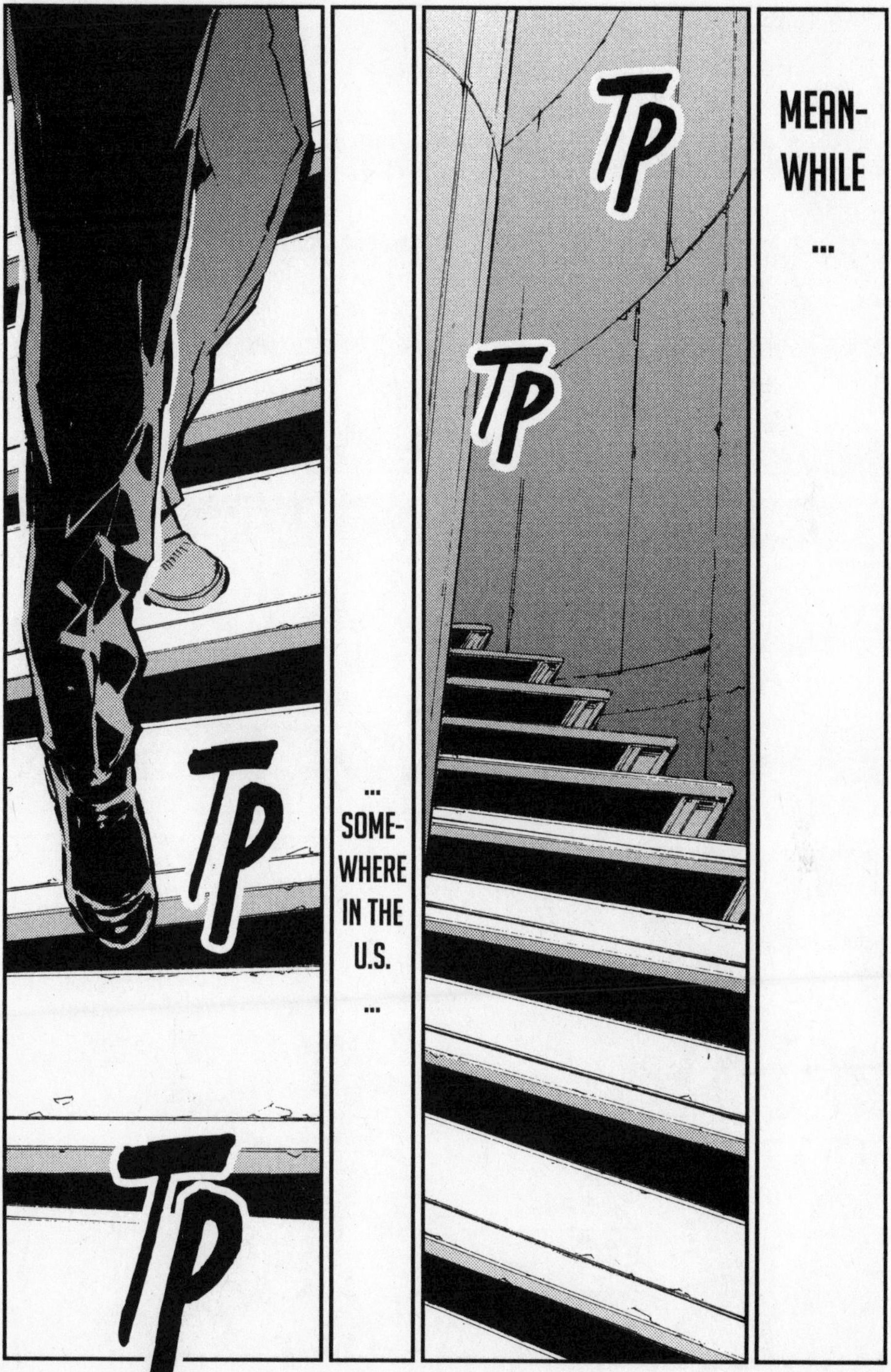
MEAN-WHILE ...
TP
TP
... SOME-WHERE IN THE U.S. ...
TP
TP

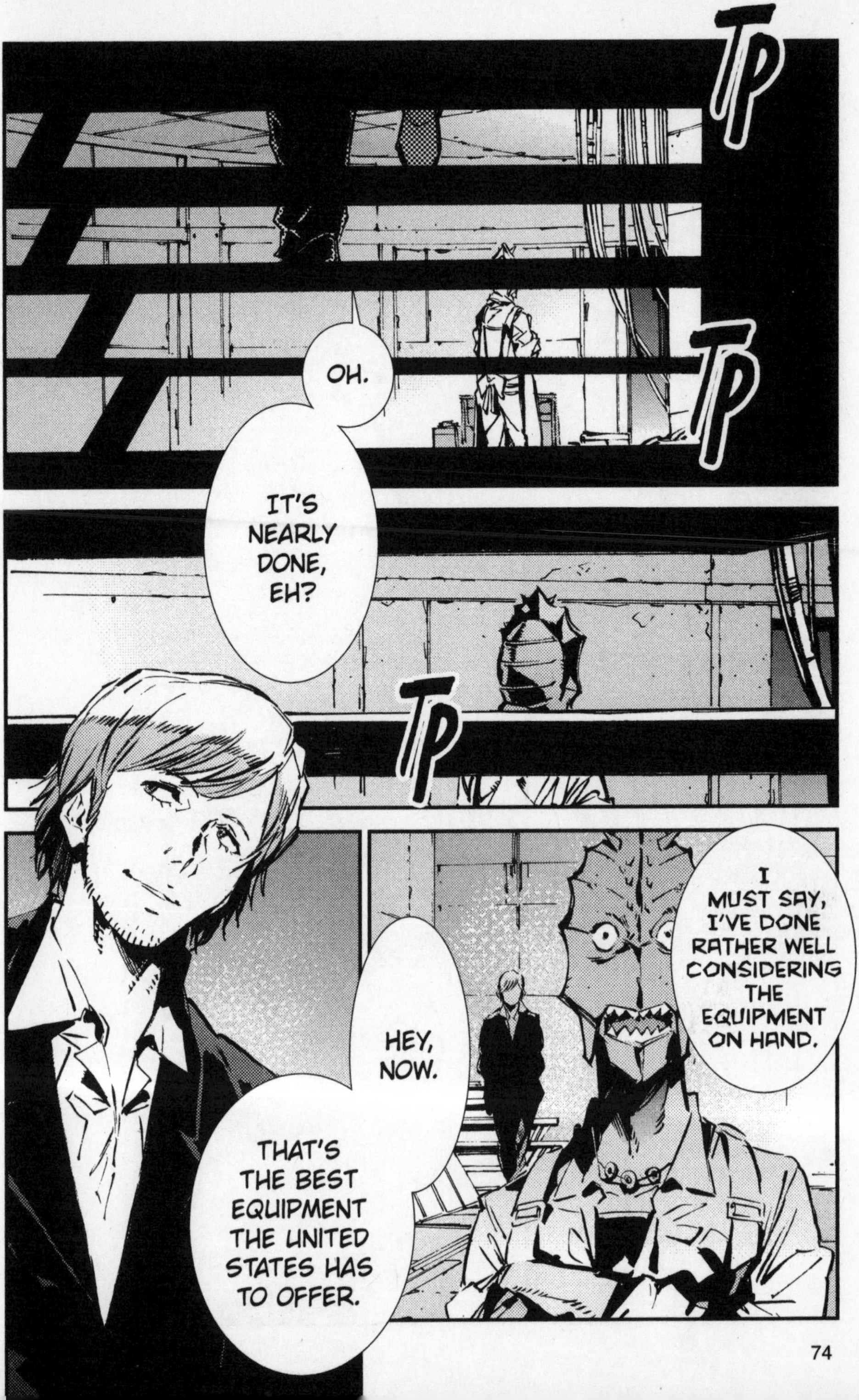
TP
TP
OH.
IT'S NEARLY DONE, EH?
TP
I MUST SAY, I'VE DONE RATHER WELL CONSIDERING THE EQUIPMENT ON HAND.
HEY, NOW.
THAT'S THE BEST EQUIPMENT THE UNITED STATES HAS TO OFFER.

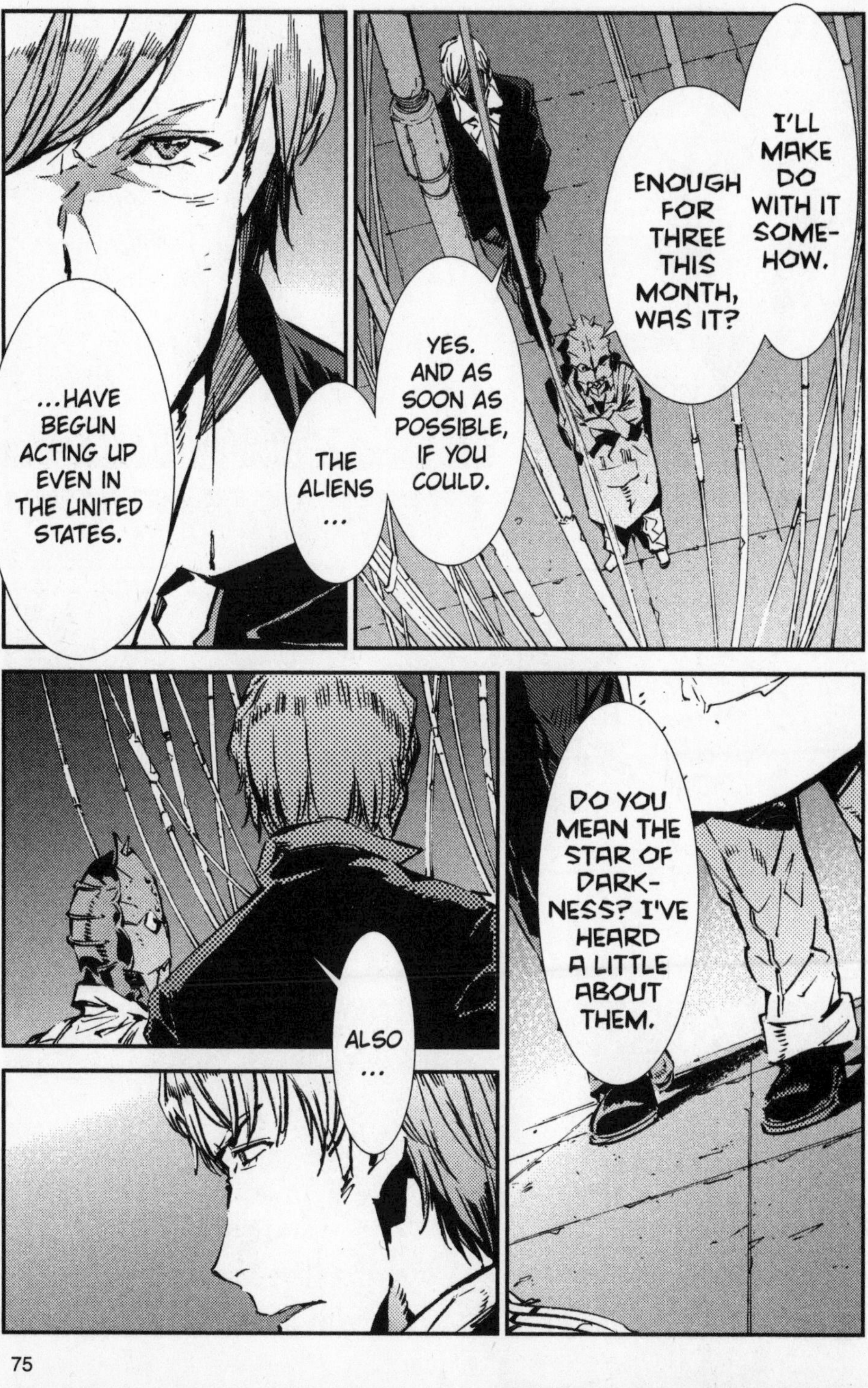
I'LL MAKE DO WITH IT SOME-HOW.
ENOUGH FOR THREE THIS MONTH, WAS IT?
YES. AND AS SOON AS POSSIBLE, IF YOU COULD.
THE ALIENS...
...HAVE BEGUN ACTING UP EVEN IN THE UNITED STATES.
DO YOU MEAN THE STAR OF DARK-NESS? I'VE HEARD A LITTLE ABOUT THEM.
ALSO...

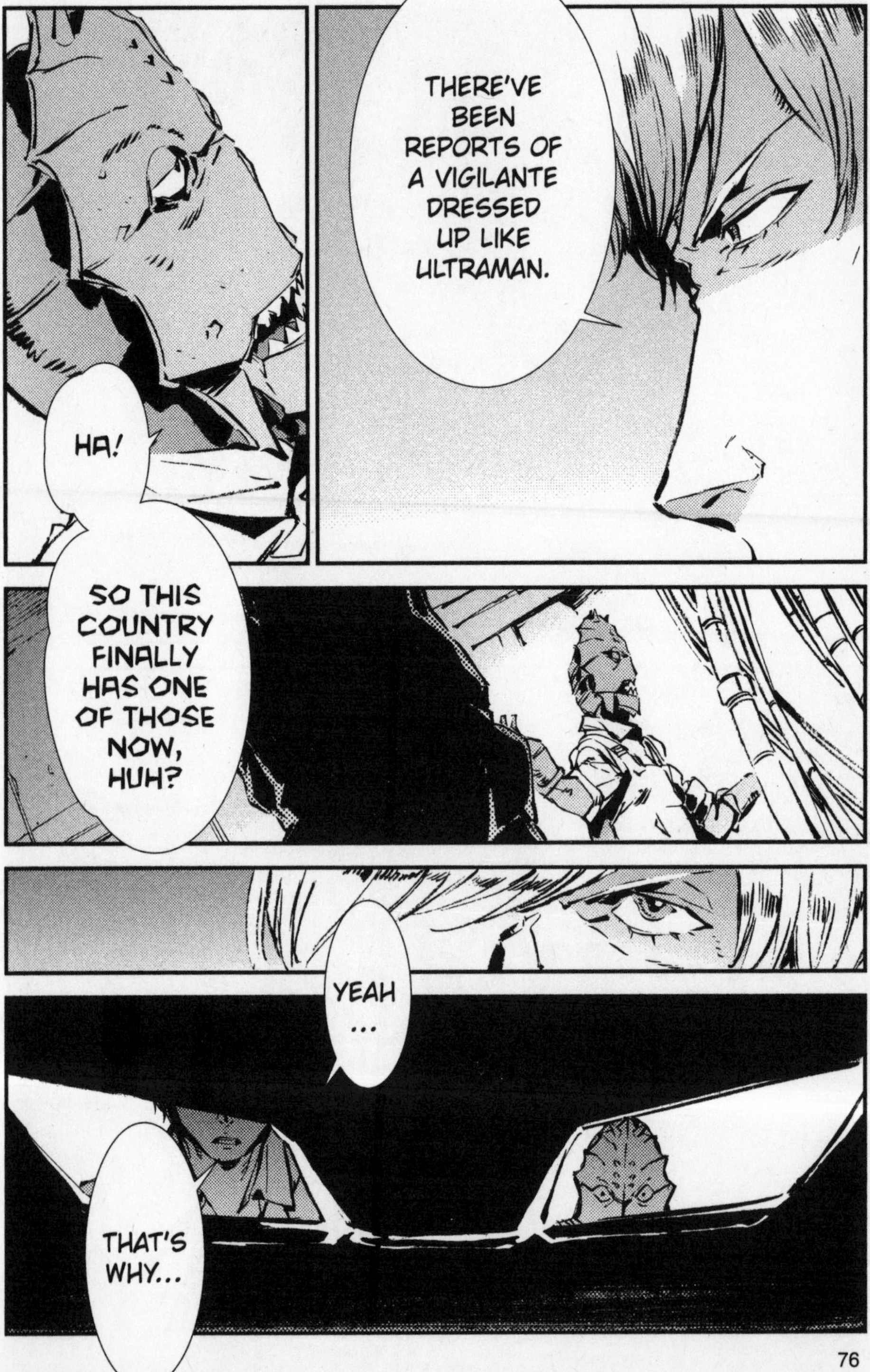
THERE'VE BEEN REPORTS OF A VIGILANTE DRESSED UP LIKE ULTRAMAN.
HA!
SO THIS COUNTRY FINALLY HAS ONE OF THOSE NOW, HUH?
YEAH ...
THAT'S WHY...

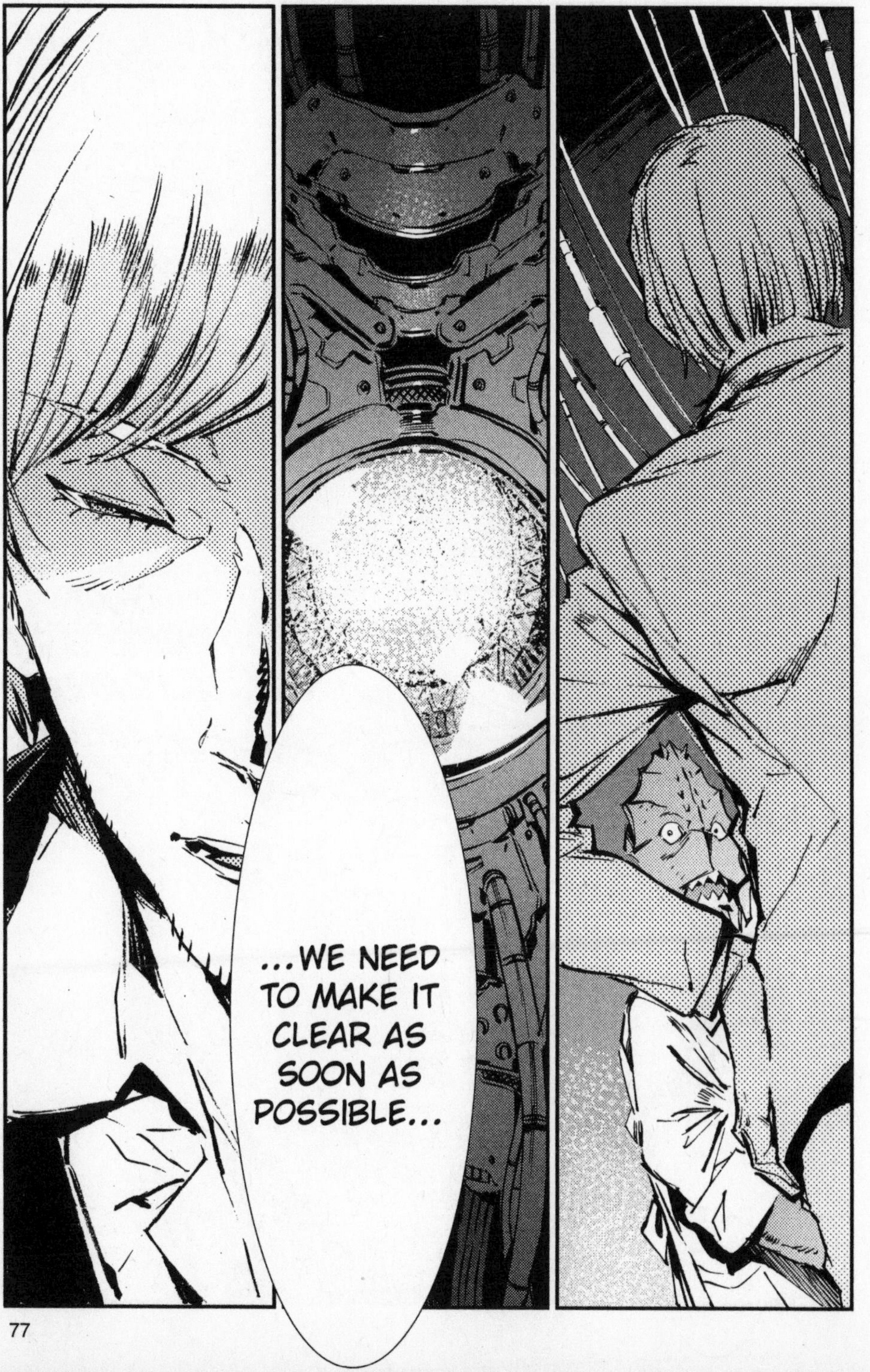
...WE NEED TO MAKE IT CLEAR AS SOON AS POSSIBLE...

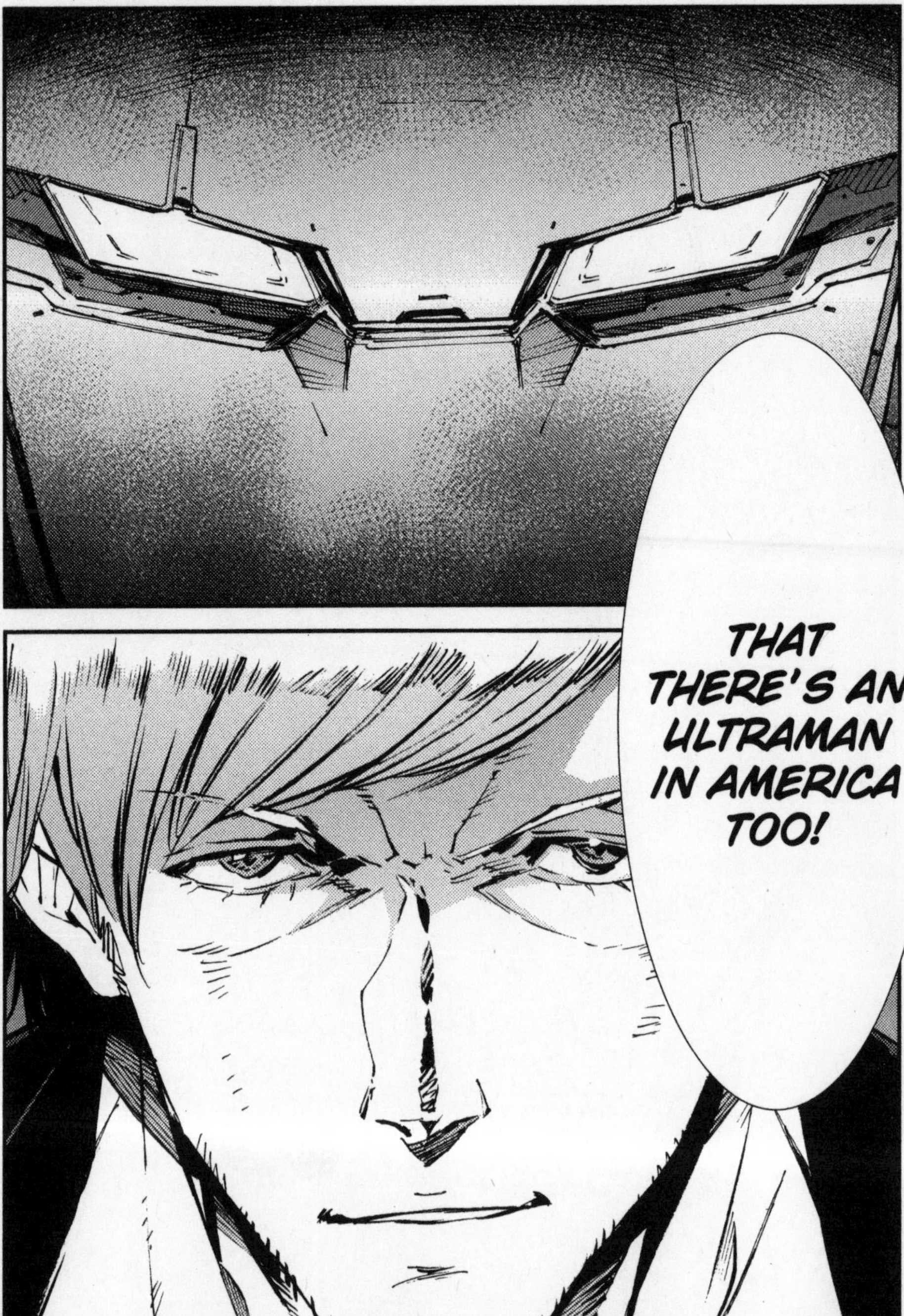
THAT THERE'S AN ULTRAMAN IN AMERICA TOO!

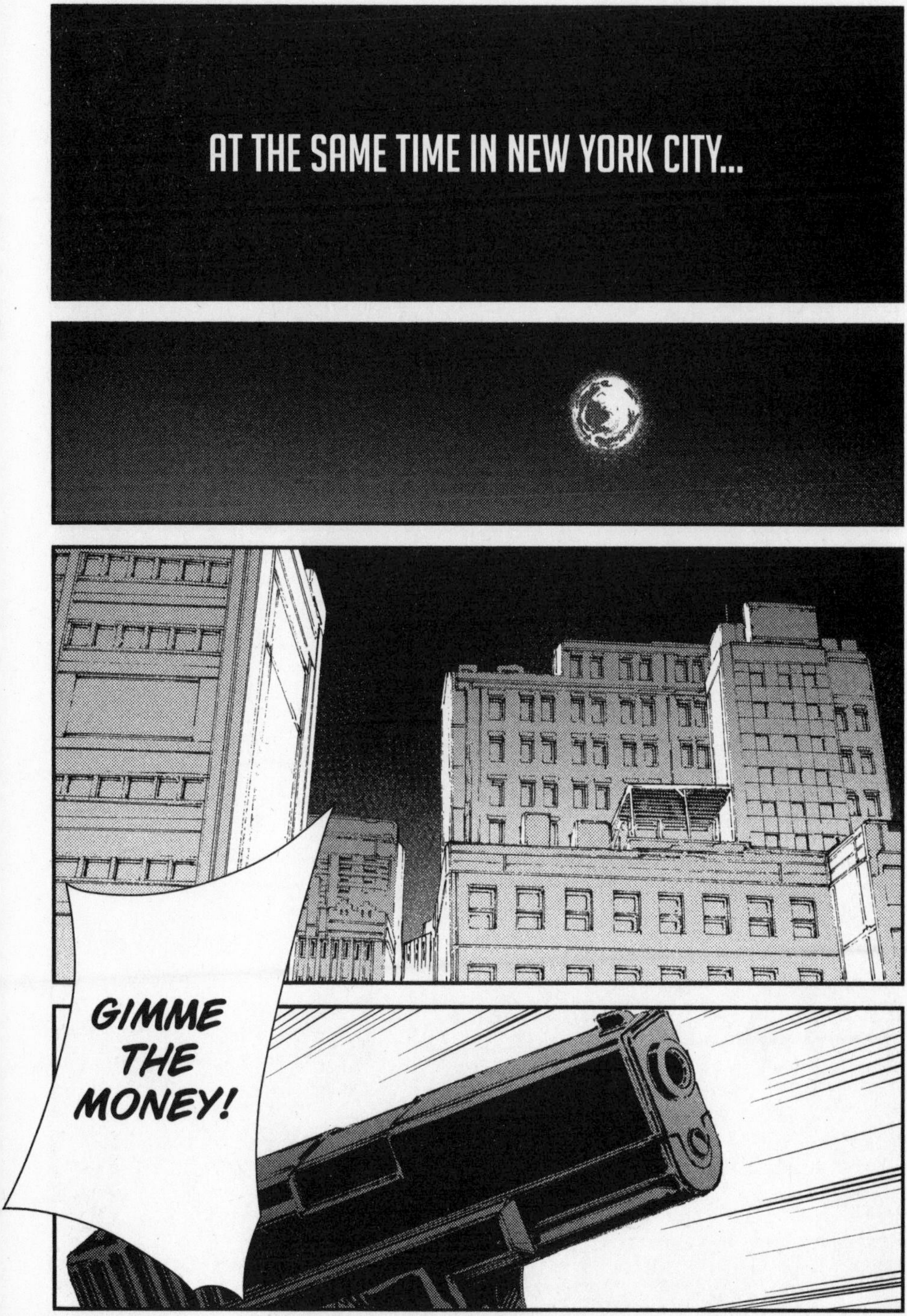
AT THE SAME TIME IN NEW YORK CITY...
GIMME THE MONEY!

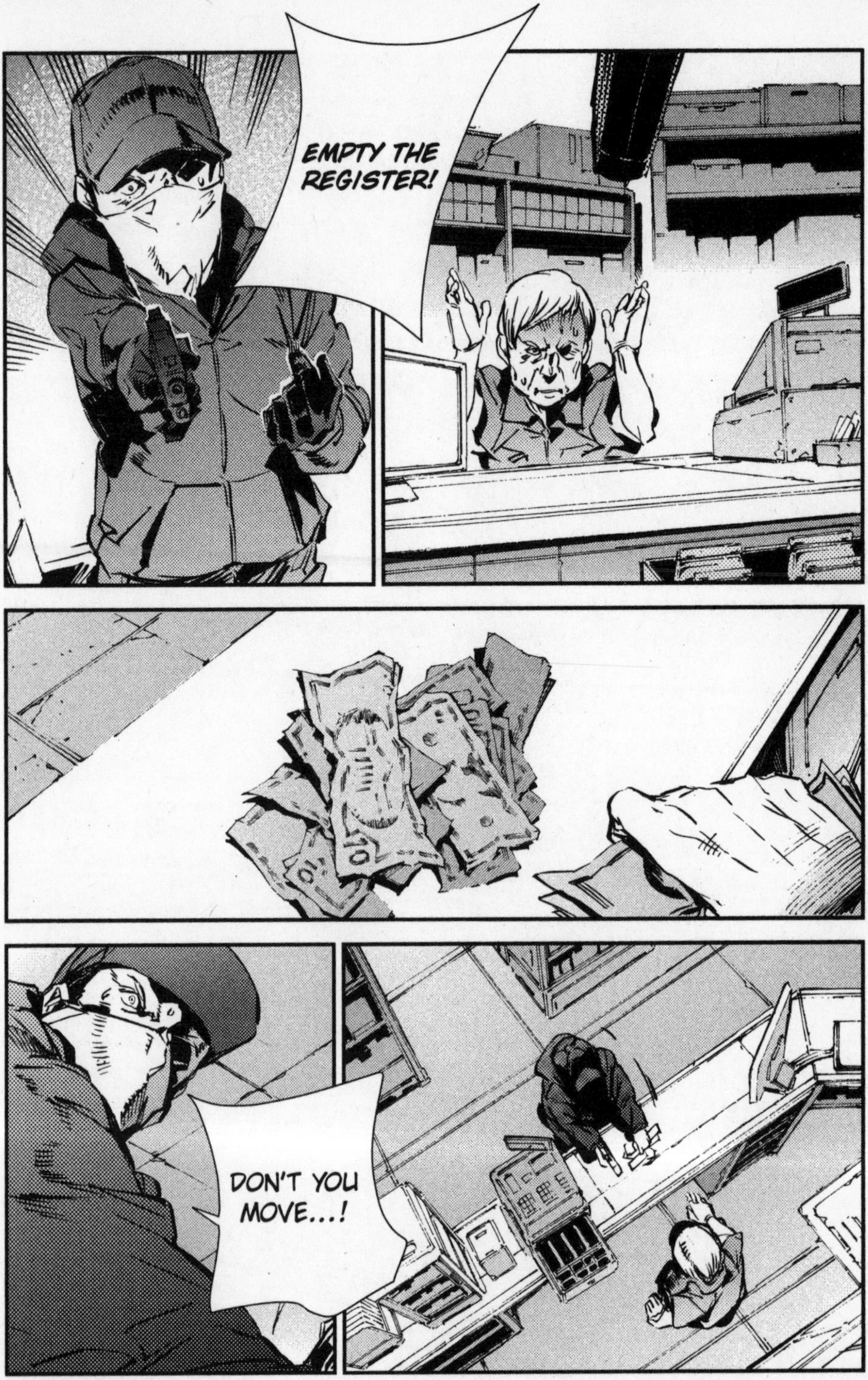
EMPTY THE REGISTER!
DON'T YOU MOVE...!

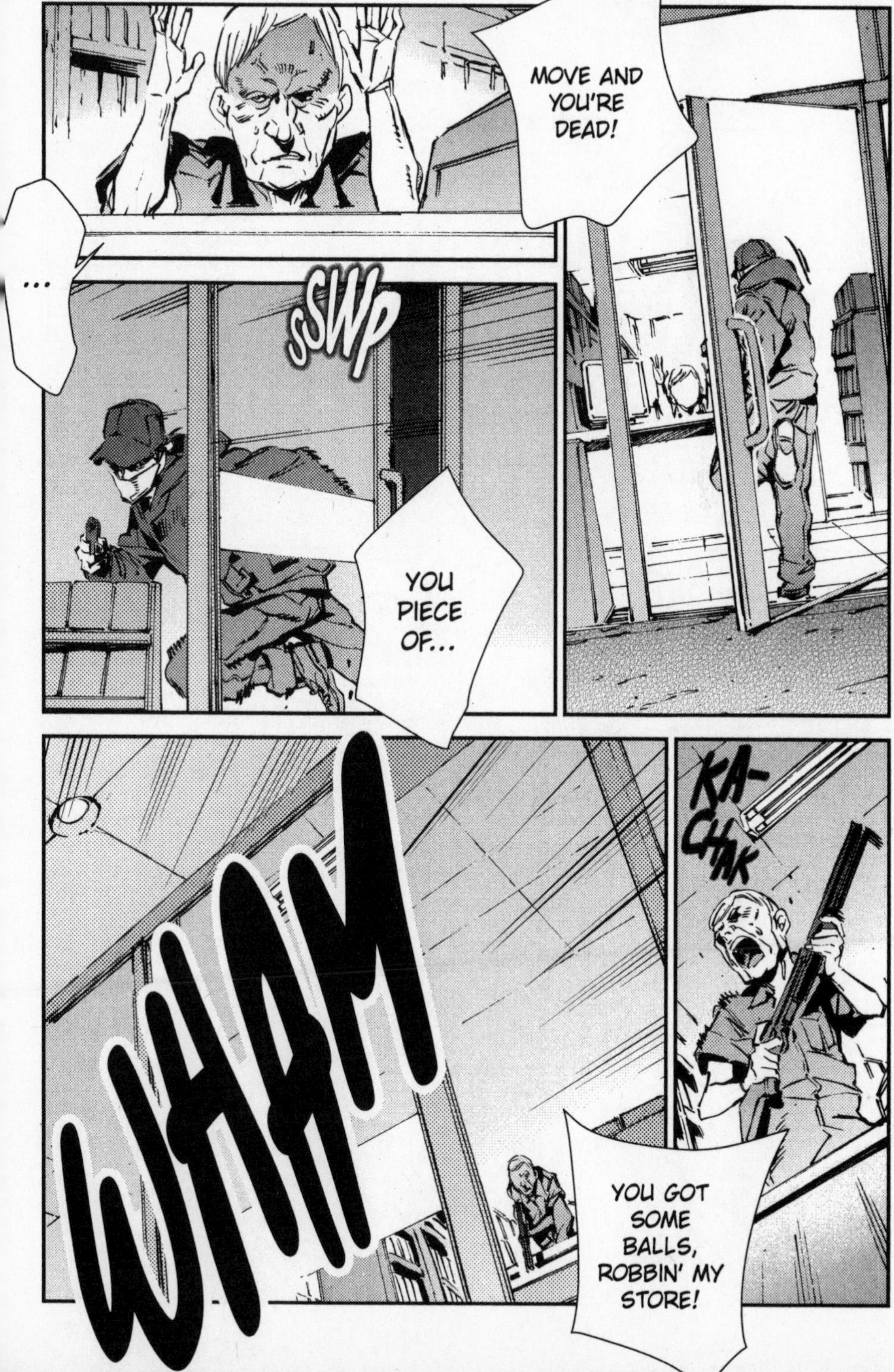
MOVE AND YOU'RE DEAD!
...
SSWP
YOU PIECE OF...
KA-CHAK
YOU GOT SOME BALLS, ROBBIN' MY STORE!
WHAM

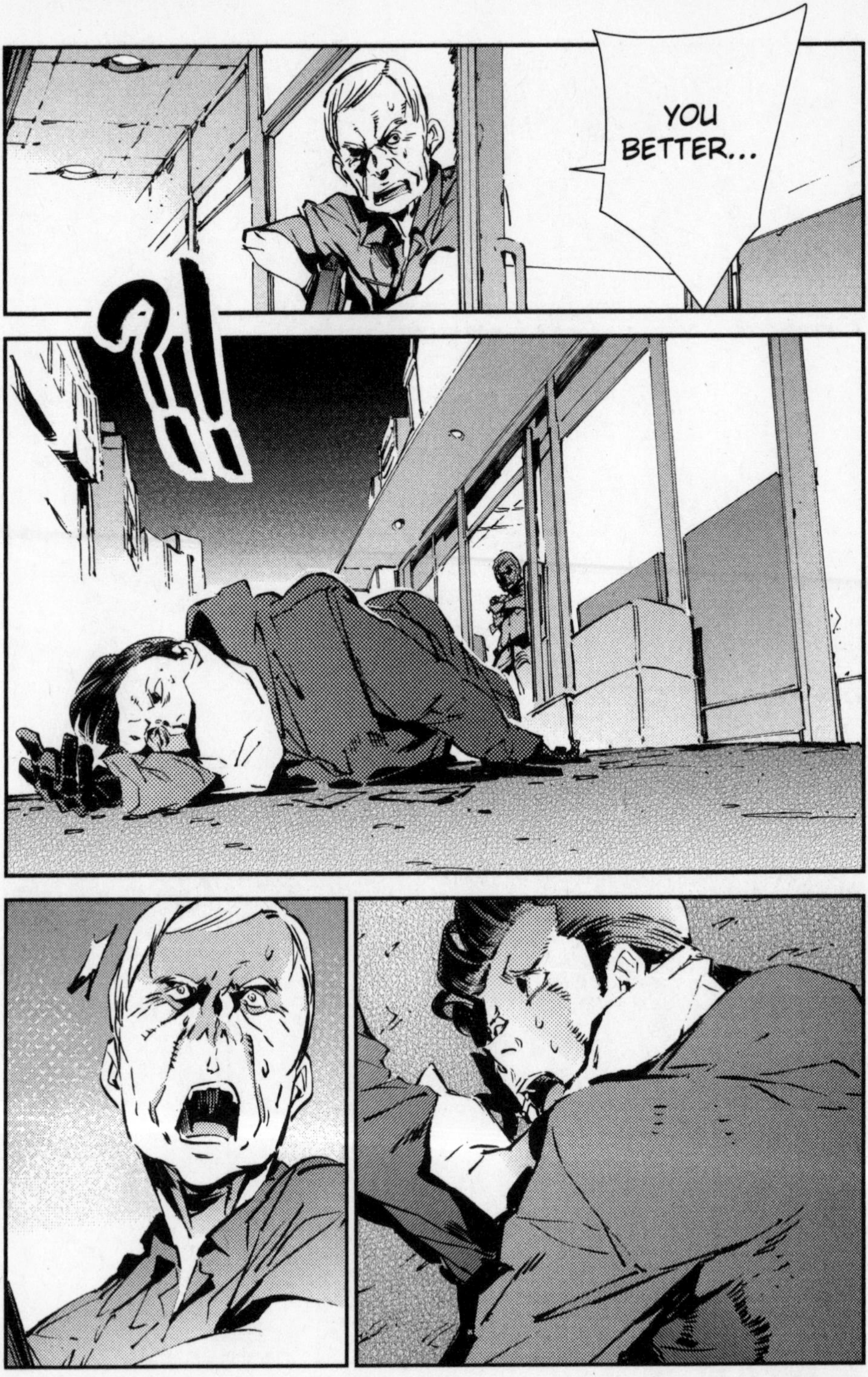
YOU BETTER...
?!!

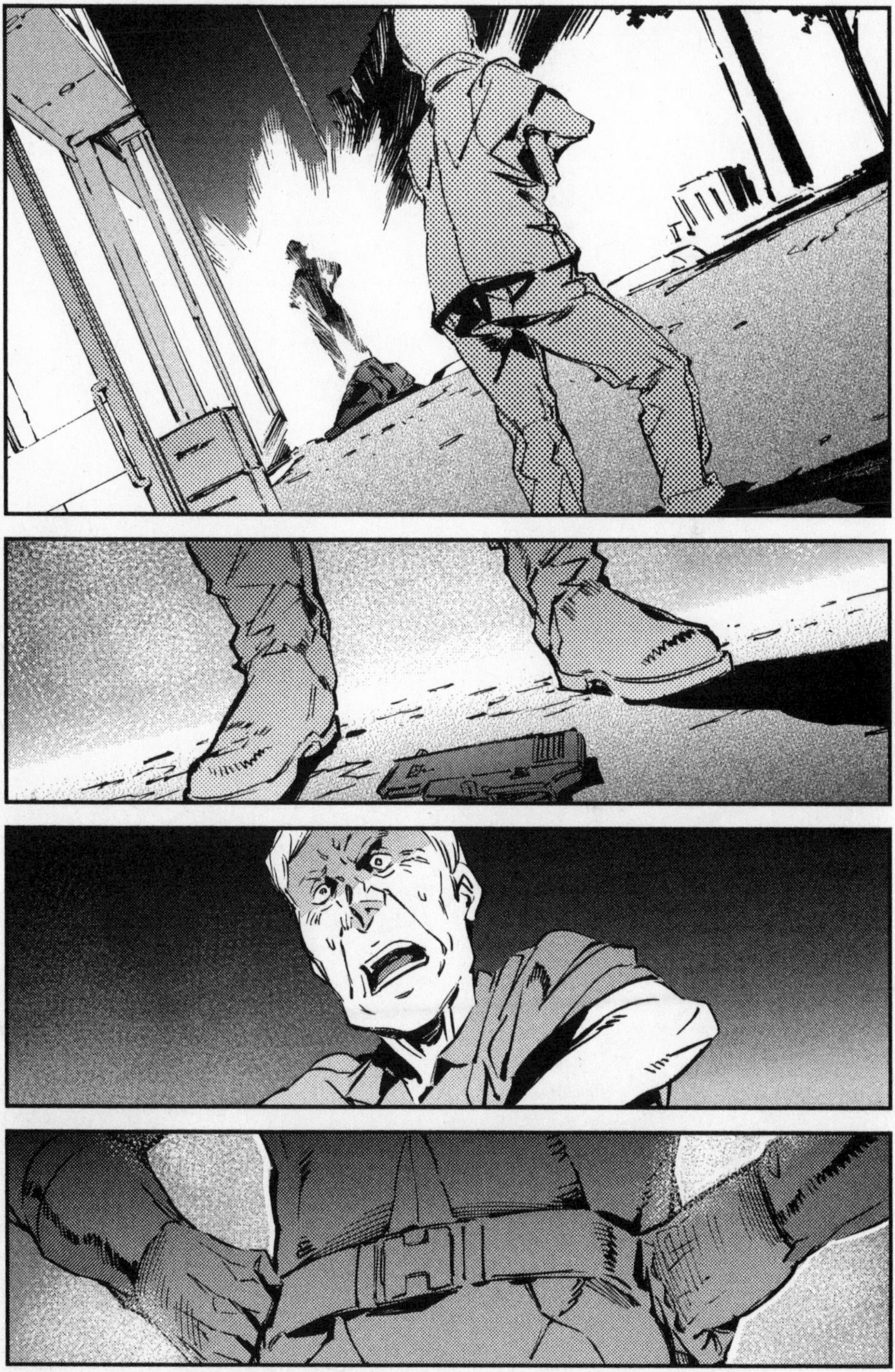

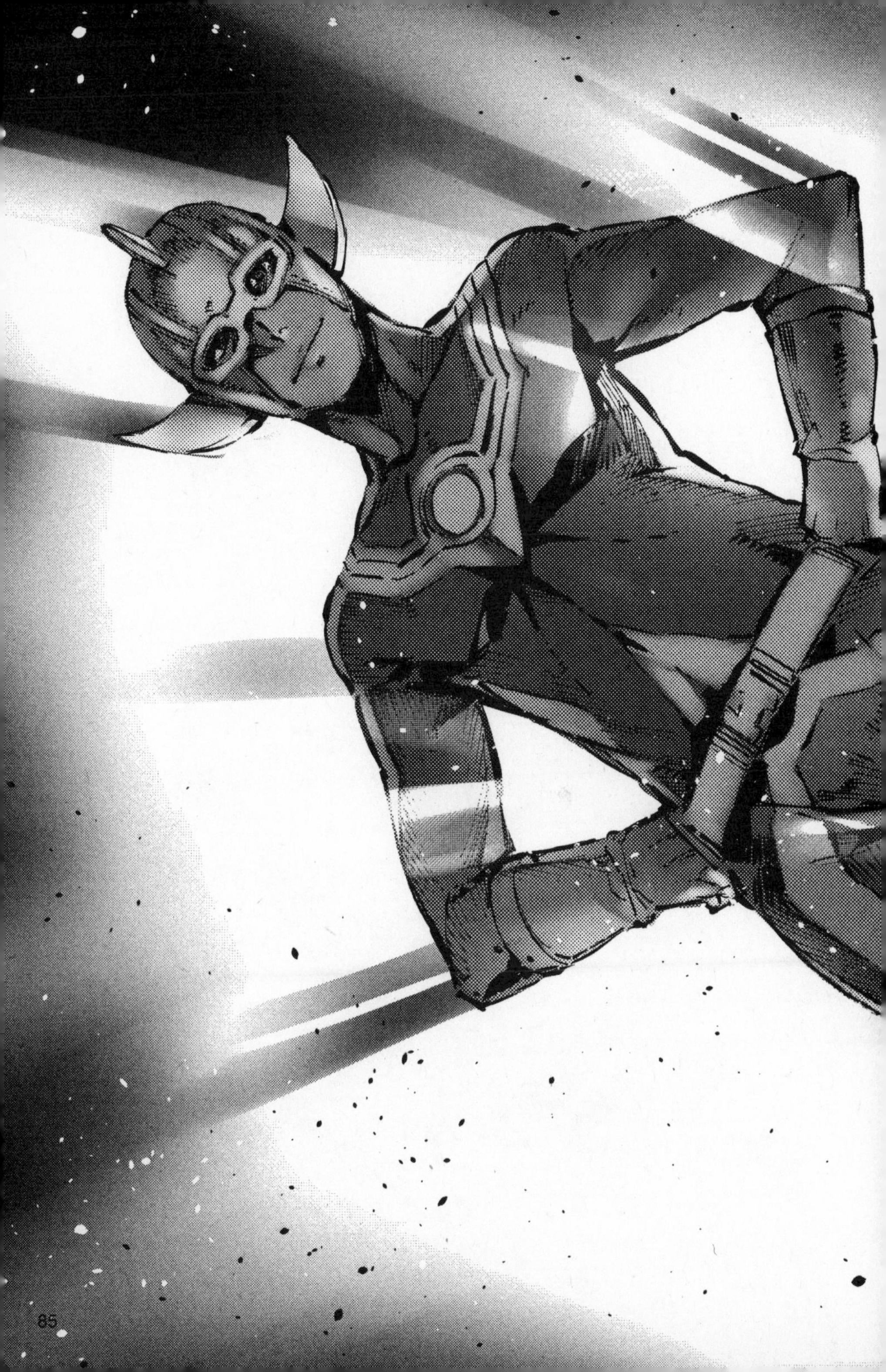

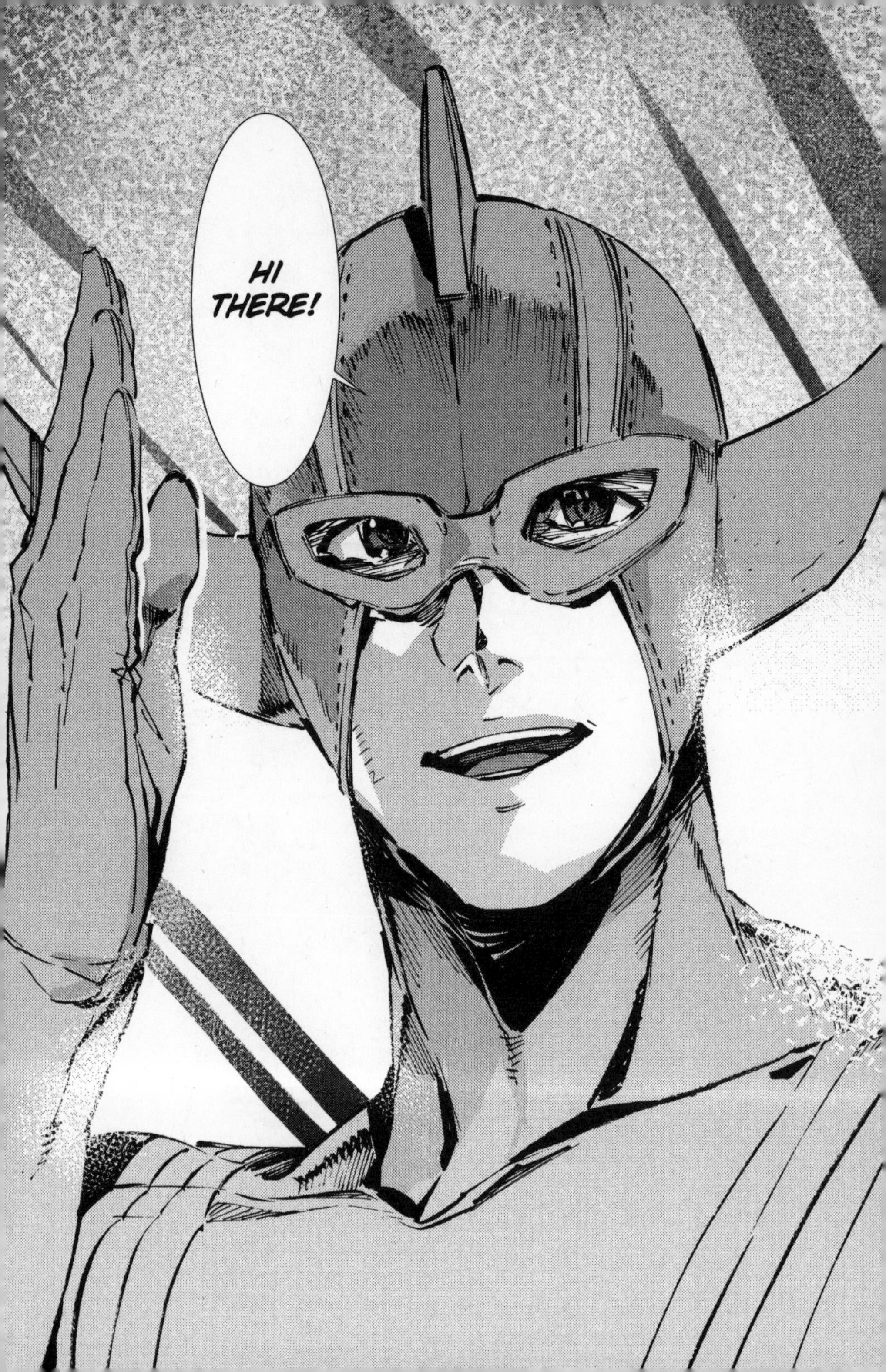
HI THERE!

ULTRAMAN

CHAPTER 57 - THE DISTANCE BETWEEN

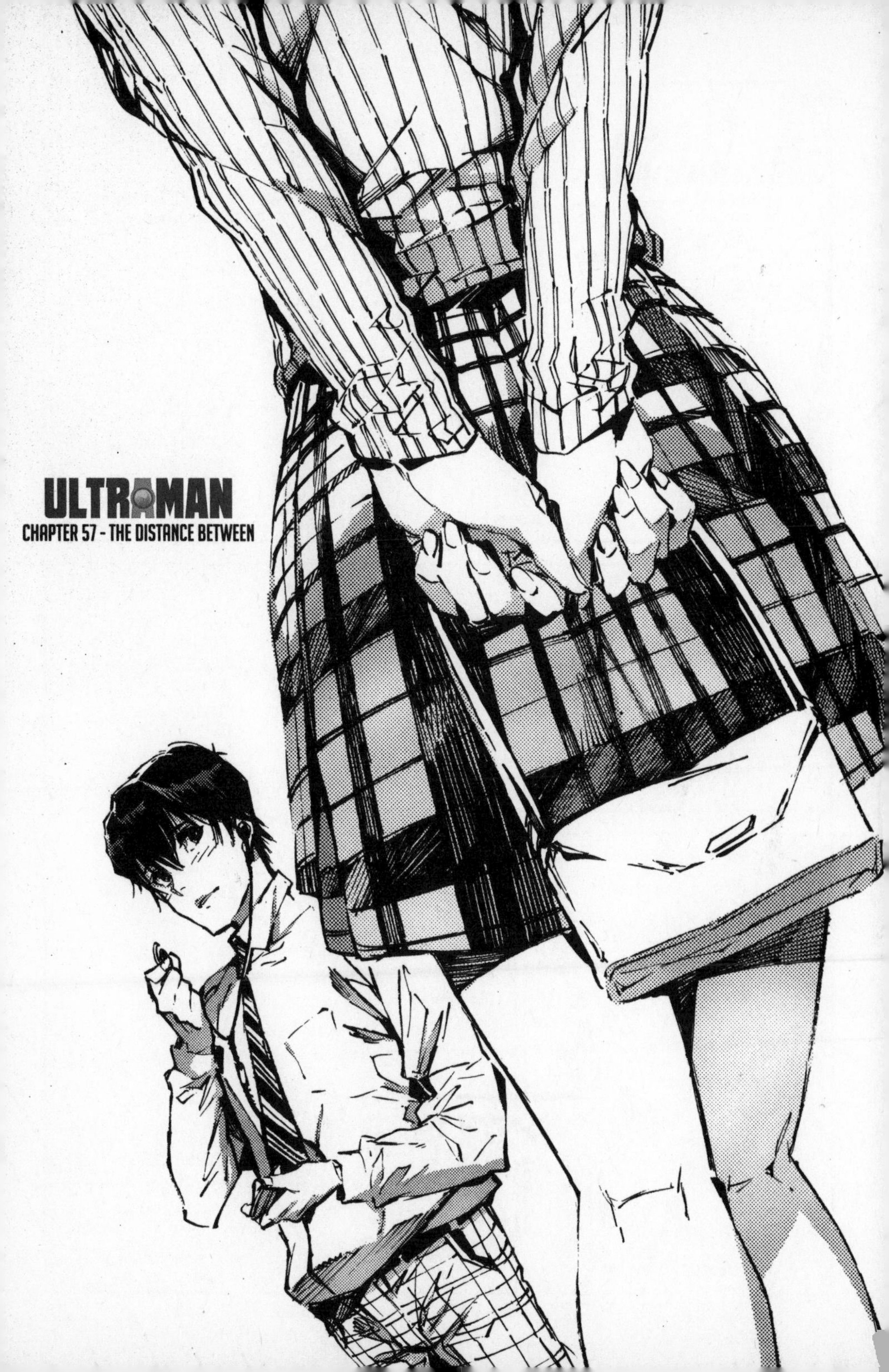

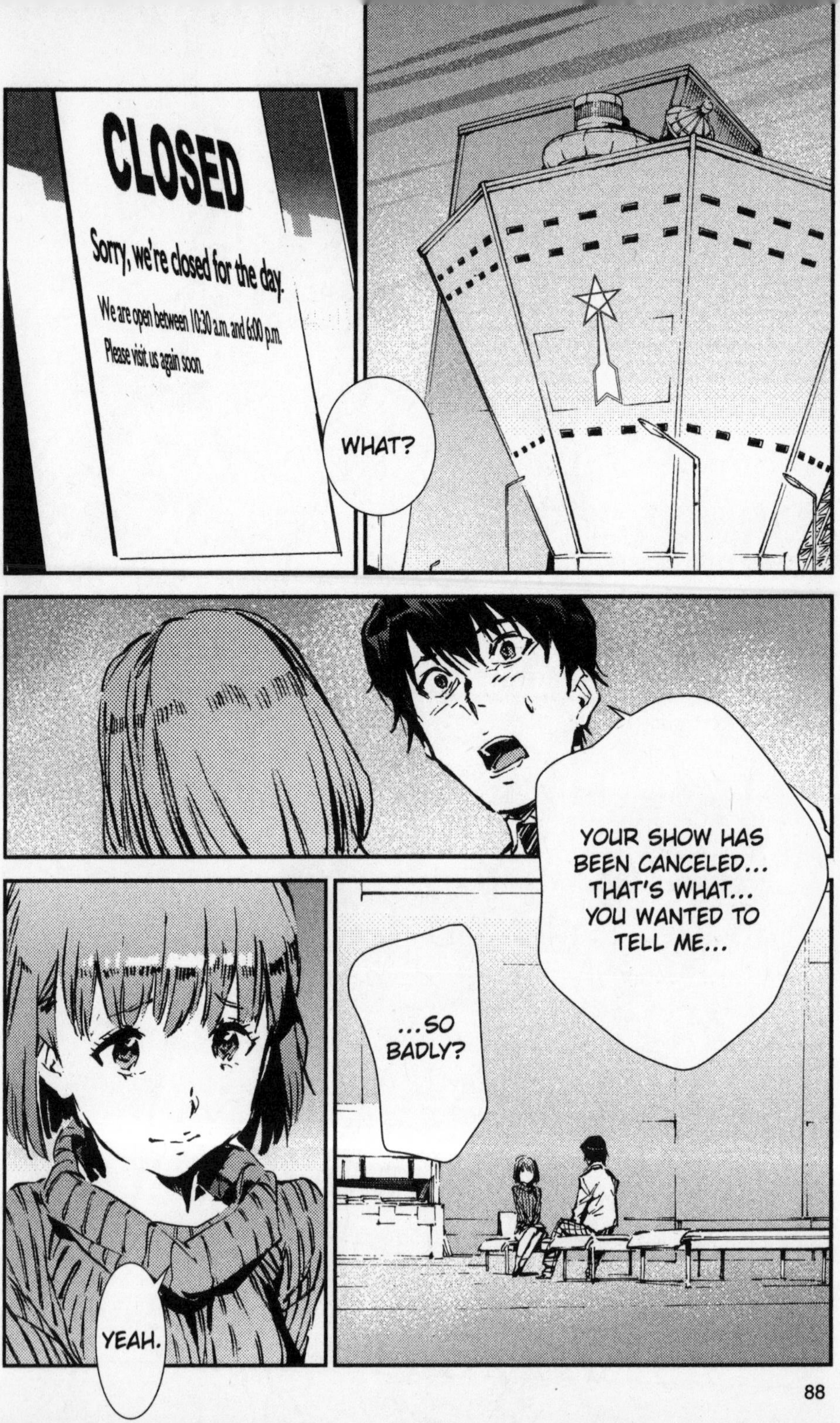
WHAT?
CLOSED
Sorry, we're closed for the day.
We are open between 10:30 a.m. and 6:00 p.m.
Please visit us again soon.
YOUR SHOW HAS BEEN CANCELED... THAT'S WHAT... YOU WANTED TO TELL ME...
...SO BADLY?
YEAH.

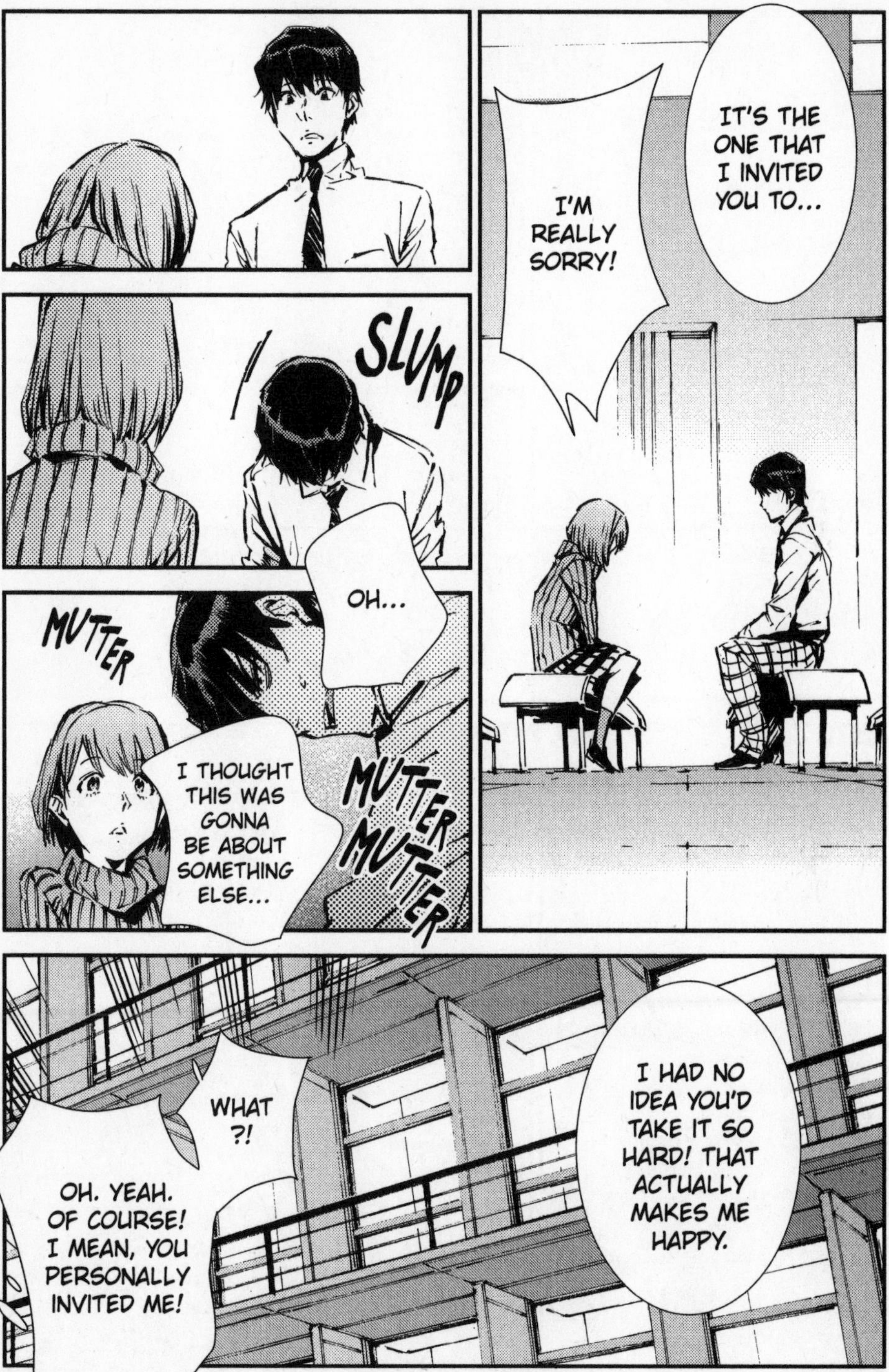
IT'S THE ONE THAT I INVITED YOU TO...
I'M REALLY SORRY!
SLUMP
OH...
MUTTER
MUTTER MUTTER
I THOUGHT THIS WAS GONNA BE ABOUT SOMETHING ELSE...
I HAD NO IDEA YOU'D TAKE IT SO HARD! THAT ACTUALLY MAKES ME HAPPY.
WHAT?!
OH. YEAH. OF COURSE! I MEAN, YOU PERSONALLY INVITED ME!

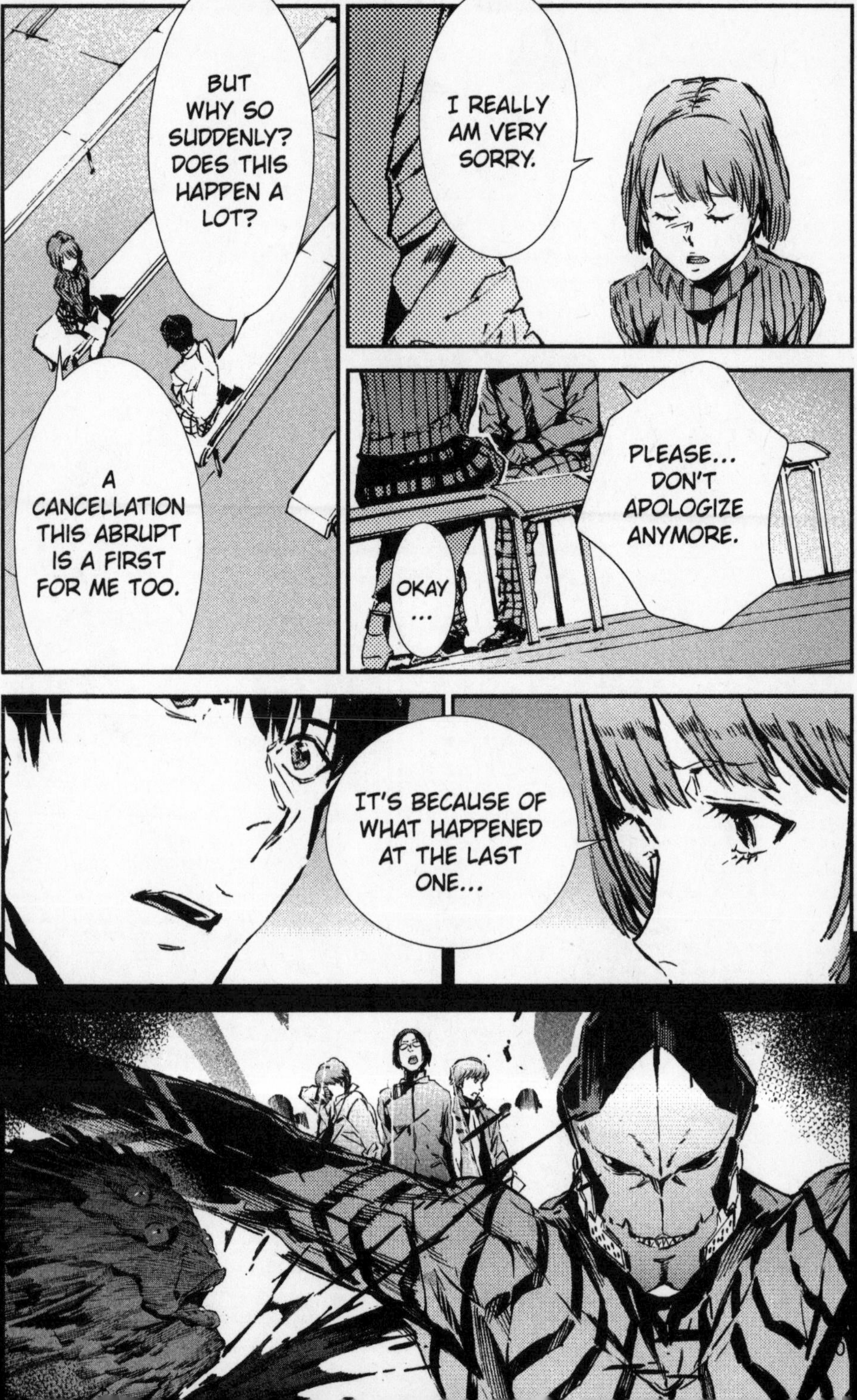
I REALLY AM VERY SORRY.
PLEASE... DON'T APOLOGIZE ANYMORE.
OKAY ...
BUT WHY SO SUDDENLY? DOES THIS HAPPEN A LOT?
A CANCELLATION THIS ABRUPT IS A FIRST FOR ME TOO.
IT'S BECAUSE OF WHAT HAPPENED AT THE LAST ONE...

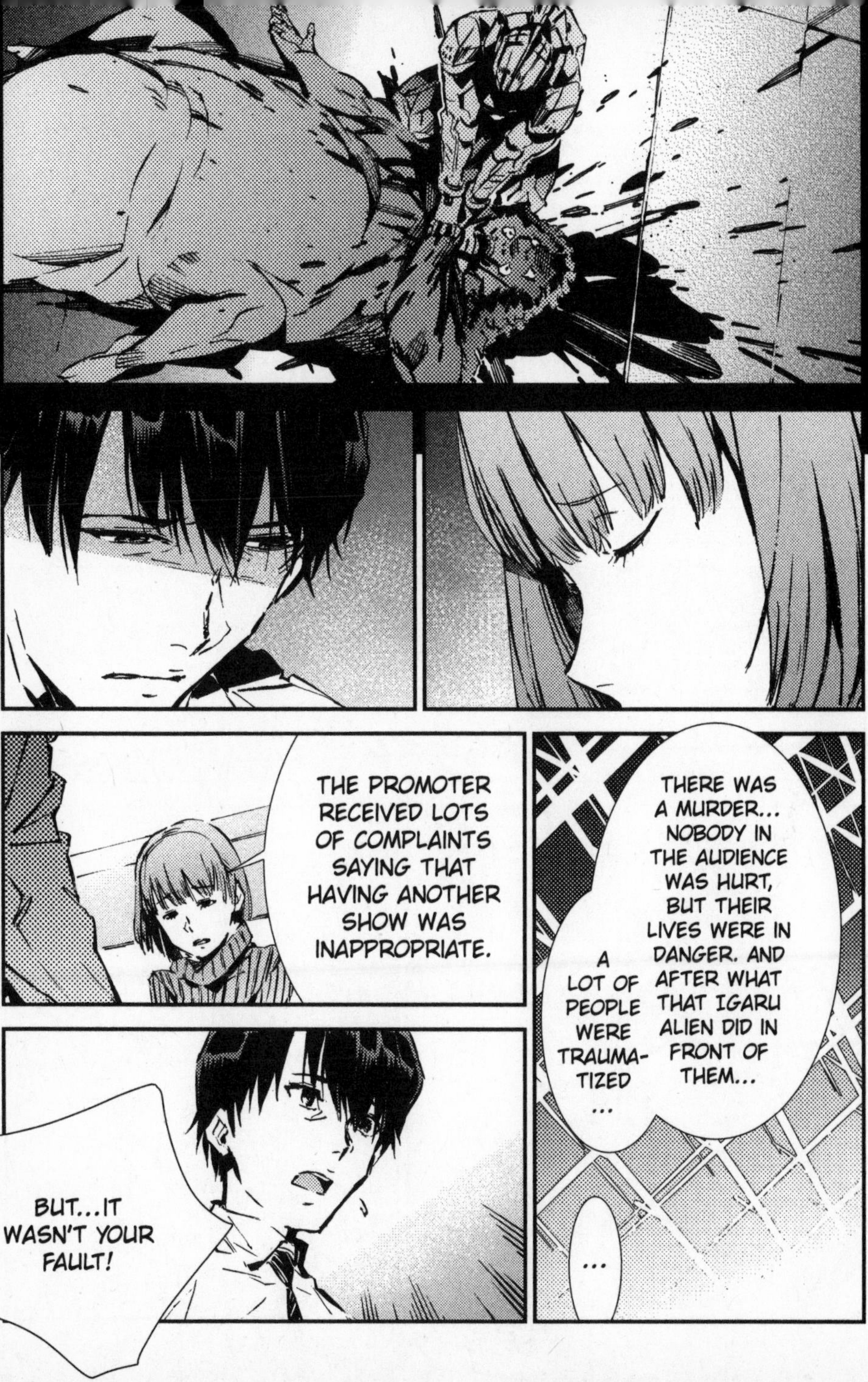
THE PROMOTER RECEIVED LOTS OF COMPLAINTS SAYING THAT HAVING ANOTHER SHOW WAS INAPPROPRIATE.
THERE WAS A MURDER... NOBODY IN THE AUDIENCE WAS HURT, BUT THEIR LIVES WERE IN DANGER. AND AFTER WHAT THAT IGARU ALIEN DID IN FRONT OF THEM...
A LOT OF PEOPLE WERE TRAUMA-TIZED...
BUT...IT WASN'T YOUR FAULT!
...

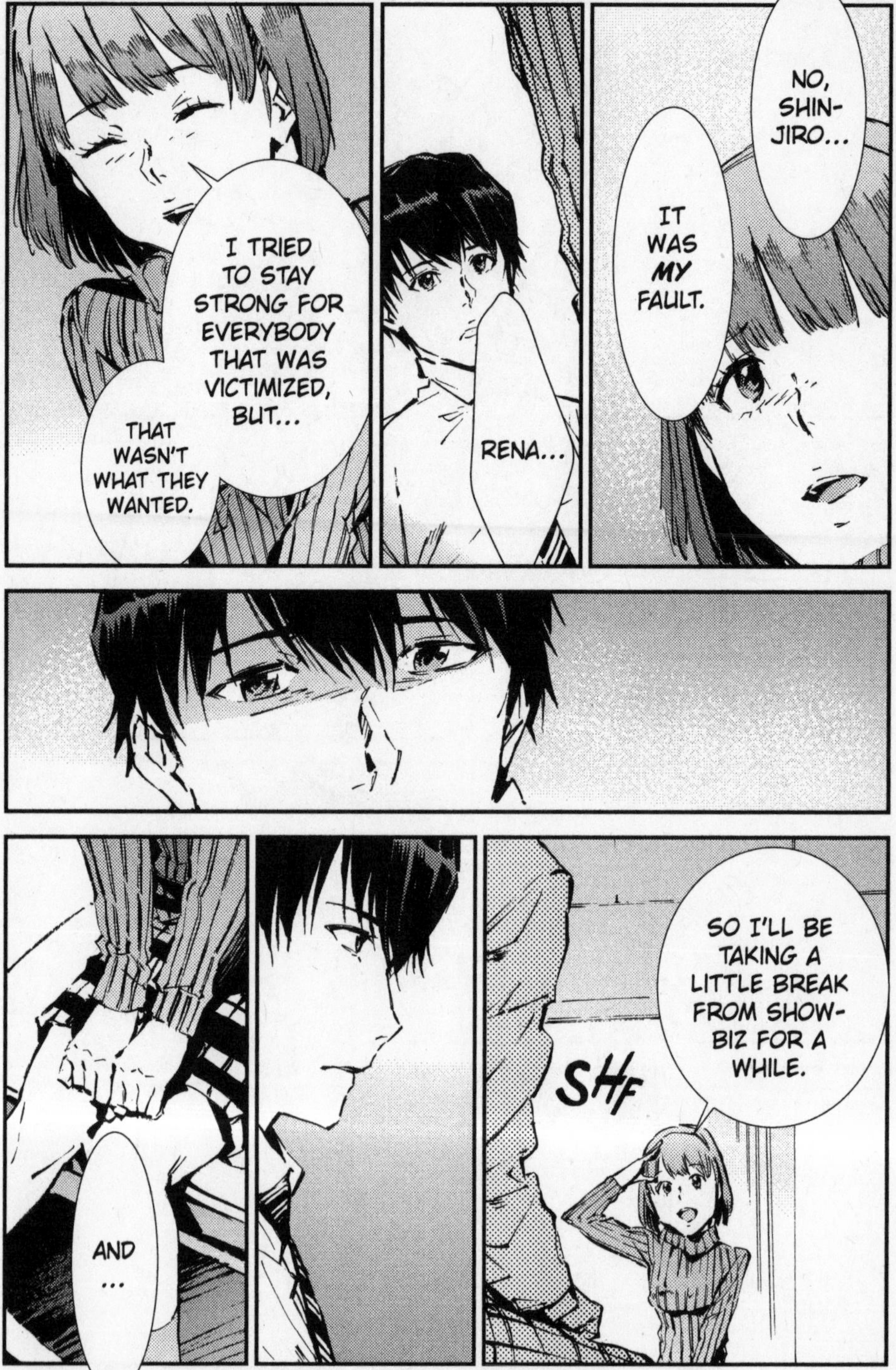
NO, SHIN-JIRO...
IT WAS *MY* FAULT.
RENA...
I TRIED TO STAY STRONG FOR EVERYBODY THAT WAS VICTIMIZED, BUT...
THAT WASN'T WHAT THEY WANTED.
SO I'LL BE TAKING A LITTLE BREAK FROM SHOW-BIZ FOR A WHILE.
SHF
AND ...

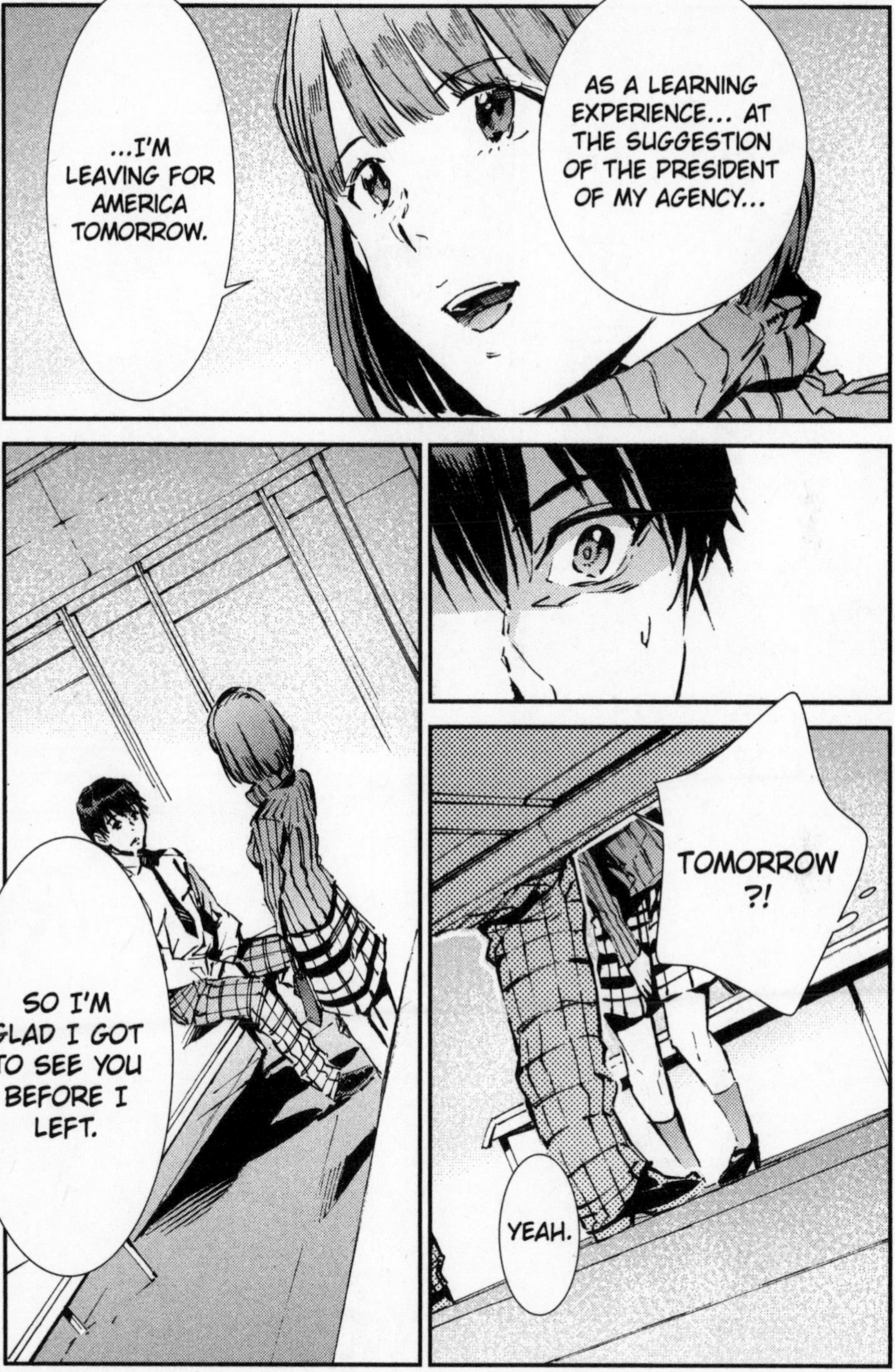

AS A LEARNING EXPERIENCE... AT THE SUGGESTION OF THE PRESIDENT OF MY AGENCY...
...I'M LEAVING FOR AMERICA TOMORROW.
TOMORROW ?!
YEAH.
SO I'M GLAD I GOT TO SEE YOU BEFORE I LEFT.

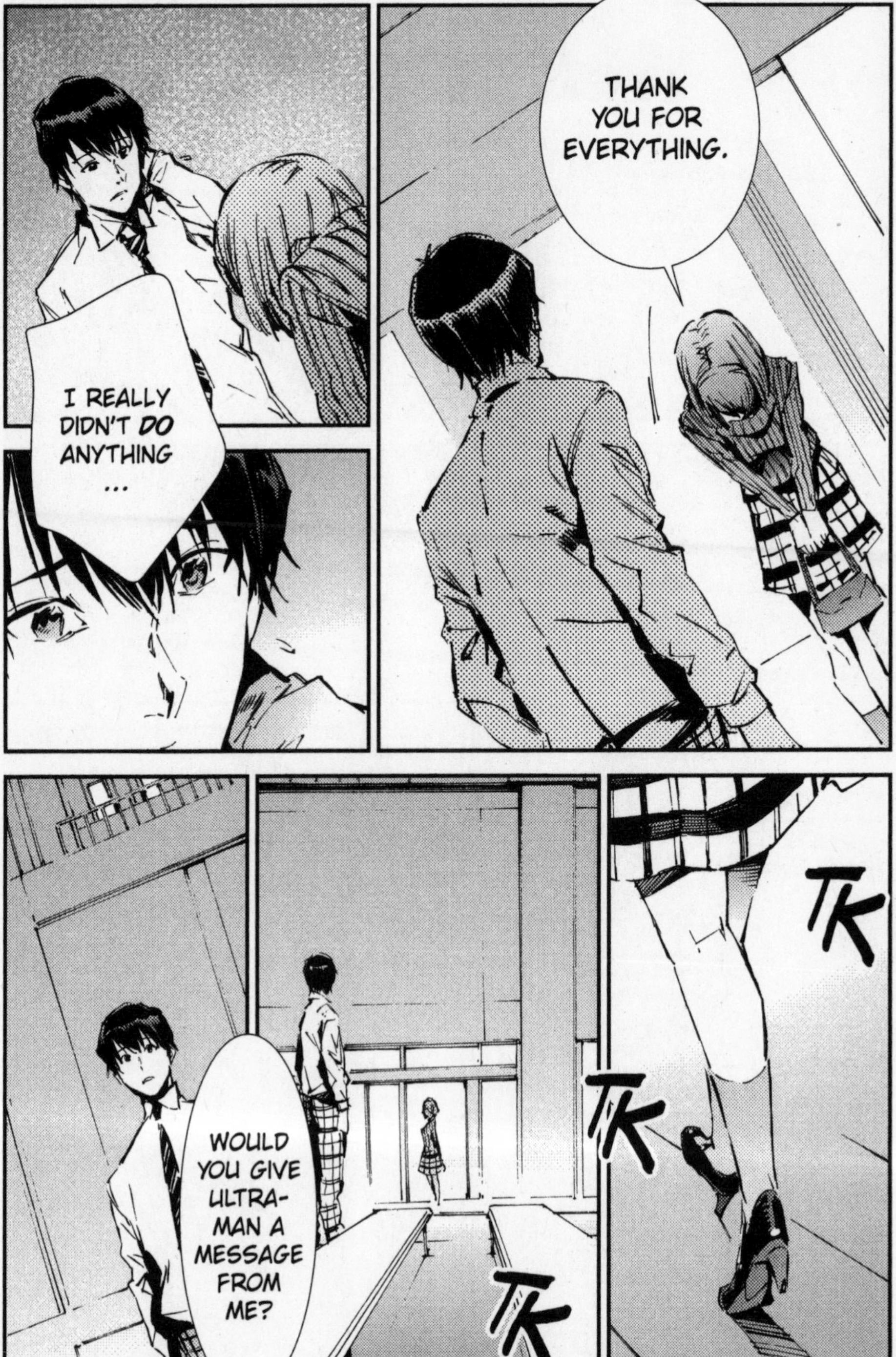
THANK YOU FOR EVERYTHING.
I REALLY DIDN'T DO ANYTHING ...
TK
TK
TK
WOULD YOU GIVE ULTRA-MAN A MESSAGE FROM ME?

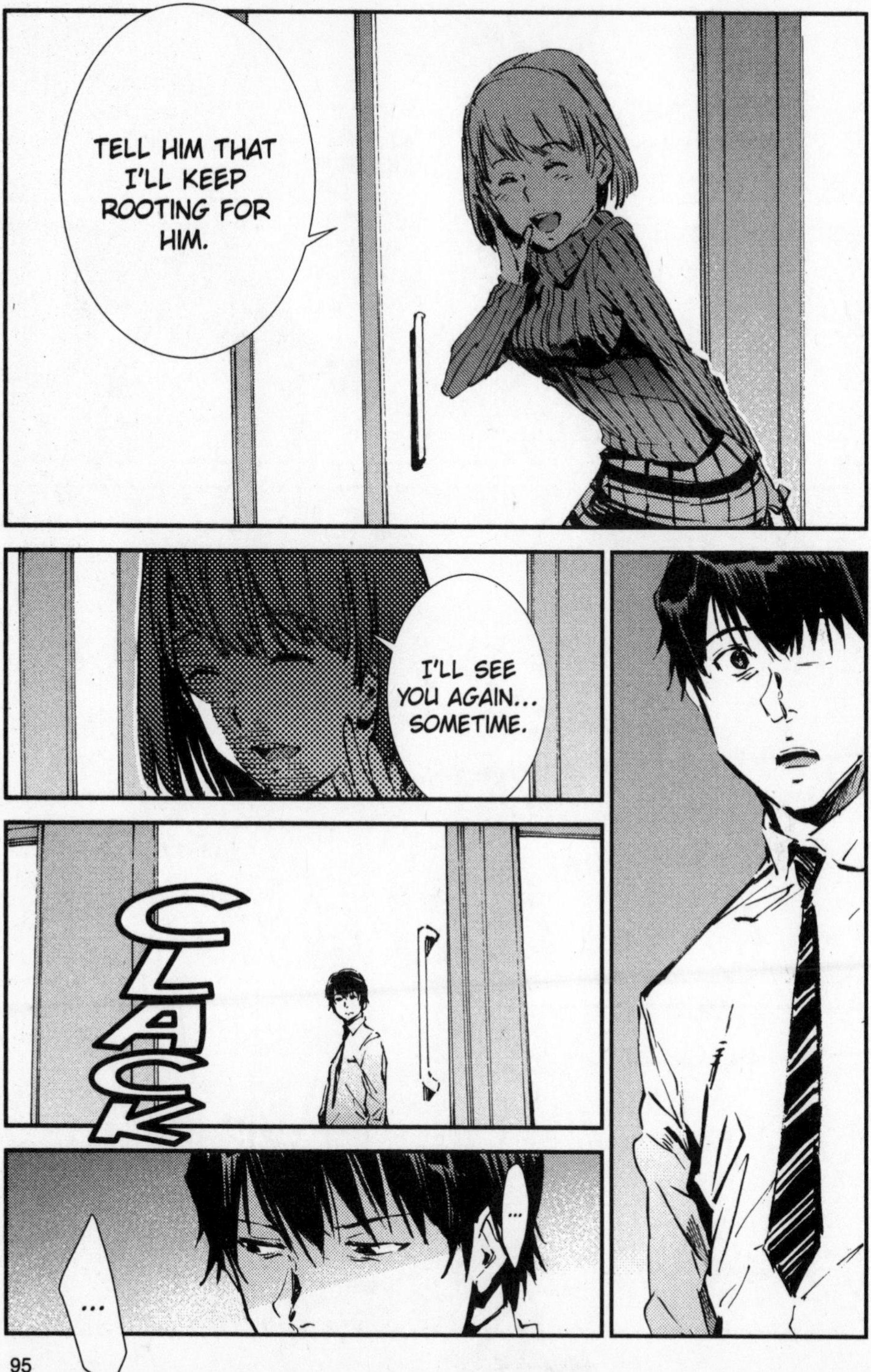
TELL HIM THAT I'LL KEEP ROOTING FOR HIM.
I'LL SEE YOU AGAIN... SOMETIME.
CLACK
...
...

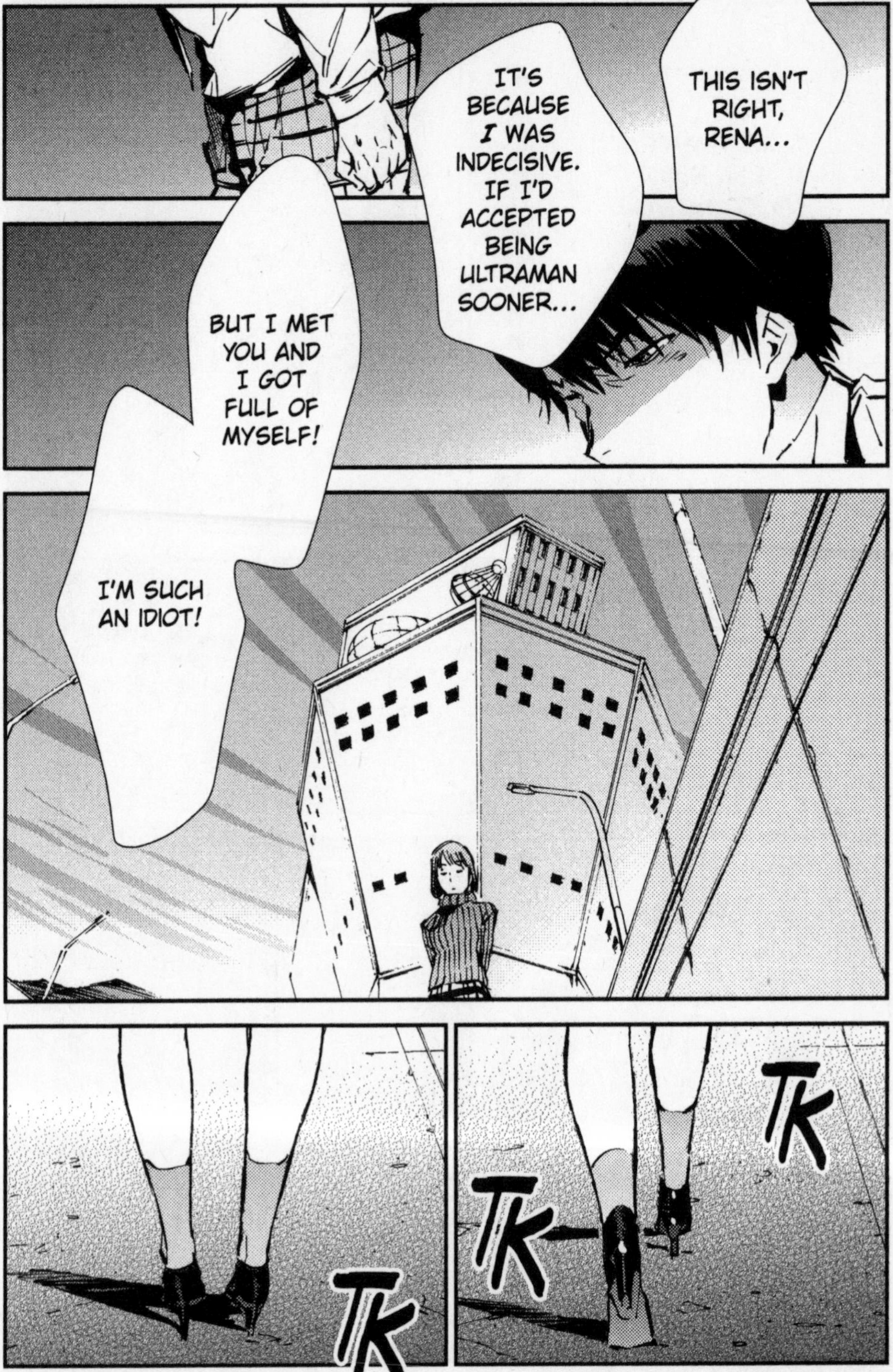
THIS ISN'T RIGHT, RENA...
IT'S BECAUSE *I* WAS INDECISIVE. IF I'D ACCEPTED BEING ULTRAMAN SOONER...
BUT I MET YOU AND I GOT FULL OF MYSELF!
I'M SUCH AN IDIOT!
TK
TK
TK

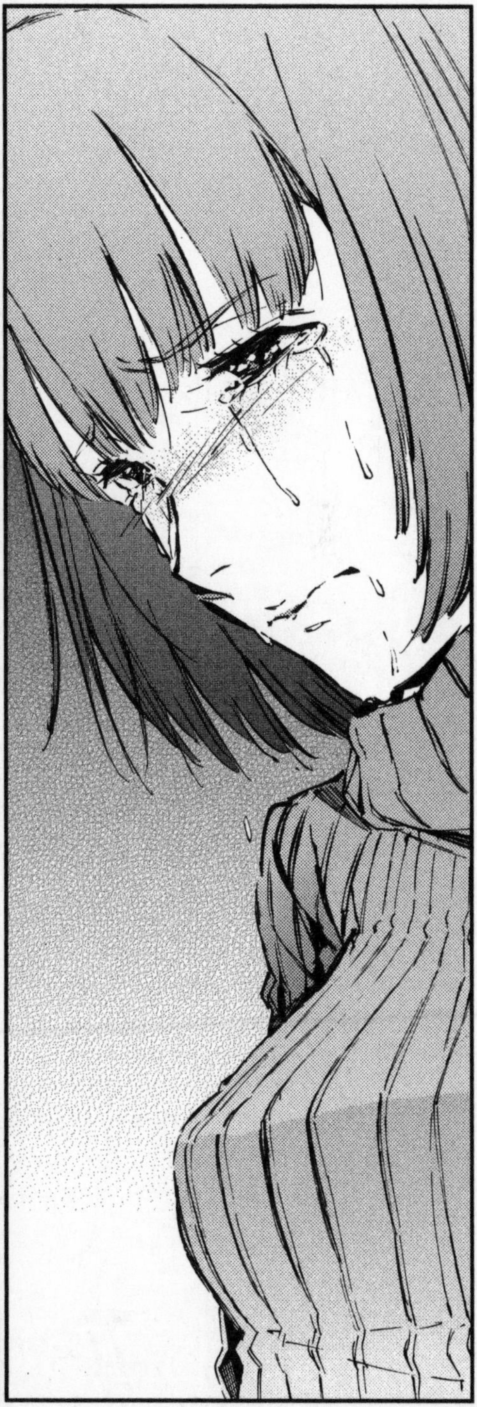
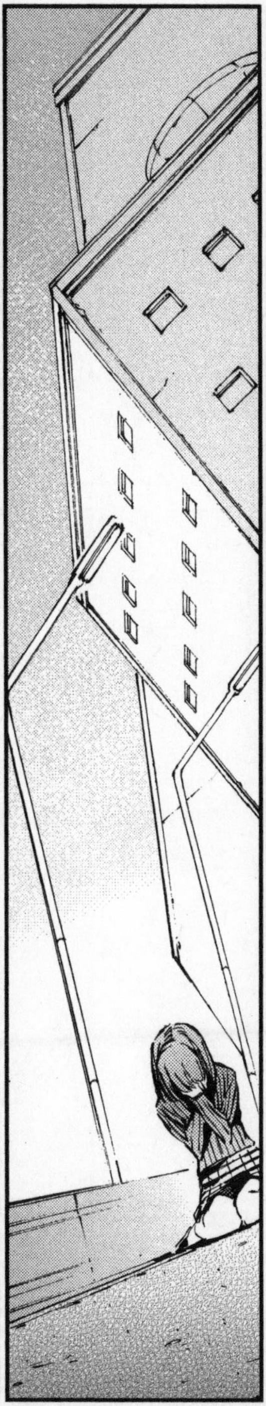
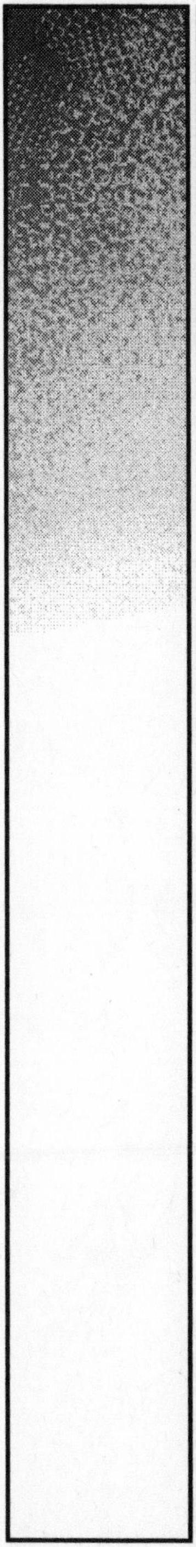

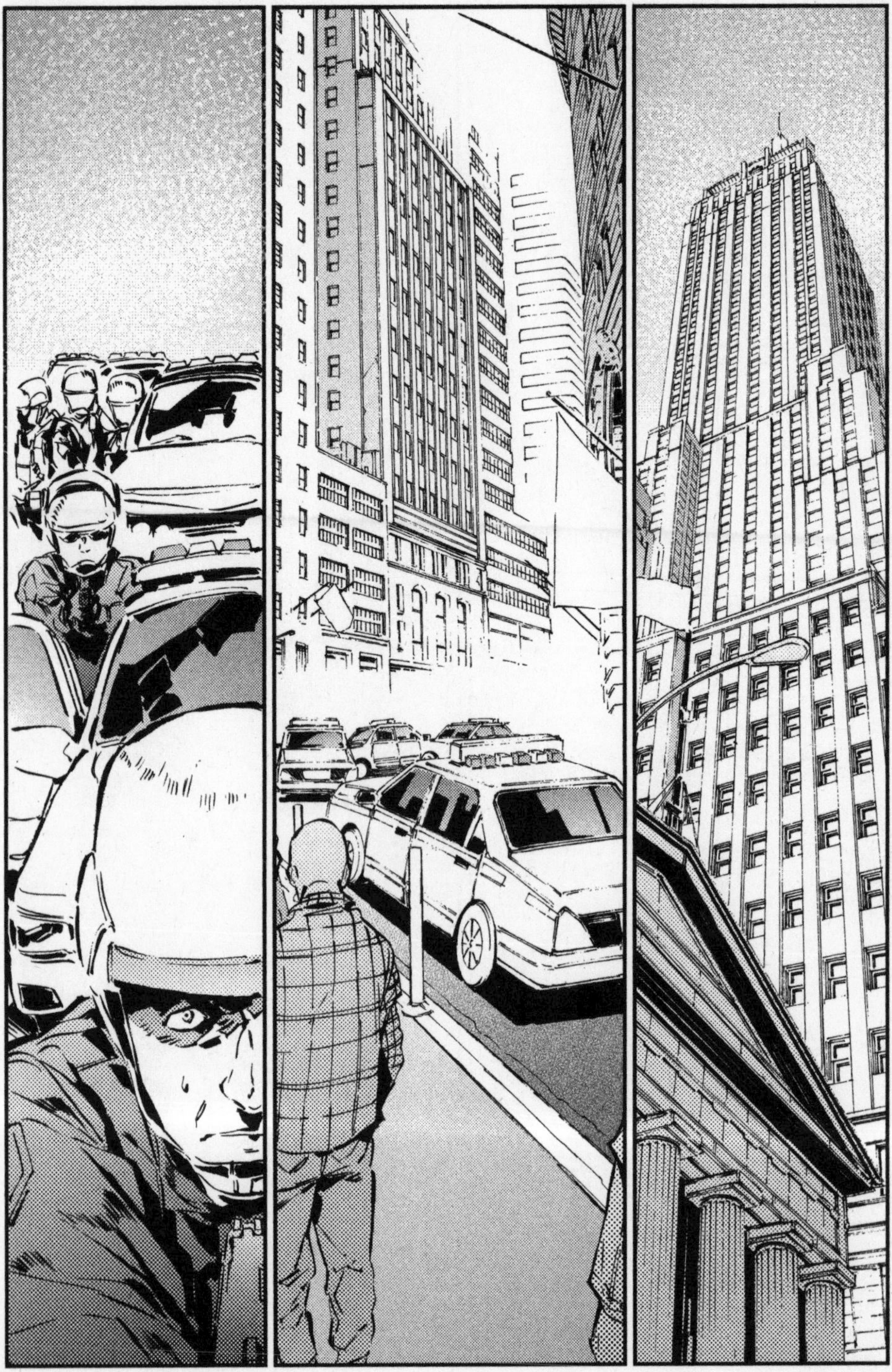

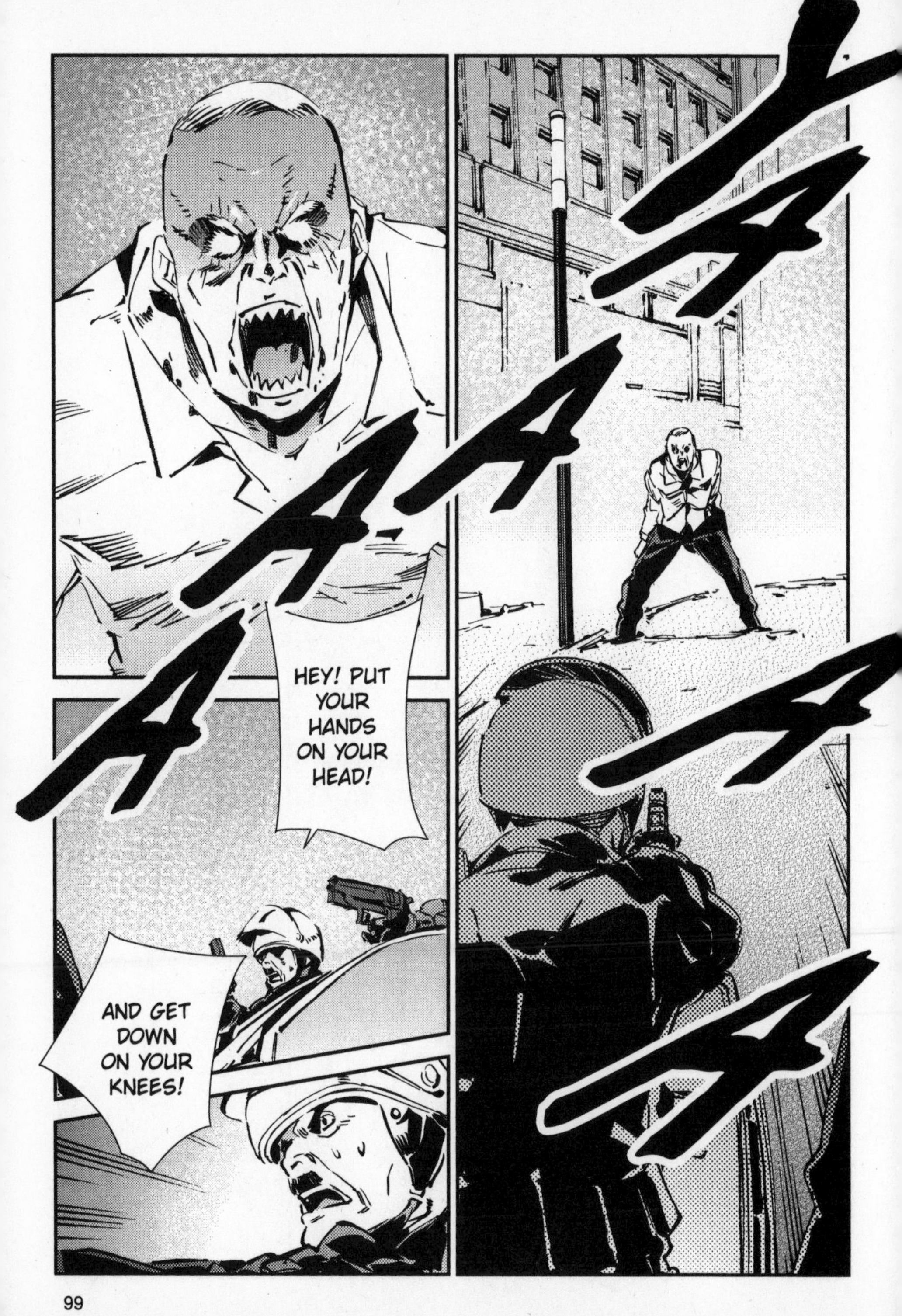
HEY! PUT YOUR HANDS ON YOUR HEAD!
AND GET DOWN ON YOUR KNEES!

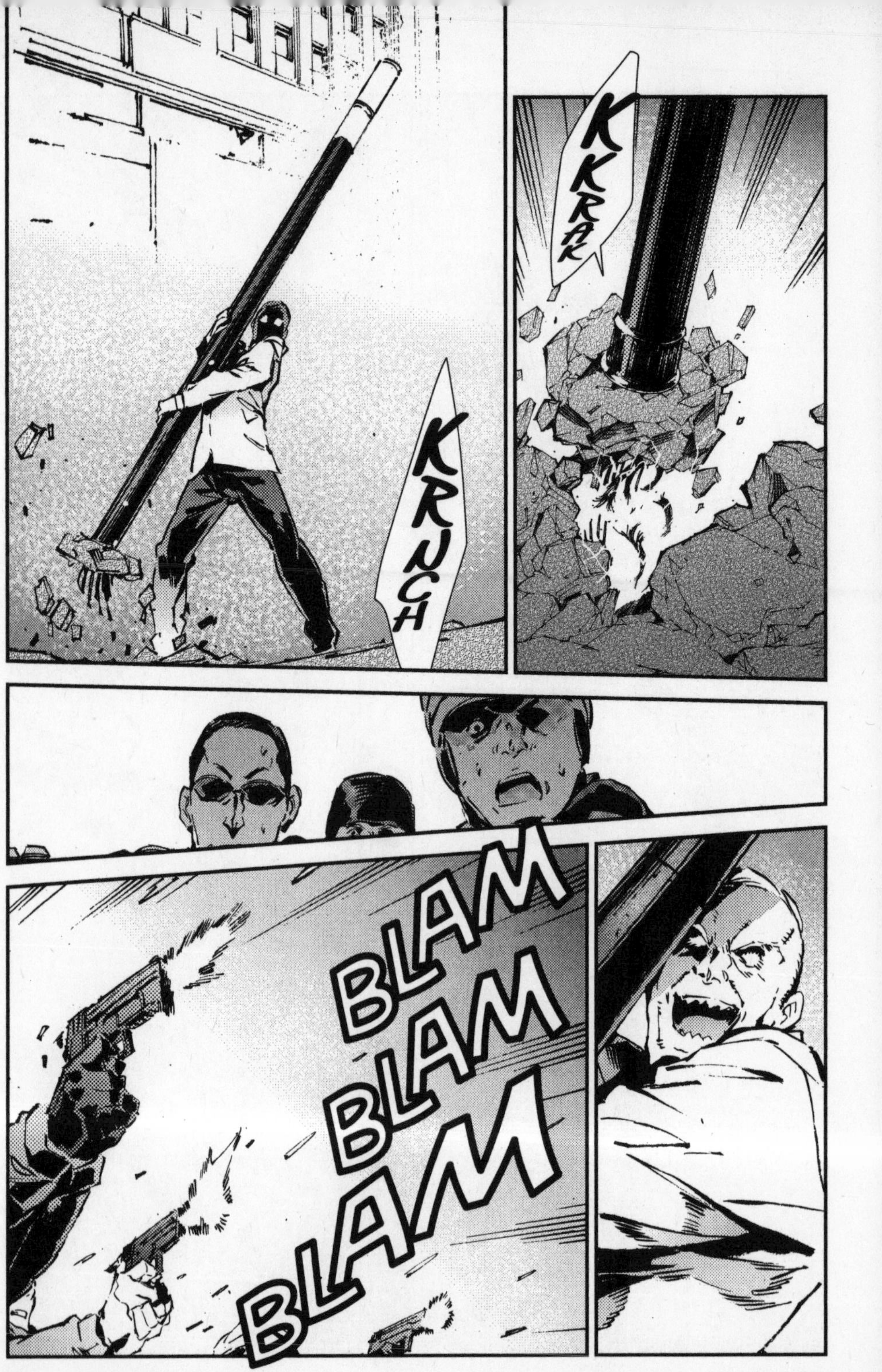
KKRAK
KRUNCH
BLAM
BLAM
BLAM
BLAM

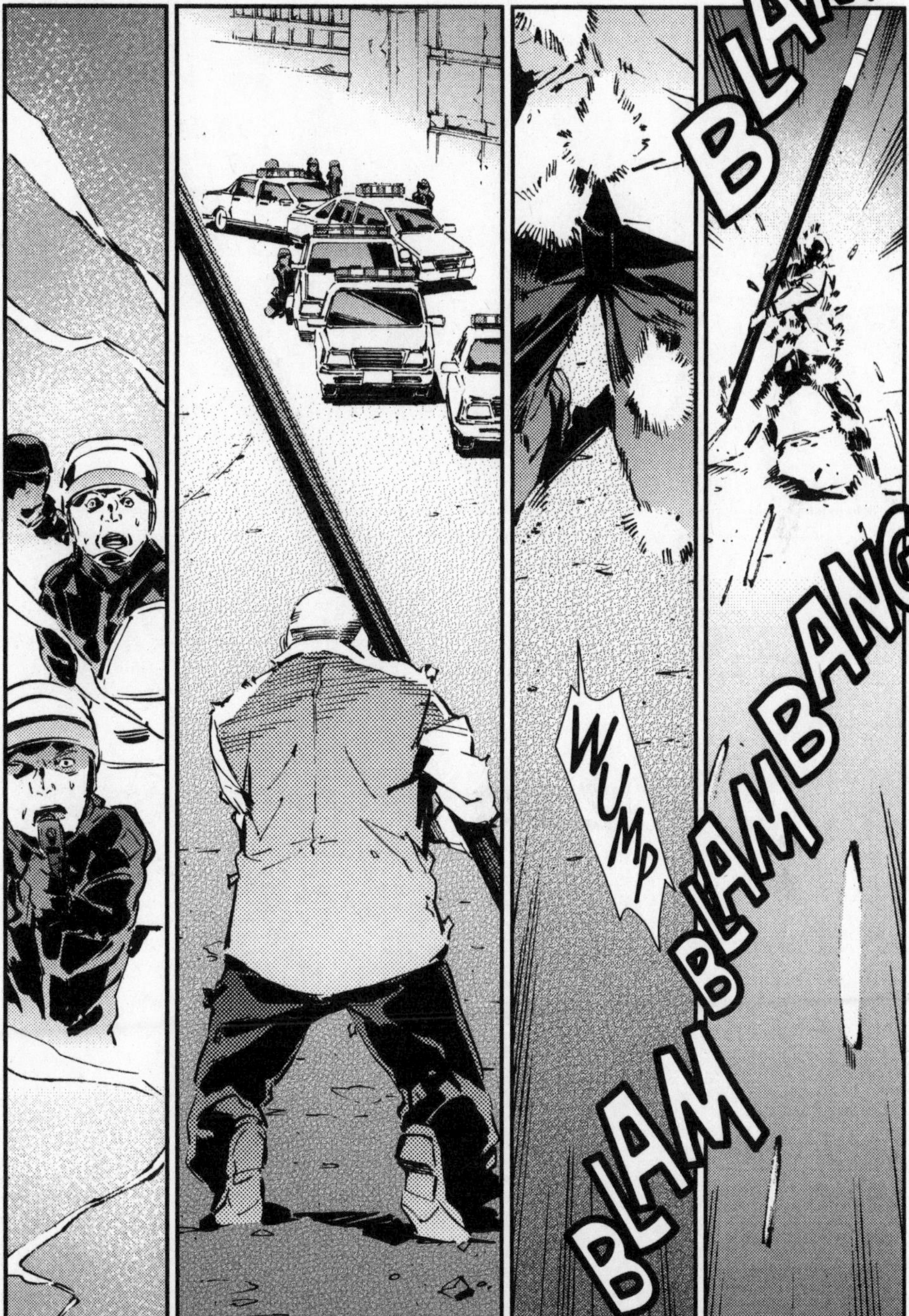
BLAM
WUMP
BLAM BLAM BANG

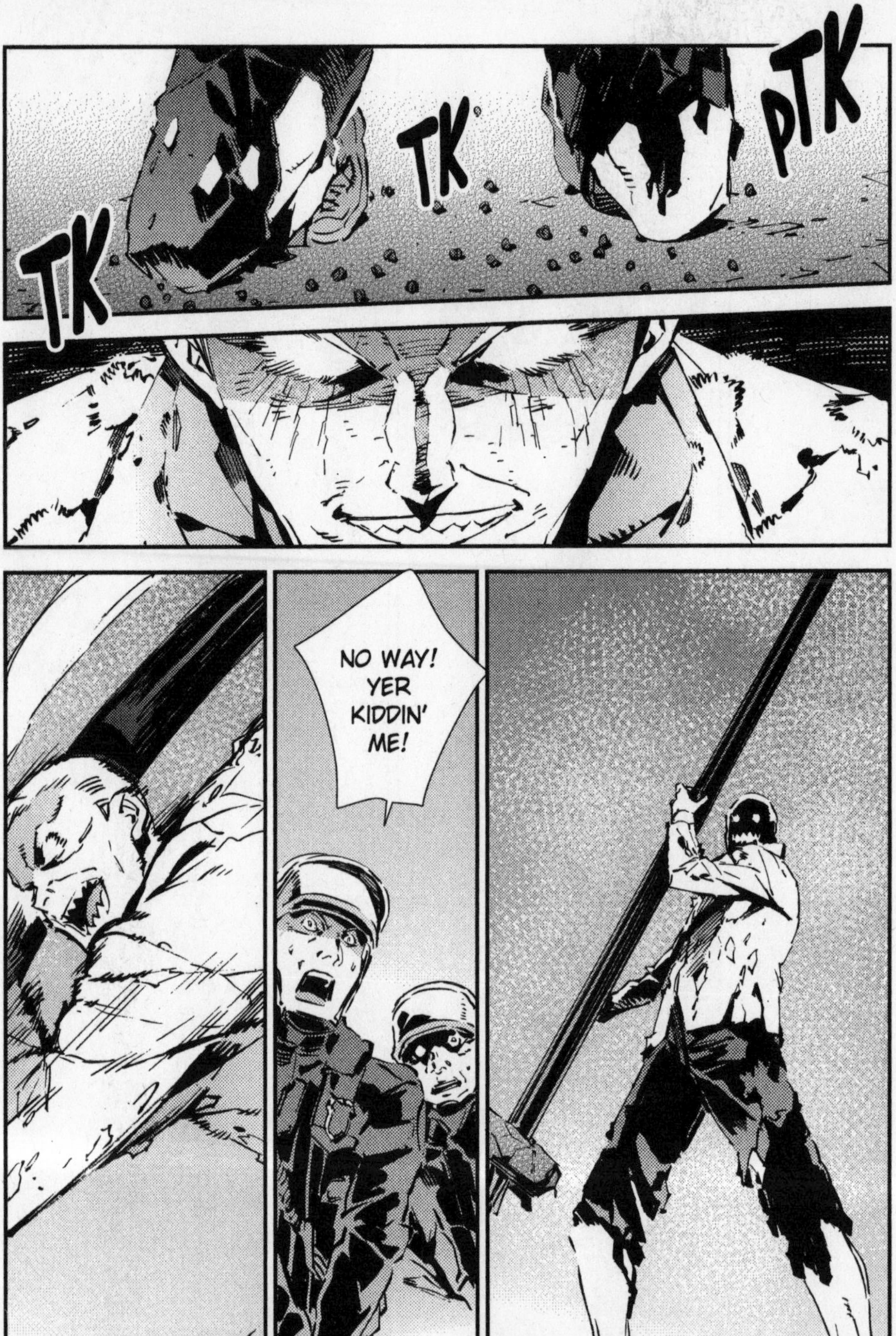
PTK
TK
TK
NO WAY! YER KIDDIN' ME!

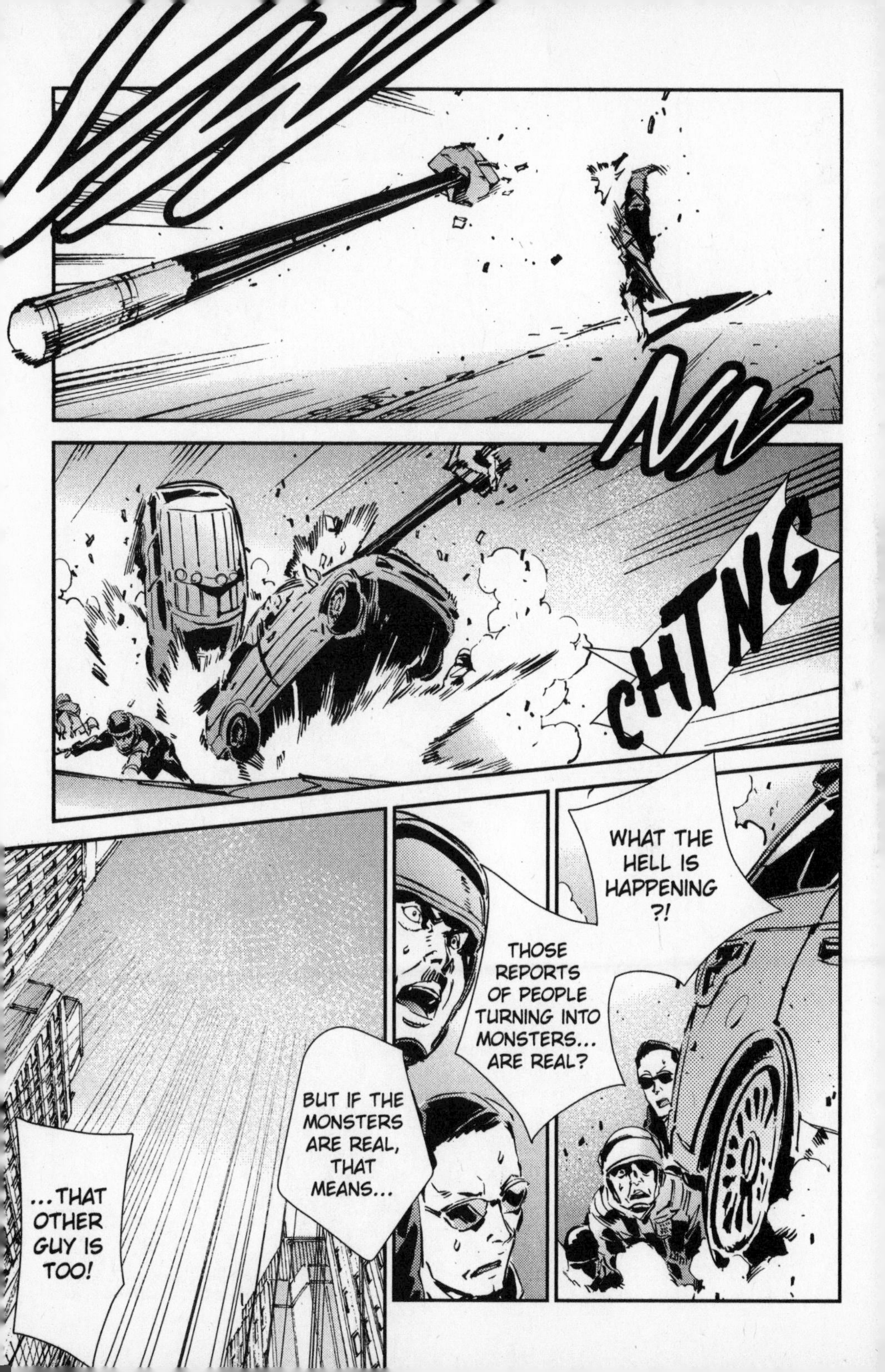
WHAT THE HELL IS HAPPENING?!
THOSE REPORTS OF PEOPLE TURNING INTO MONSTERS... ARE REAL?
BUT IF THE MONSTERS ARE REAL, THAT MEANS...
...THAT OTHER GUY IS TOO!

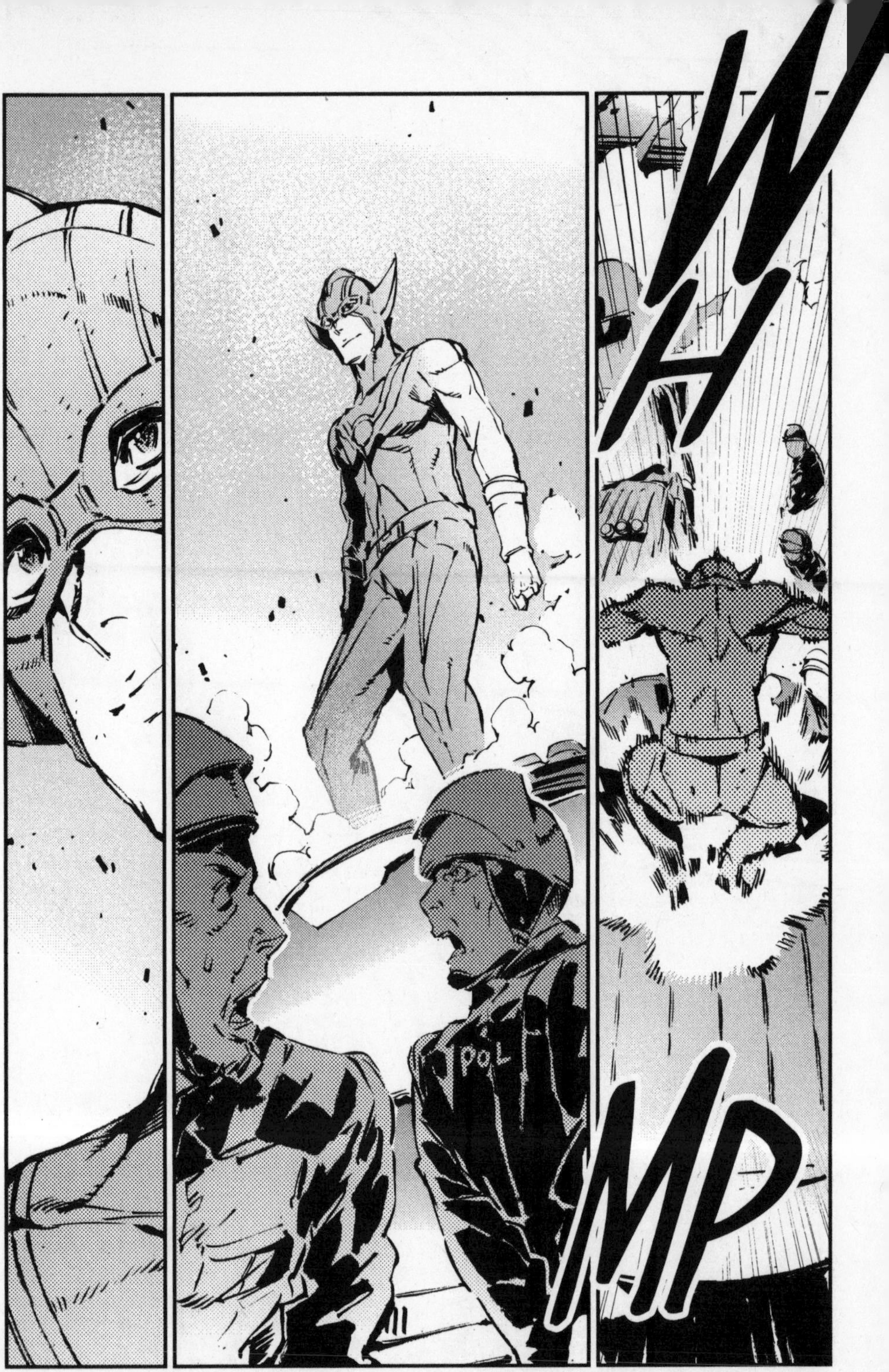
WHUMP

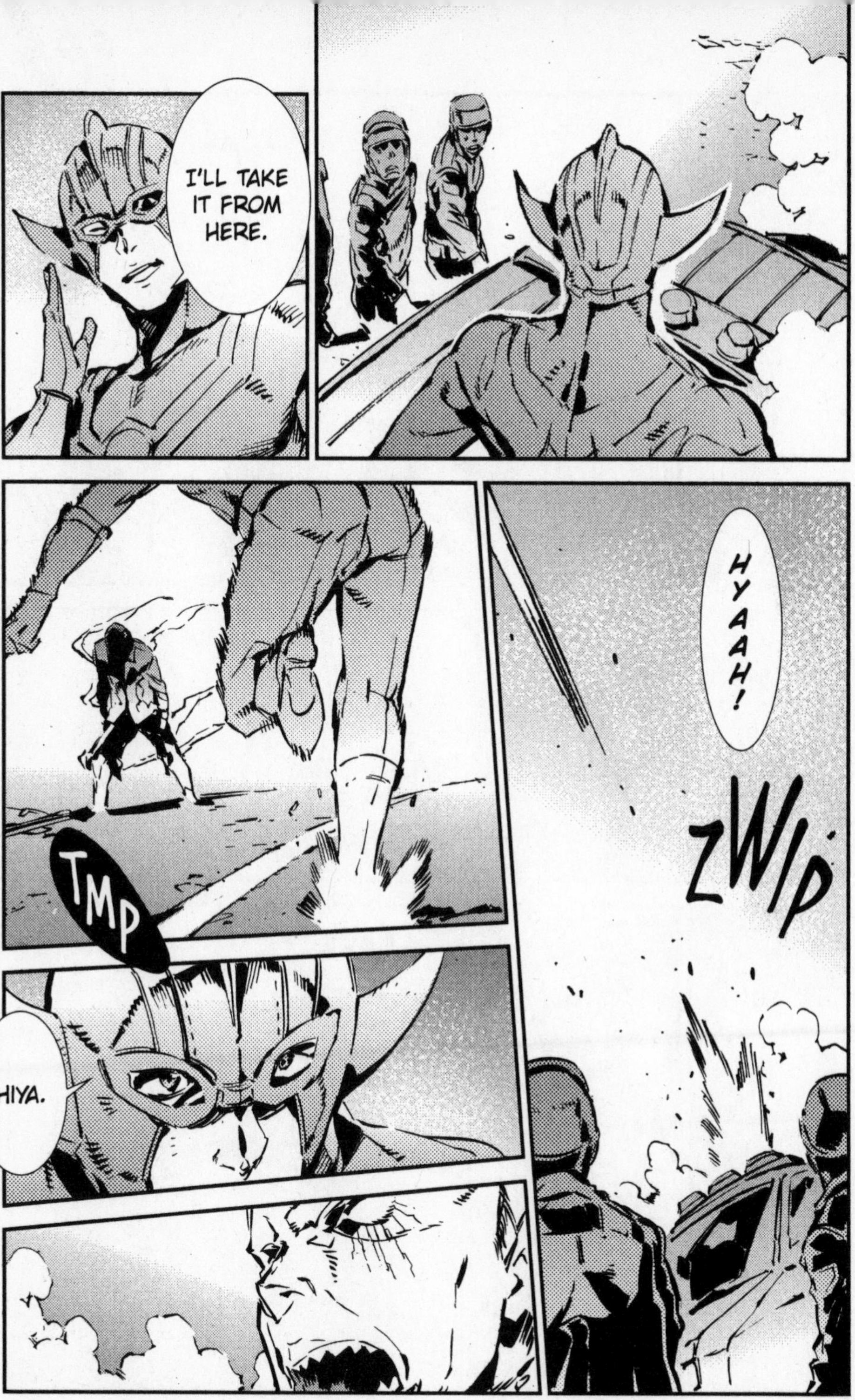
I'LL TAKE IT FROM HERE.
HYAAAH!
ZWIP
TMP
HIYA.

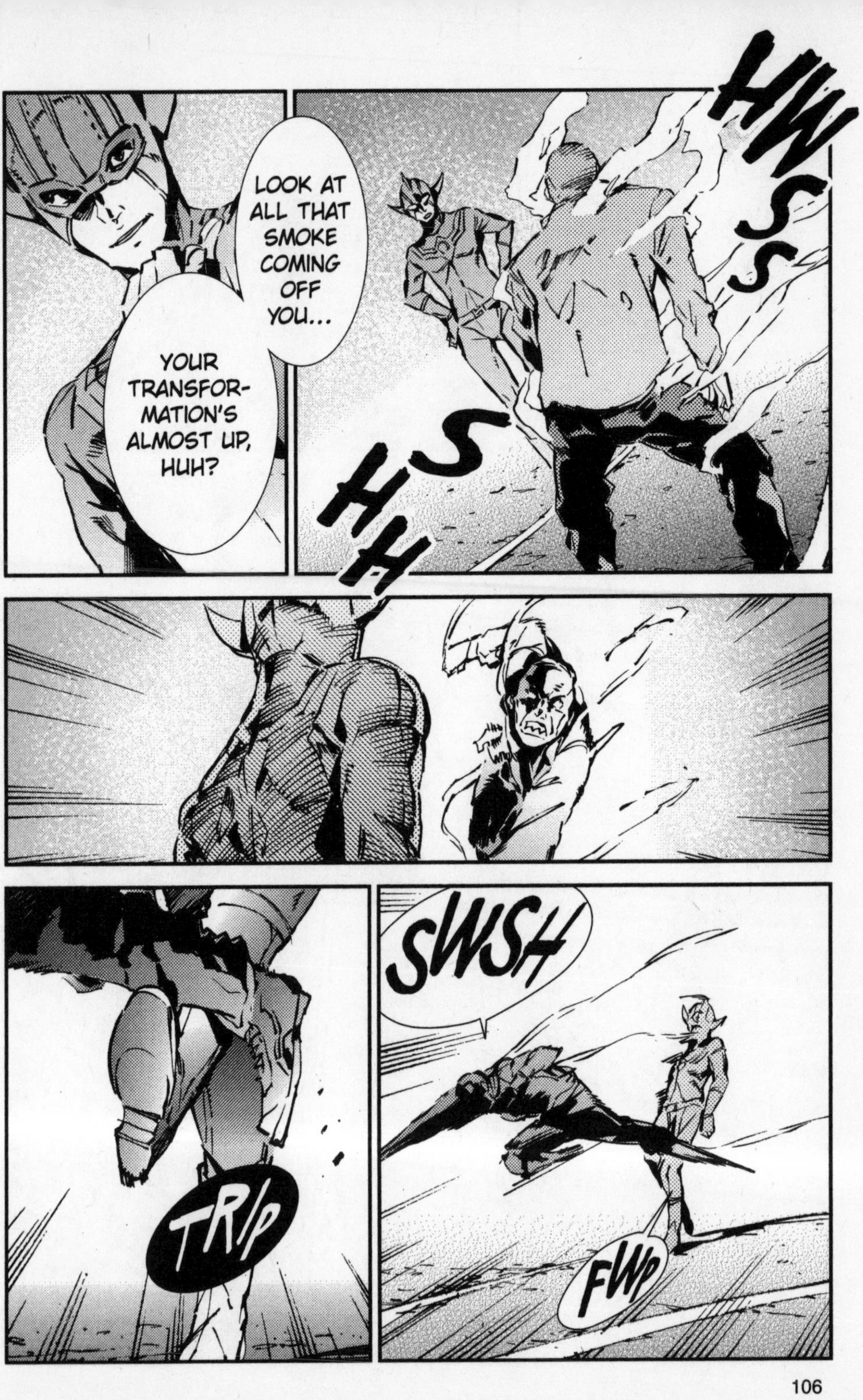
HWSSS
SHH
LOOK AT ALL THAT SMOKE COMING OFF YOU...
YOUR TRANSFOR-MATION'S ALMOST UP, HUH?
SWSH
FWP
TRIP

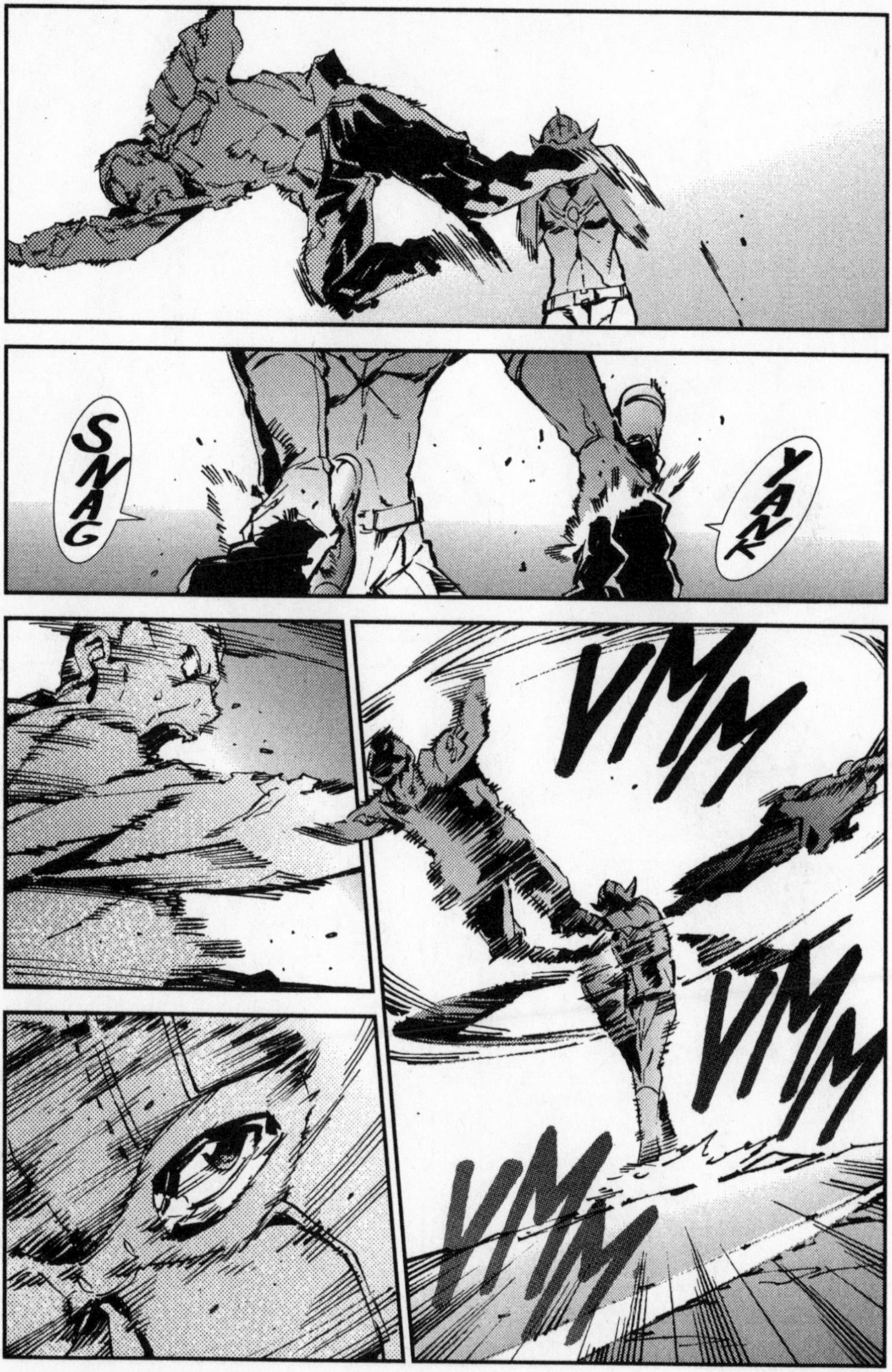
YANK
SNAG
VMM
VMM
VMM

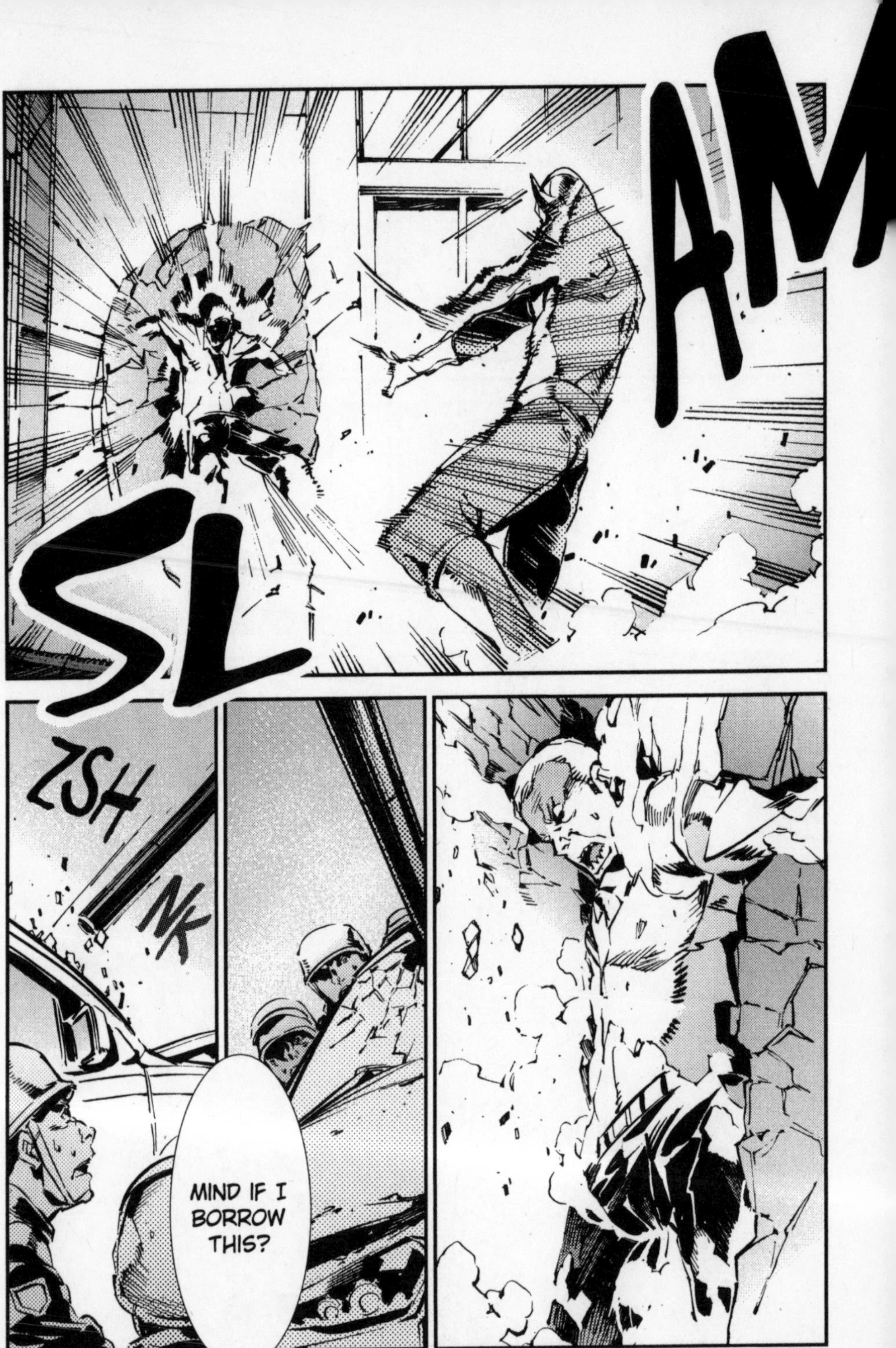
AM
SL
MIND IF I BORROW THIS?
ZSH
NK

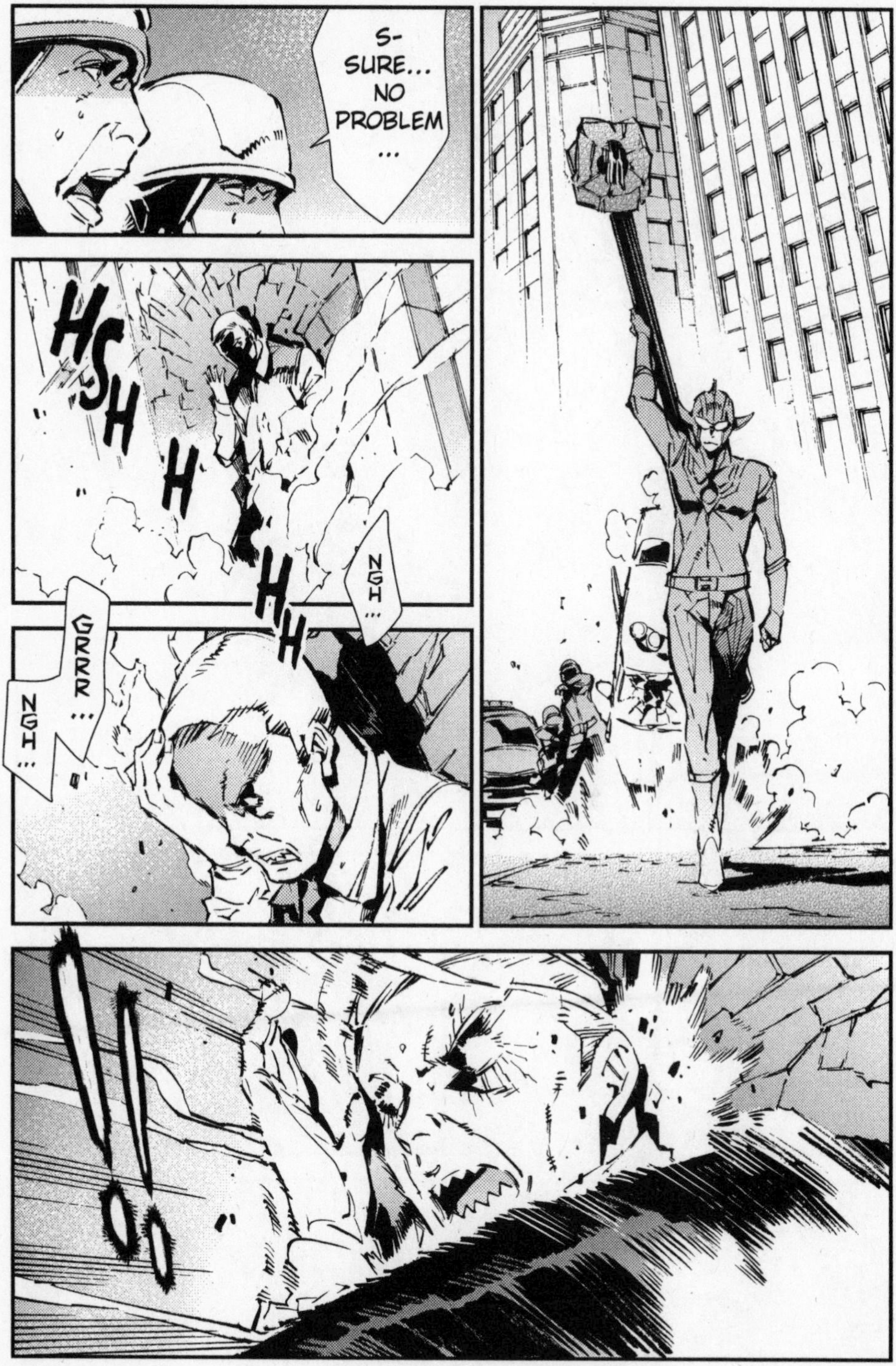
S-SURE... NO PROBLEM ...
HSHHHH
NGH...
GRRR...
NGH...
!!

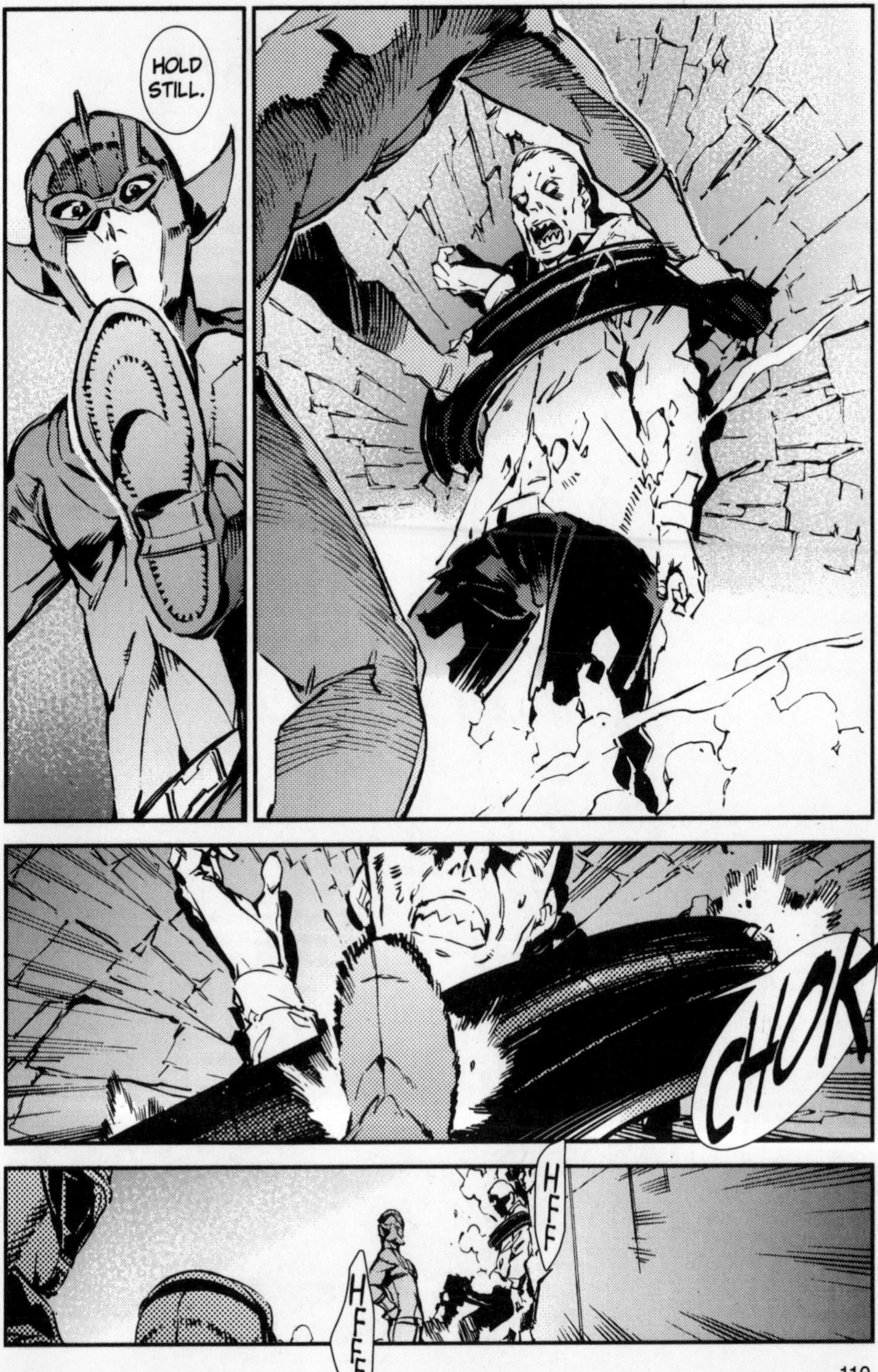
HOLD STILL.
CHOK
HFFF
HFFF

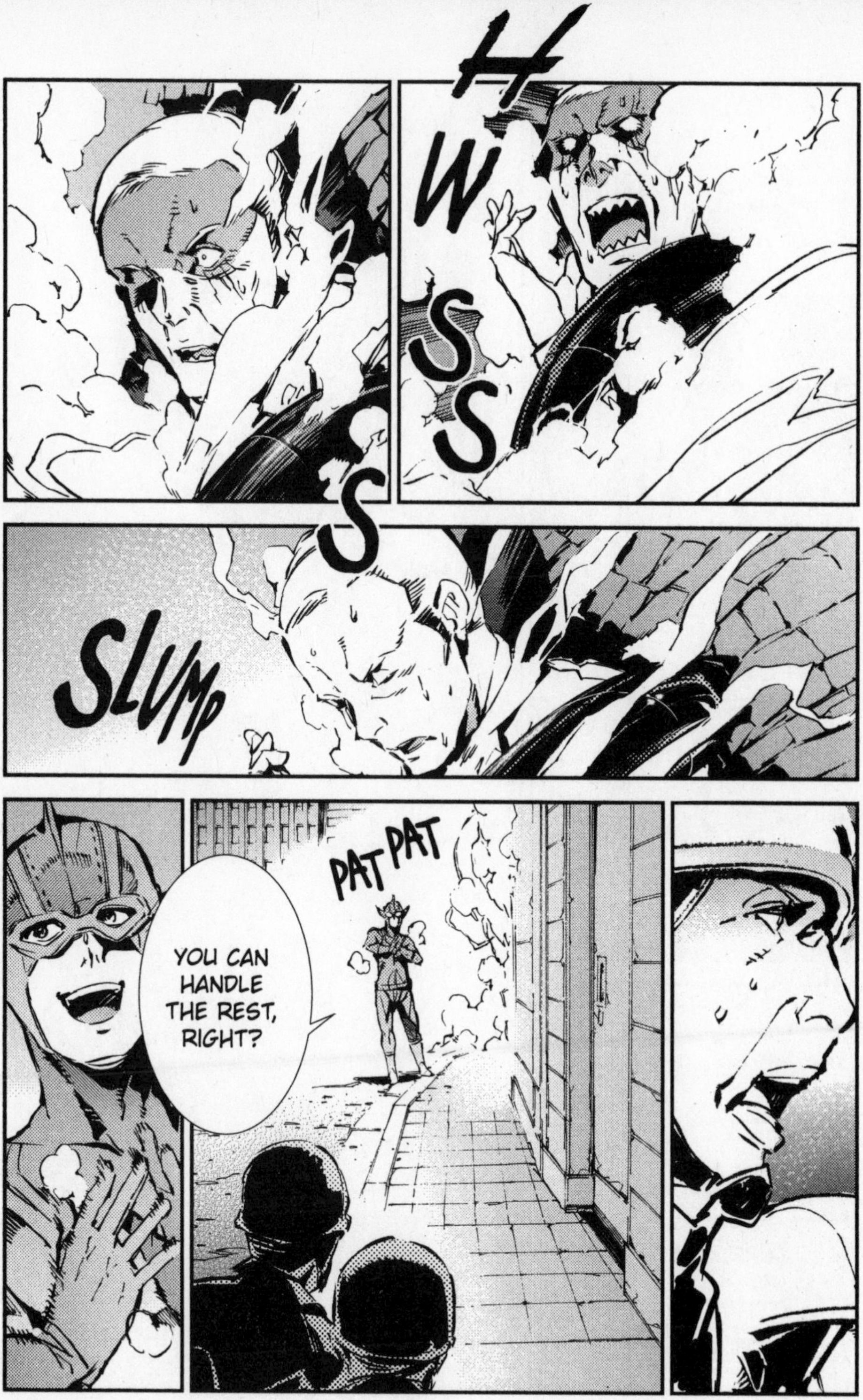
HWSSSS
SLUMP
PAT PAT
YOU CAN HANDLE THE REST, RIGHT?

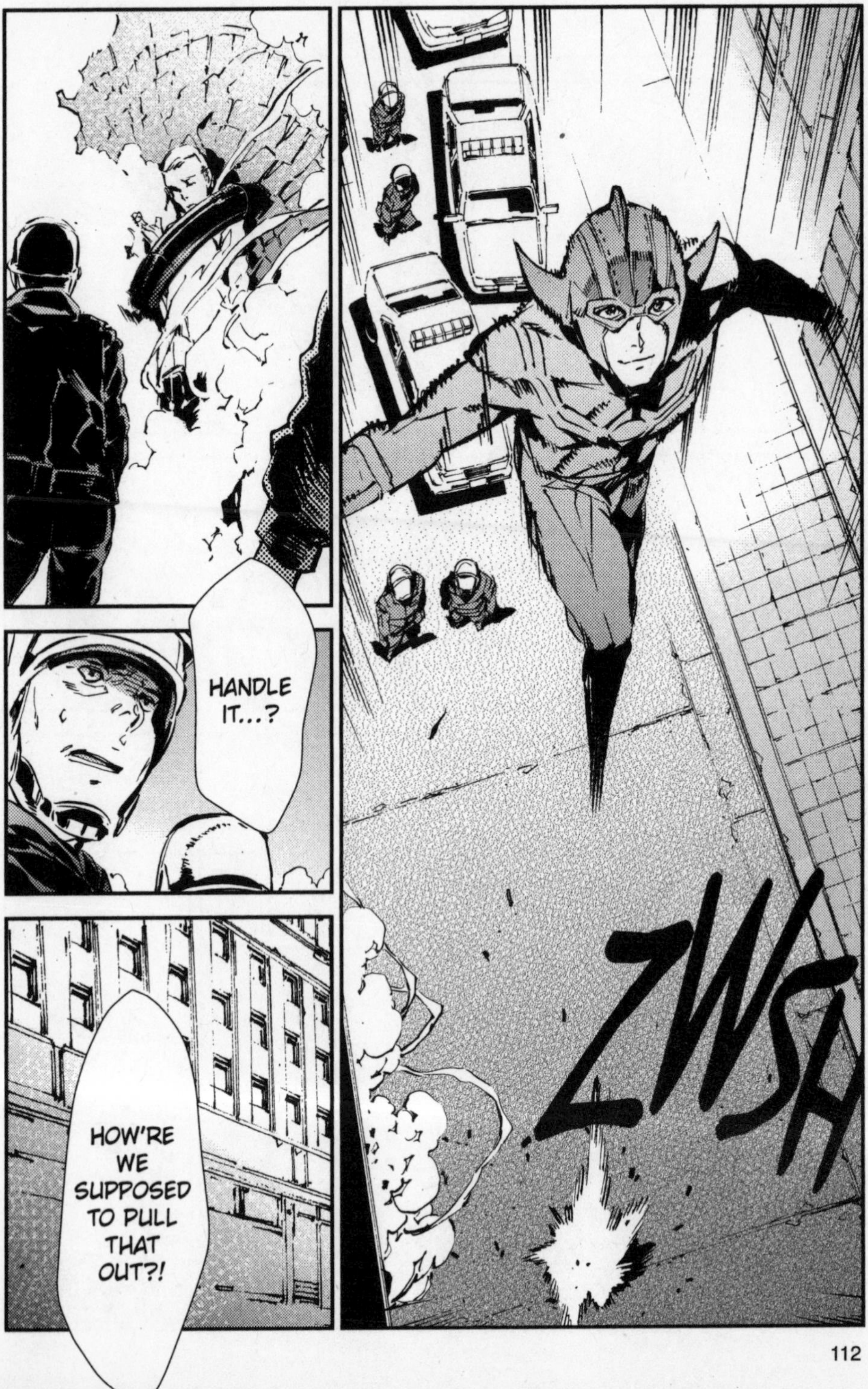
ZWSH
HANDLE IT...?
HOW'RE WE SUPPOSED TO PULL THAT OUT?!

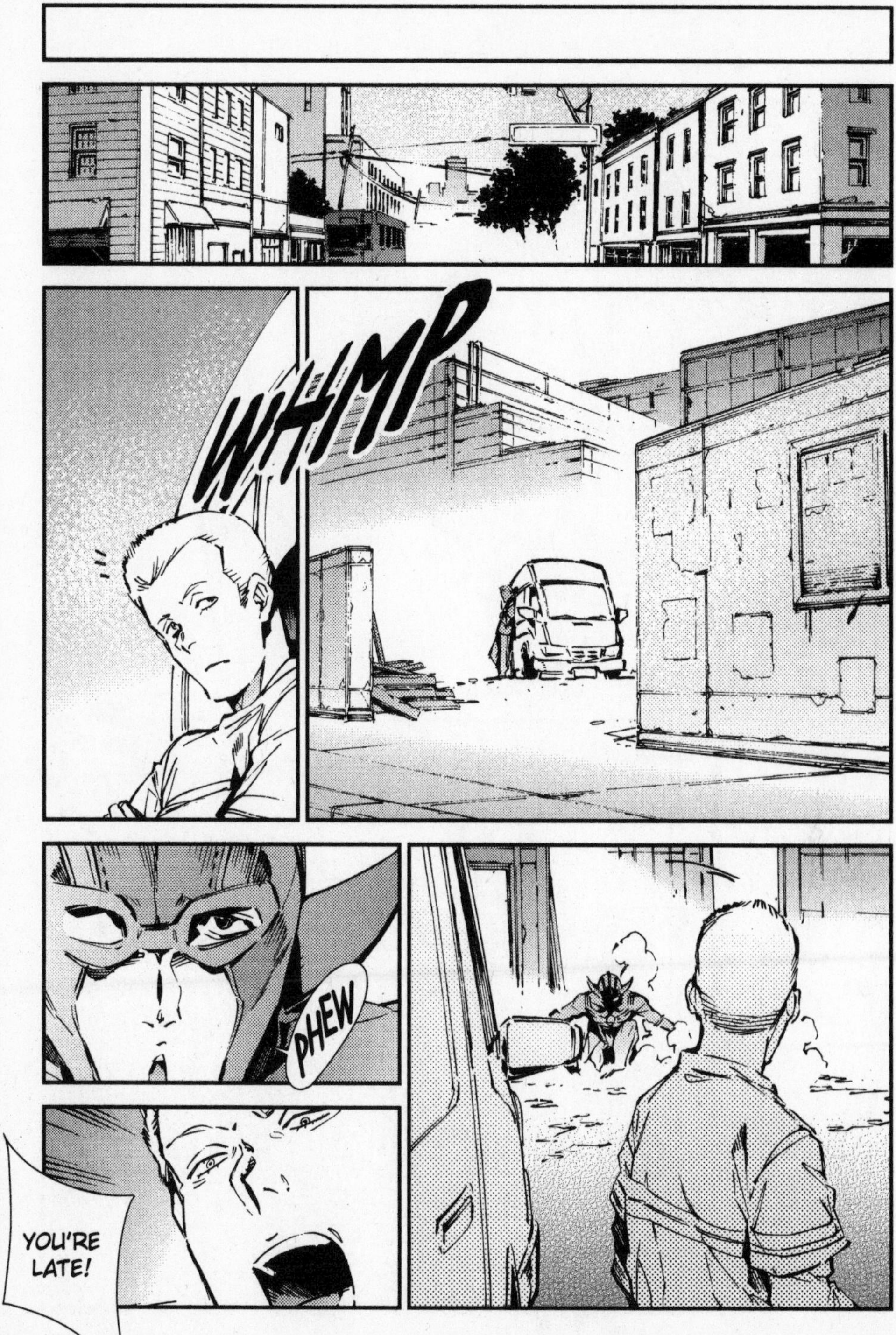
WHMP
PHEW
YOU'RE LATE!

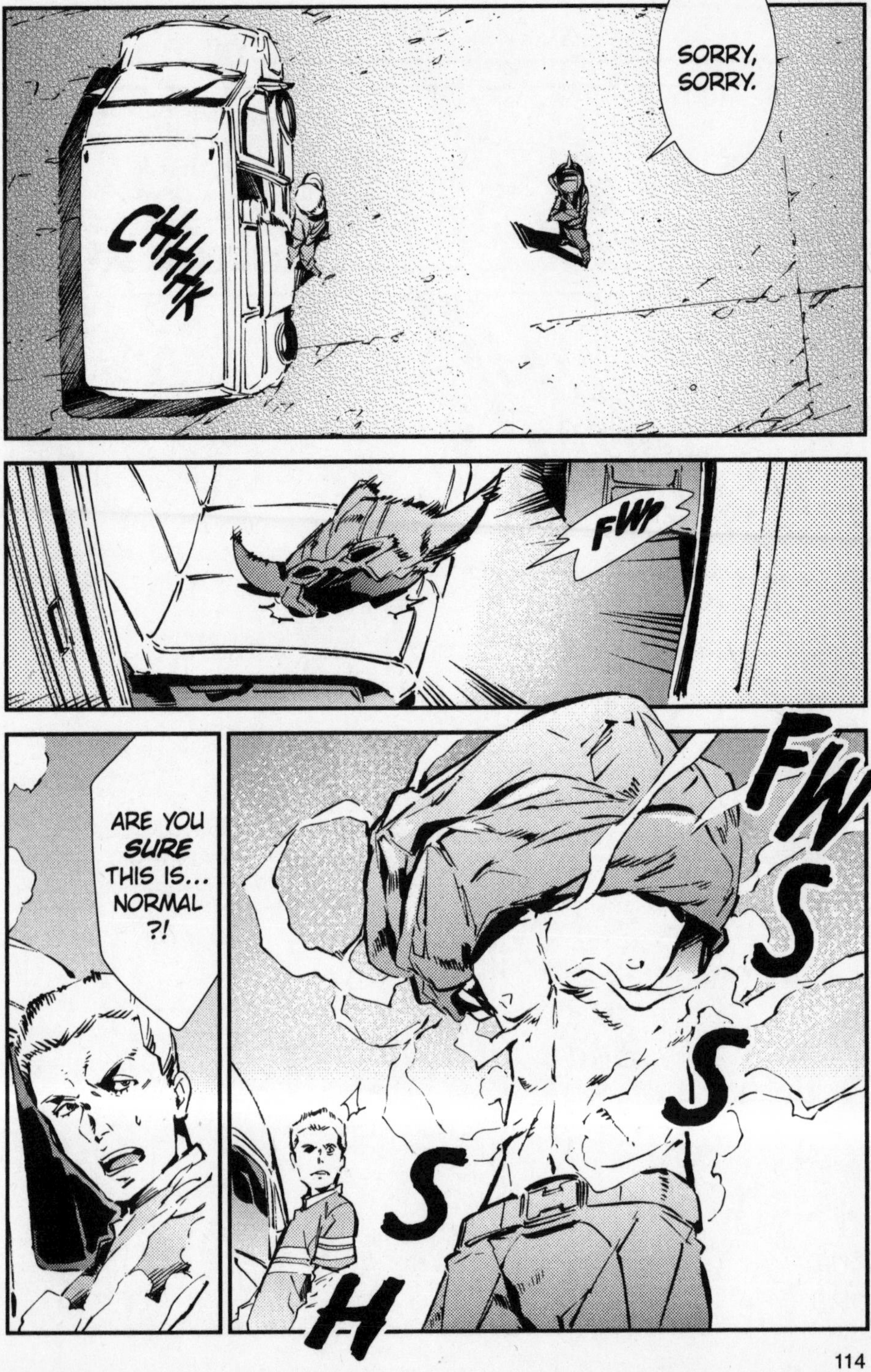
SORRY, SORRY.
CHHKK
FWI
FWSSSSH
ARE YOU SURE THIS IS... NORMAL?!

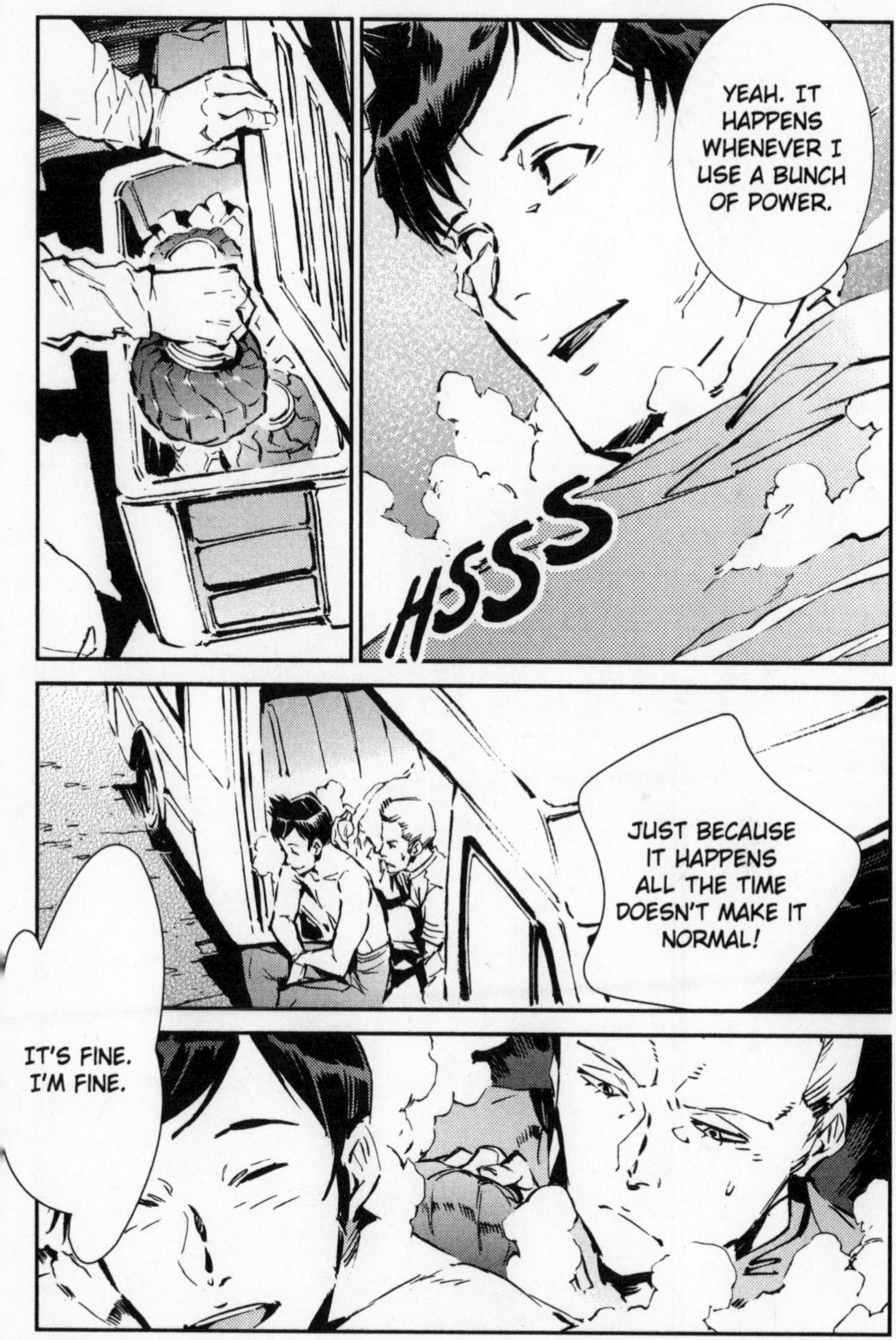
YEAH. IT HAPPENS WHENEVER I USE A BUNCH OF POWER.
HSSSS
JUST BECAUSE IT HAPPENS ALL THE TIME DOESN'T MAKE IT NORMAL!
IT'S FINE. I'M FINE.

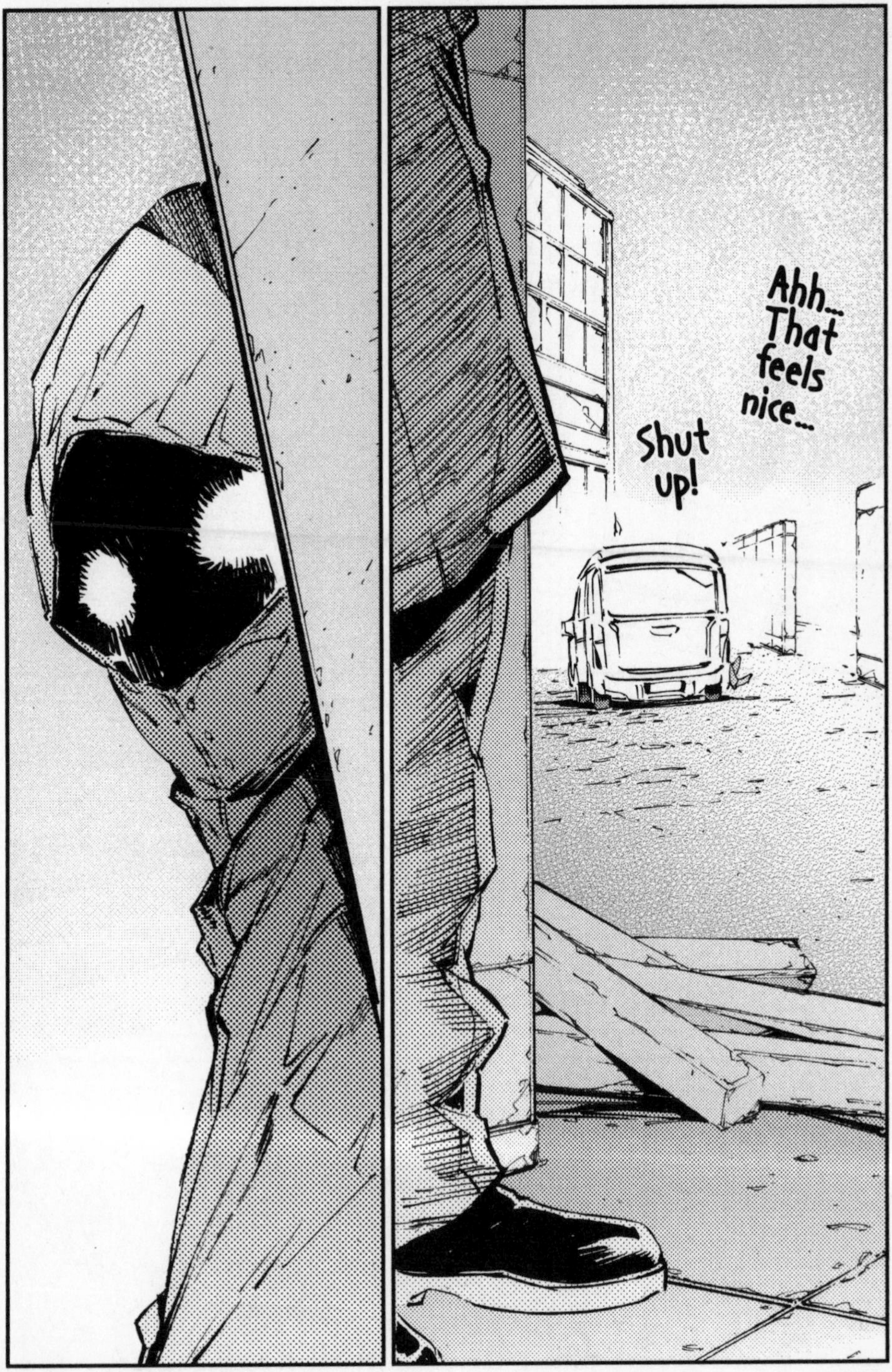
Ahh... That feels nice...
Shut up!

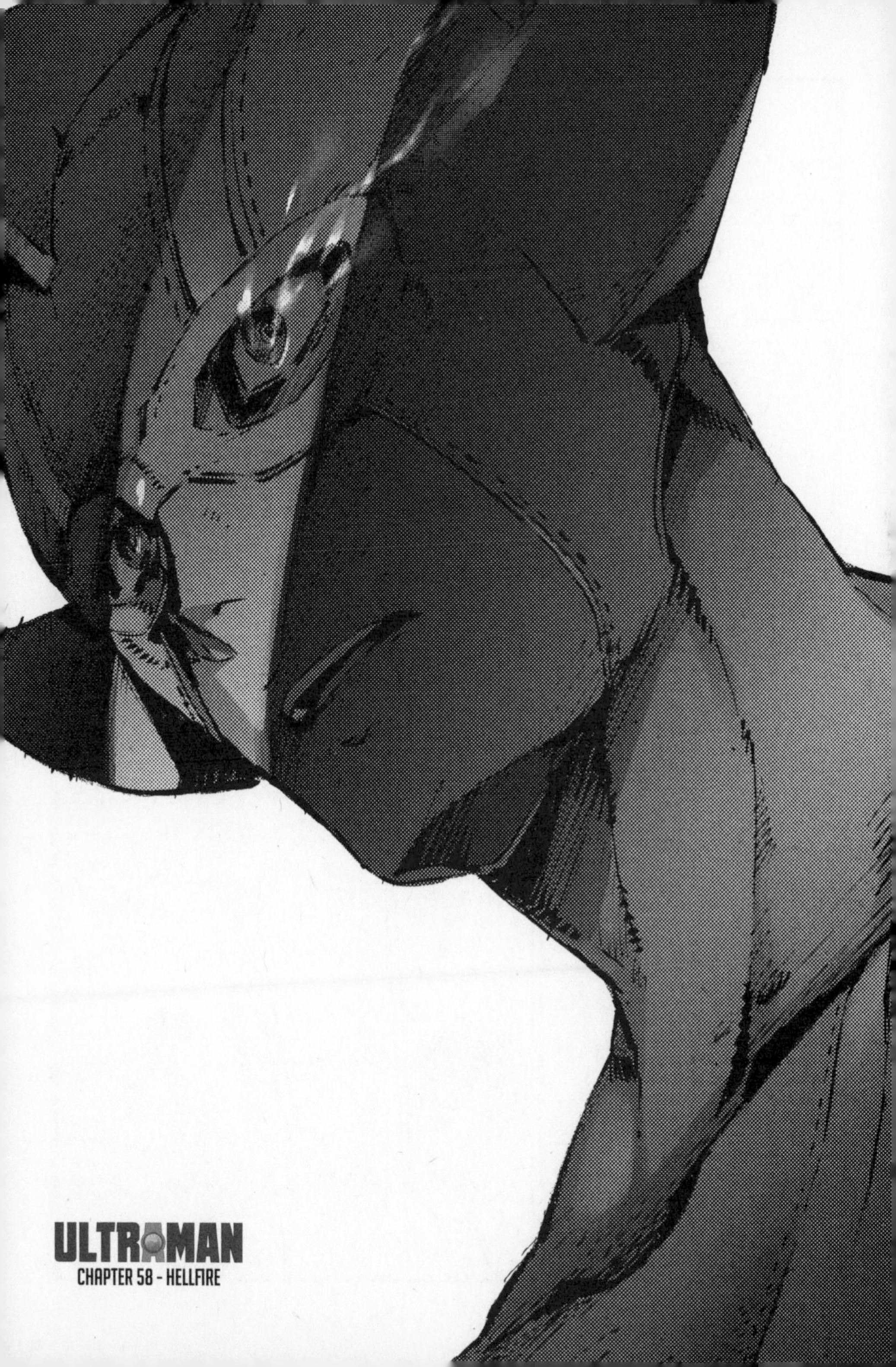

ULTRAMAN

CHAPTER 58 - HELLFIRE

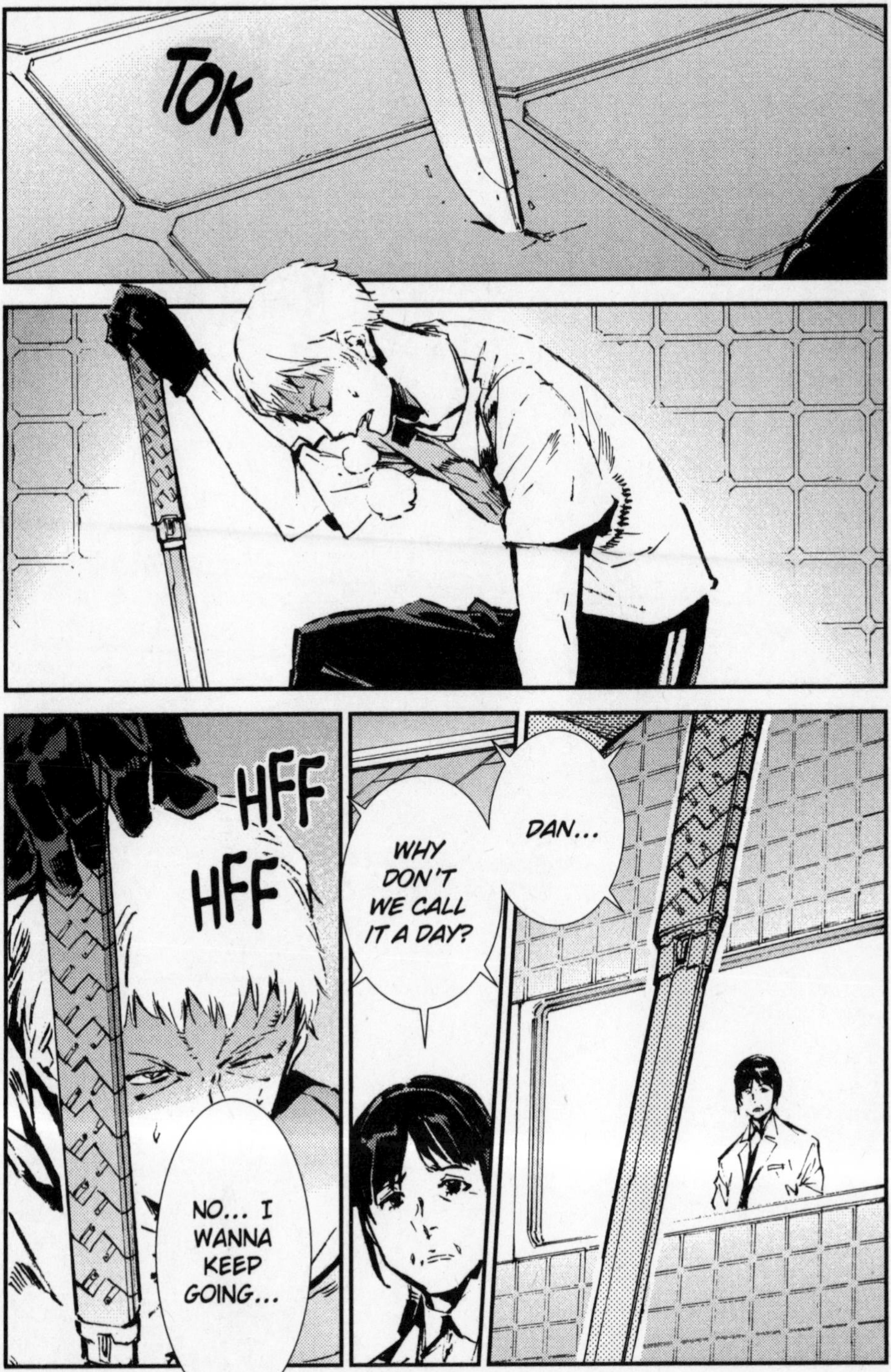
TOK
DAN...
WHY DON'T WE CALL IT A DAY?
HFF HFF
NO... I WANNA KEEP GOING...

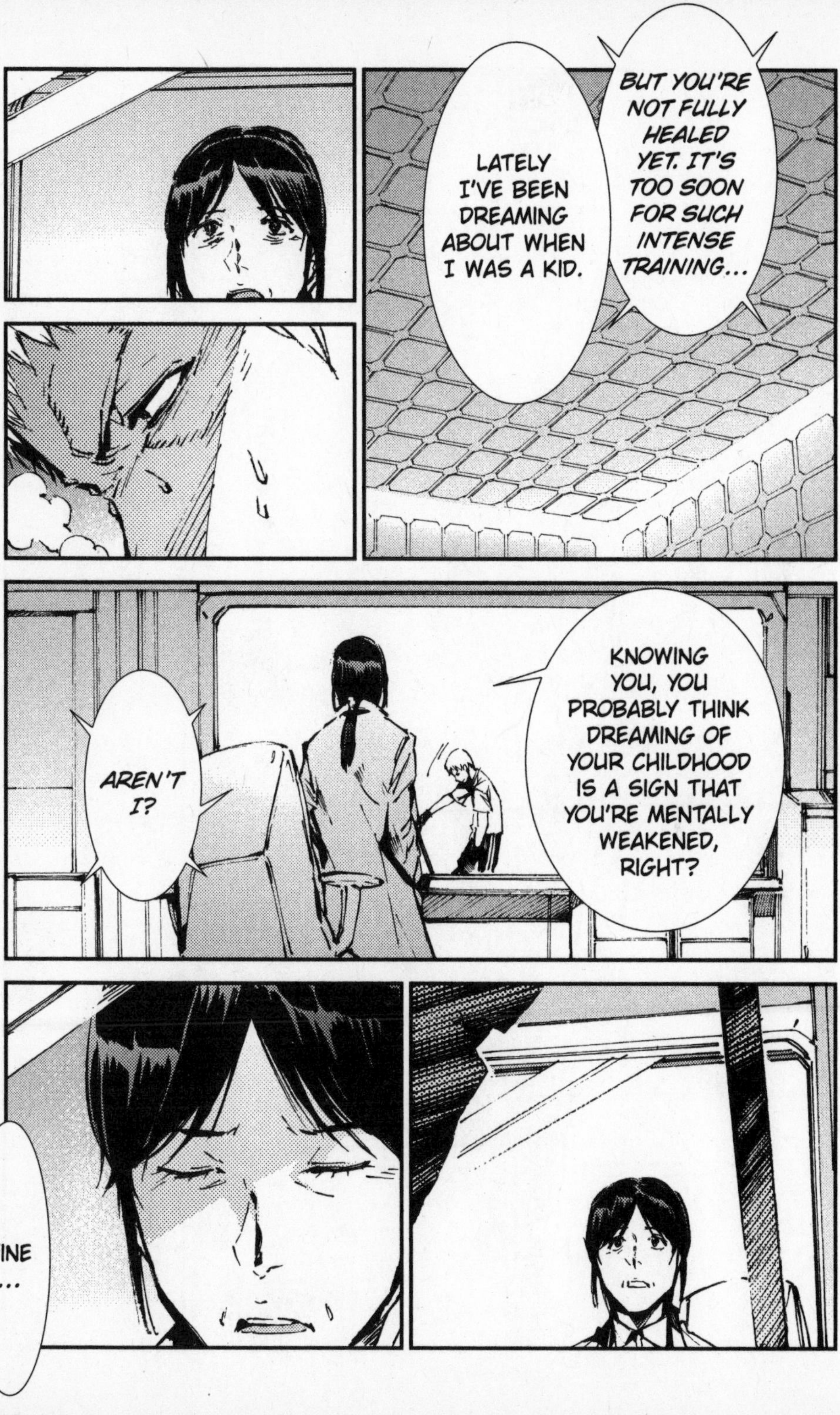
BUT YOU'RE NOT FULLY HEALED YET. IT'S TOO SOON FOR SUCH INTENSE TRAINING...
LATELY I'VE BEEN DREAMING ABOUT WHEN I WAS A KID.
KNOWING YOU, YOU PROBABLY THINK DREAMING OF YOUR CHILDHOOD IS A SIGN THAT YOU'RE MENTALLY WEAKENED, RIGHT?
AREN'T I?
FINE ...

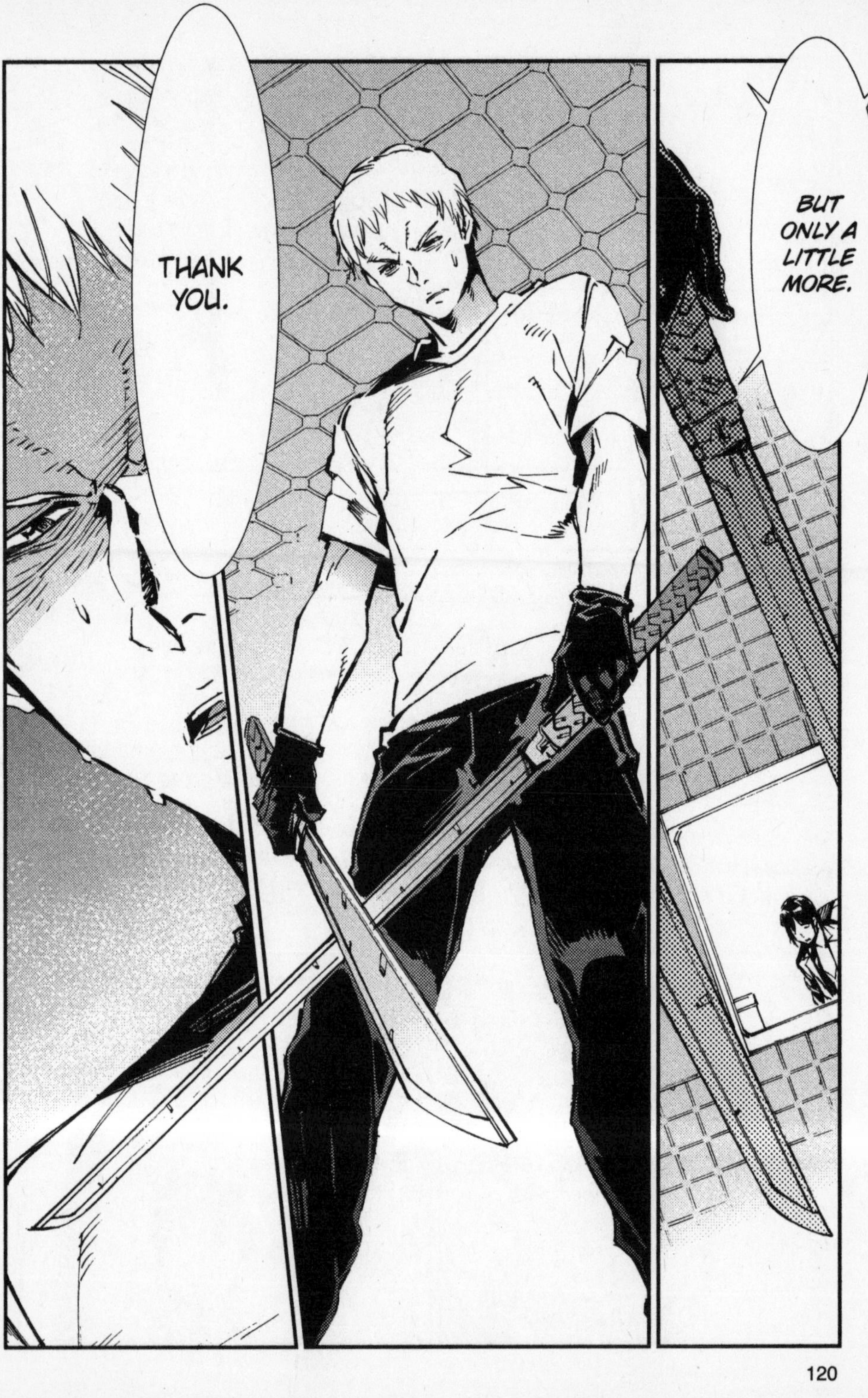
BUT ONLY A LITTLE MORE.
THANK YOU.

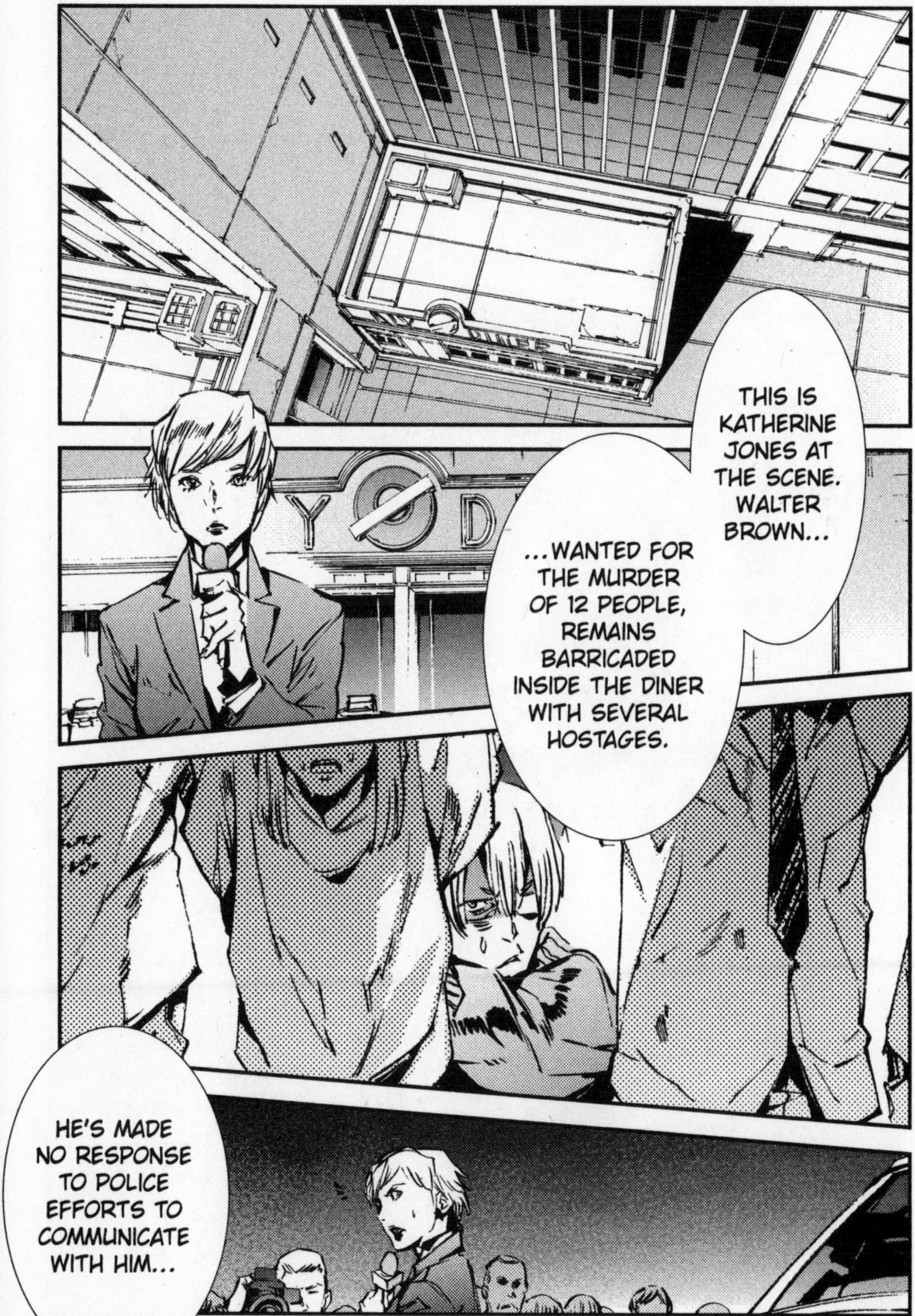
THIS IS KATHERINE JONES AT THE SCENE. WALTER BROWN...
...WANTED FOR THE MURDER OF 12 PEOPLE, REMAINS BARRICADED INSIDE THE DINER WITH SEVERAL HOSTAGES.
HE'S MADE NO RESPONSE TO POLICE EFFORTS TO COMMUNICATE WITH HIM...

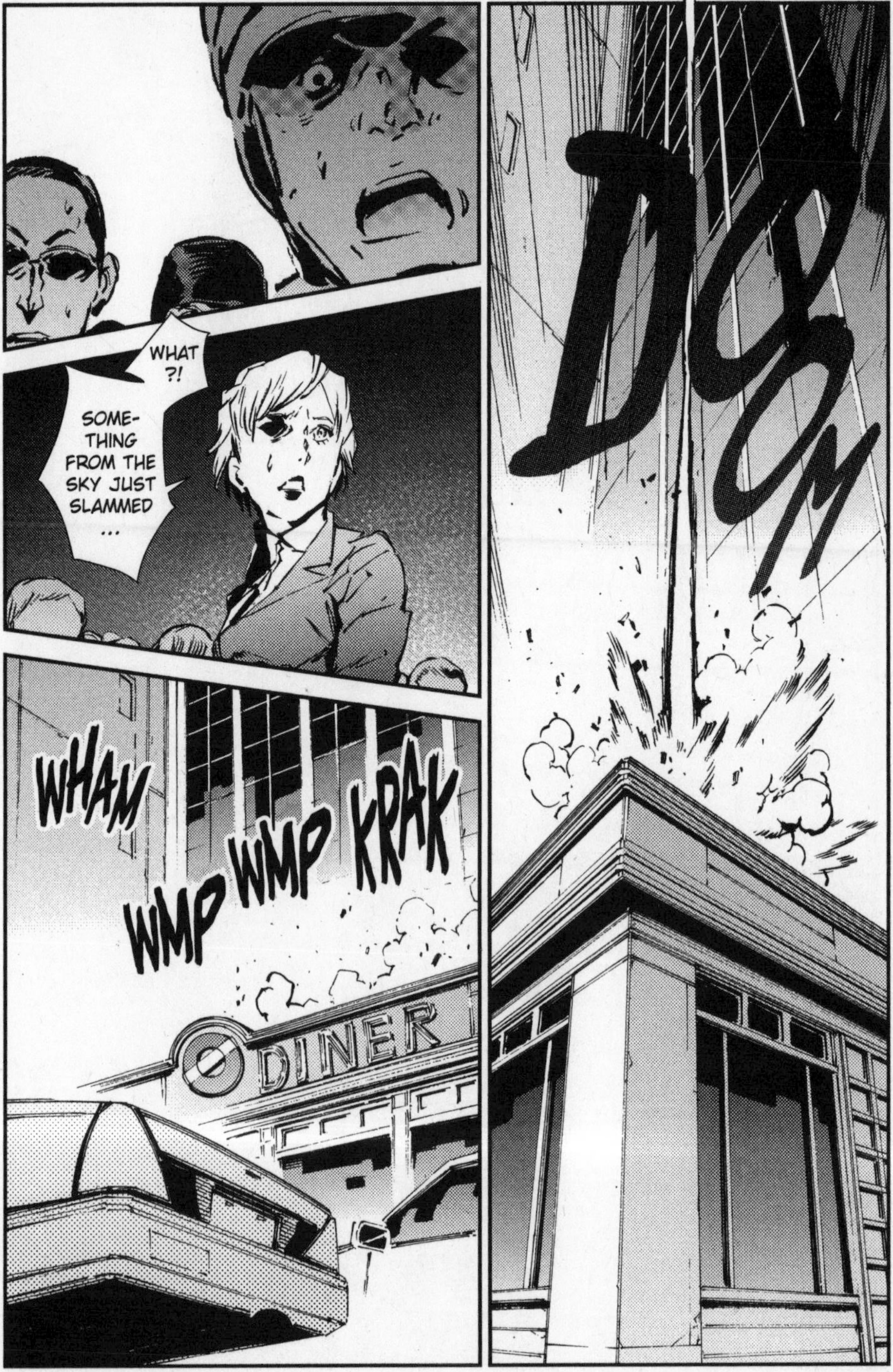
DOOM
WHAT ?!
SOME-THING FROM THE SKY JUST SLAMMED ...
WHAM
WMP WMP KRAK
DINER

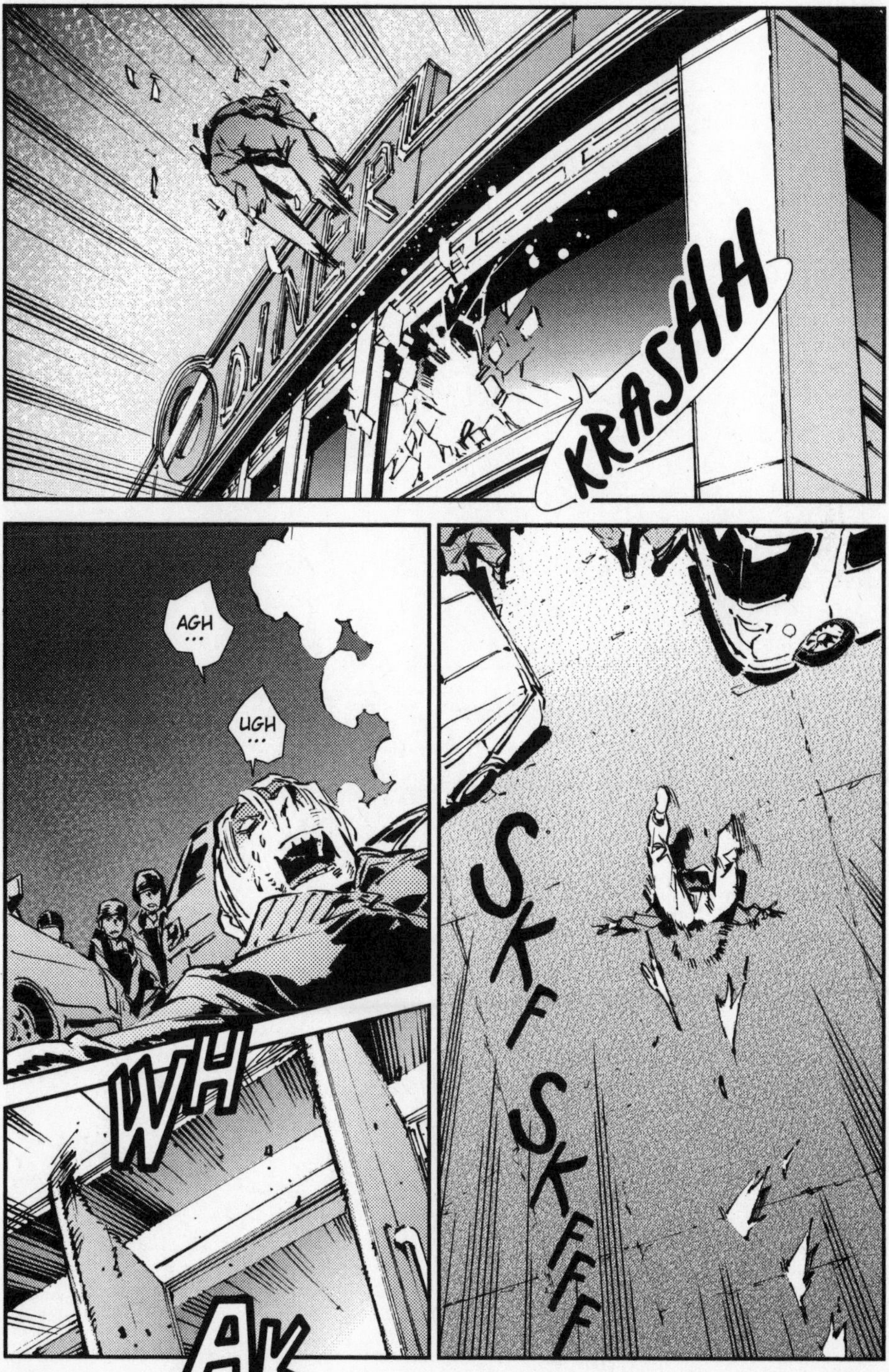
DINER
KRASHH
SKF SKFFF
AGH...
UGH...
WHAK

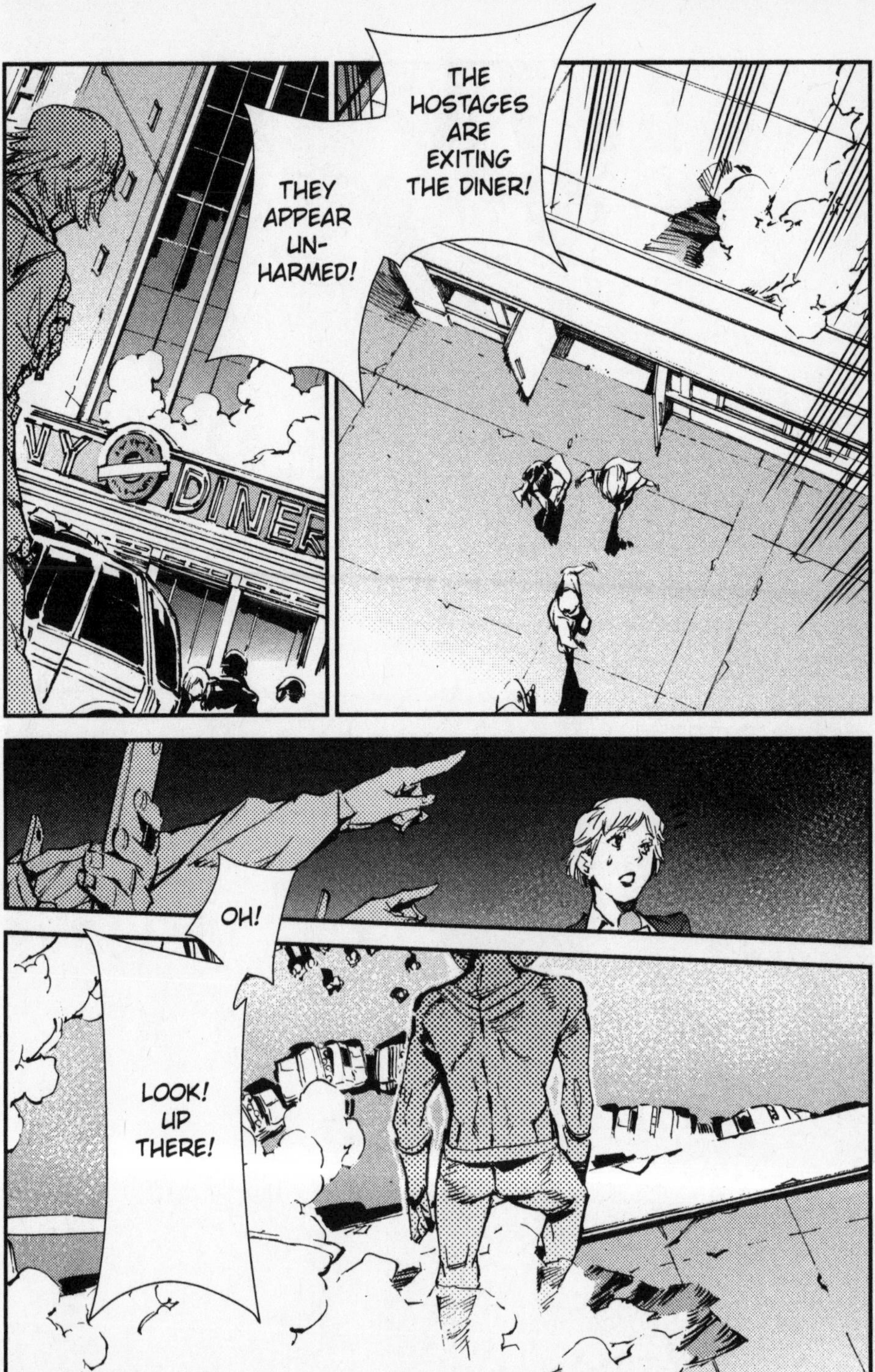
THE HOSTAGES ARE EXITING THE DINER!
THEY APPEAR UN-HARMED!
OH!
LOOK! UP THERE!

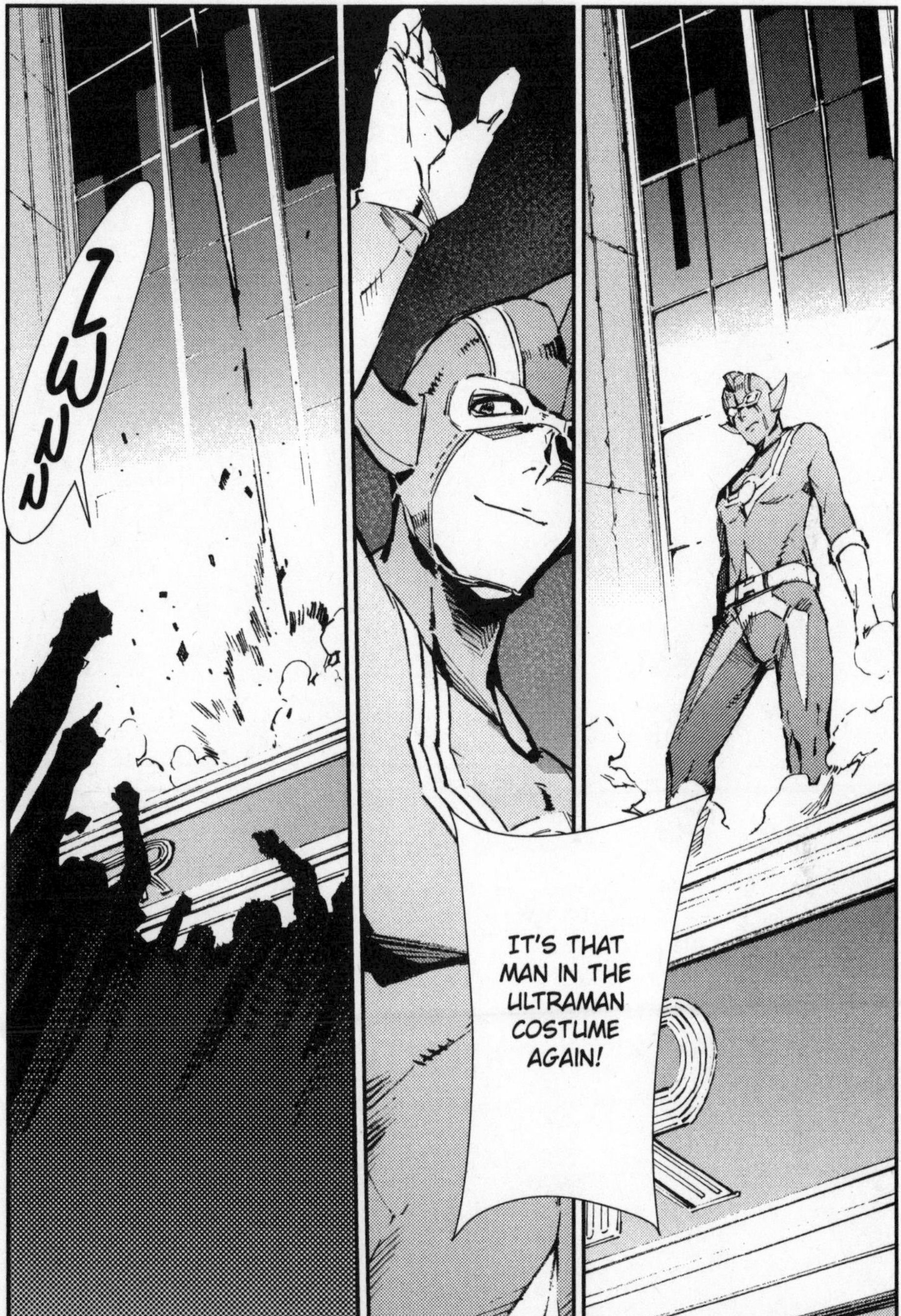

WOOO
IT'S THAT MAN IN THE ULTRAMAN COSTUME AGAIN!

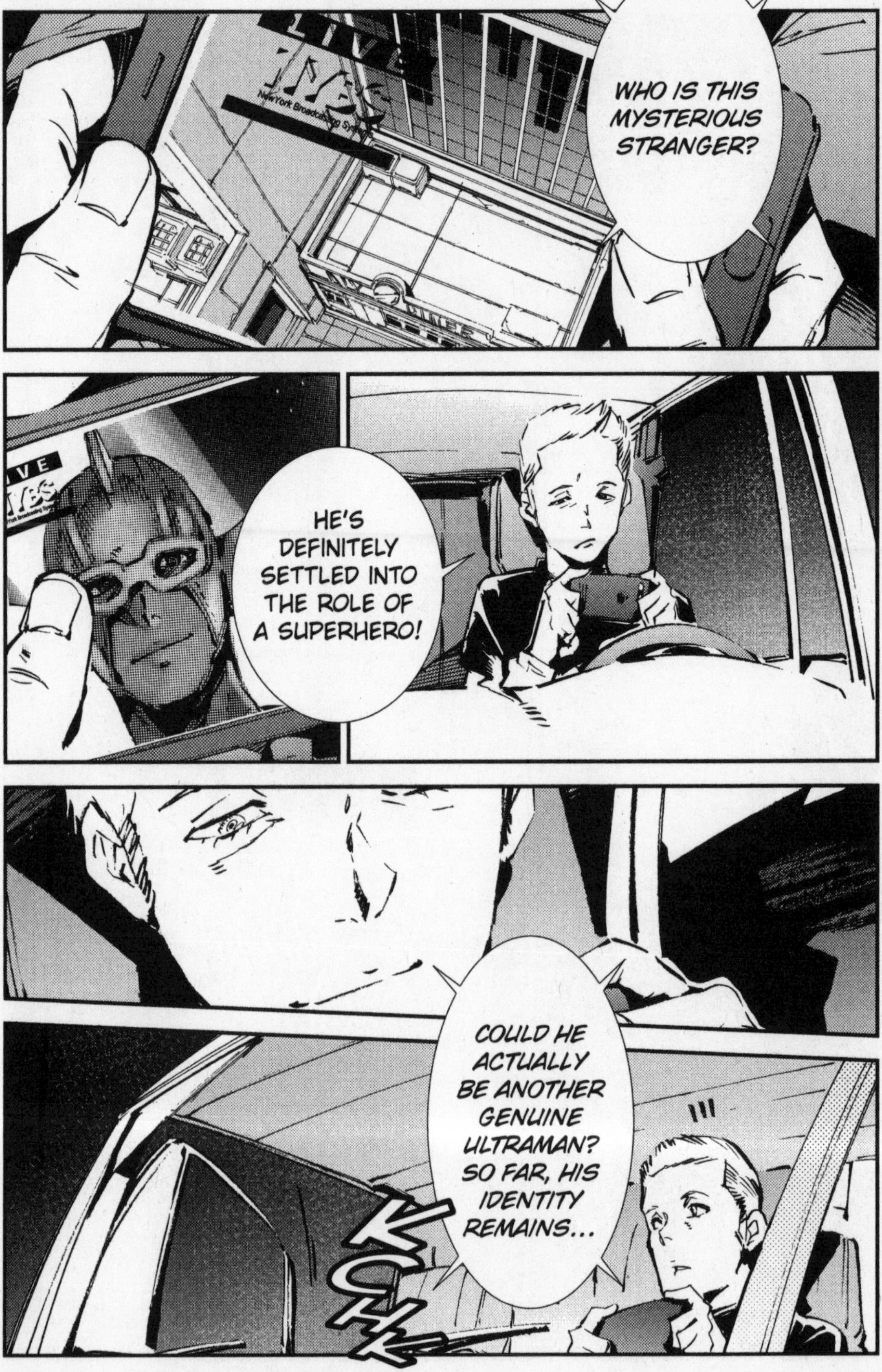
WHO IS THIS MYSTERIOUS STRANGER?
LIVE
HE'S DEFINITELY SETTLED INTO THE ROLE OF A SUPERHERO!
COULD HE ACTUALLY BE ANOTHER GENUINE ULTRAMAN? SO FAR, HIS IDENTITY REMAINS...
KCHK

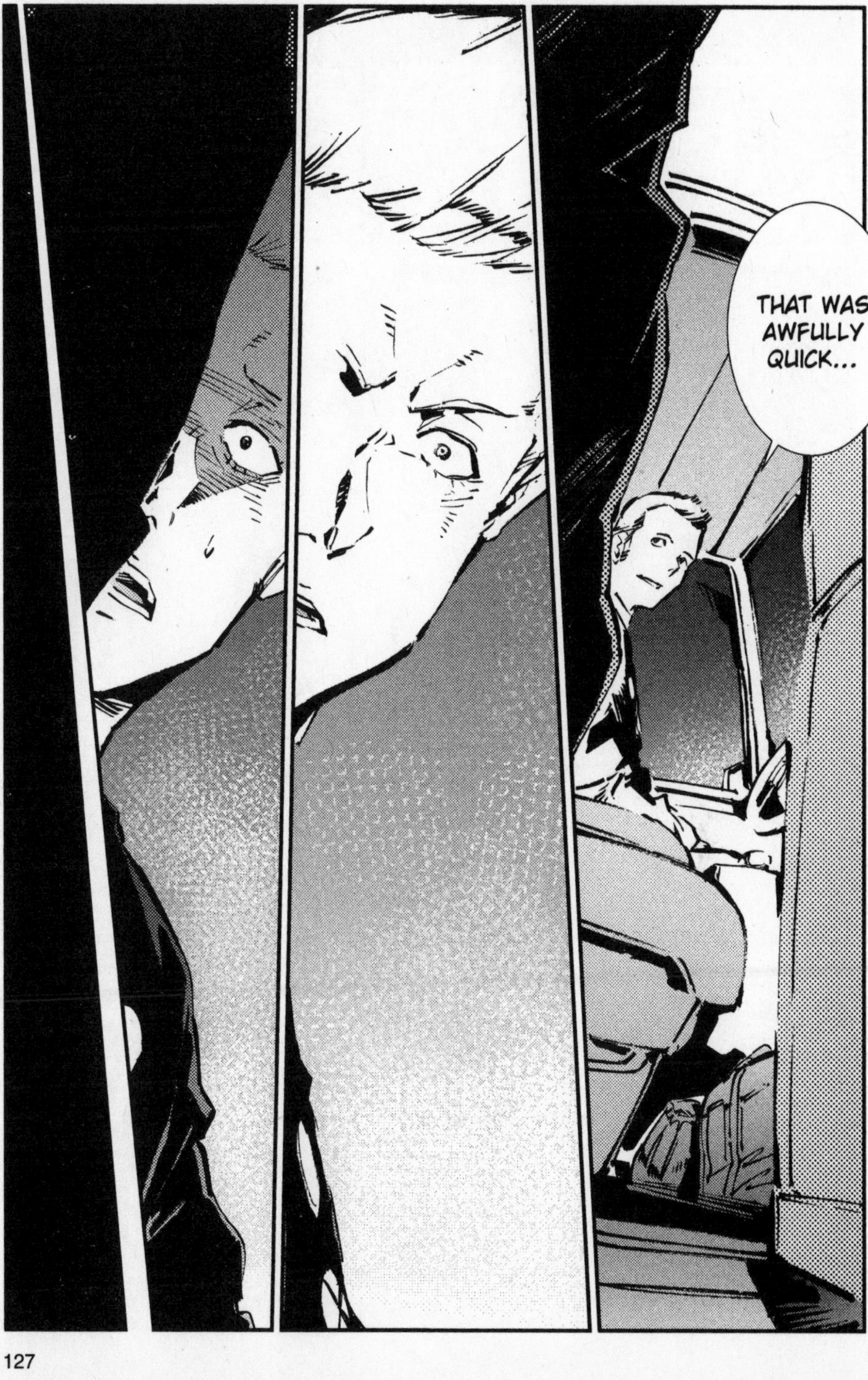
THAT WAS AWFULLY QUICK...

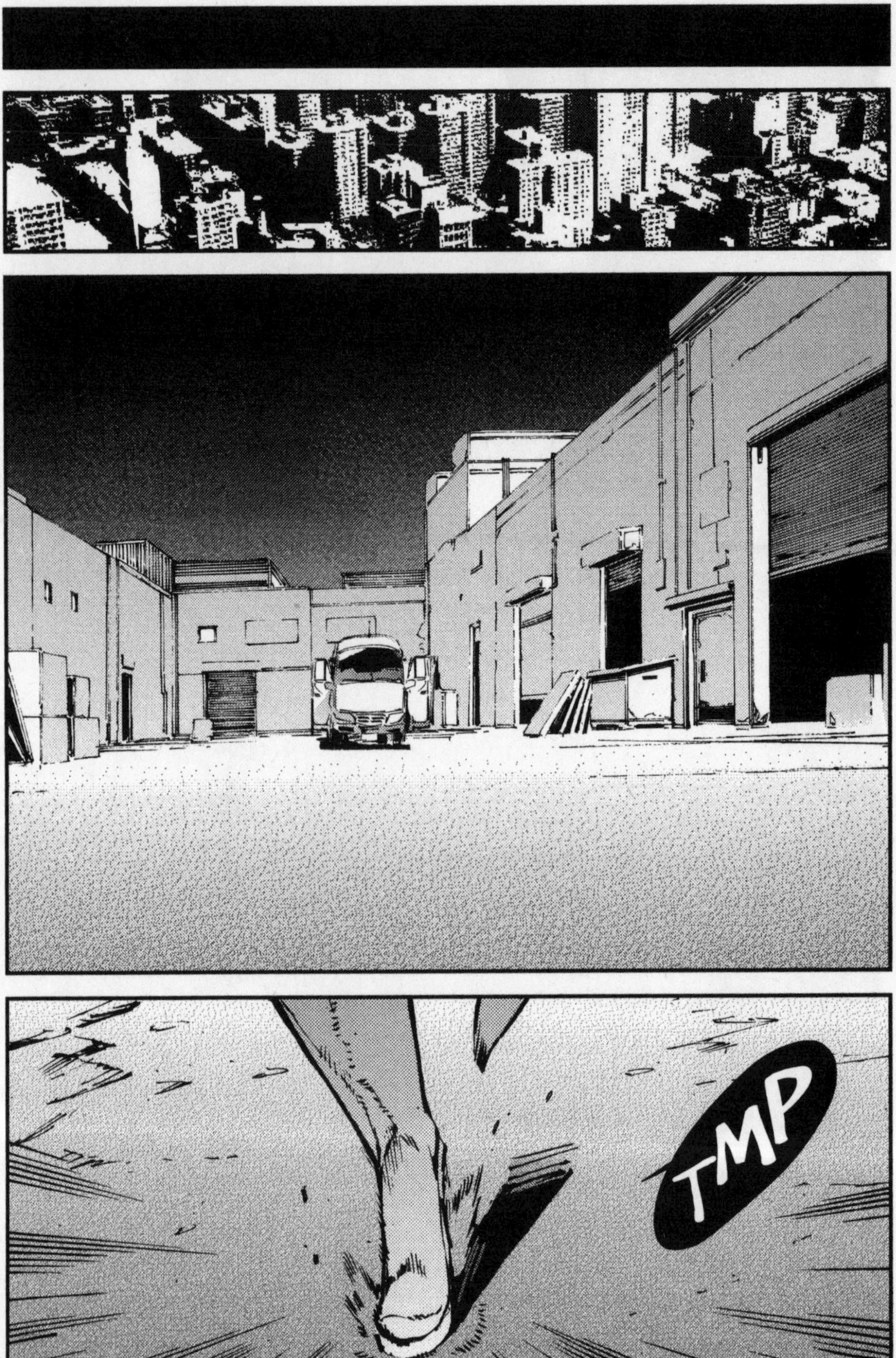
TMP

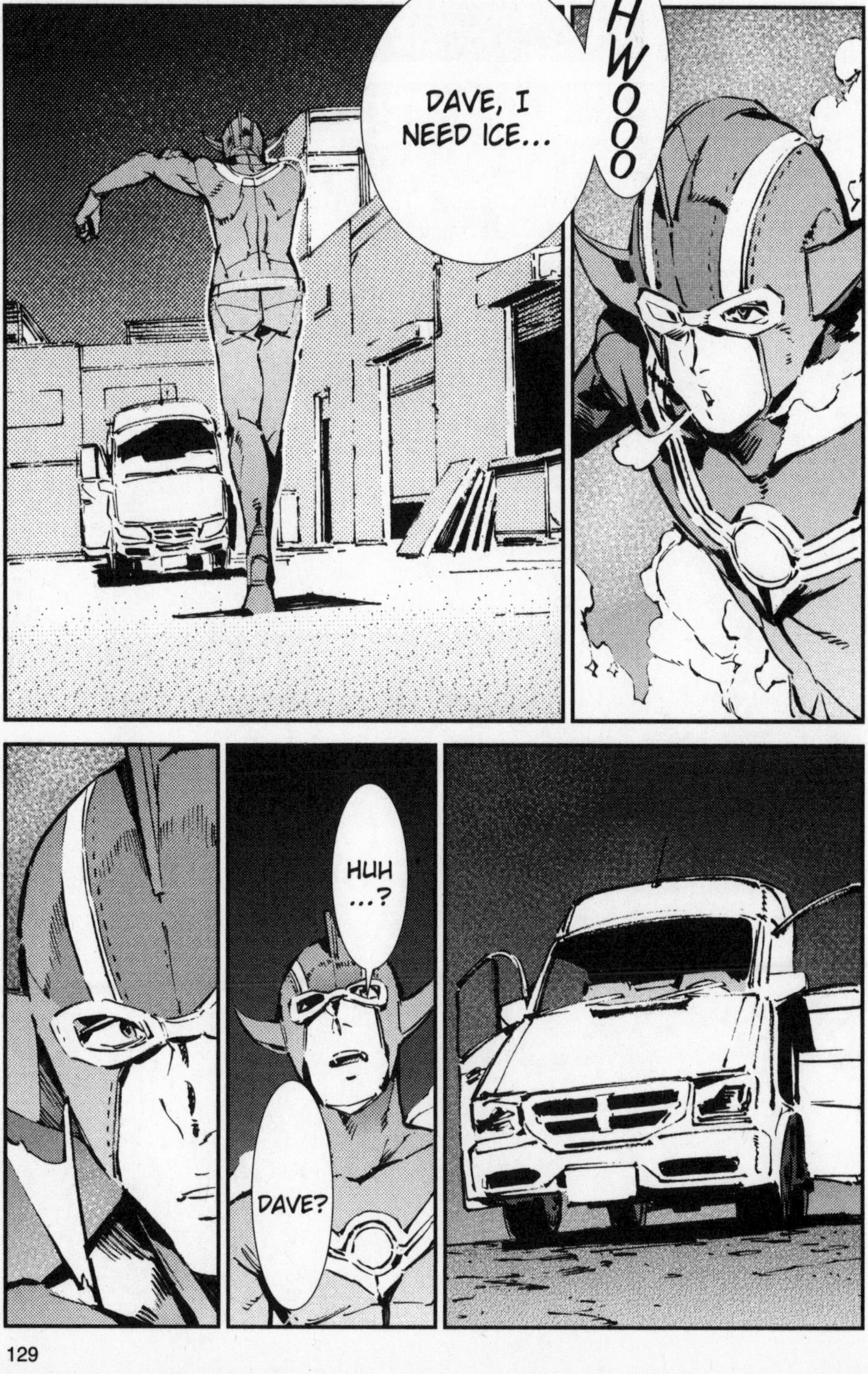
HWOOO
DAVE, I NEED ICE...
HUH ...?
DAVE?

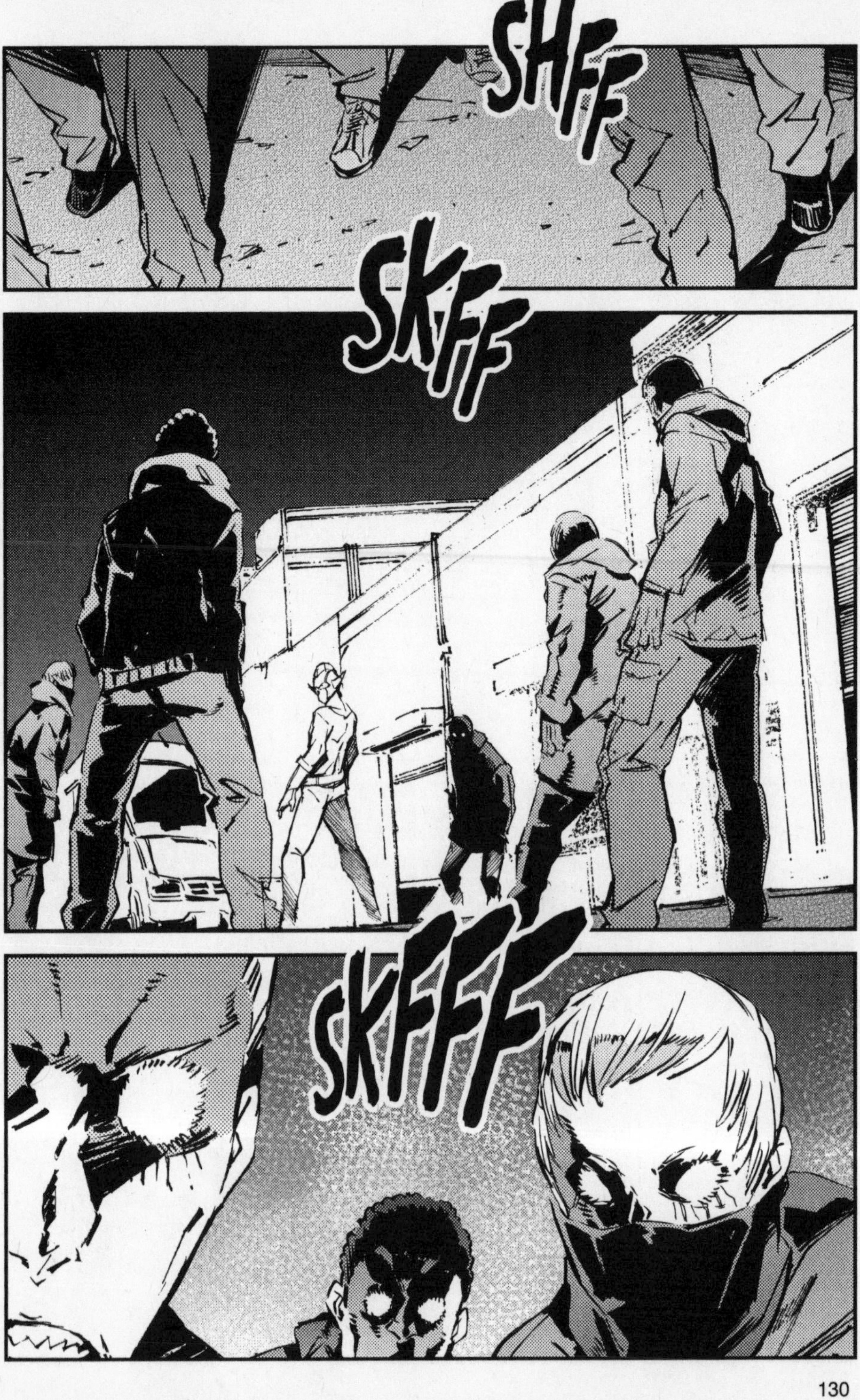
SHFF
SKFF
SKFFF

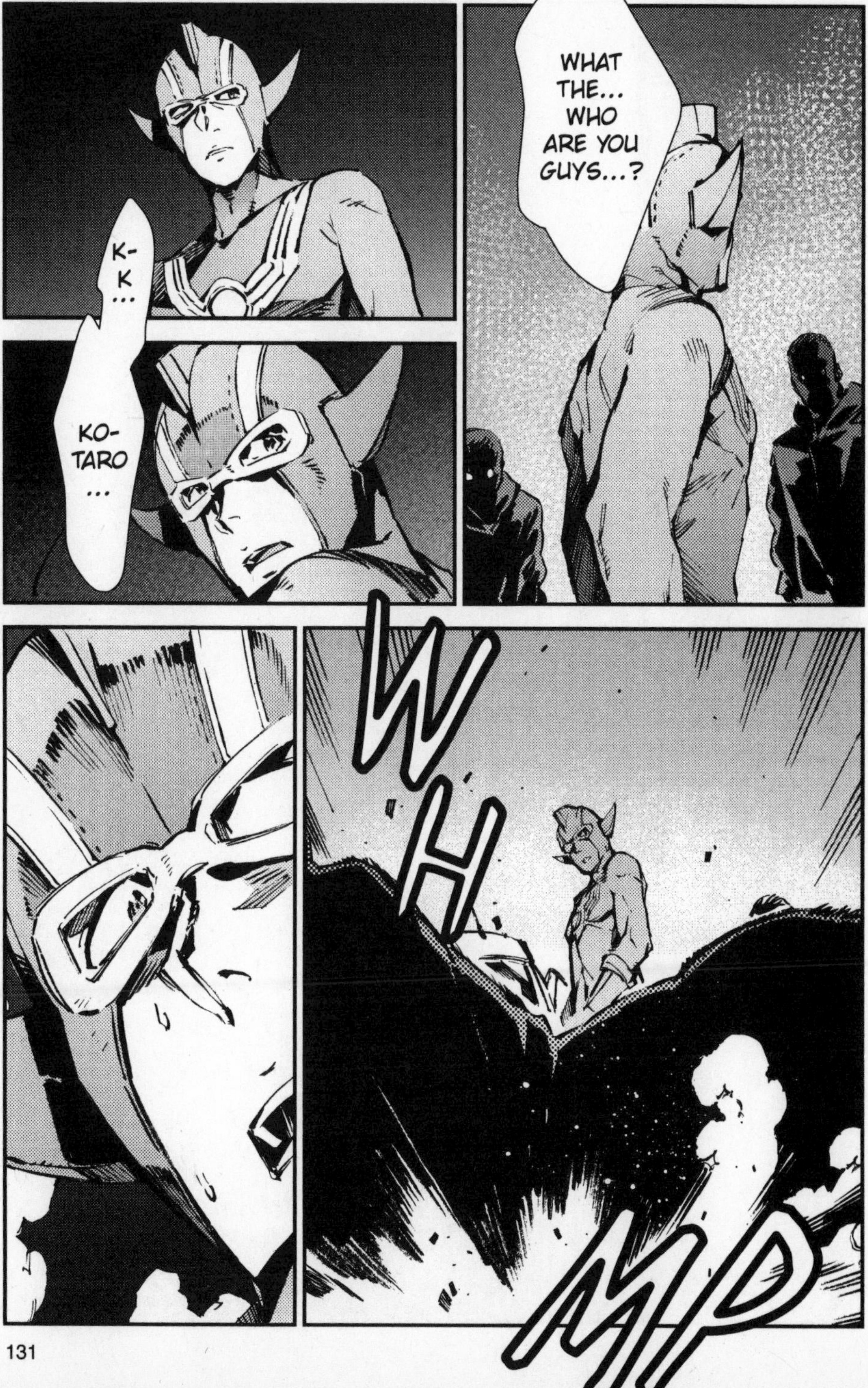
WHAT THE... WHO ARE YOU GUYS...?
K-K...
KO-TARO...
WHMP

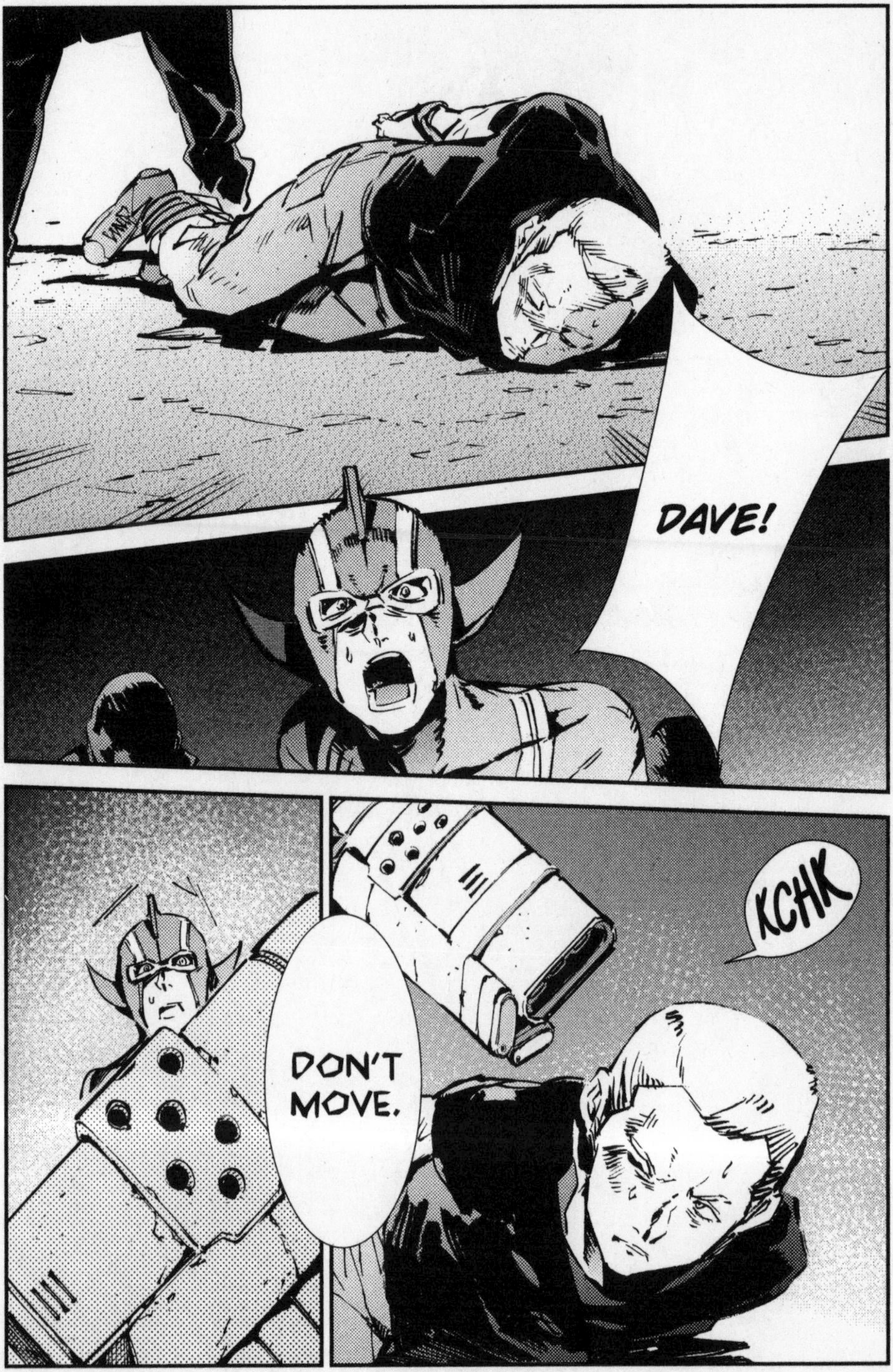
DAVE!
KCHK
DON'T MOVE.

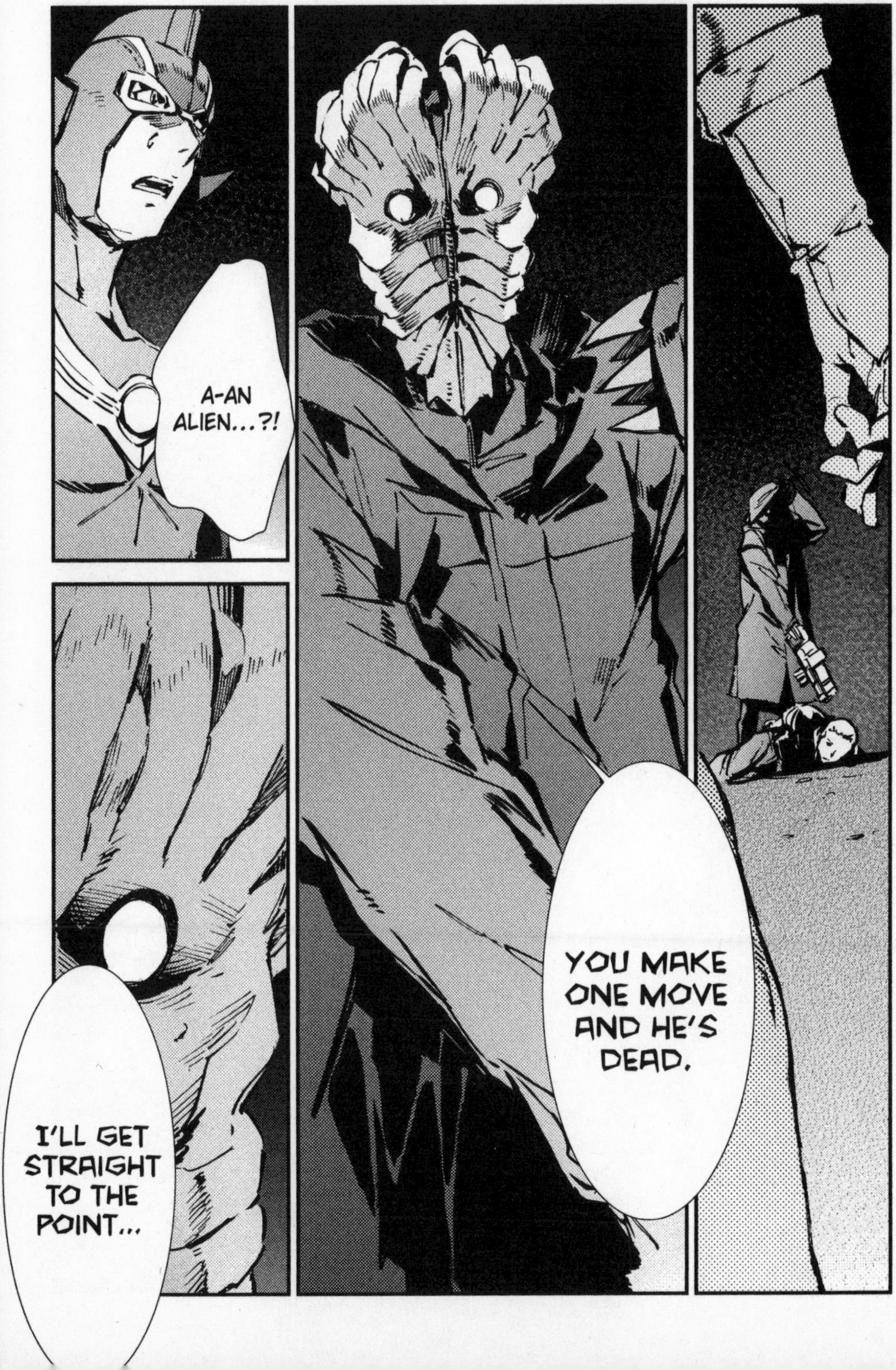
YOU MAKE ONE MOVE AND HE'S DEAD.
A-AN ALIEN...?!
I'LL GET STRAIGHT TO THE POINT...

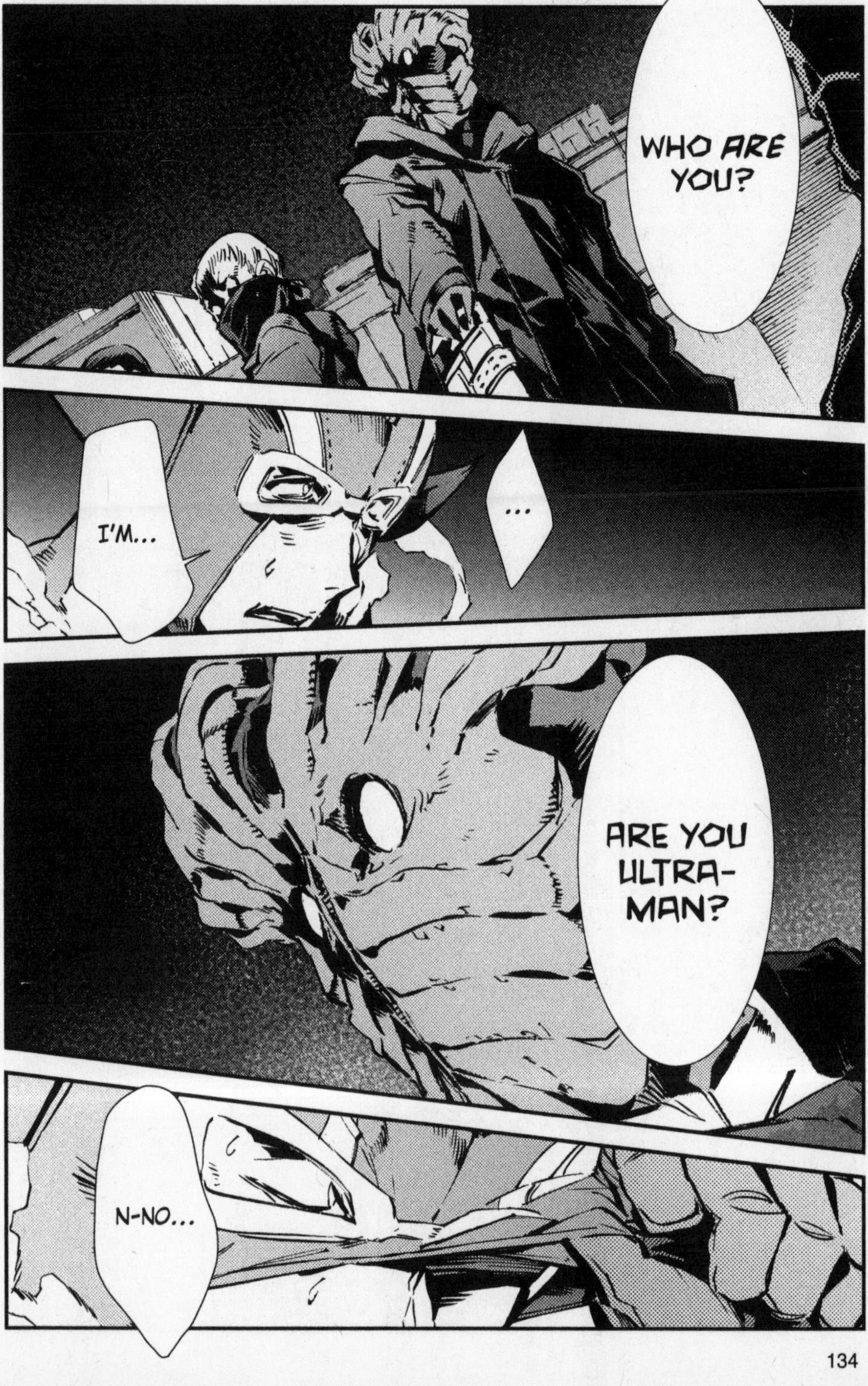
WHO ARE YOU?
...
I'M...
ARE YOU ULTRA-MAN?
N-NO...

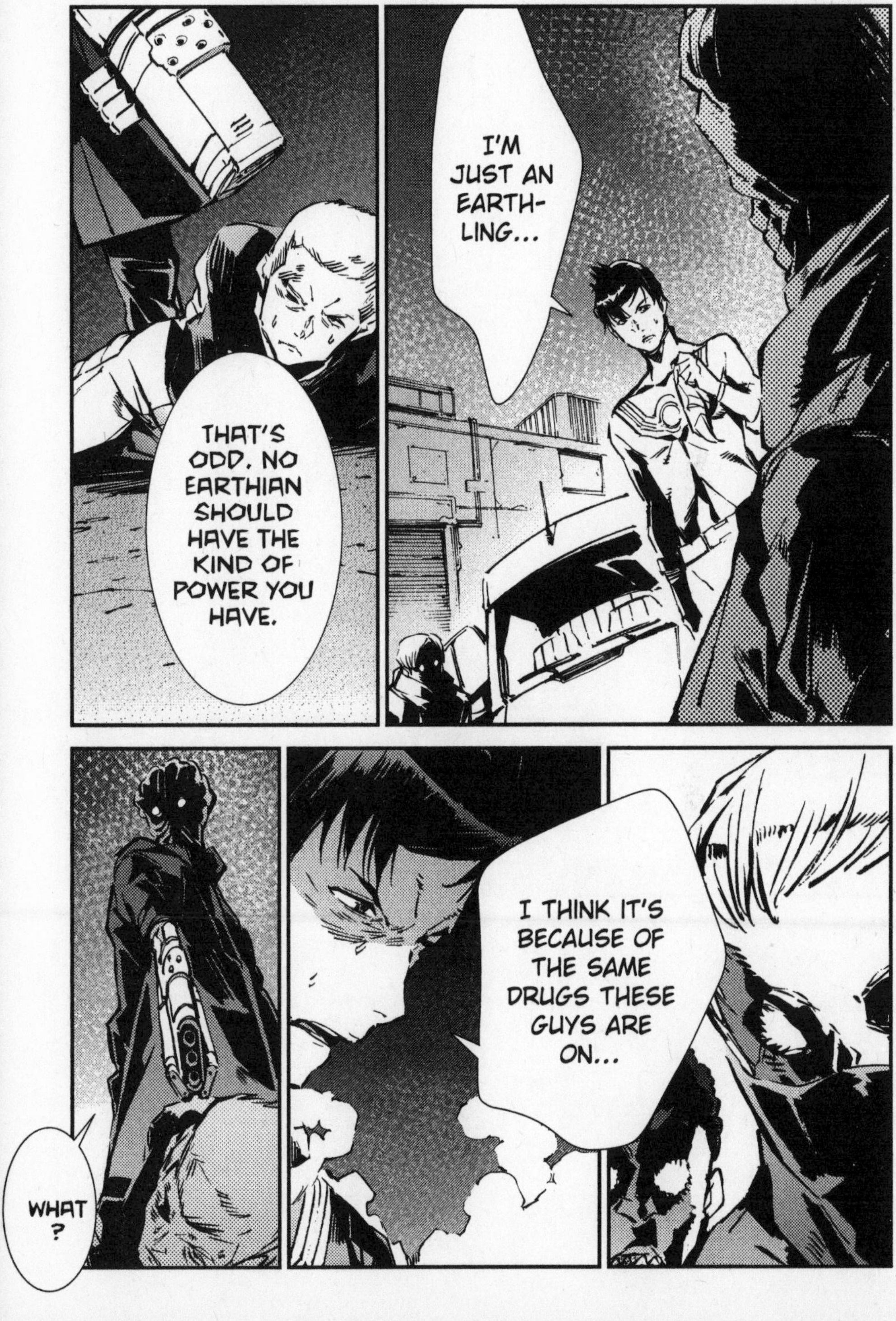
I'M JUST AN EARTH-LING...
THAT'S ODD. NO EARTHIAN SHOULD HAVE THE KIND OF POWER YOU HAVE.
I THINK IT'S BECAUSE OF THE SAME DRUGS THESE GUYS ARE ON...
WHAT?

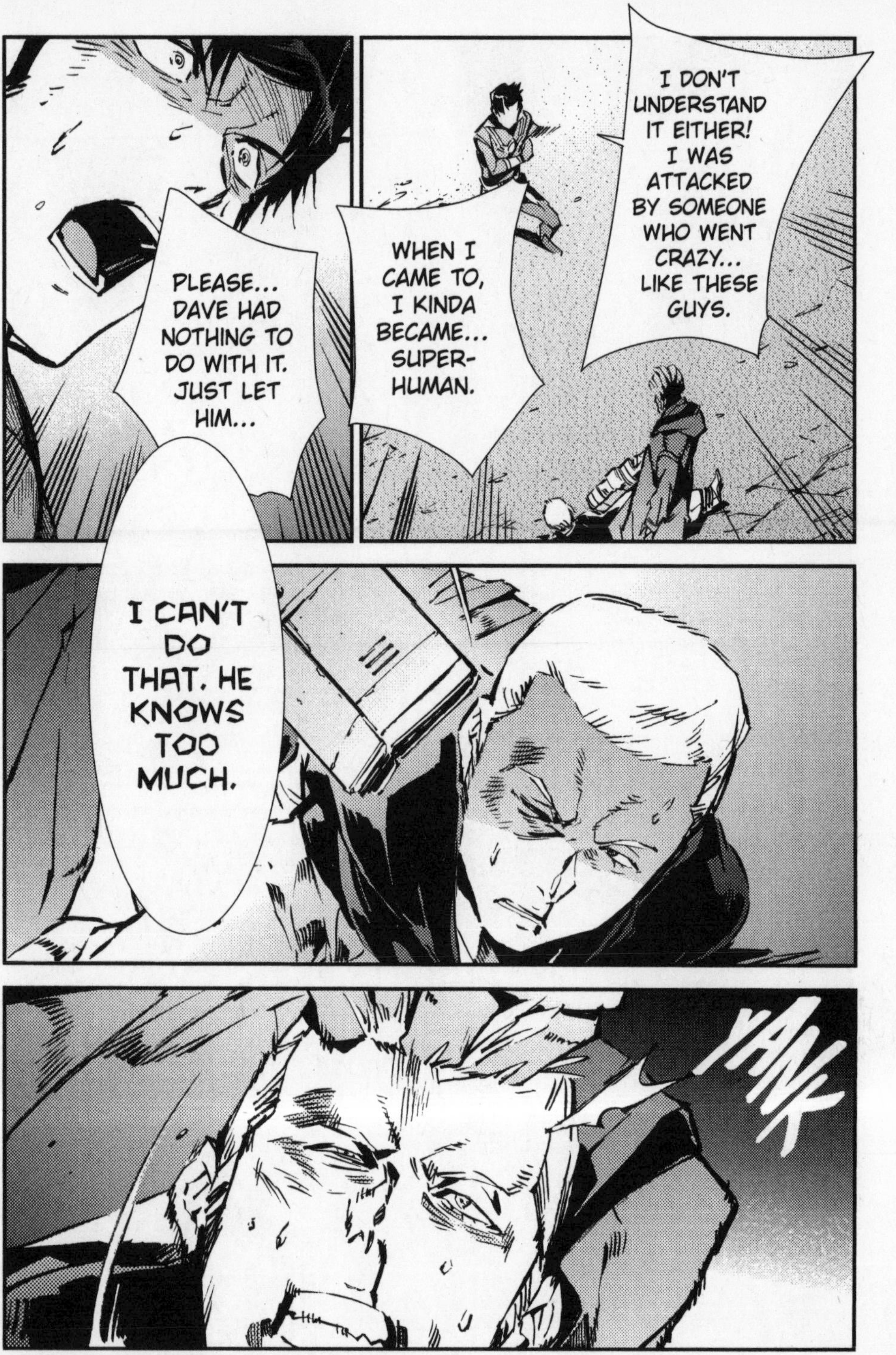
I DON'T UNDERSTAND IT EITHER! I WAS ATTACKED BY SOMEONE WHO WENT CRAZY... LIKE THESE GUYS.
WHEN I CAME TO, I KINDA BECAME... SUPER-HUMAN.
PLEASE... DAVE HAD NOTHING TO DO WITH IT. JUST LET HIM...
I CAN'T DO THAT. HE KNOWS TOO MUCH.
YANK

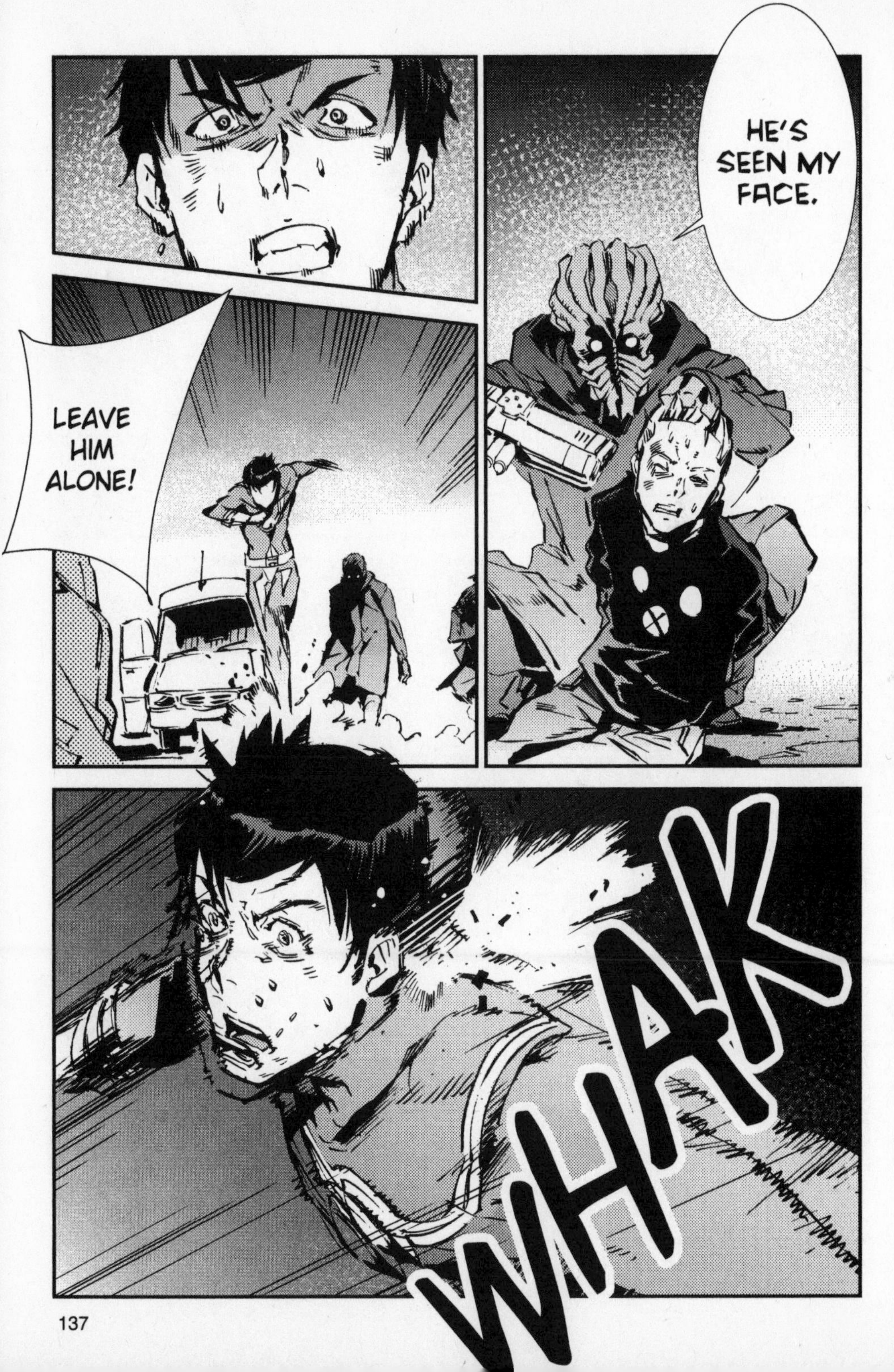
HE'S SEEN MY FACE.
LEAVE HIM ALONE!
WHAK

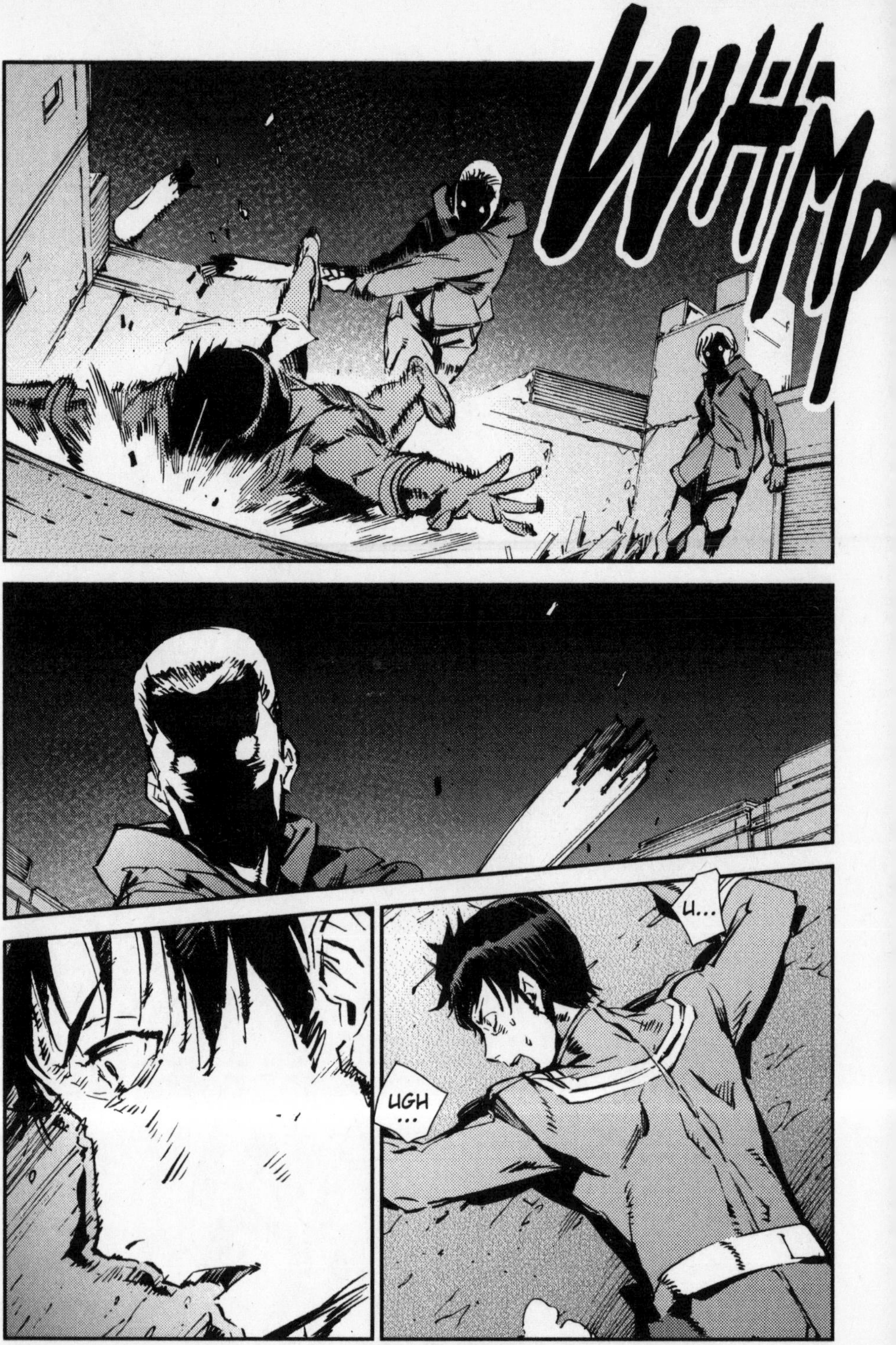
WHUMP
U...
UGH...

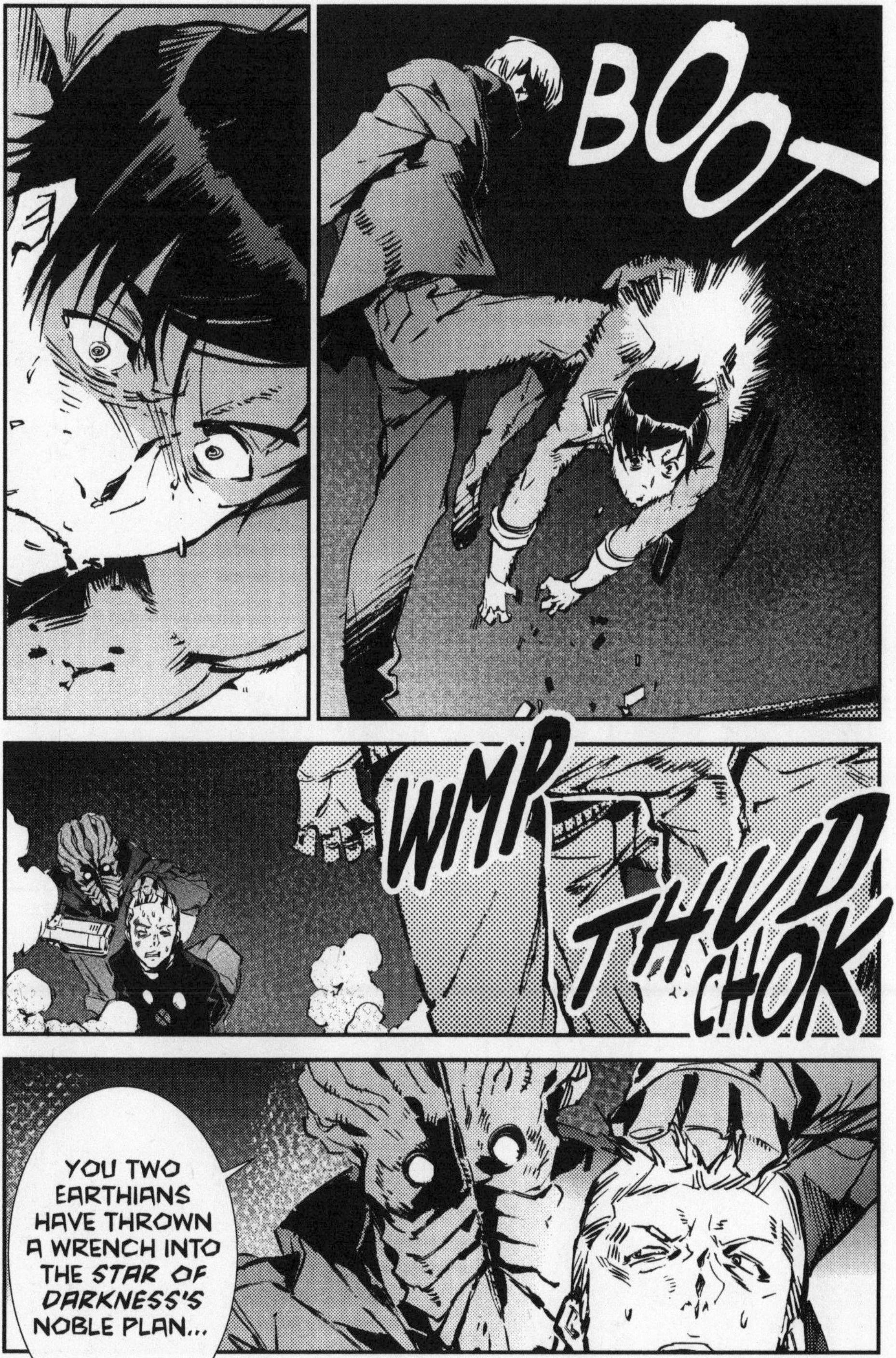
BOOT
WMP
THUD
CHOK
YOU TWO EARTHIANS HAVE THROWN A WRENCH INTO THE *STAR OF DARKNESS'S* NOBLE PLAN...

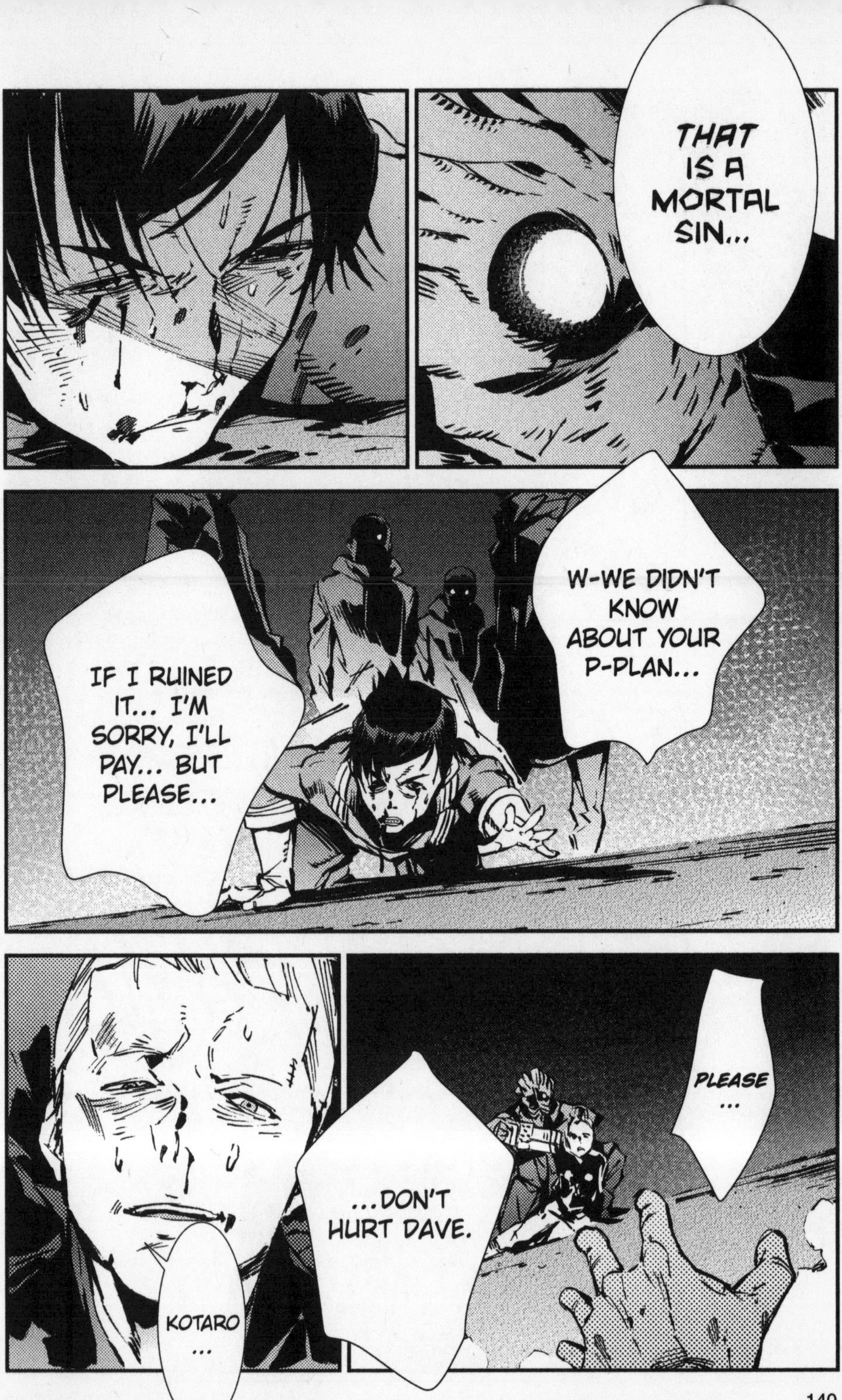
THAT IS A MORTAL SIN...
W-WE DIDN'T KNOW ABOUT YOUR P-PLAN...
IF I RUINED IT... I'M SORRY, I'LL PAY... BUT PLEASE...
PLEASE ...
...DON'T HURT DAVE.
KOTARO ...

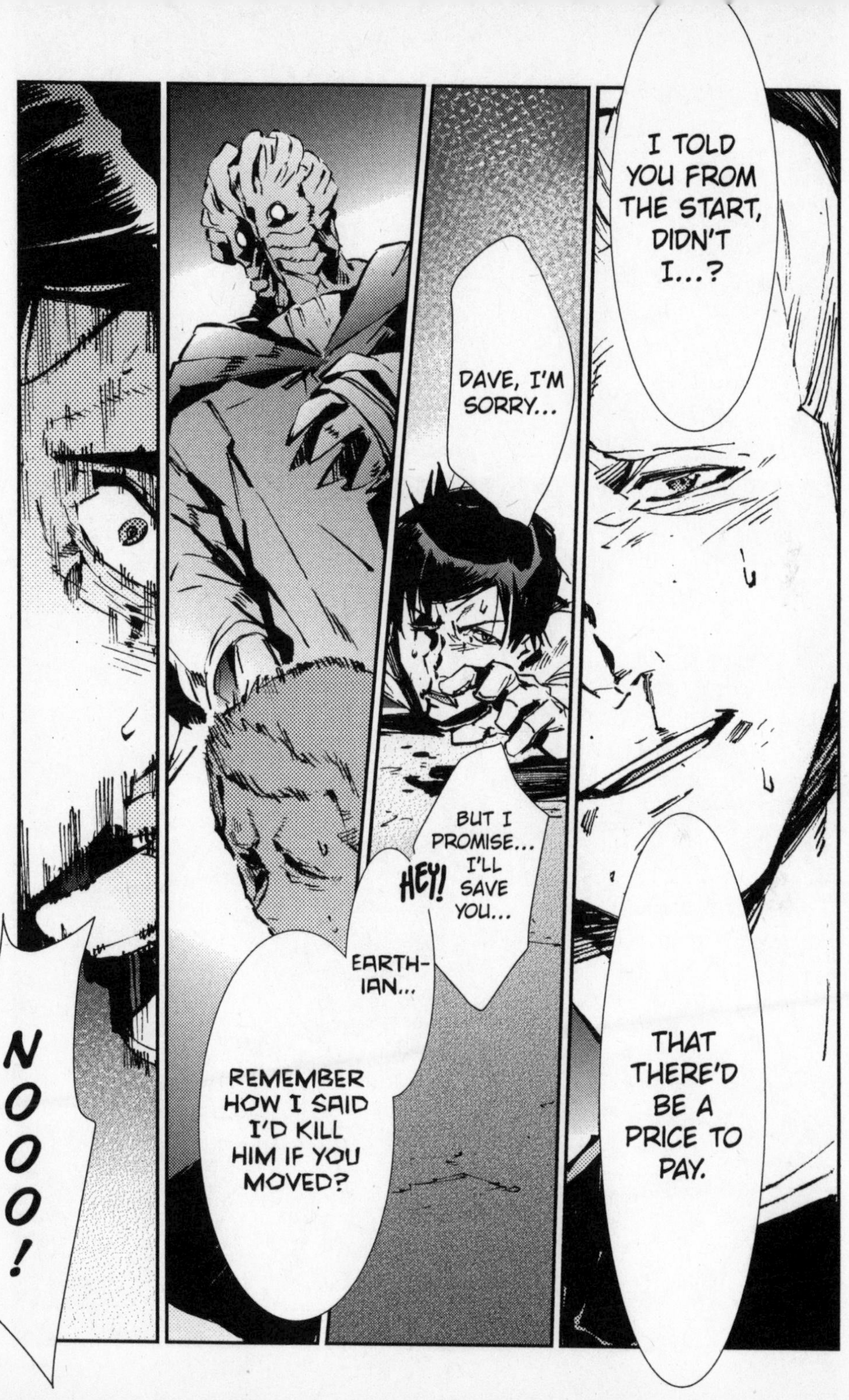
I TOLD YOU FROM THE START, DIDN'T I...?
THAT THERE'D BE A PRICE TO PAY.
DAVE, I'M SORRY...
BUT I PROMISE... I'LL SAVE YOU...
HEY!
EARTH-IAN...
REMEMBER HOW I SAID I'D KILL HIM IF YOU MOVED?
NOOOO!

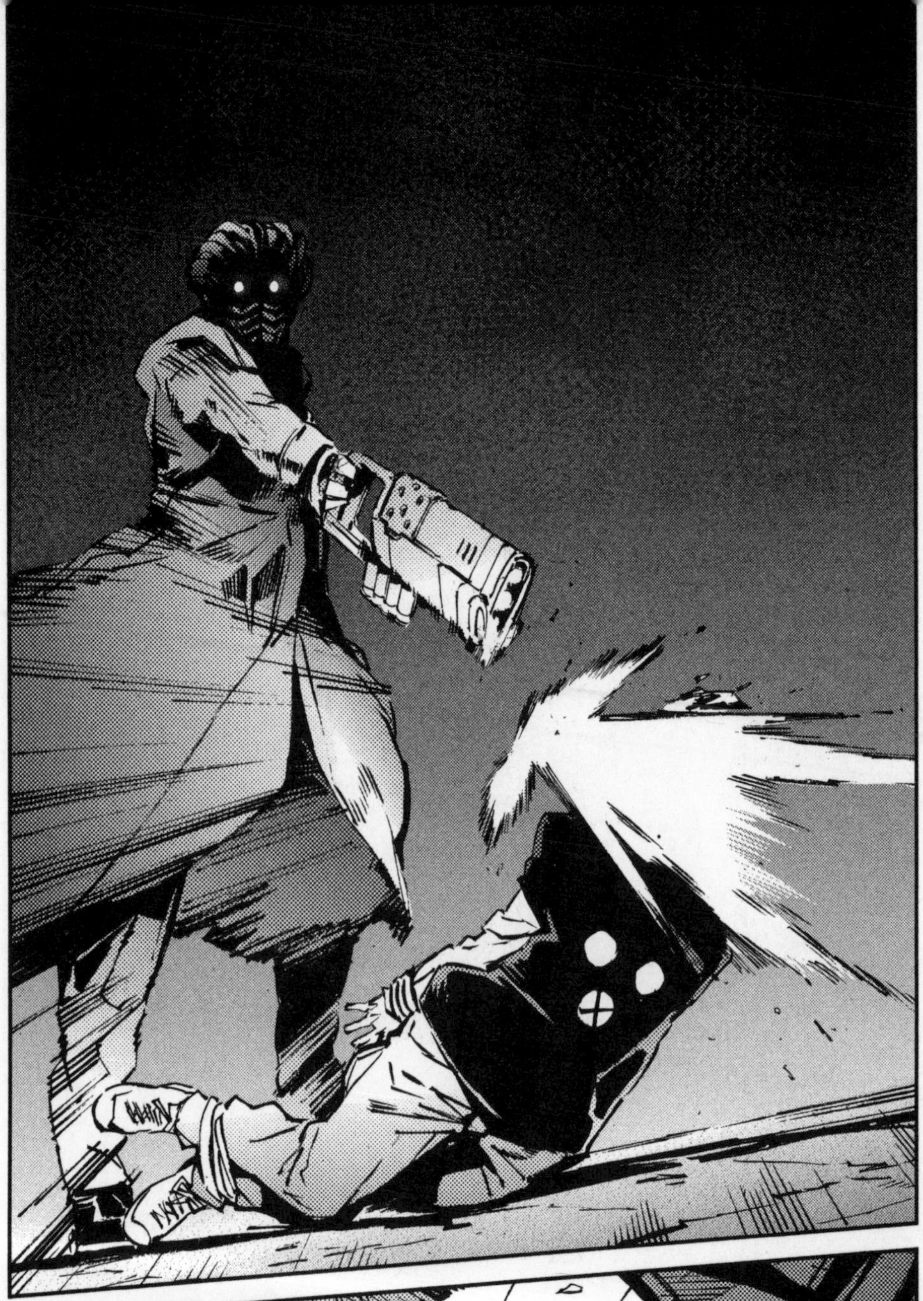

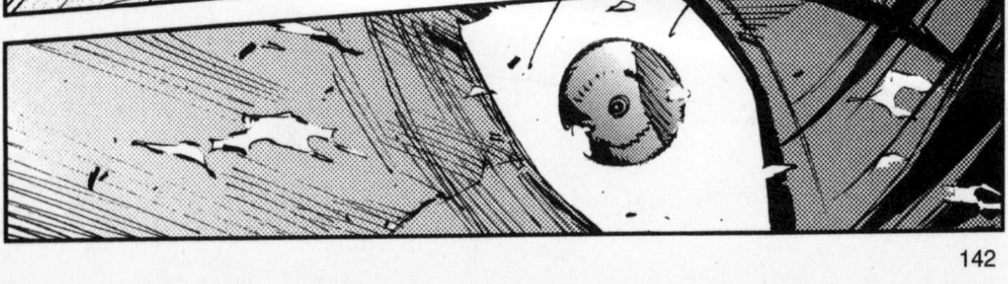

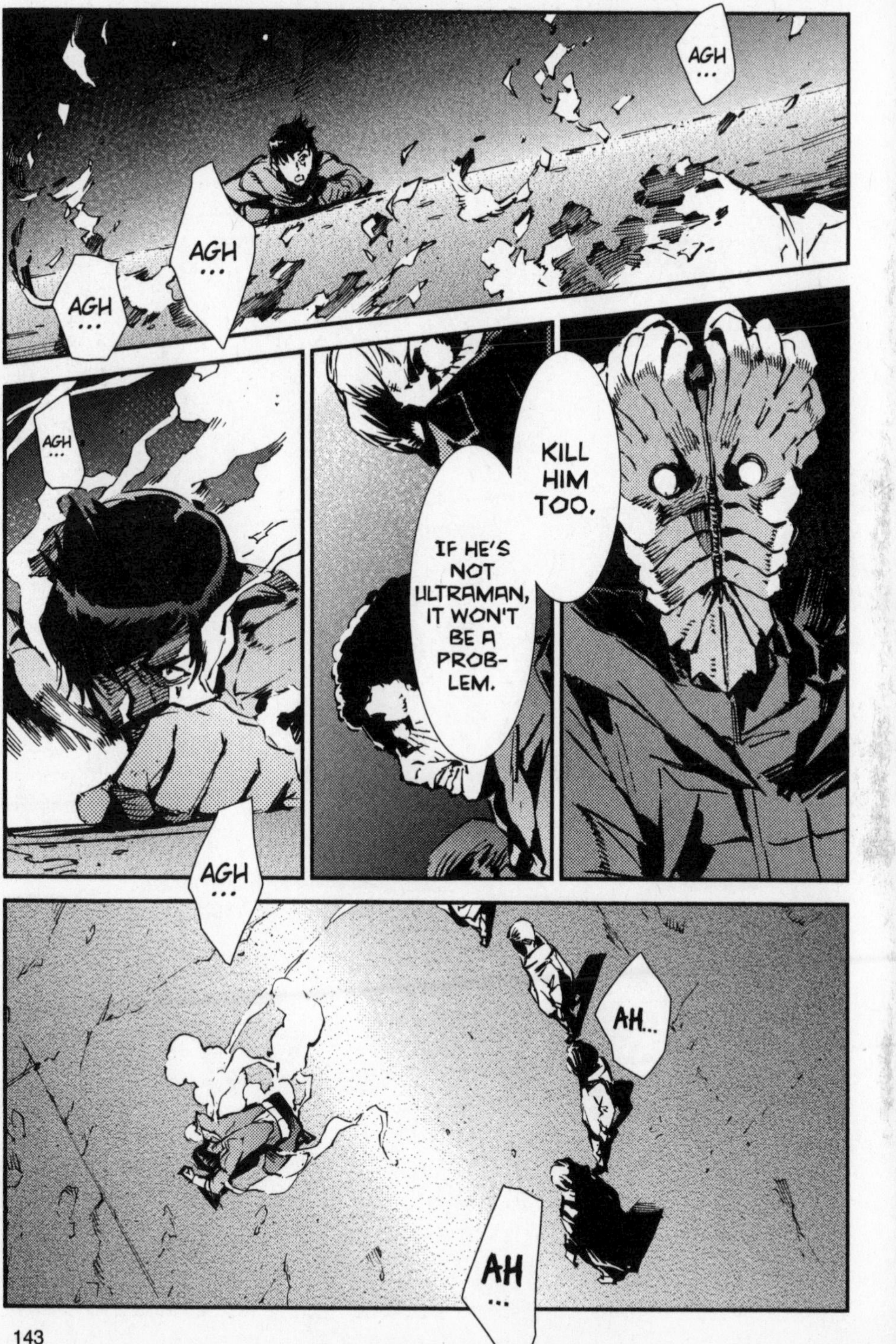
AGH ...
AGH ...
AGH ...
KILL HIM TOO.
IF HE'S NOT ULTRAMAN, IT WON'T BE A PROB-LEM.
AGH ...
AGH ...
AH...
AH ...

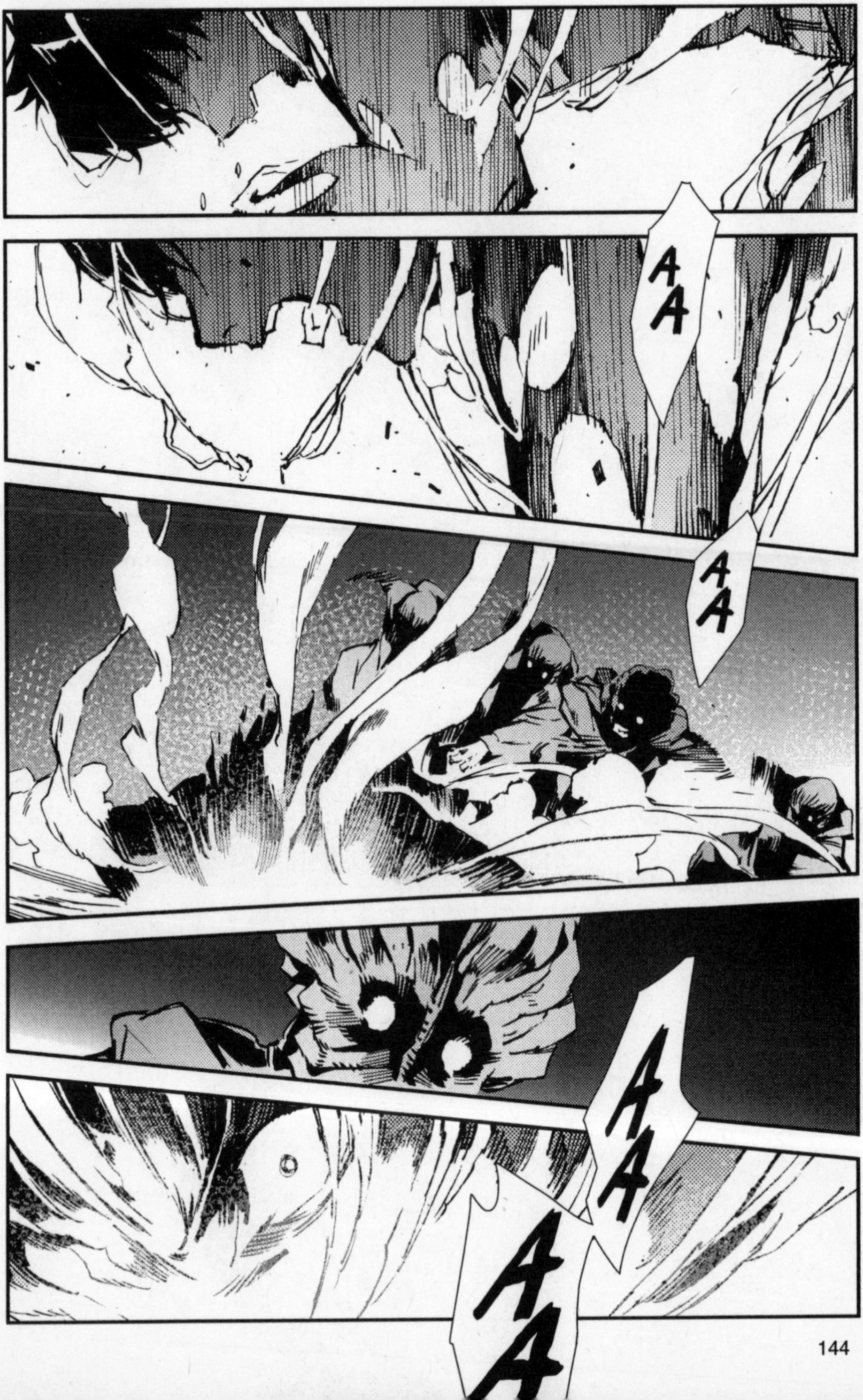
AA
AA
AAA
AA

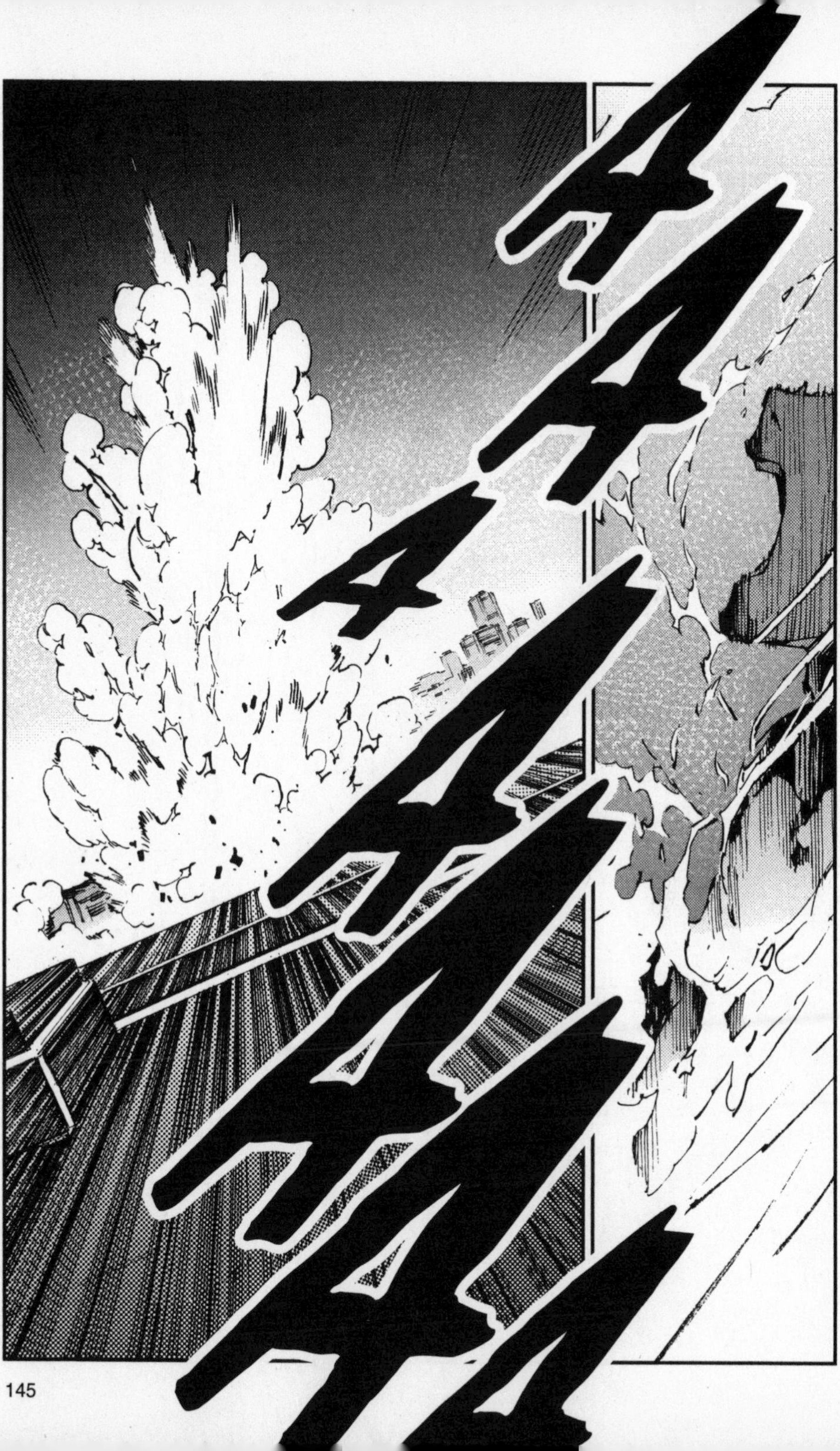

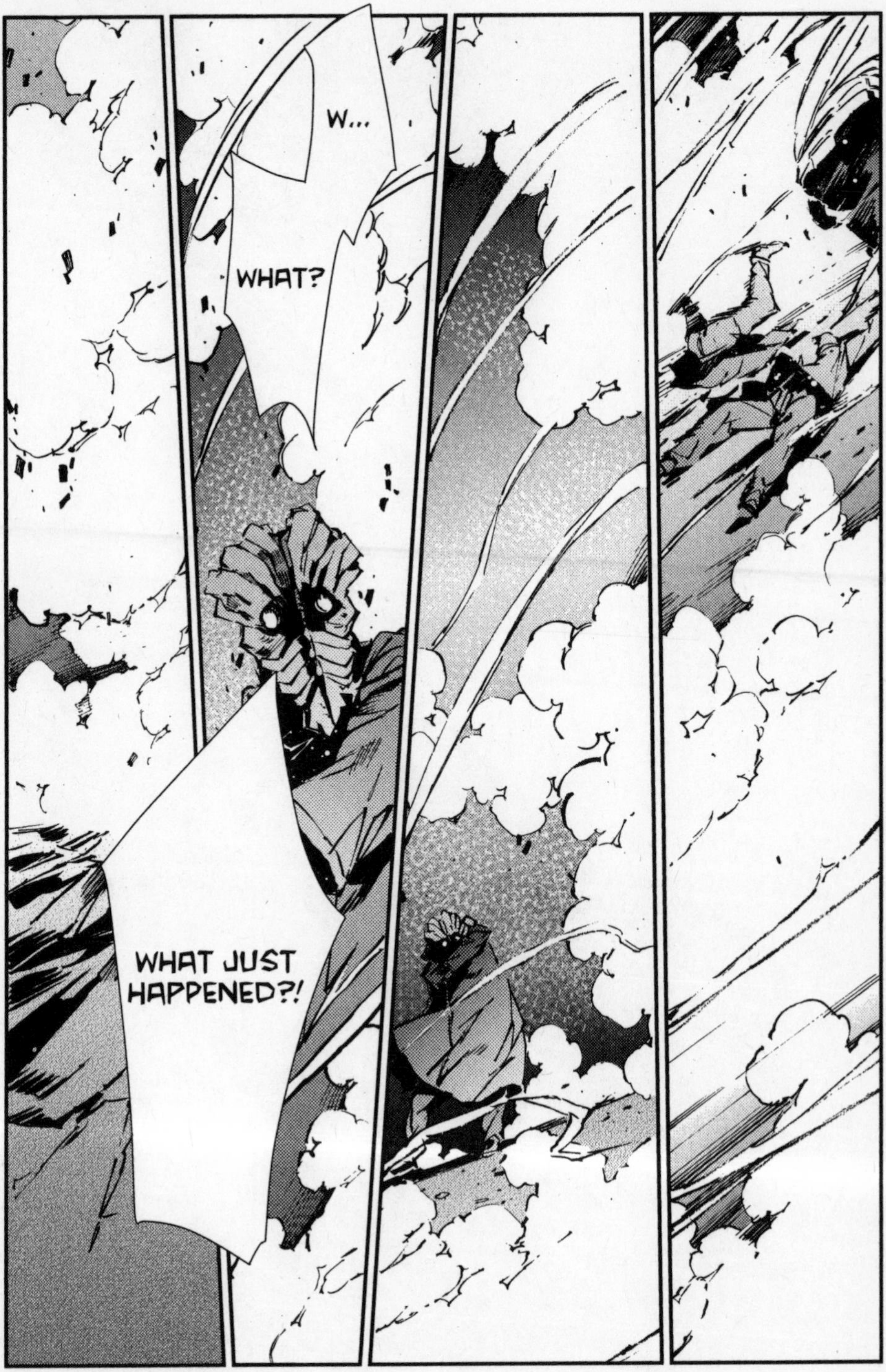
W...
WHAT?
WHAT JUST HAPPENED?!

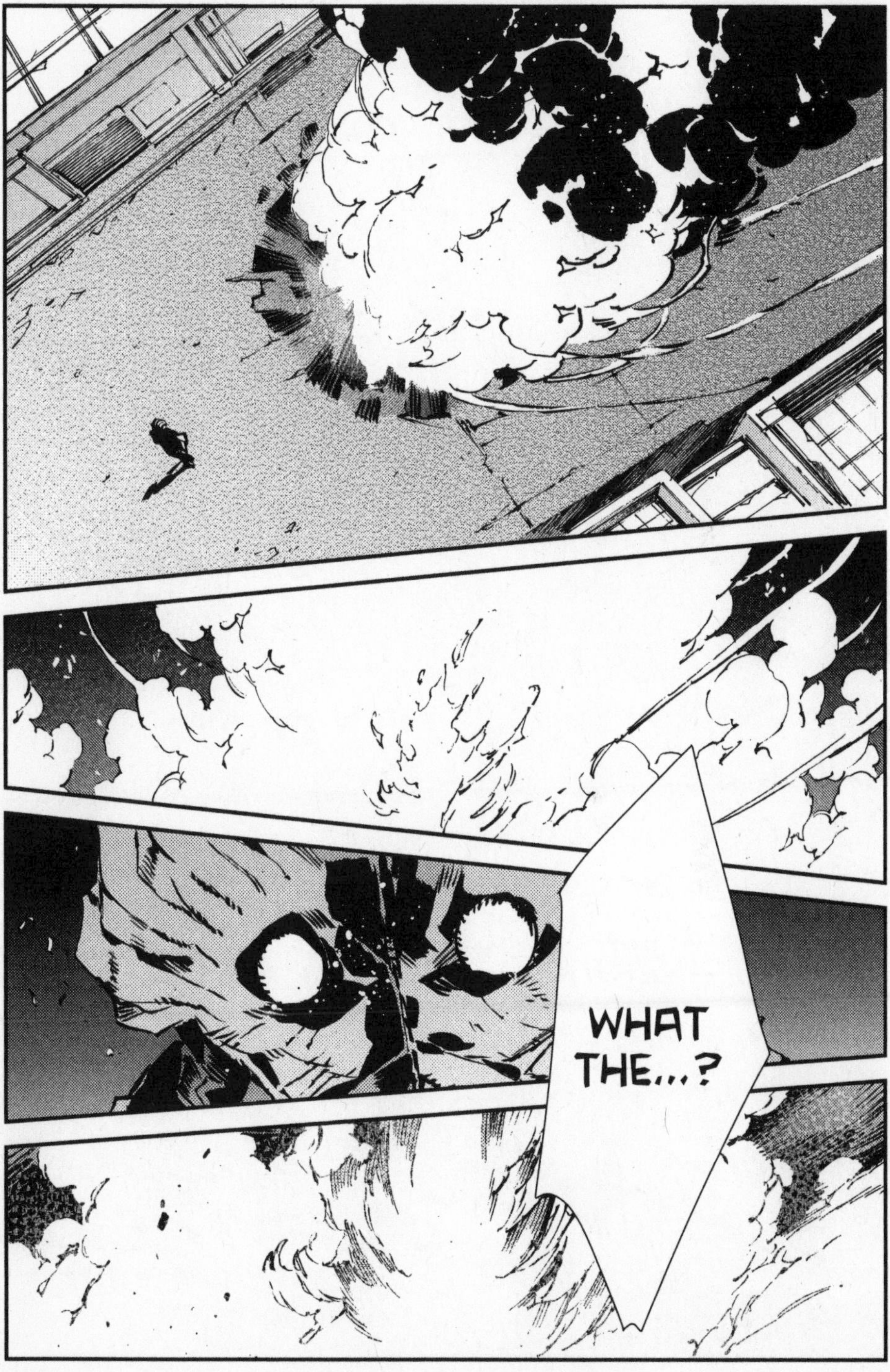
WHAT THE...?

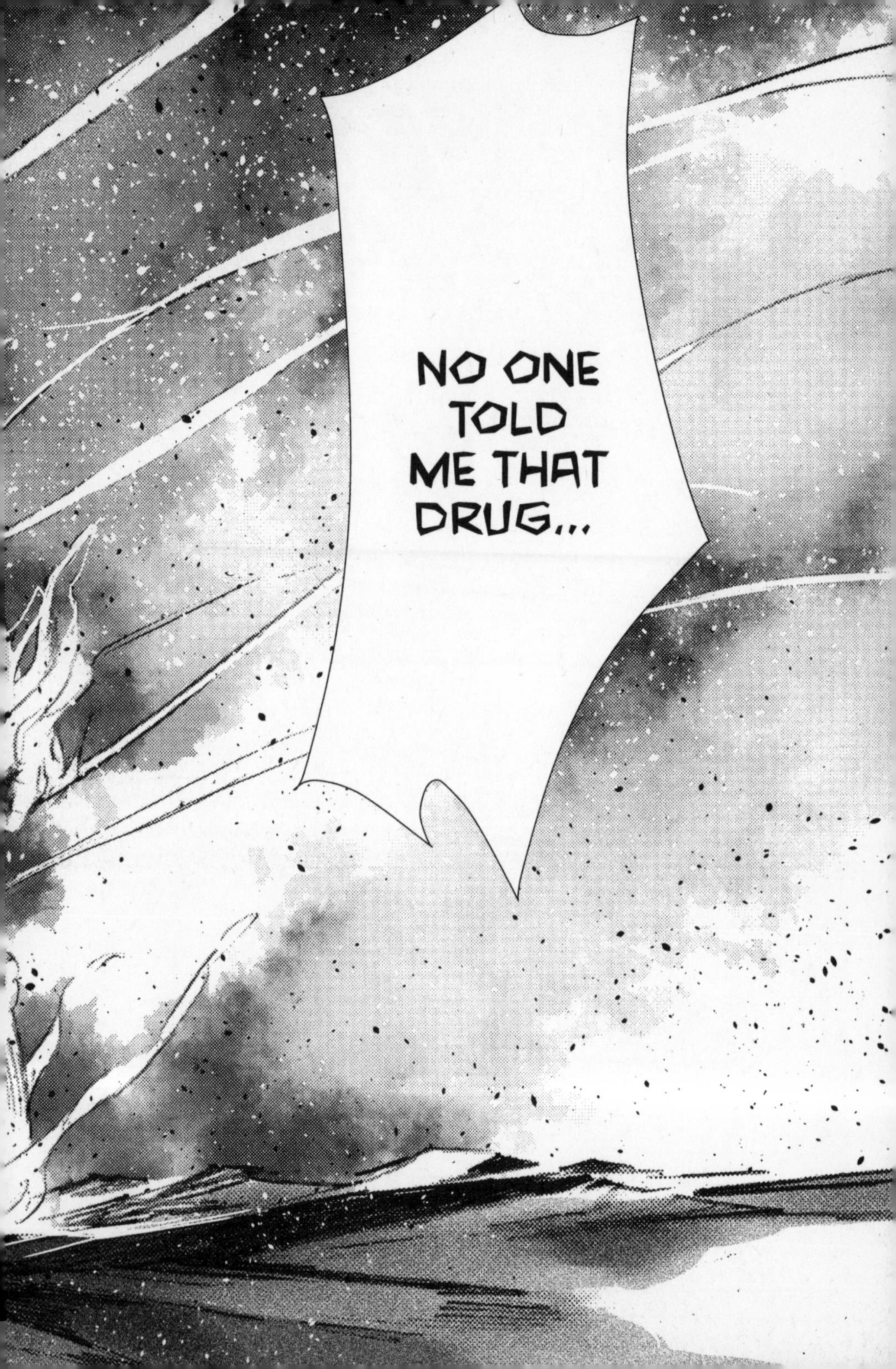
NO ONE TOLD ME THAT DRUG...

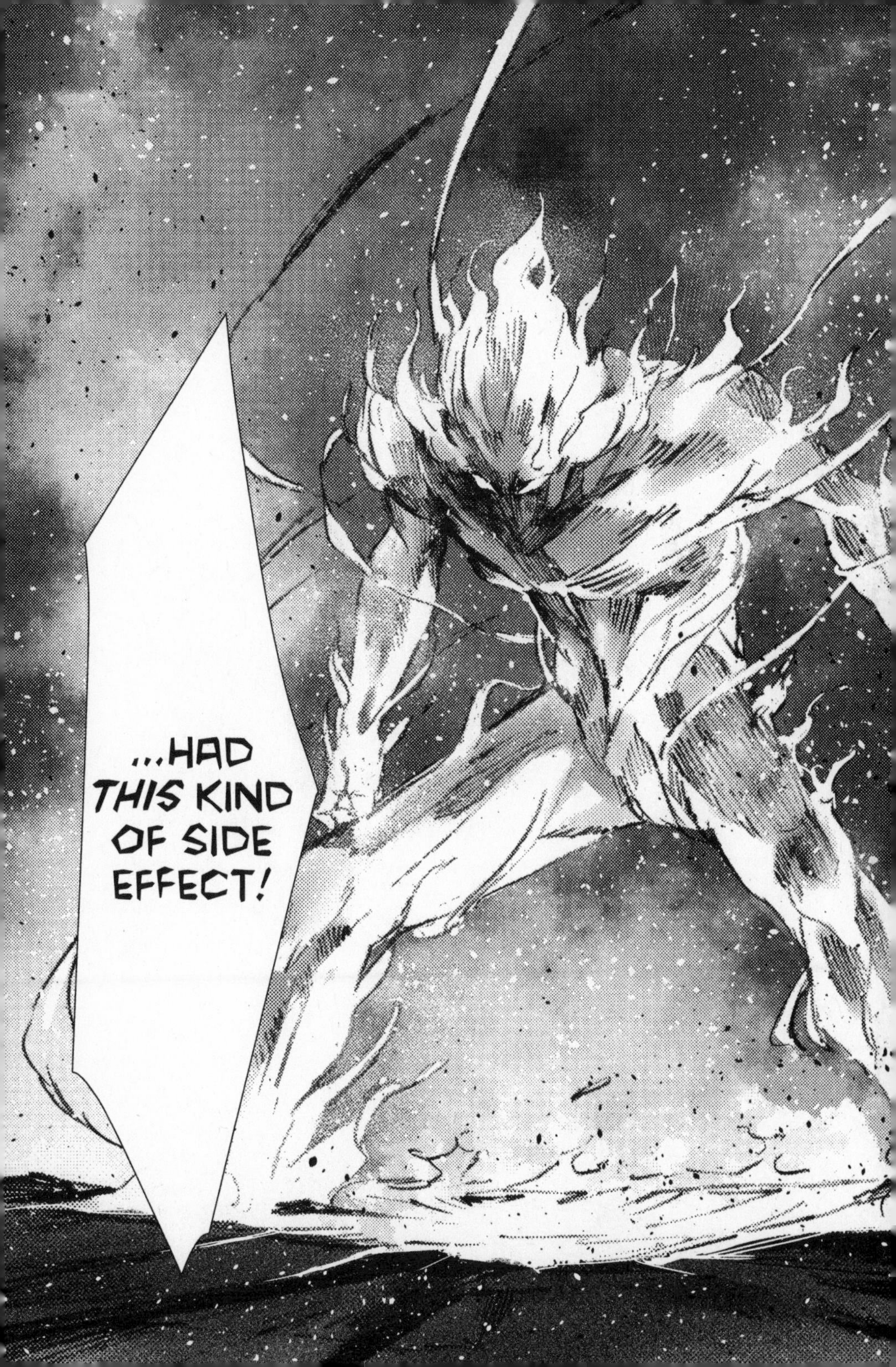
...HAD *THIS* KIND OF SIDE EFFECT!

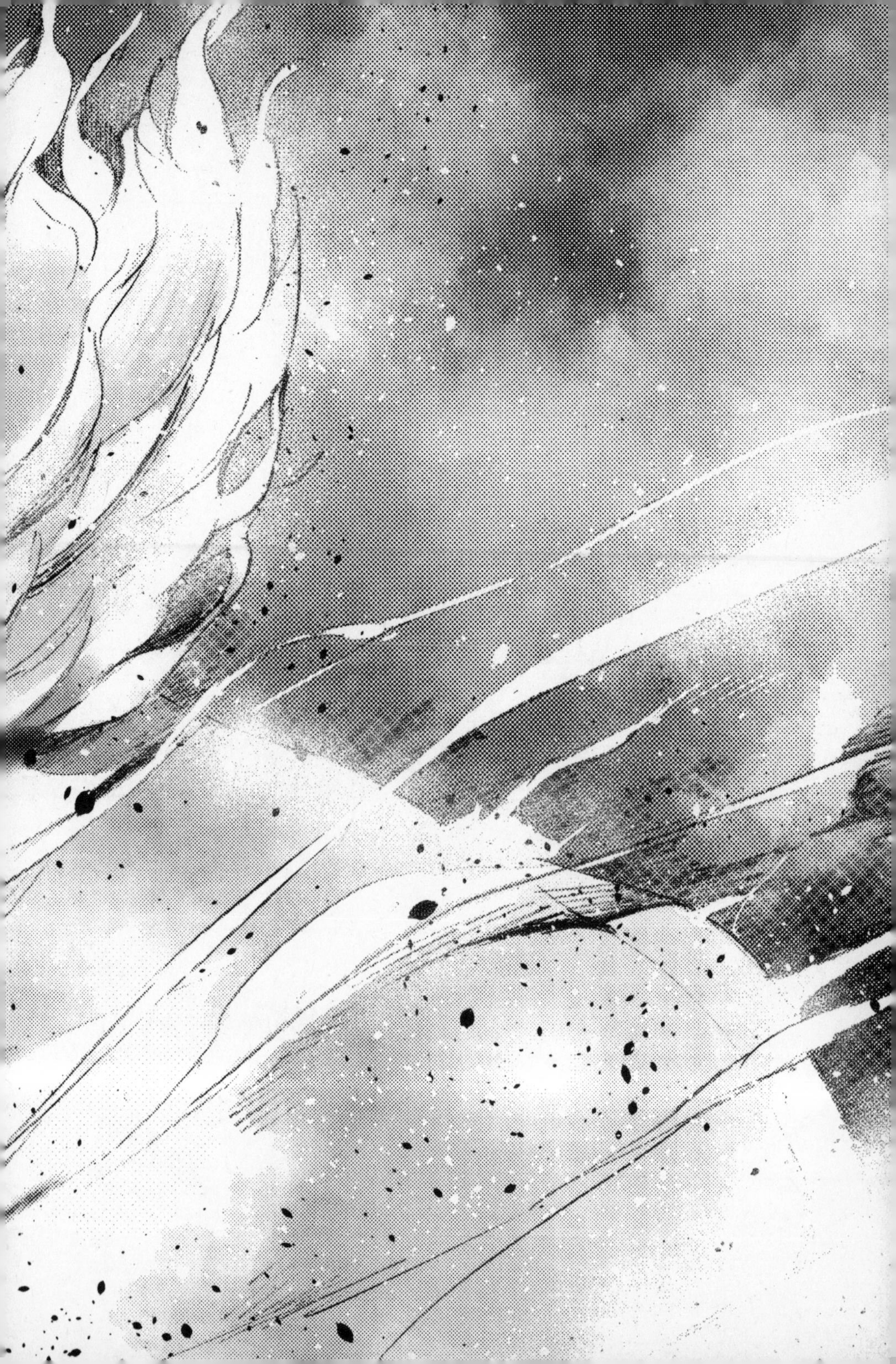

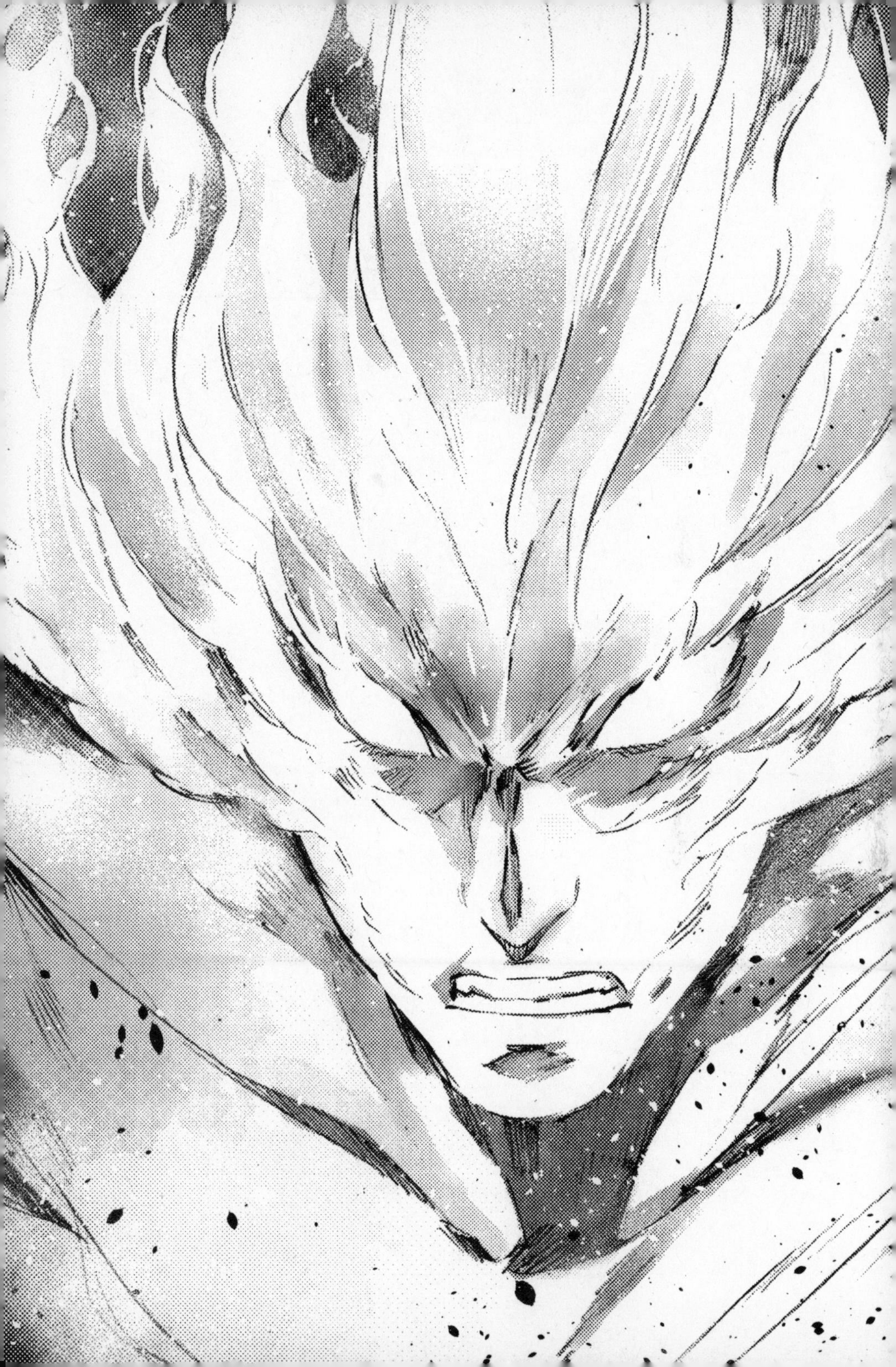

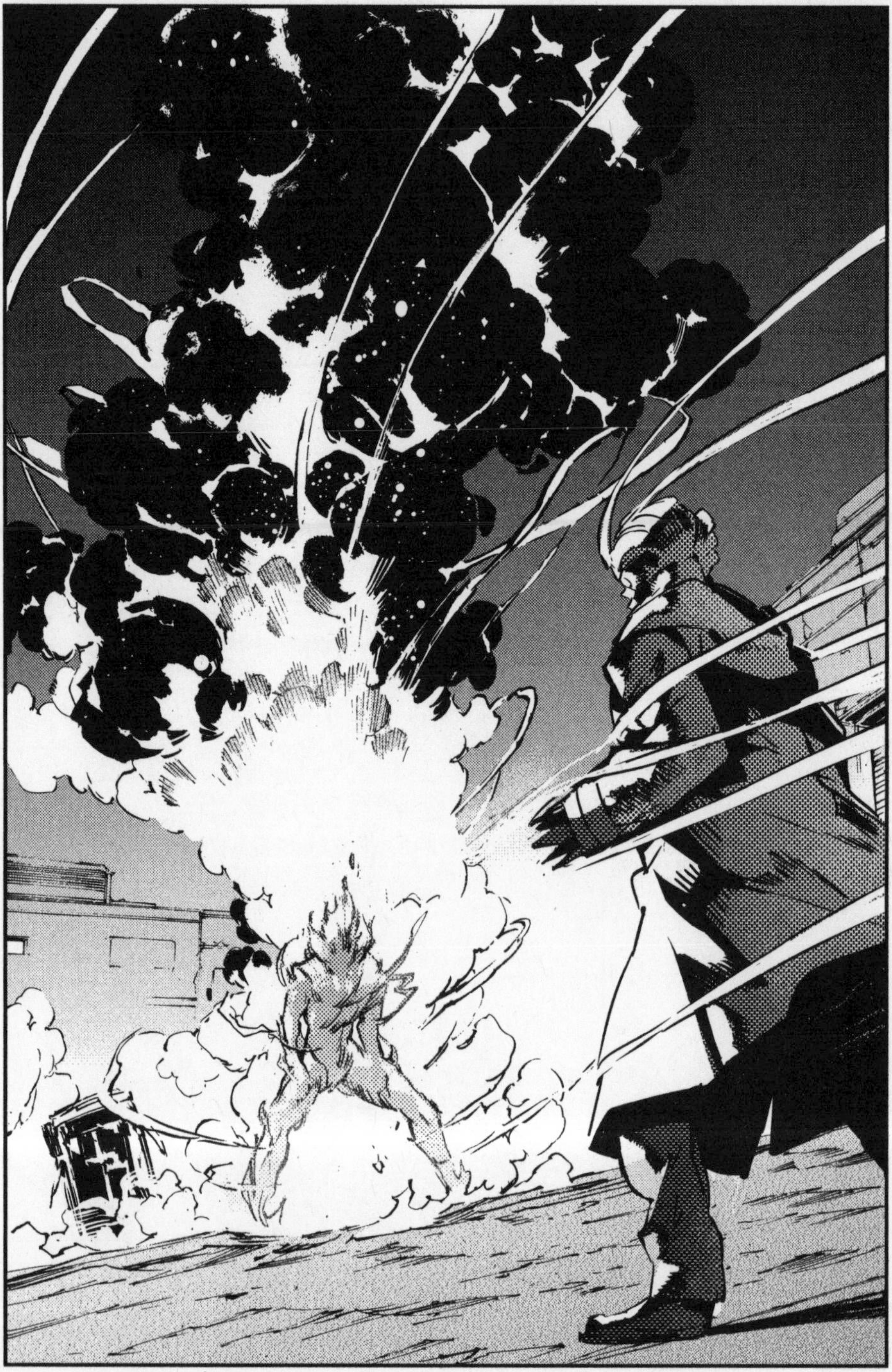

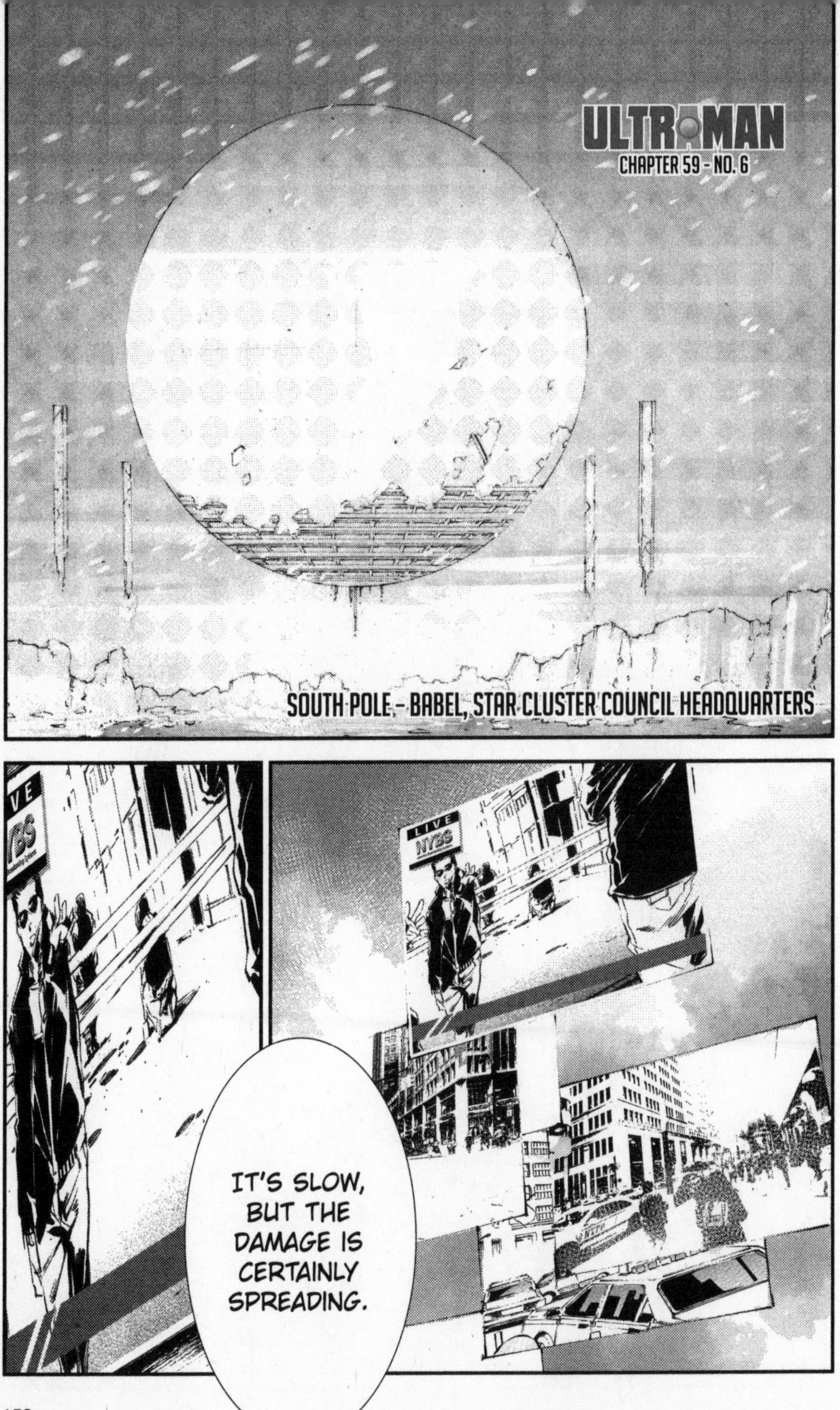
ULTRAMAN
CHAPTER 59 - NO. 6
SOUTH POLE - BABEL, STAR CLUSTER COUNCIL HEADQUARTERS
LIVE
NYBS
IT'S SLOW, BUT THE DAMAGE IS CERTAINLY SPREADING.

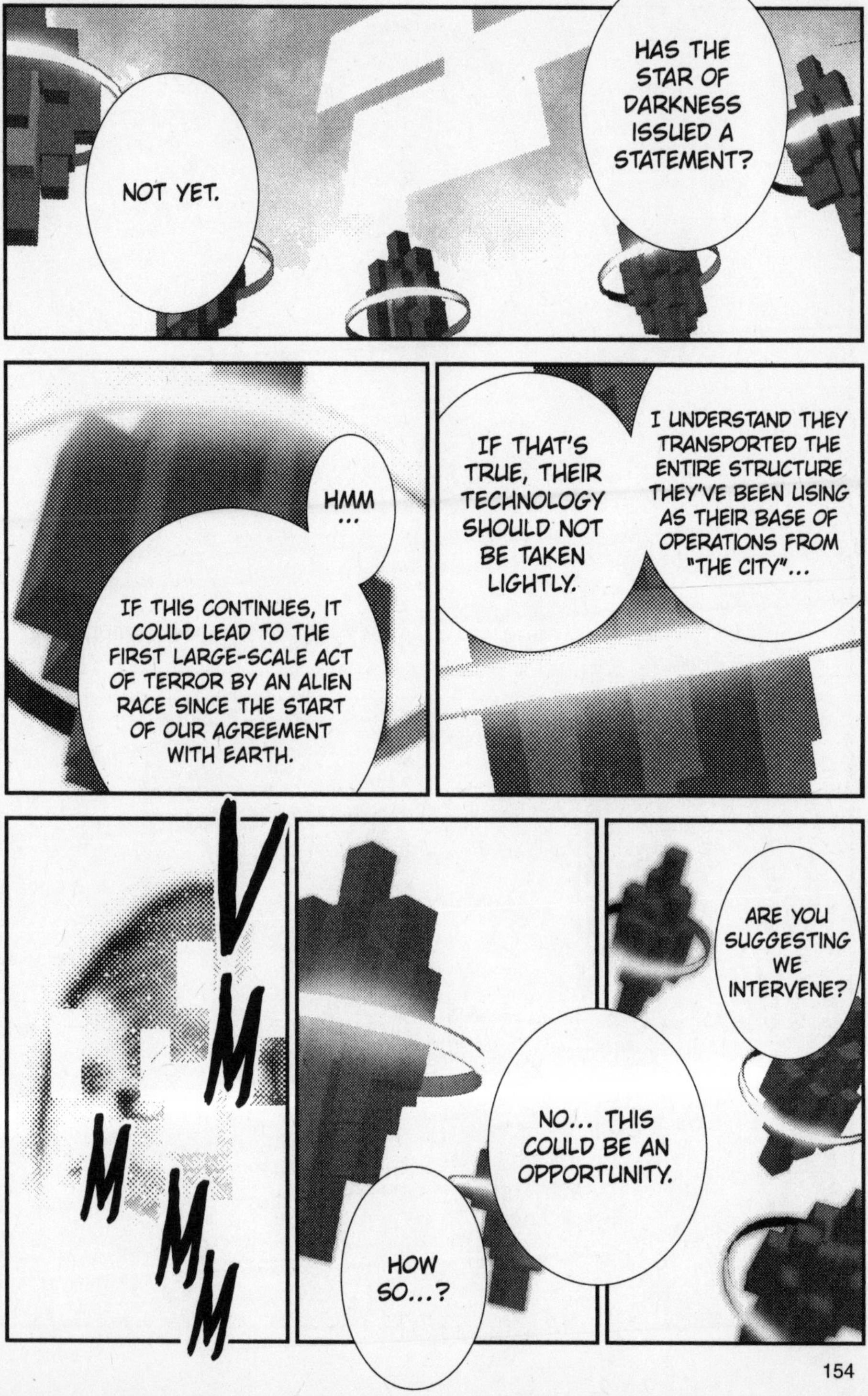
HAS THE STAR OF DARKNESS ISSUED A STATEMENT?
NOT YET.
I UNDERSTAND THEY TRANSPORTED THE ENTIRE STRUCTURE THEY'VE BEEN USING AS THEIR BASE OF OPERATIONS FROM "THE CITY"...
IF THAT'S TRUE, THEIR TECHNOLOGY SHOULD NOT BE TAKEN LIGHTLY.
HMM...
IF THIS CONTINUES, IT COULD LEAD TO THE FIRST LARGE-SCALE ACT OF TERROR BY AN ALIEN RACE SINCE THE START OF OUR AGREEMENT WITH EARTH.
ARE YOU SUGGESTING WE INTERVENE?
NO... THIS COULD BE AN OPPORTUNITY.
HOW SO...?
VMMMMM

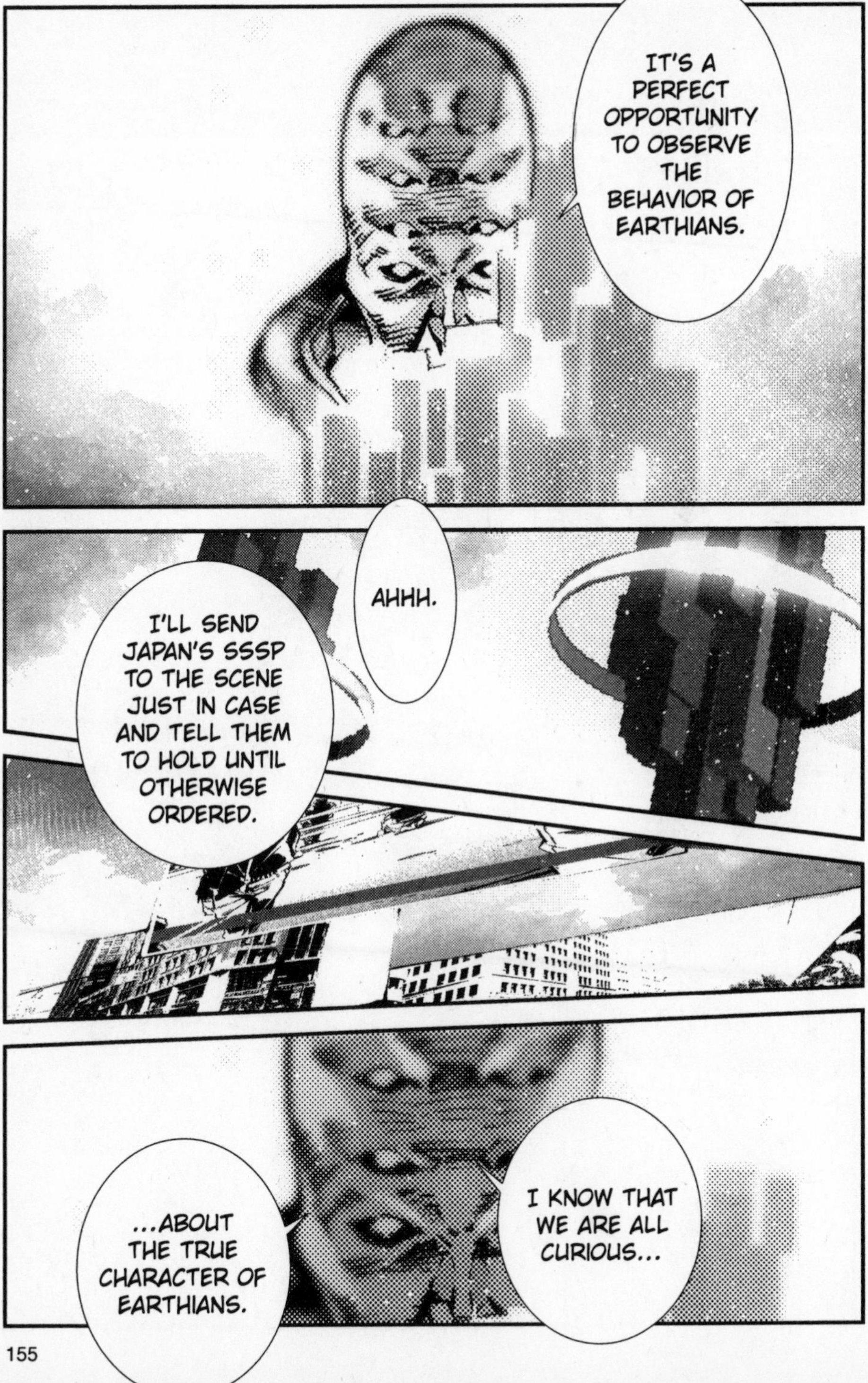
IT'S A PERFECT OPPORTUNITY TO OBSERVE THE BEHAVIOR OF EARTHIANS.
AHHH.
I'LL SEND JAPAN'S SSSP TO THE SCENE JUST IN CASE AND TELL THEM TO HOLD UNTIL OTHERWISE ORDERED.
I KNOW THAT WE ARE ALL CURIOUS...
...ABOUT THE TRUE CHARACTER OF EARTHIANS.

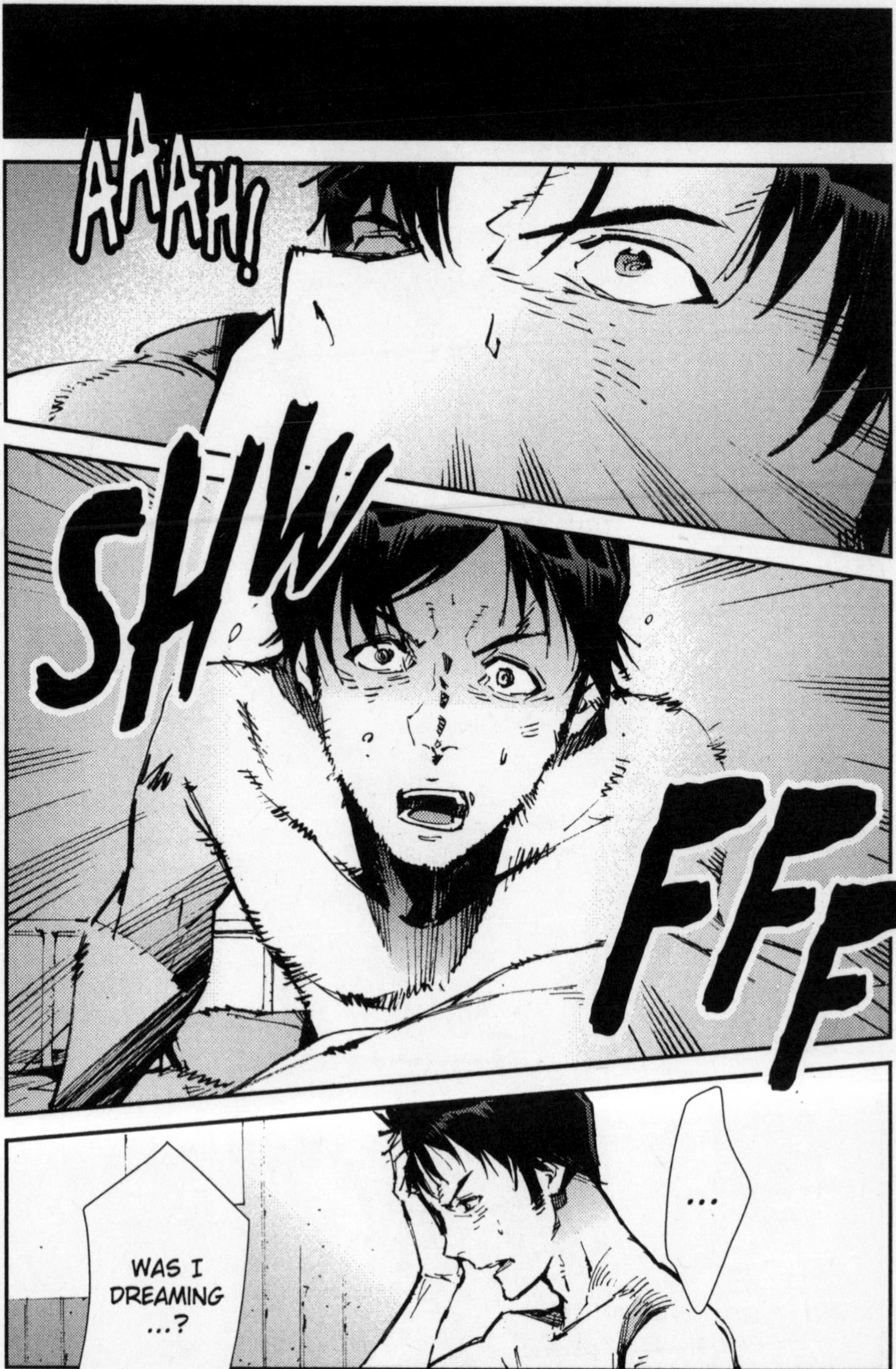
AAAH!
SHWFFF
...
WAS I DREAMING ...?

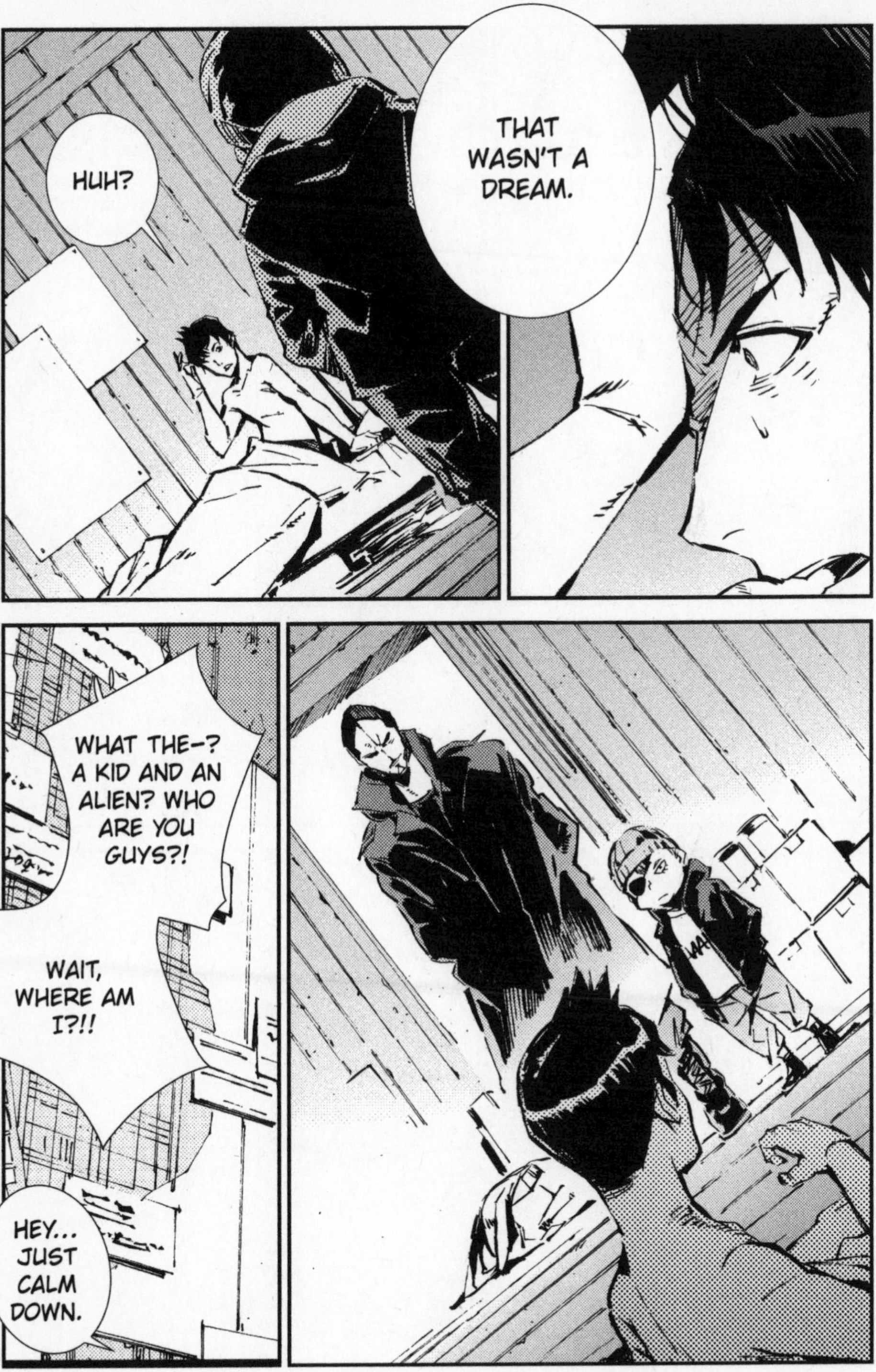
THAT WASN'T A DREAM.
HUH?
WHAT THE-? A KID AND AN ALIEN? WHO ARE YOU GUYS?!
WAIT, WHERE AM I?!!
HEY... JUST CALM DOWN.

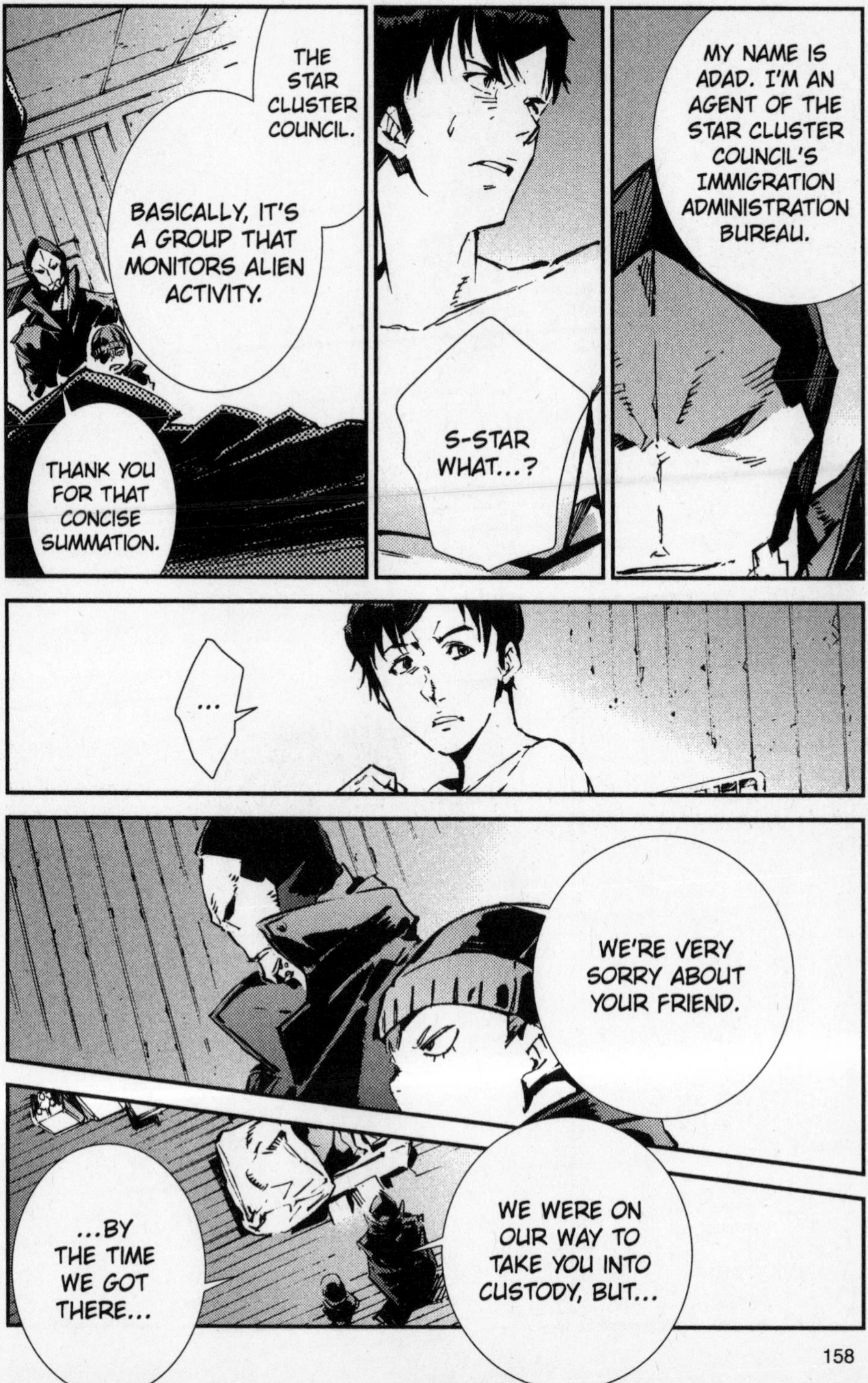
MY NAME IS ADAD. I'M AN AGENT OF THE STAR CLUSTER COUNCIL'S IMMIGRATION ADMINISTRATION BUREAU.
S-STAR WHAT...?
THE STAR CLUSTER COUNCIL.
BASICALLY, IT'S A GROUP THAT MONITORS ALIEN ACTIVITY.
THANK YOU FOR THAT CONCISE SUMMATION.
...
WE'RE VERY SORRY ABOUT YOUR FRIEND.
WE WERE ON OUR WAY TO TAKE YOU INTO CUSTODY, BUT...
...BY THE TIME WE GOT THERE...

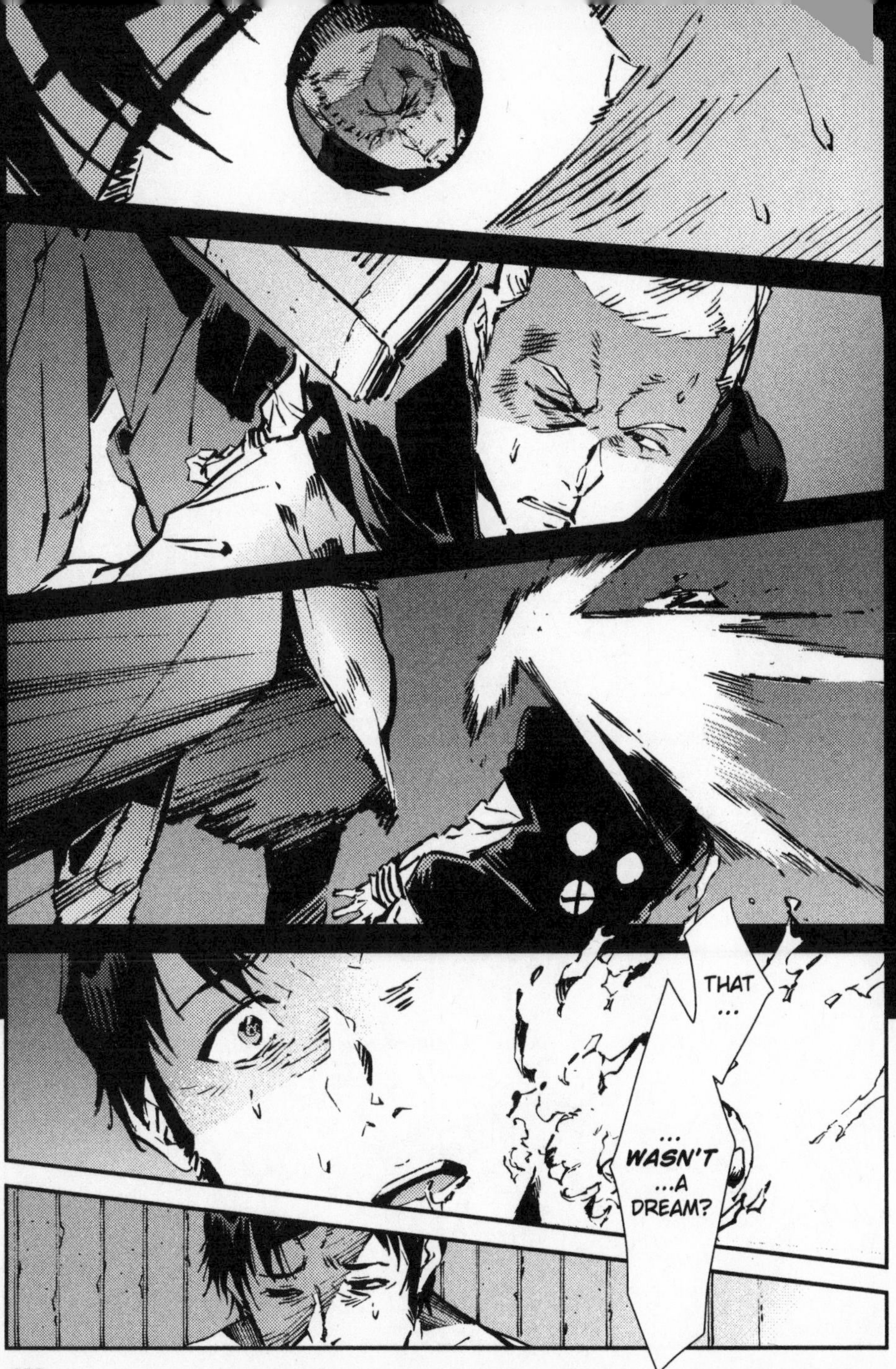
THAT ...
... WASN'T ...A DREAM?

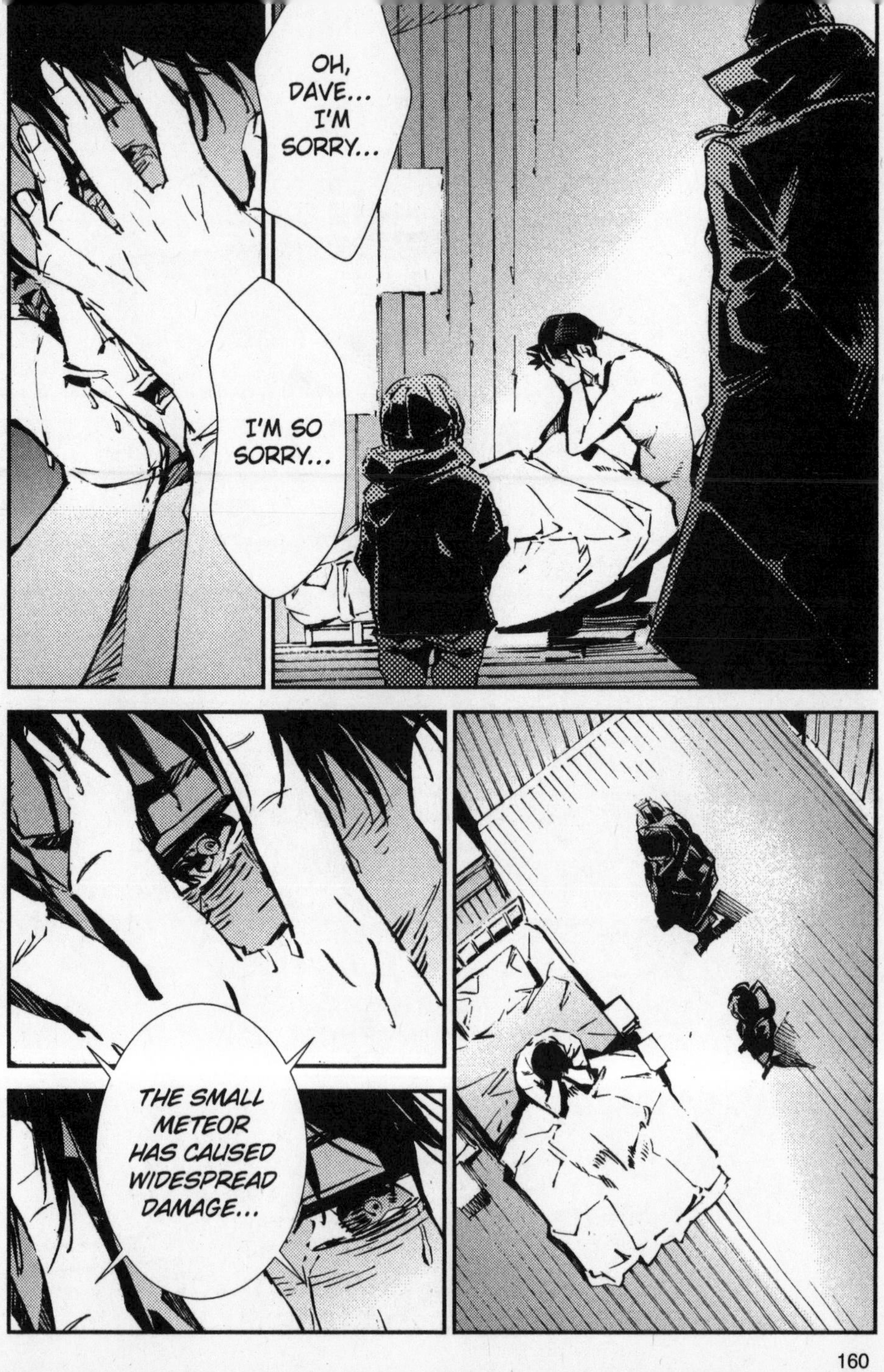
OH, DAVE... I'M SORRY...
I'M SO SORRY...
THE SMALL METEOR HAS CAUSED WIDESPREAD DAMAGE...

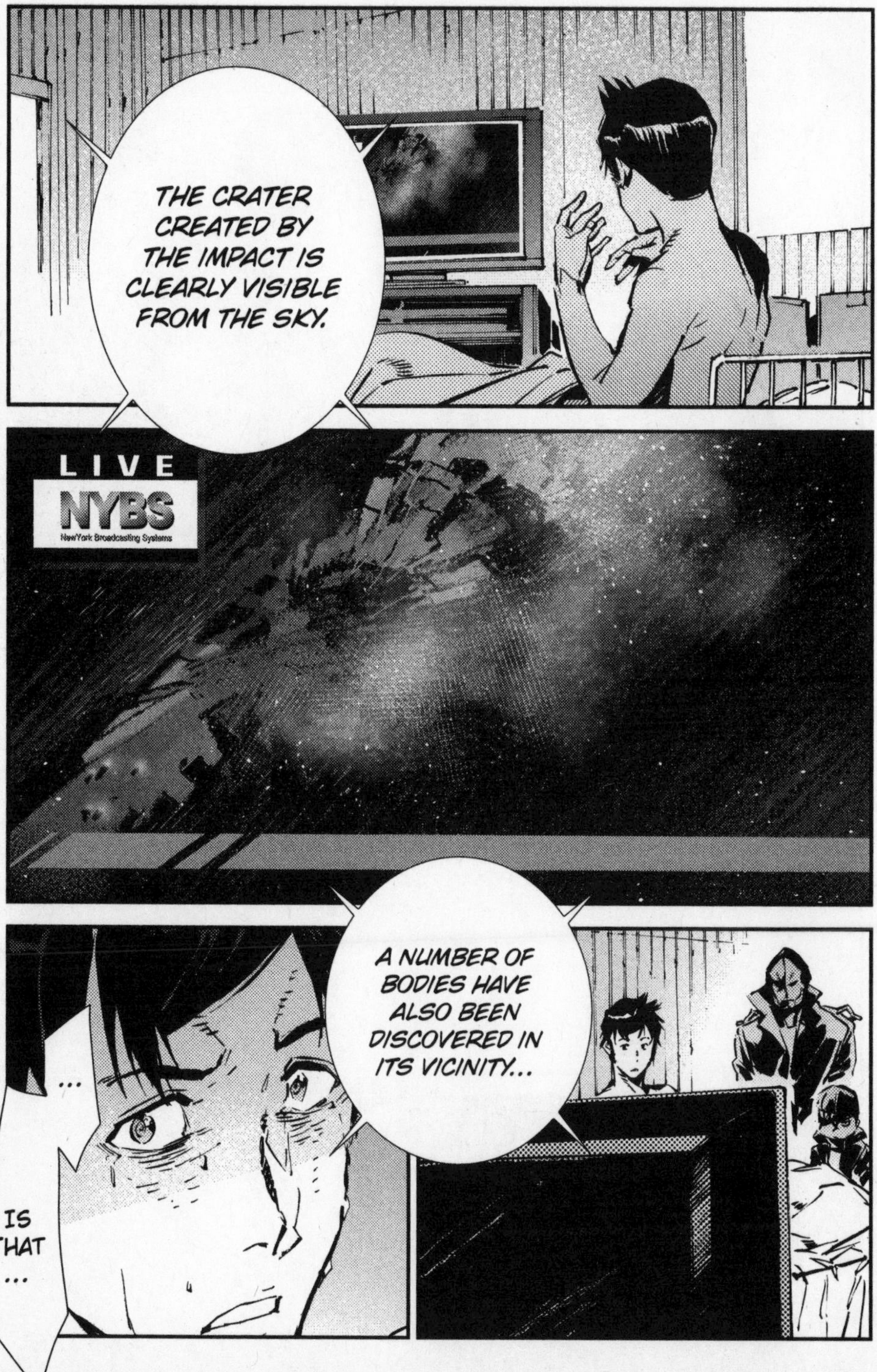
THE CRATER CREATED BY THE IMPACT IS CLEARLY VISIBLE FROM THE SKY.
LIVE
NYBS
NewYork Broadcasting Systems
A NUMBER OF BODIES HAVE ALSO BEEN DISCOVERED IN ITS VICINITY...
...
IS THAT ...

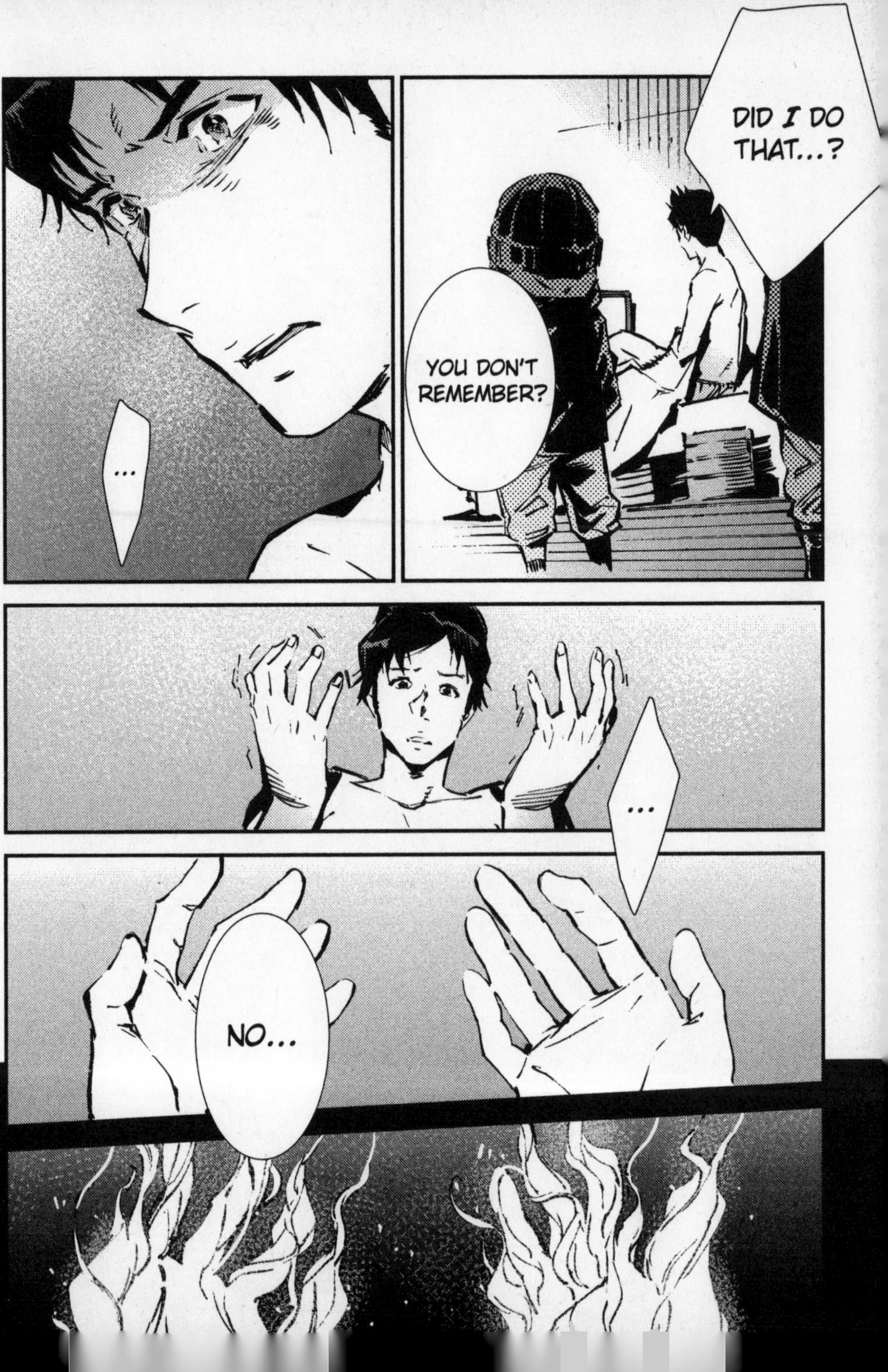
DID I DO THAT...?
YOU DON'T REMEMBER?
...
...
NO...

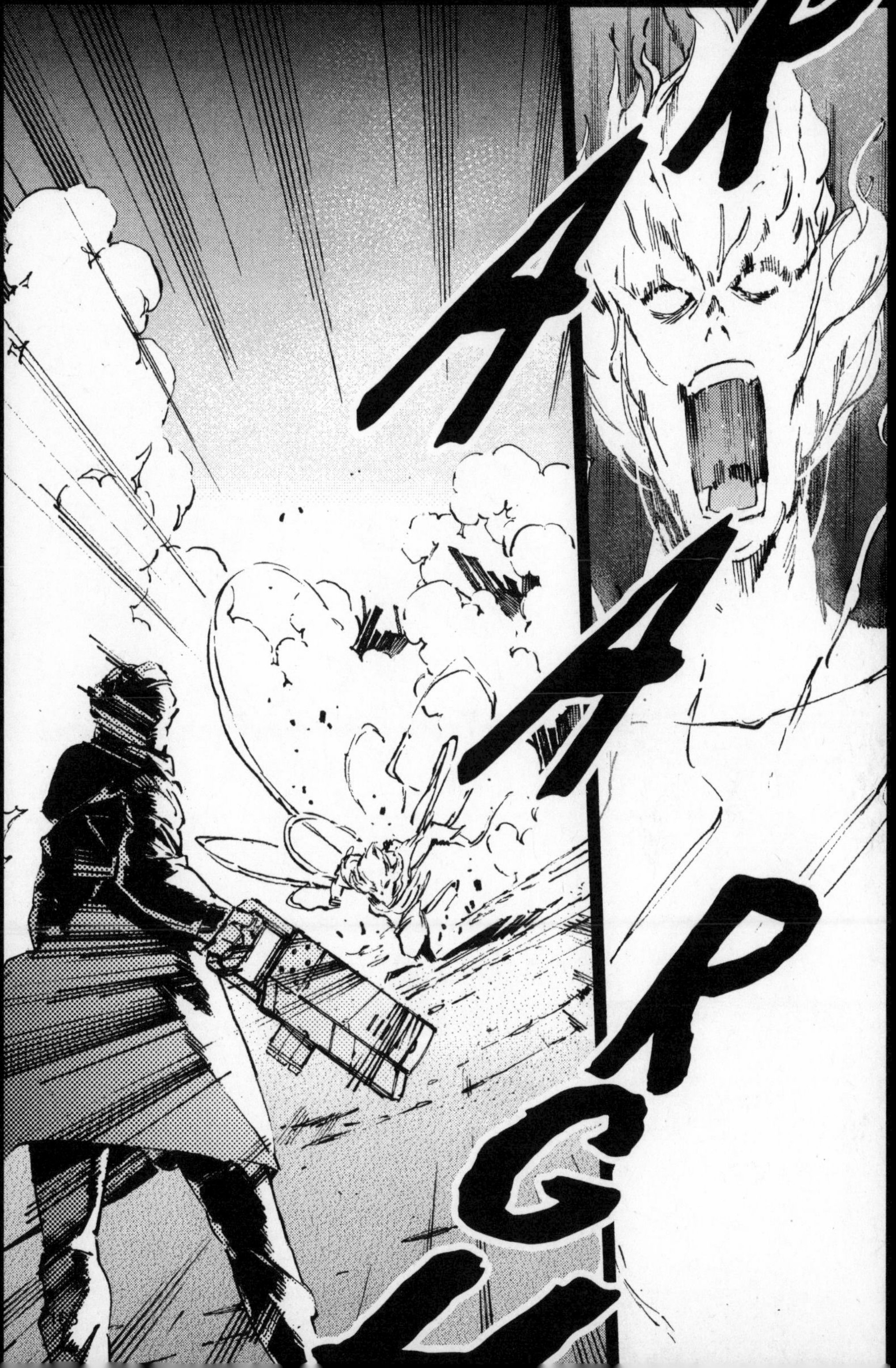
AAARGH

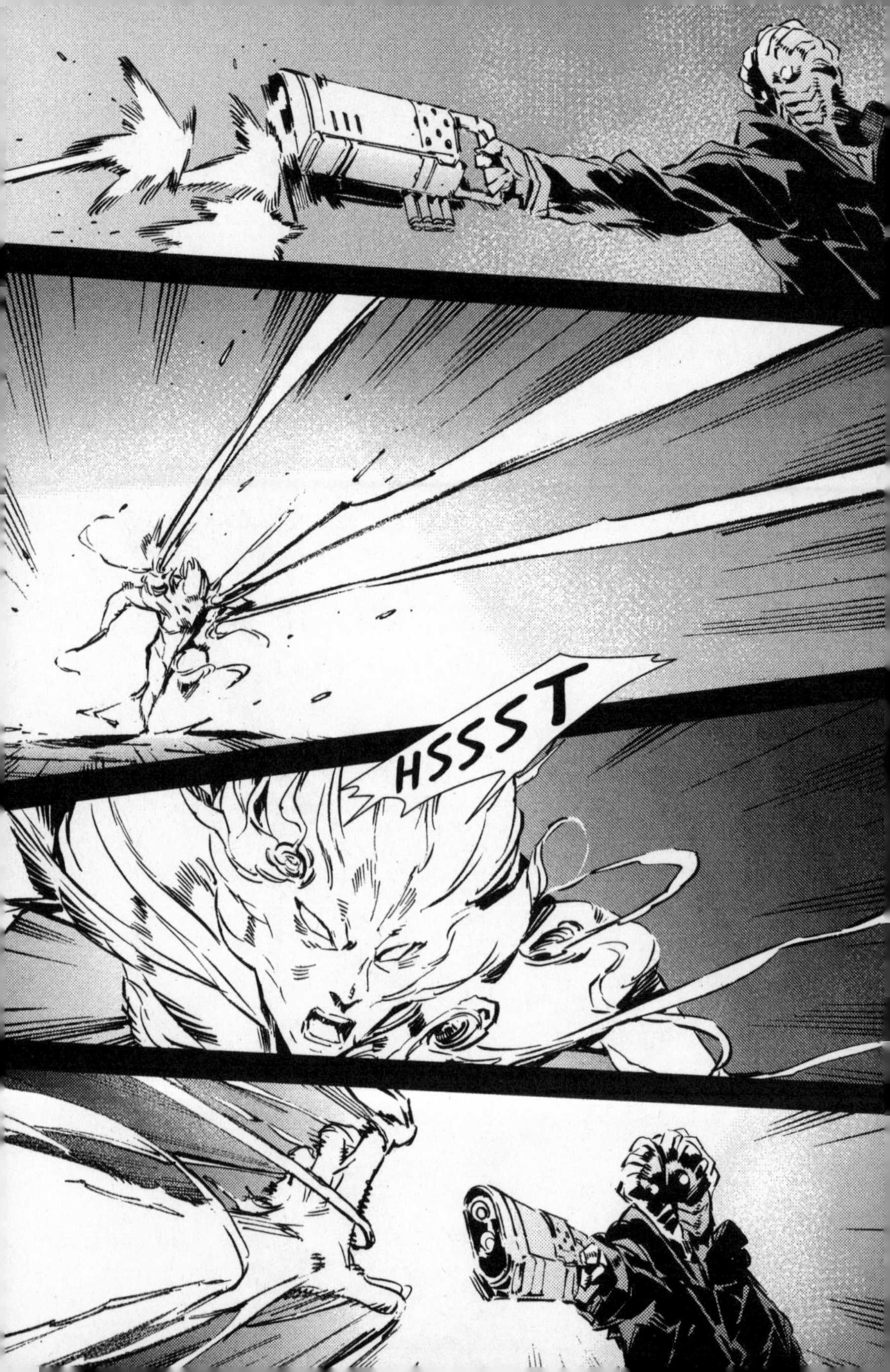
HSSST

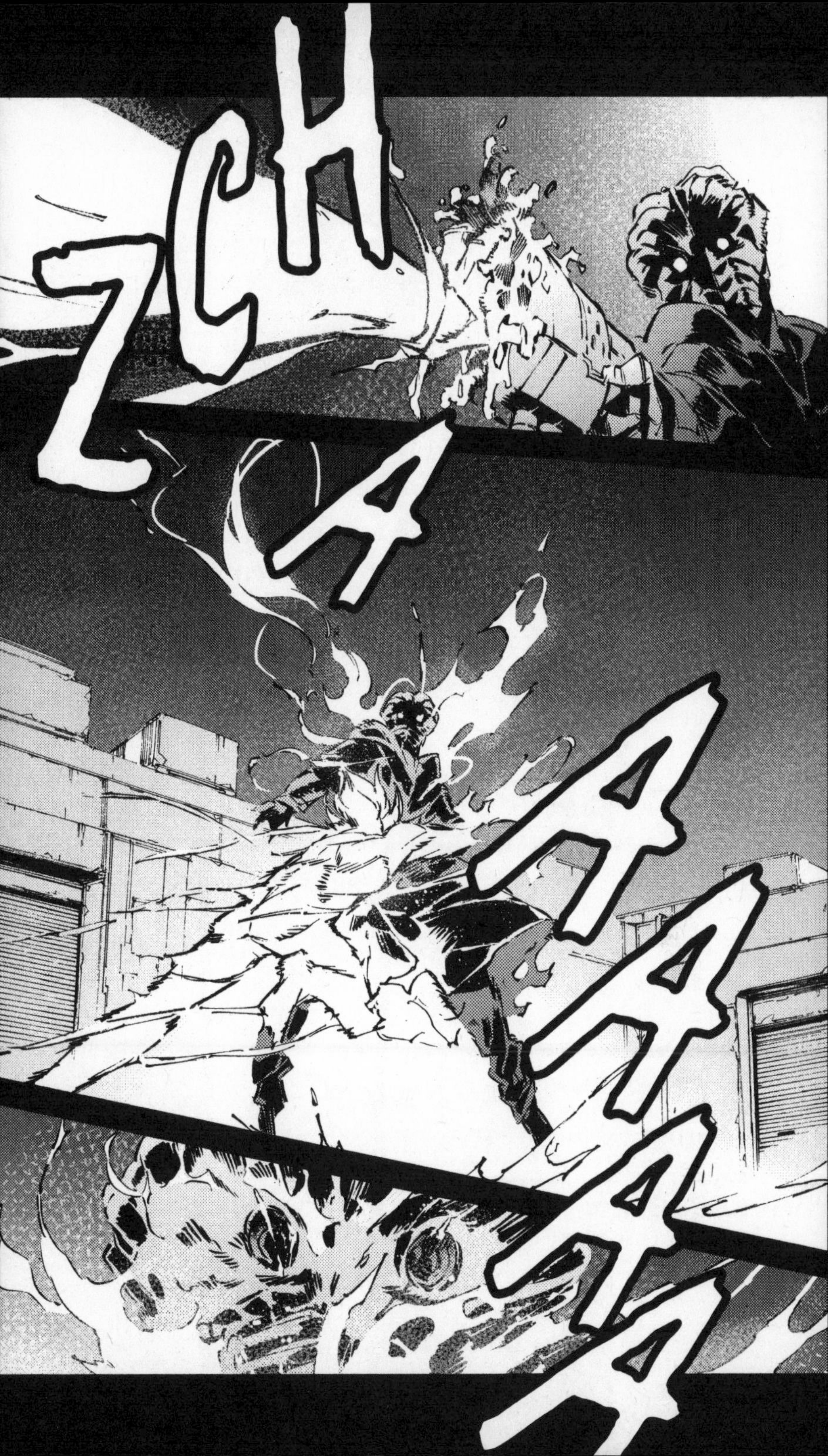
ZCHAAAAA

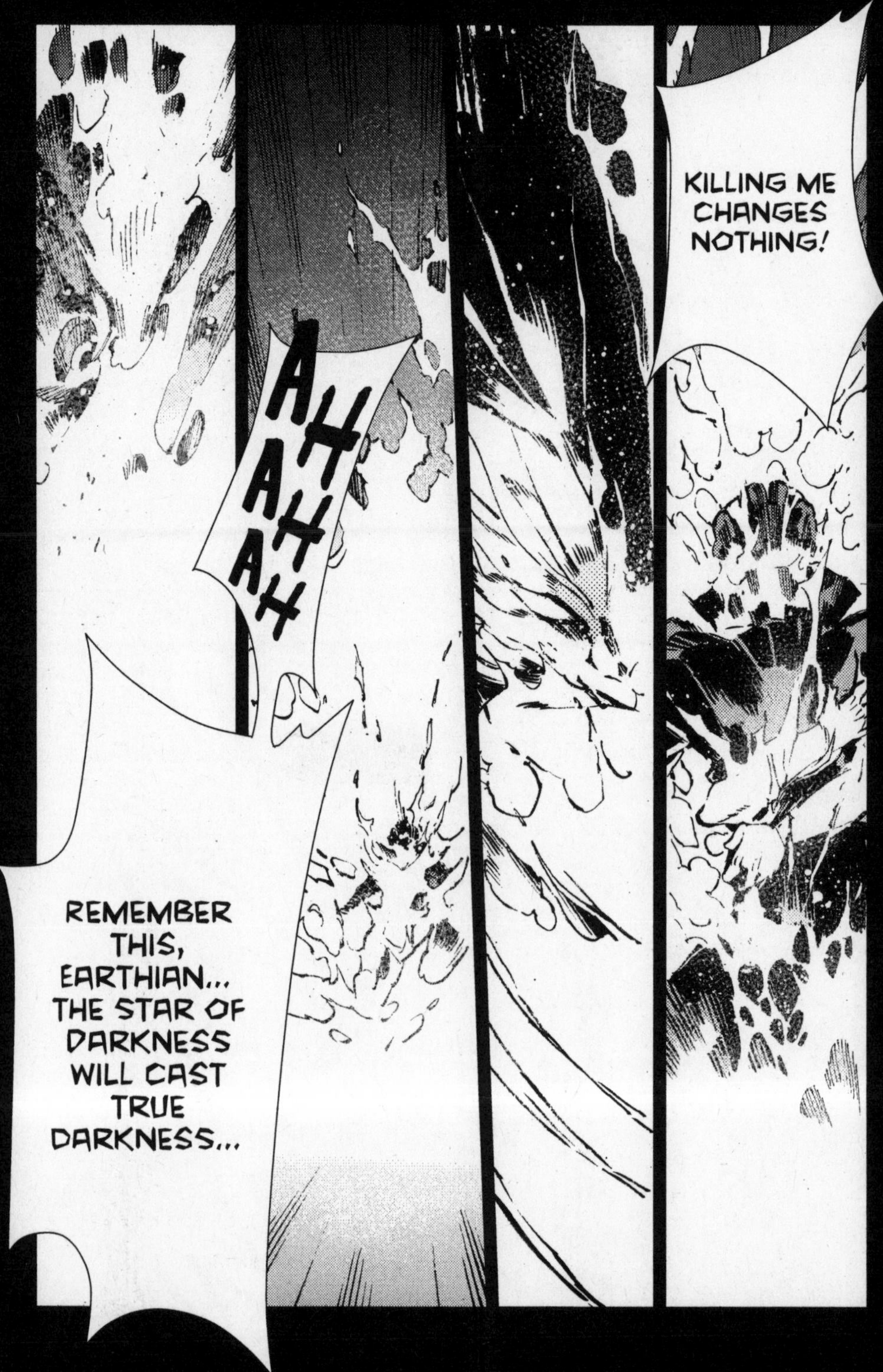
KILLING ME CHANGES NOTHING!
AHAHAH
REMEMBER THIS, EARTHIAN... THE STAR OF DARKNESS WILL CAST TRUE DARKNESS...

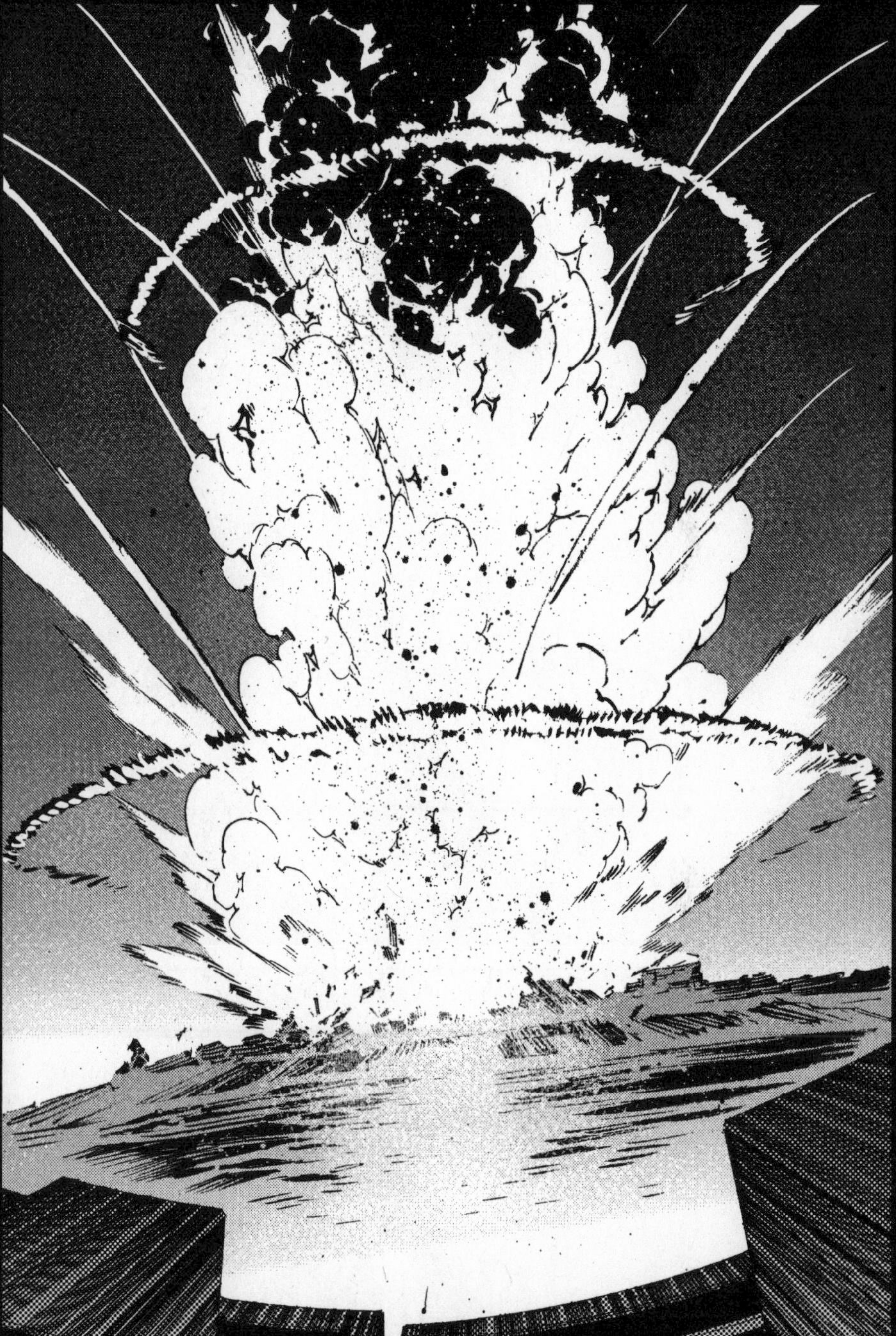

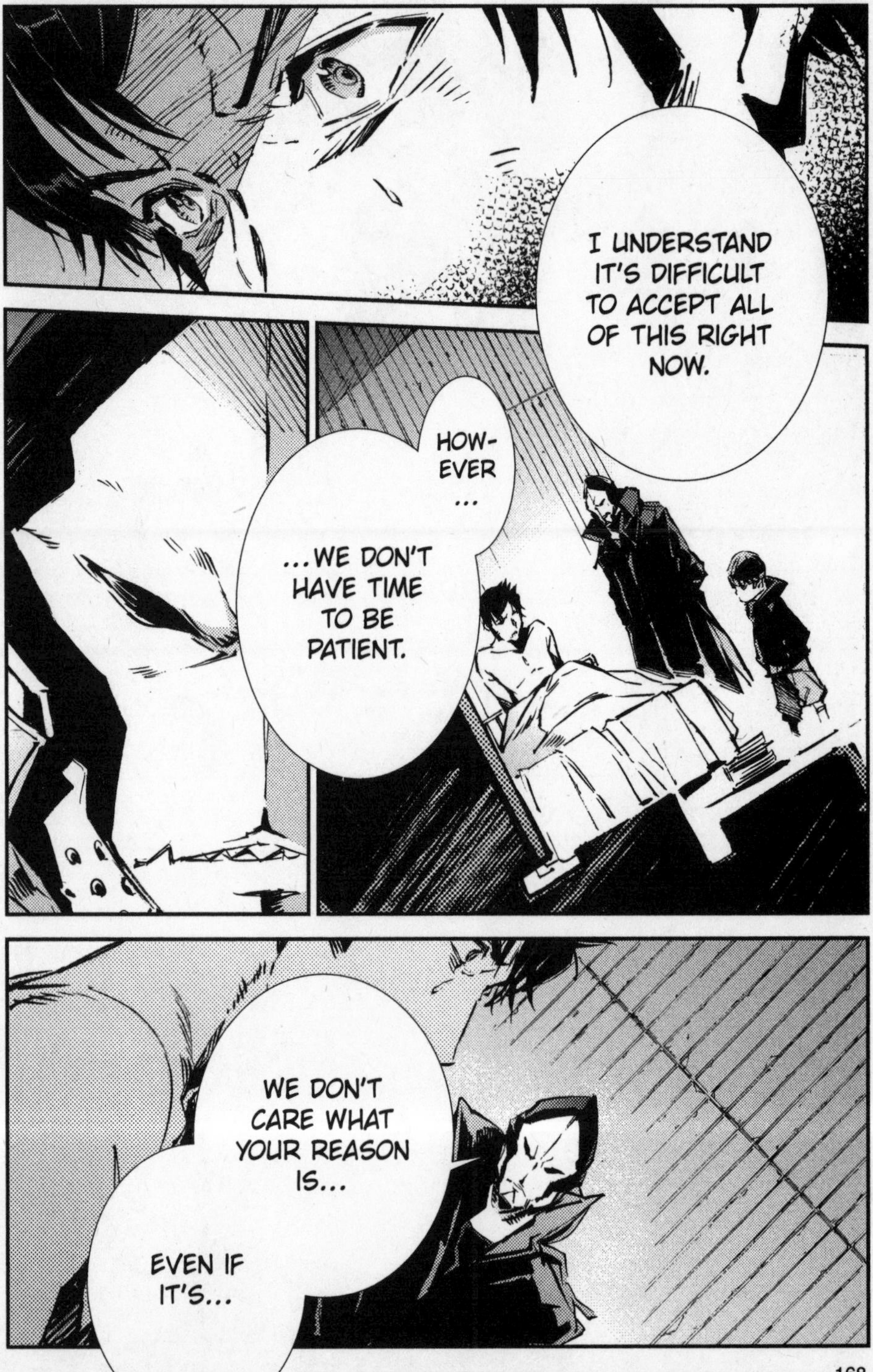
I UNDERSTAND IT'S DIFFICULT TO ACCEPT ALL OF THIS RIGHT NOW.
HOW-EVER ...
...WE DON'T HAVE TIME TO BE PATIENT.
WE DON'T CARE WHAT YOUR REASON IS...
EVEN IF IT'S...

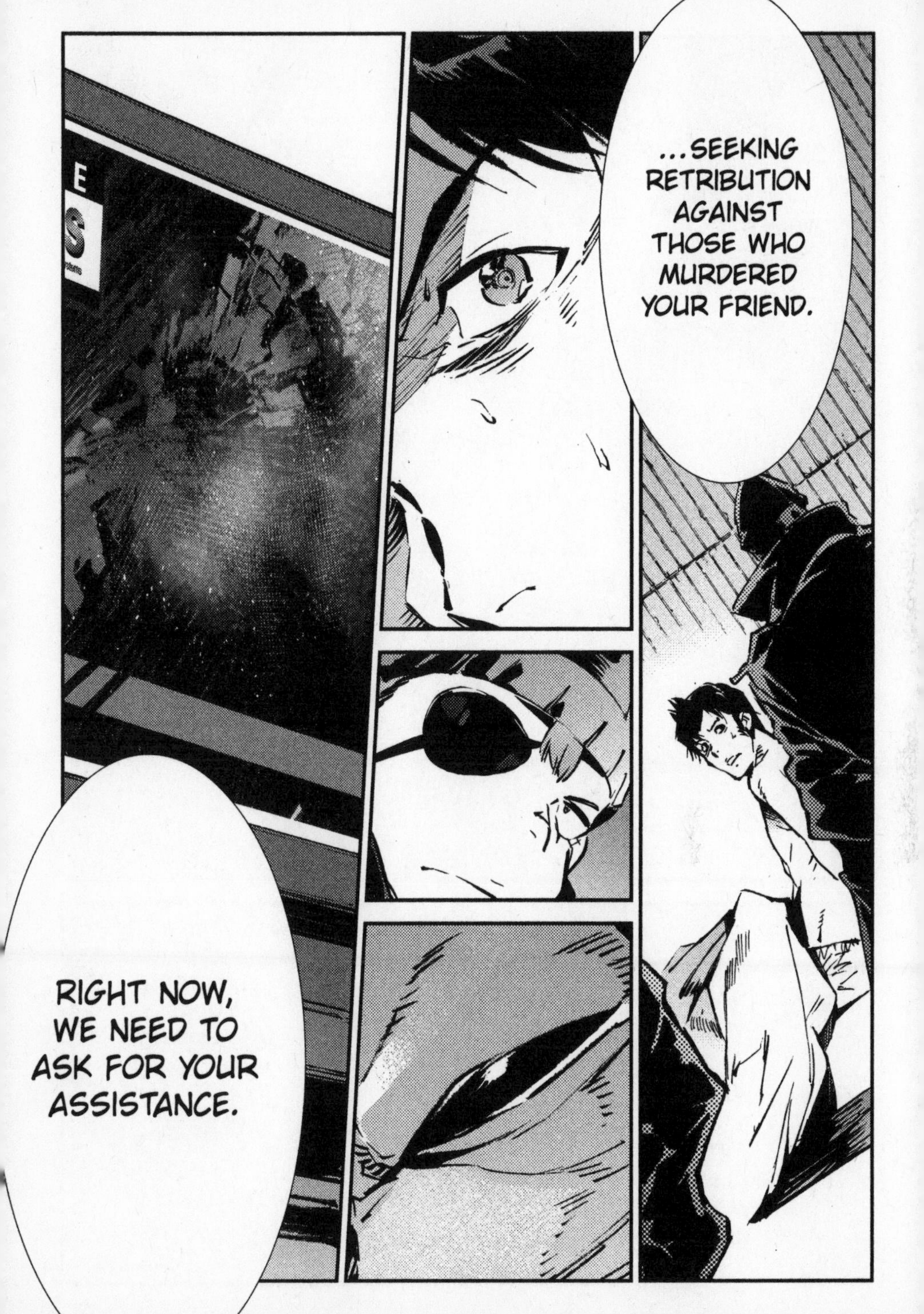
...SEEKING RETRIBUTION AGAINST THOSE WHO MURDERED YOUR FRIEND.
RIGHT NOW, WE NEED TO ASK FOR YOUR ASSISTANCE.

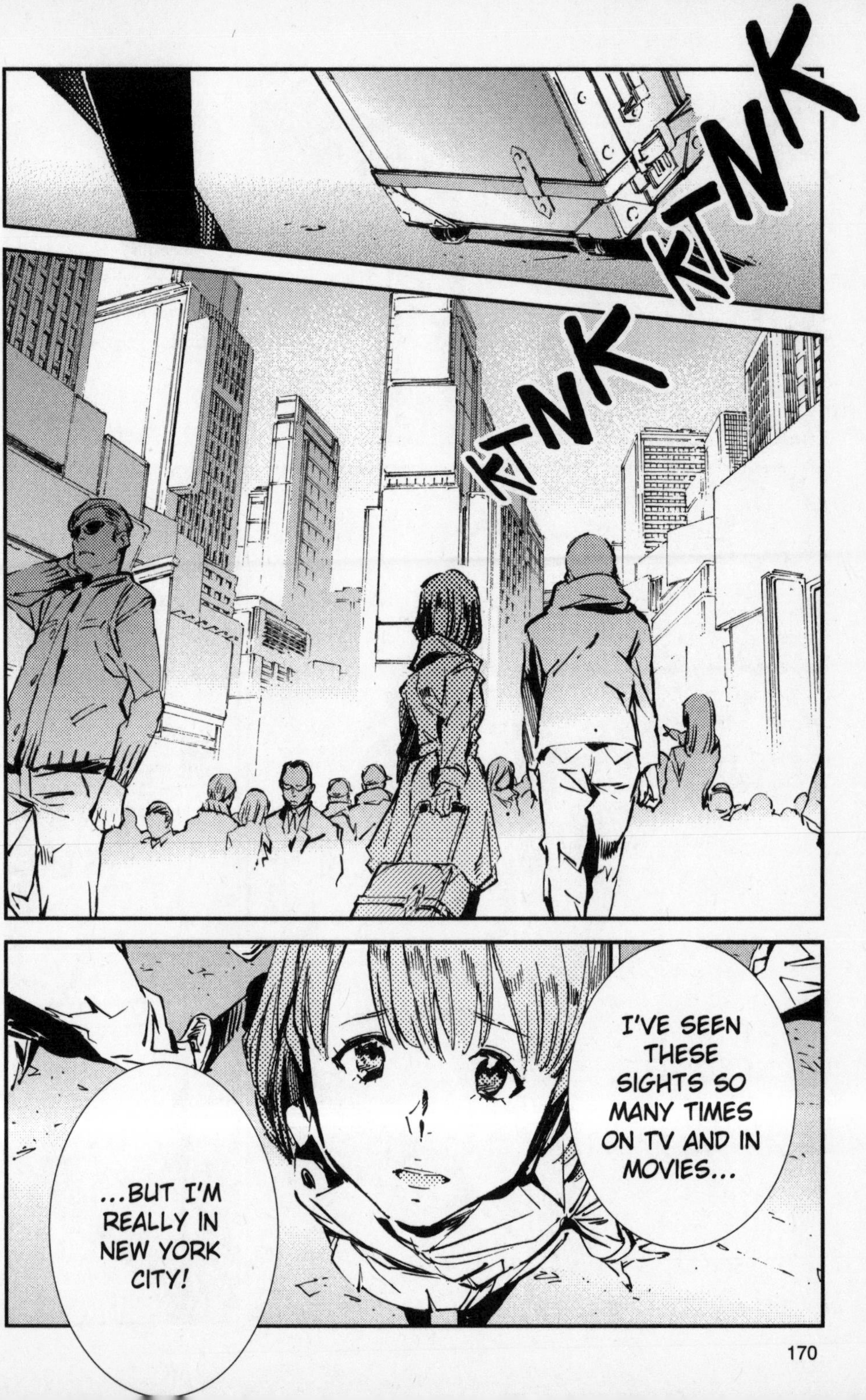
KTNK KTNK
KTNK
I'VE SEEN THESE SIGHTS SO MANY TIMES ON TV AND IN MOVIES...
...BUT I'M REALLY IN NEW YORK CITY!

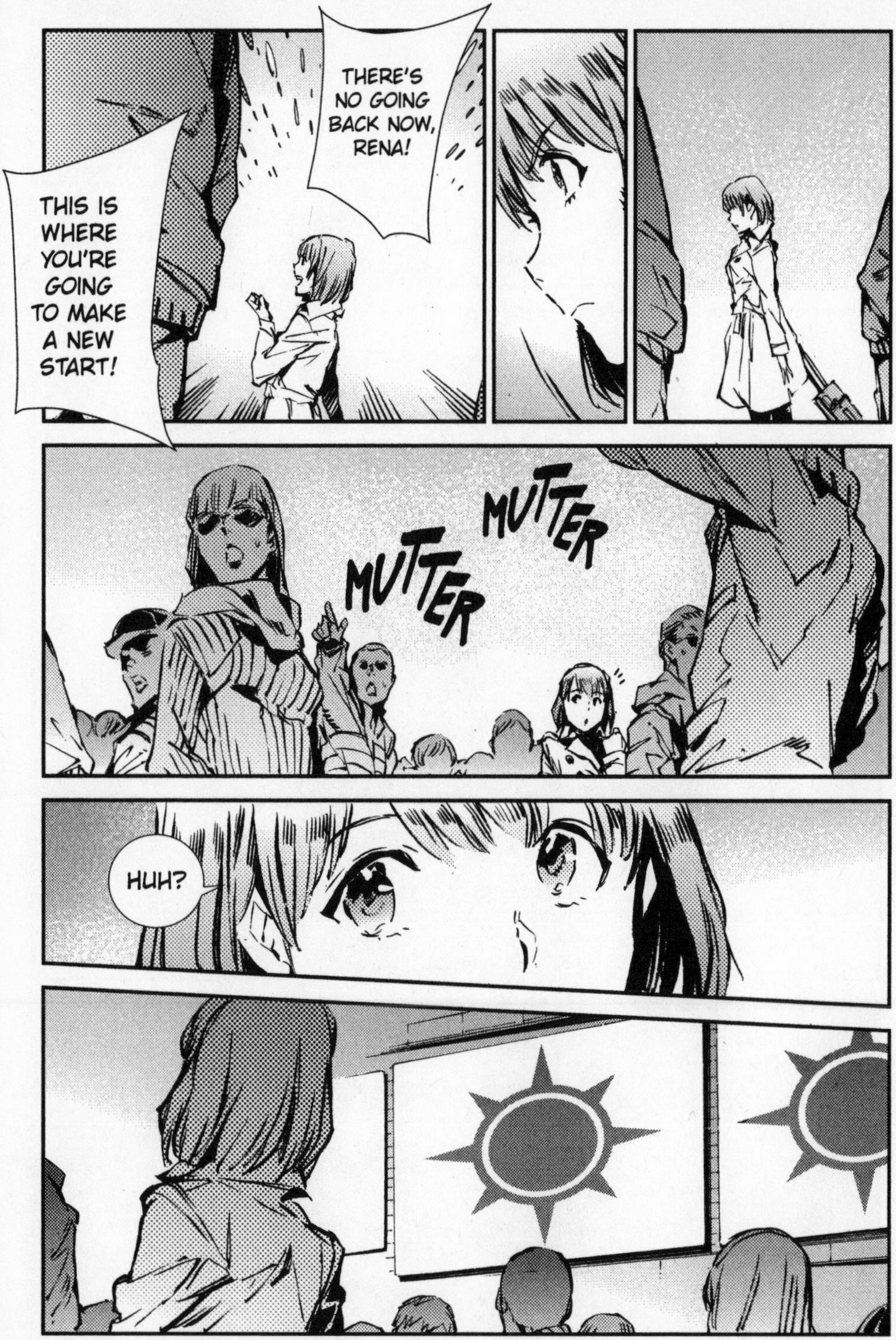
THERE'S NO GOING BACK NOW, RENA!
THIS IS WHERE YOU'RE GOING TO MAKE A NEW START!
MUTTER
MUTTER
HUH?

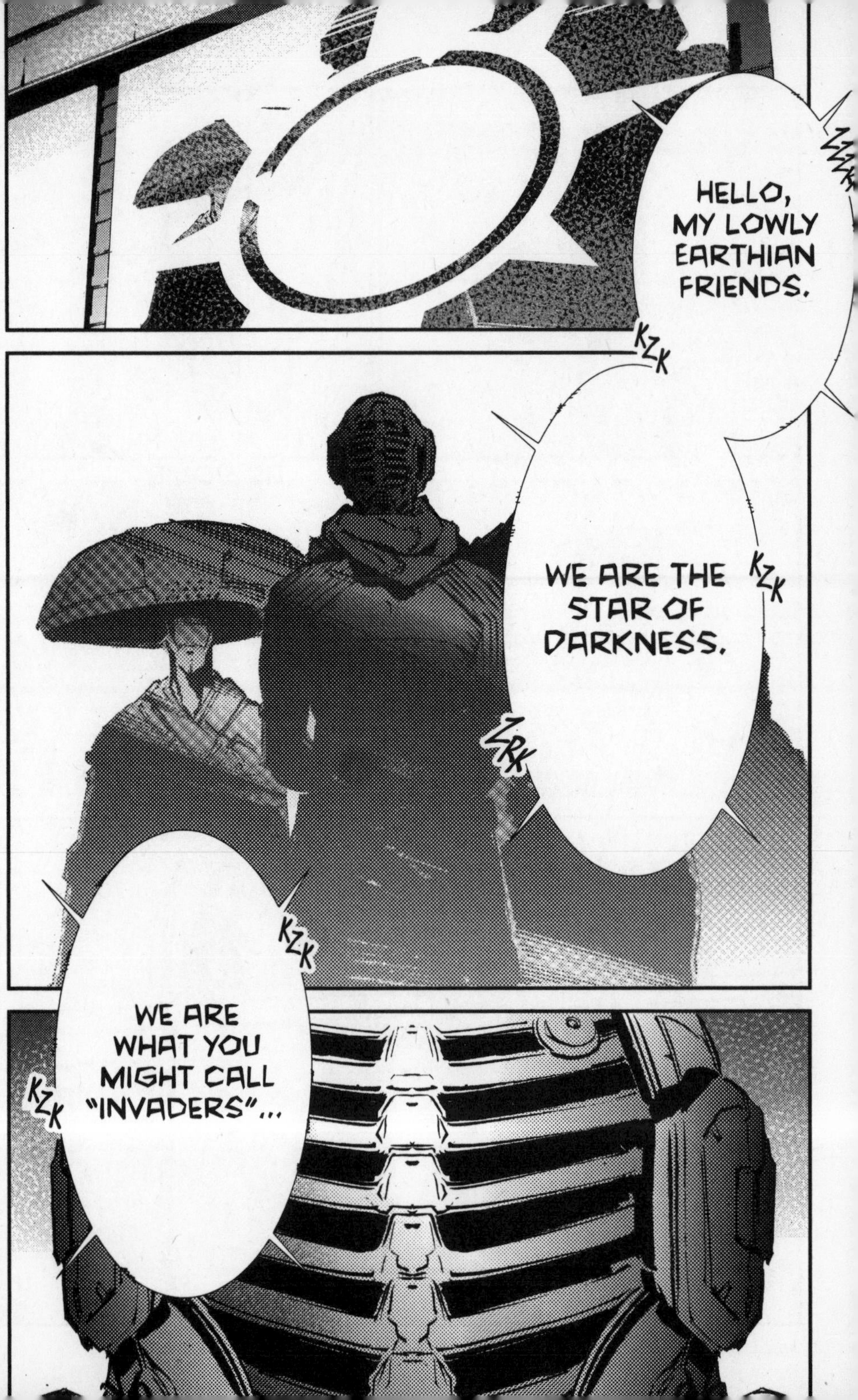
HELLO, MY LOWLY EARTHIAN FRIENDS.
KZK
WE ARE THE STAR OF DARKNESS.
KZK
ZRK
KZK
WE ARE WHAT YOU MIGHT CALL "INVADERS"...
KZK

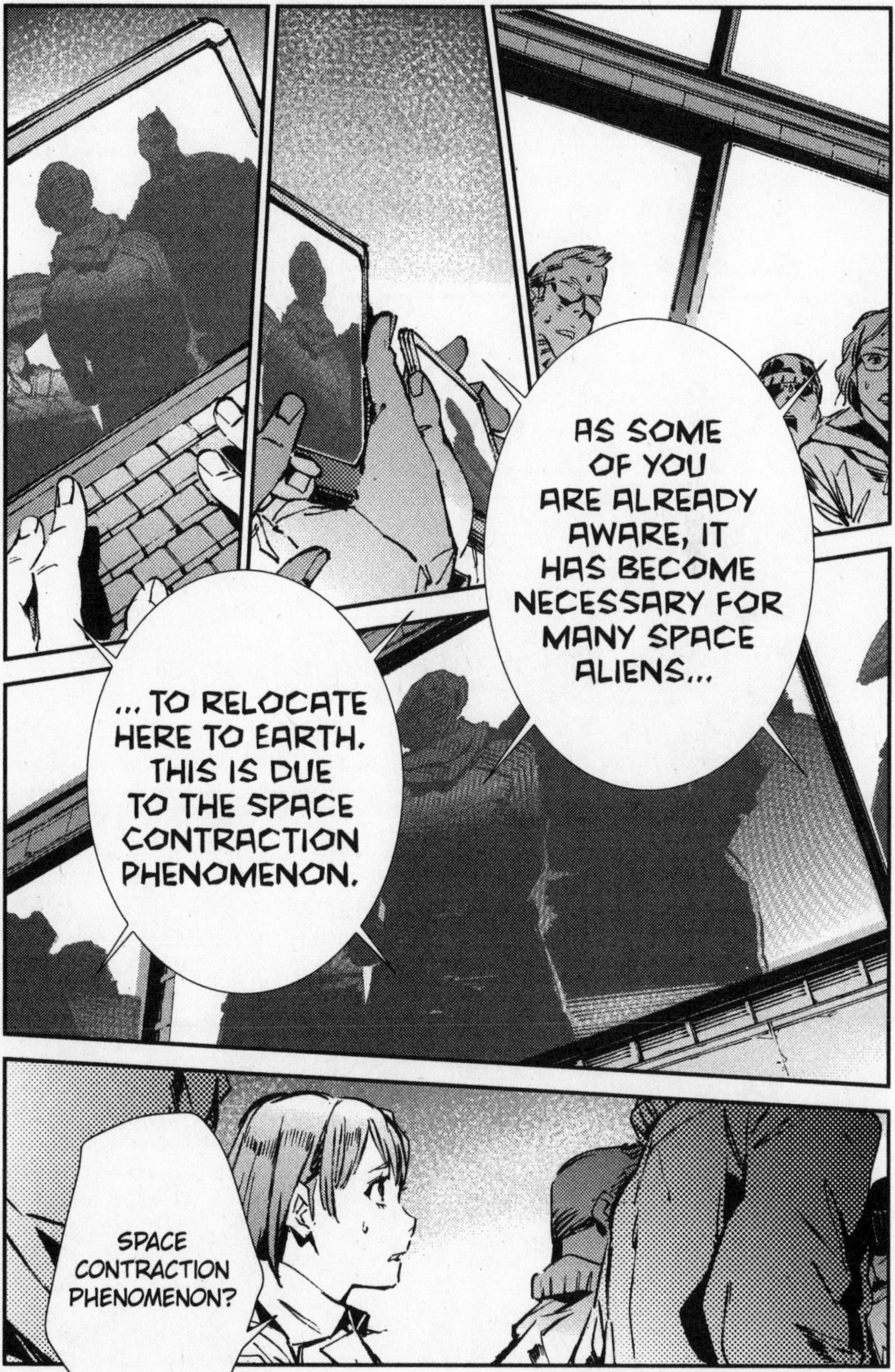
AS SOME OF YOU ARE ALREADY AWARE, IT HAS BECOME NECESSARY FOR MANY SPACE ALIENS...
...TO RELOCATE HERE TO EARTH. THIS IS DUE TO THE SPACE CONTRACTION PHENOMENON.
SPACE CONTRACTION PHENOMENON?

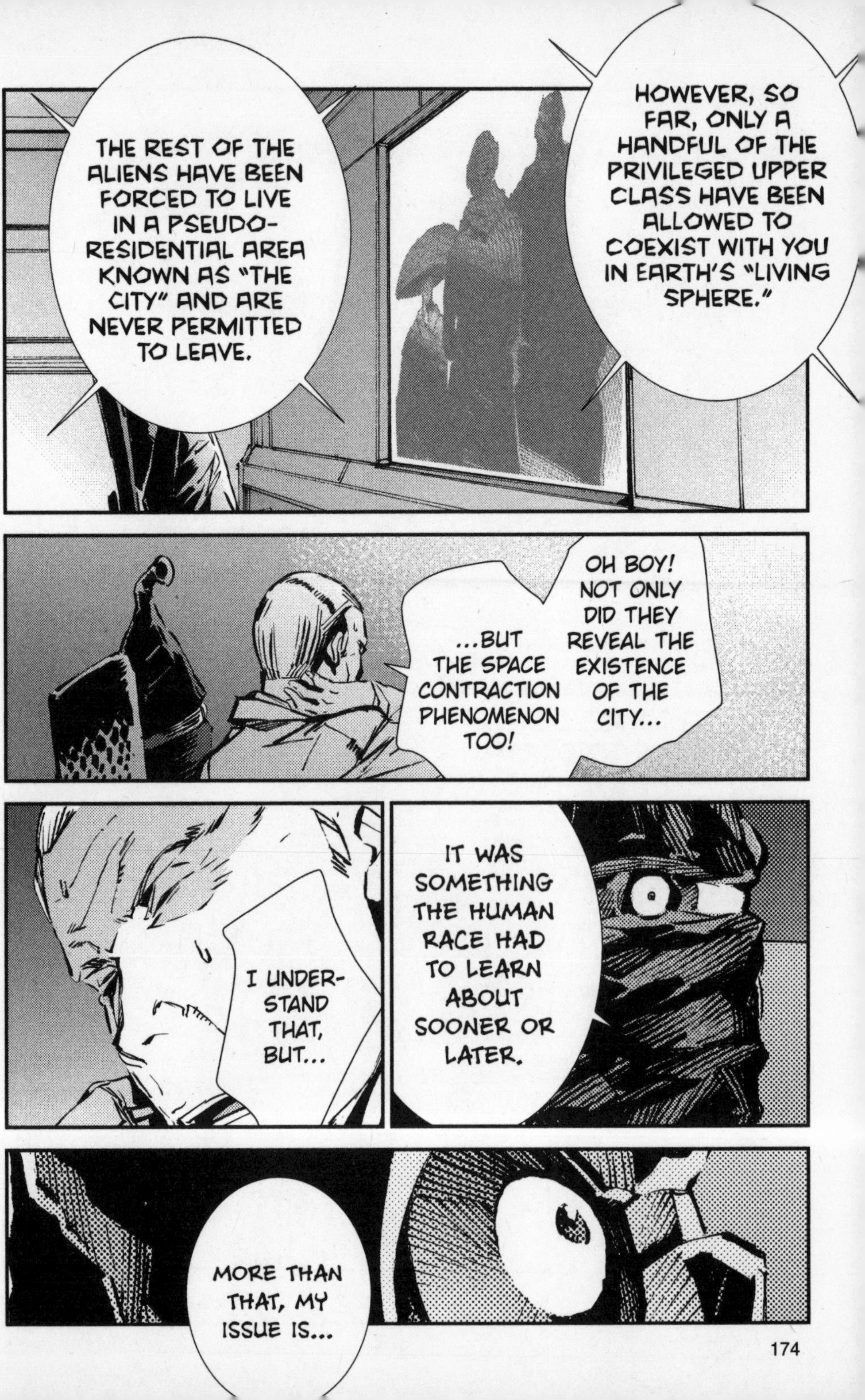
HOWEVER, SO FAR, ONLY A HANDFUL OF THE PRIVILEGED UPPER CLASS HAVE BEEN ALLOWED TO COEXIST WITH YOU IN EARTH'S "LIVING SPHERE."
THE REST OF THE ALIENS HAVE BEEN FORCED TO LIVE IN A PSEUDO-RESIDENTIAL AREA KNOWN AS "THE CITY" AND ARE NEVER PERMITTED TO LEAVE.
OH BOY! NOT ONLY DID THEY REVEAL THE EXISTENCE OF THE CITY...
...BUT THE SPACE CONTRACTION PHENOMENON TOO!
IT WAS SOMETHING THE HUMAN RACE HAD TO LEARN ABOUT SOONER OR LATER.
I UNDER-STAND THAT, BUT...
MORE THAN THAT, MY ISSUE IS...

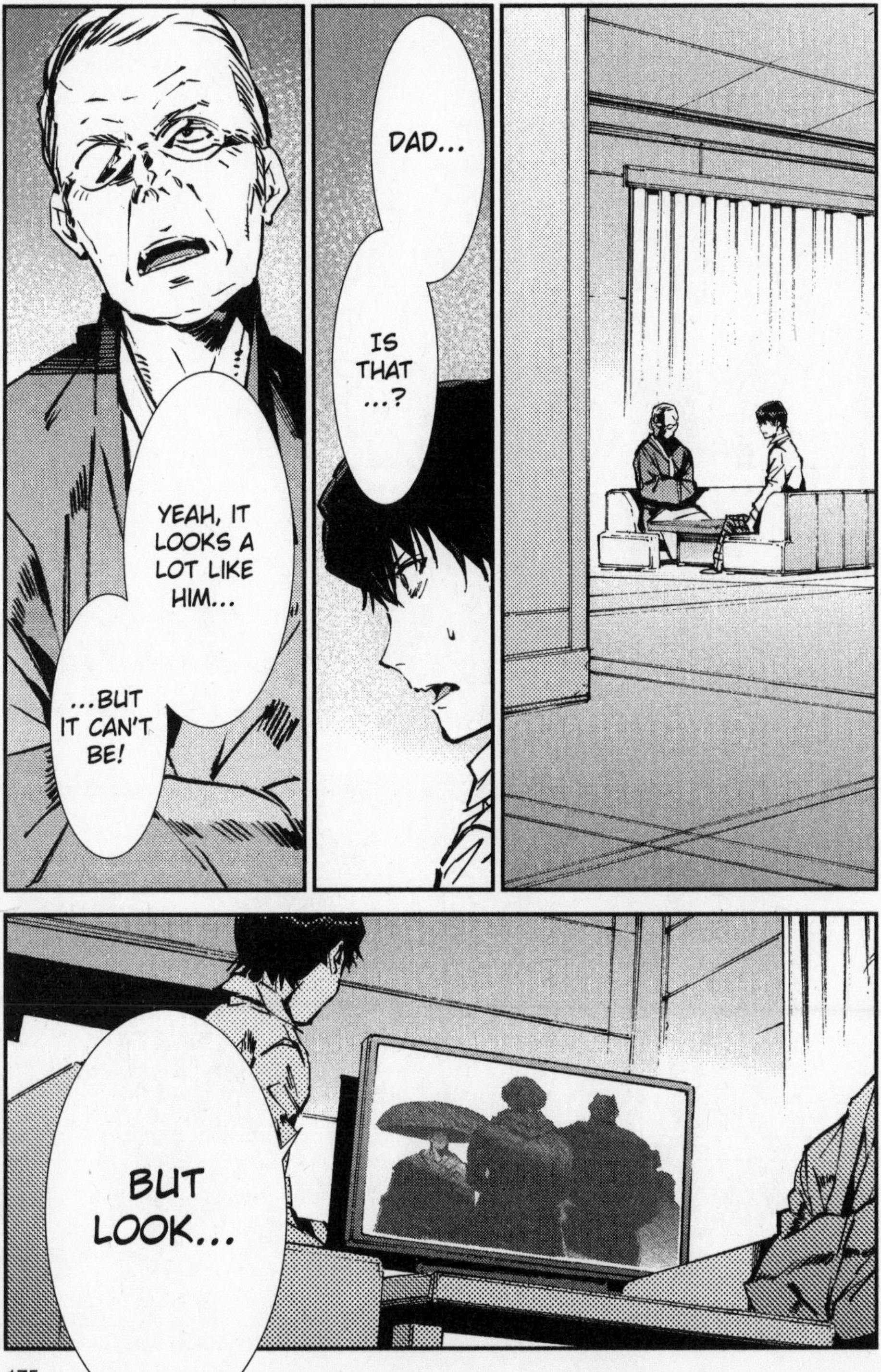
DAD...
IS THAT ...?
YEAH, IT LOOKS A LOT LIKE HIM...
...BUT IT CAN'T BE!
BUT LOOK...

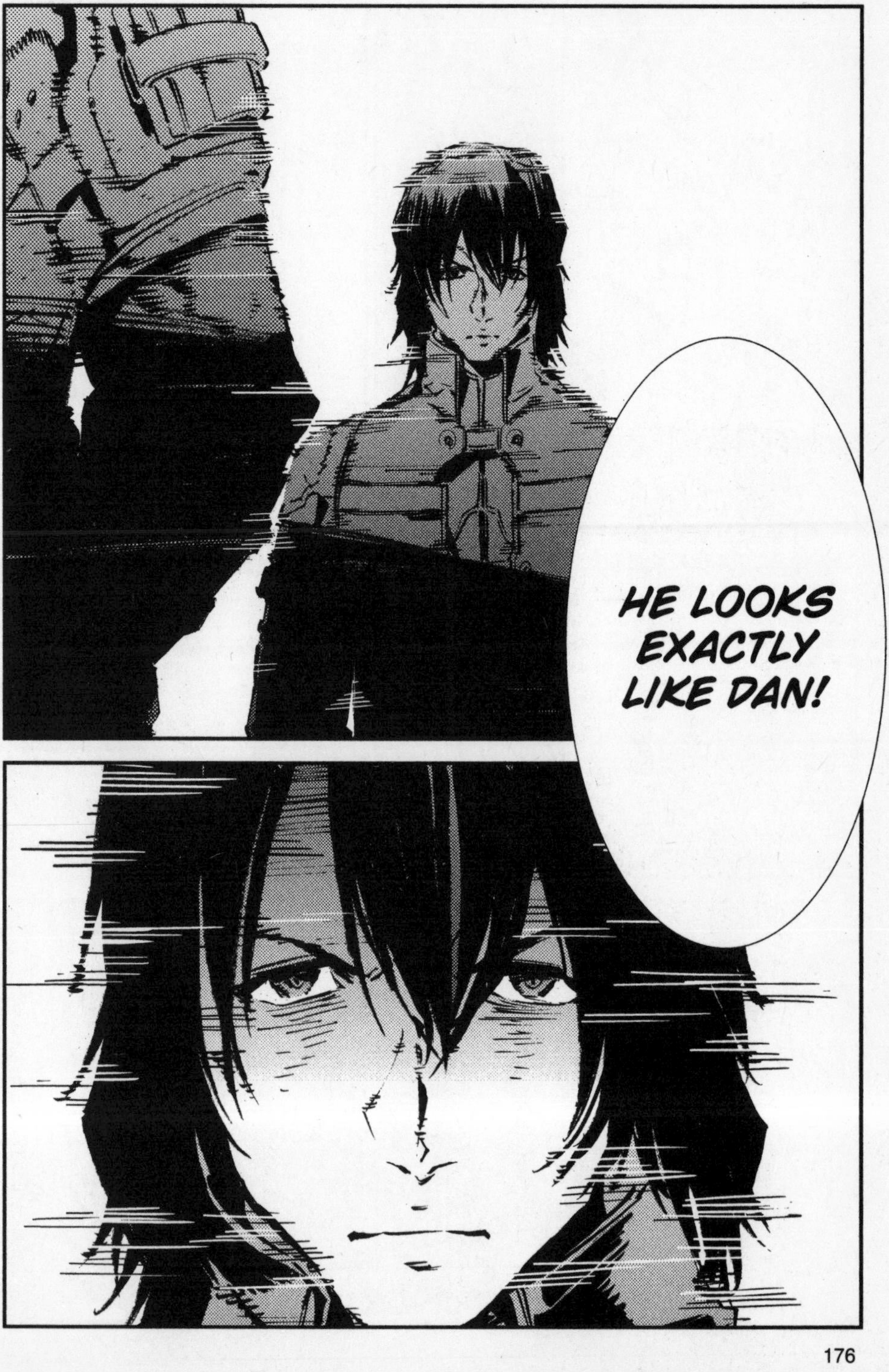
HE LOOKS EXACTLY LIKE DAN!

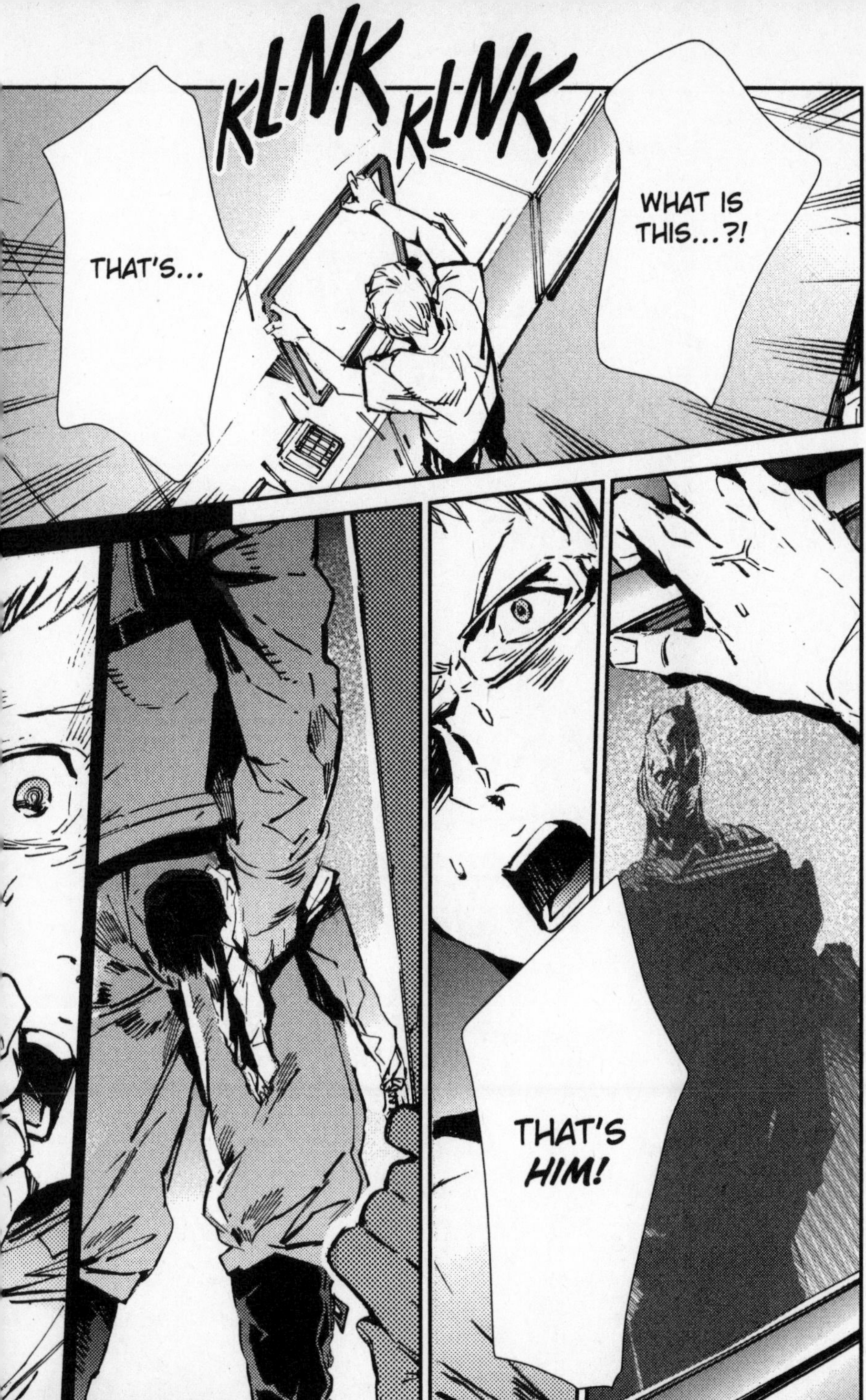
KLNK KLNK
WHAT IS THIS...?!
THAT'S...
THAT'S *HIM!*

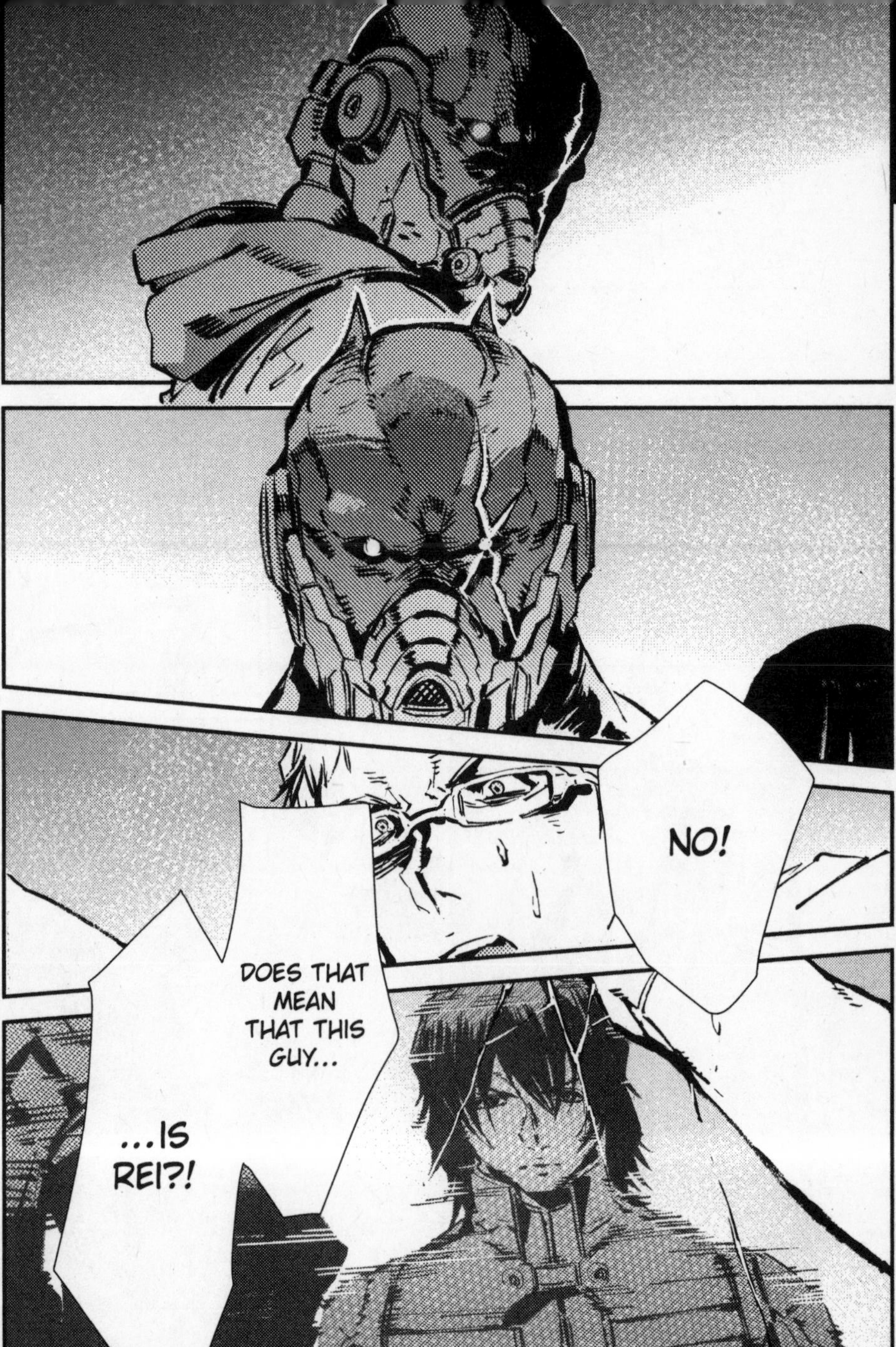
NO!
DOES THAT MEAN THAT THIS GUY...
...IS REI?!

YOU EARTHIANS... *ARE MORONS!*

I WILL STOP SPEAKING SO OMINOUSLY AND SAY IT PLAINLY LIKE YOU EARTHIANS WOULD.

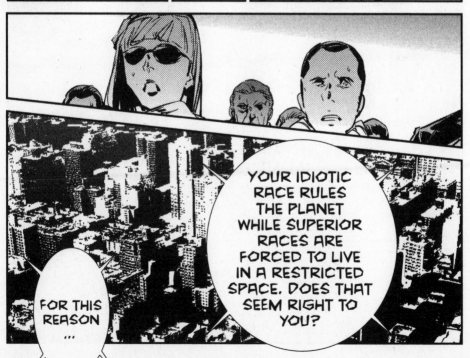

YOUR IDIOTIC RACE RULES THE PLANET WHILE SUPERIOR RACES ARE FORCED TO LIVE IN A RESTRICTED SPACE. DOES THAT SEEM RIGHT TO YOU?

FOR THIS REASON ...

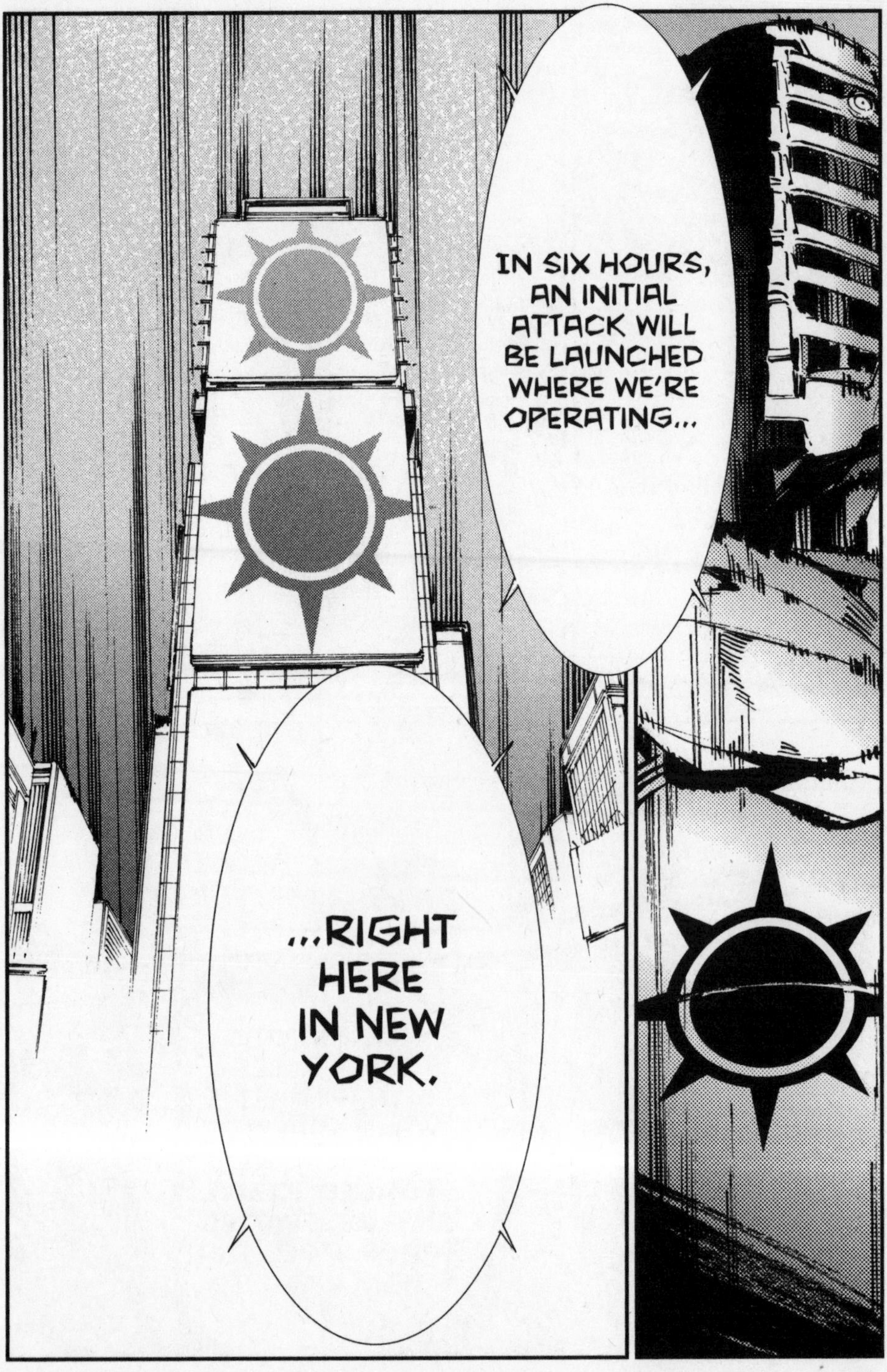
IN SIX HOURS, AN INITIAL ATTACK WILL BE LAUNCHED WHERE WE'RE OPERATING...
...RIGHT HERE IN NEW YORK.

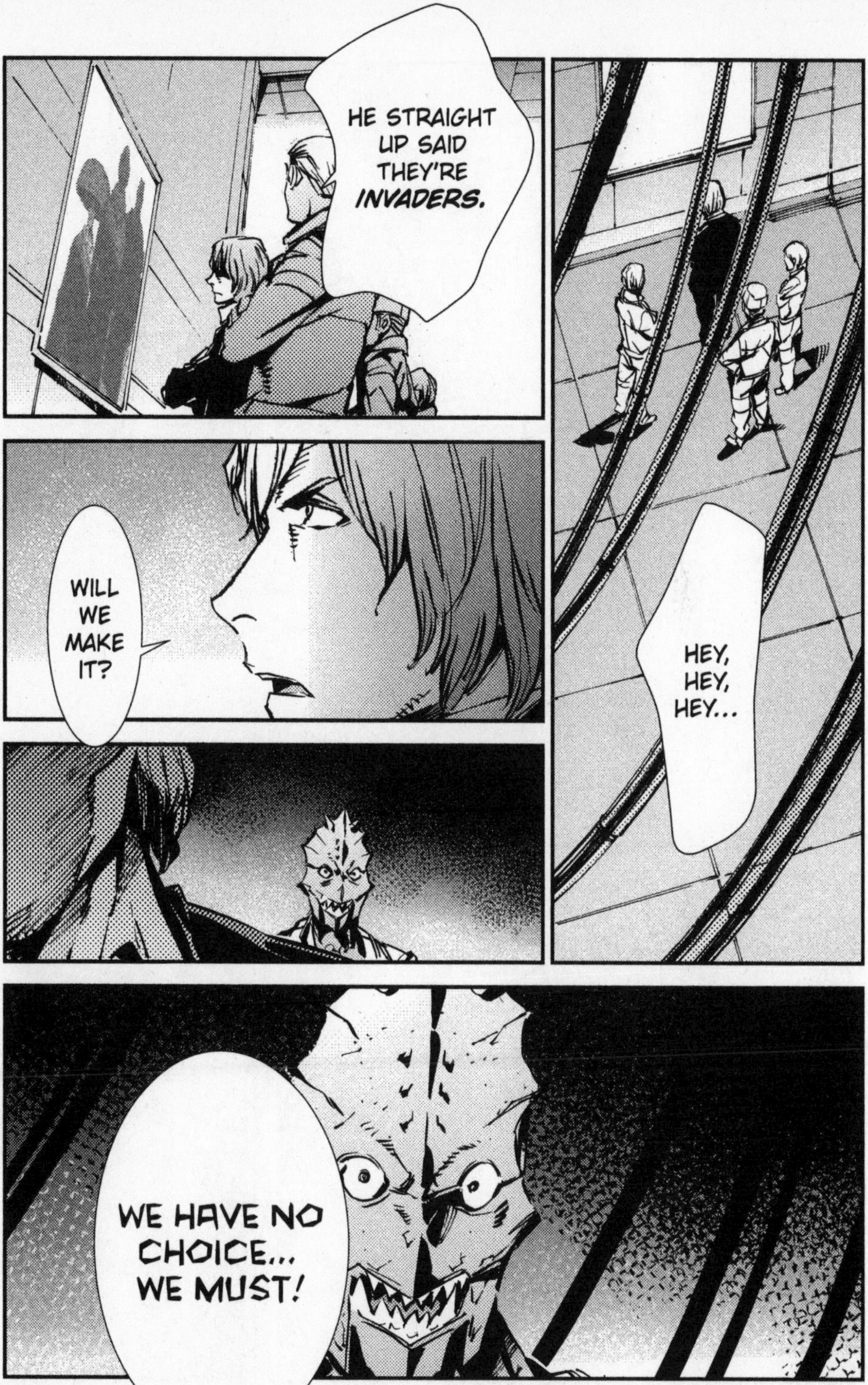
HEY, HEY, HEY...
HE STRAIGHT UP SAID THEY'RE *INVADERS.*
WILL WE MAKE IT?
WE HAVE NO CHOICE... WE MUST!

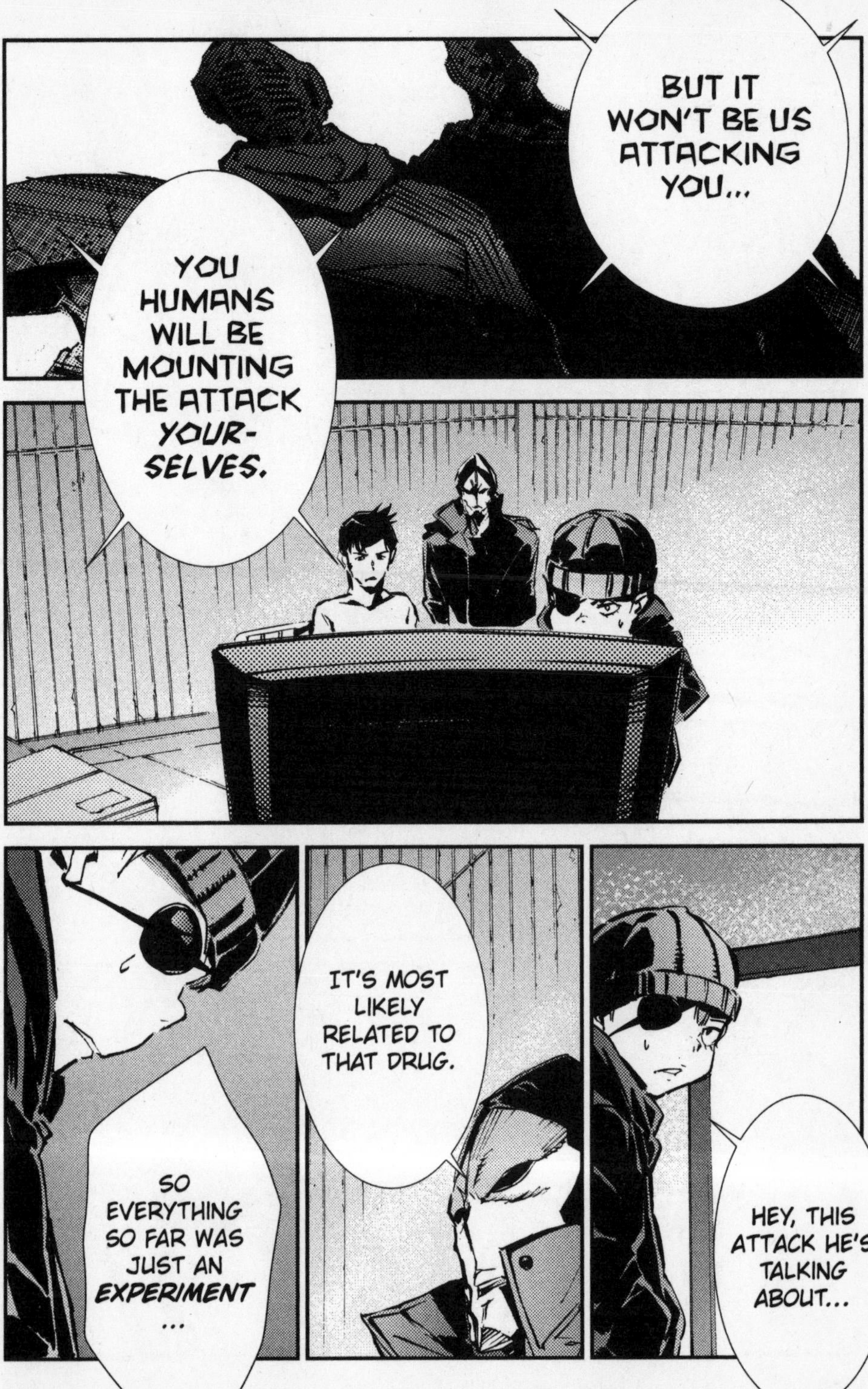
BUT IT WON'T BE US ATTACKING YOU...
YOU HUMANS WILL BE MOUNTING THE ATTACK *YOUR-SELVES.*
HEY, THIS ATTACK HE'S TALKING ABOUT...
IT'S MOST LIKELY RELATED TO THAT DRUG.
SO EVERYTHING SO FAR WAS JUST AN *EXPERIMENT* ...

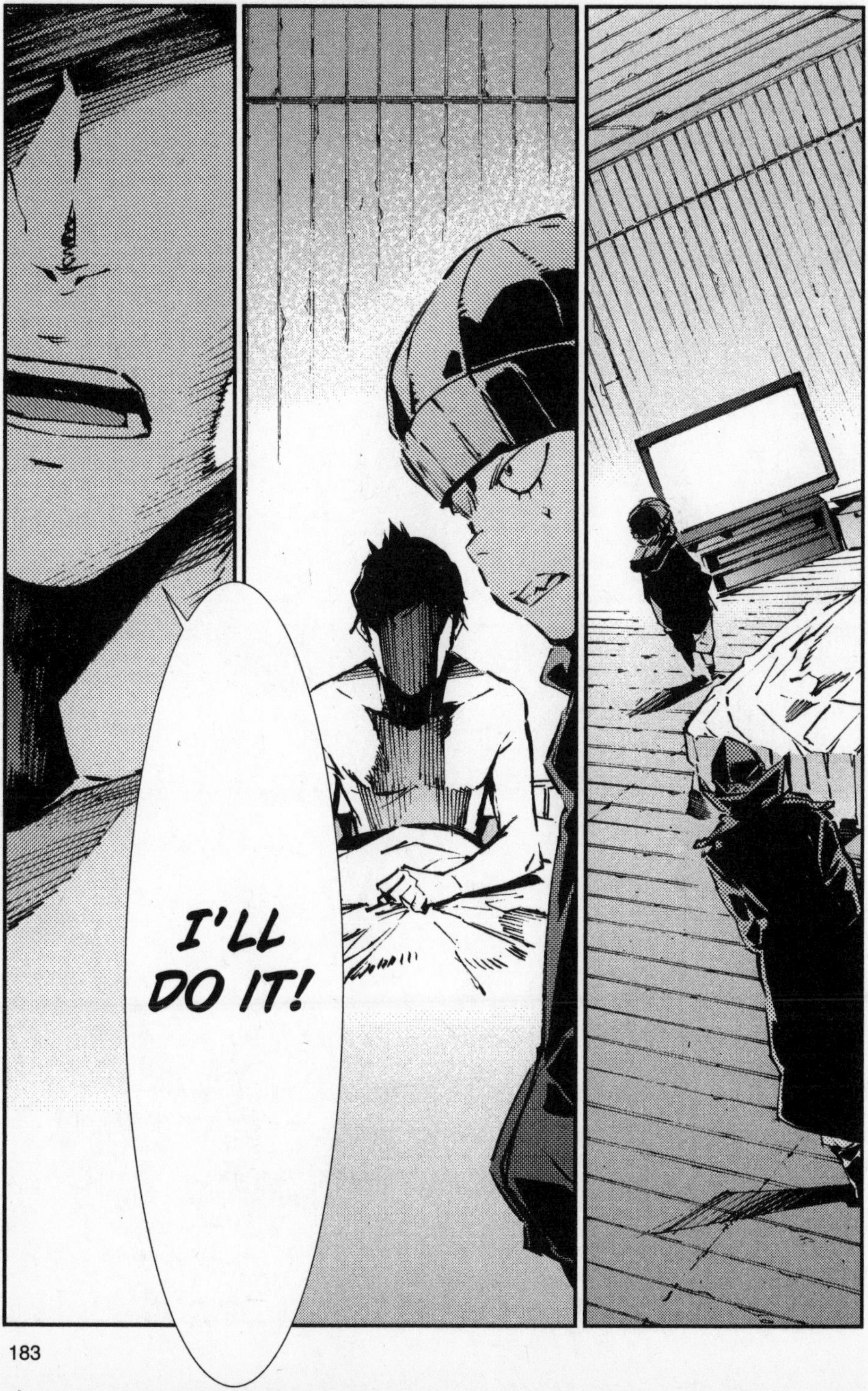
I'LL DO IT!

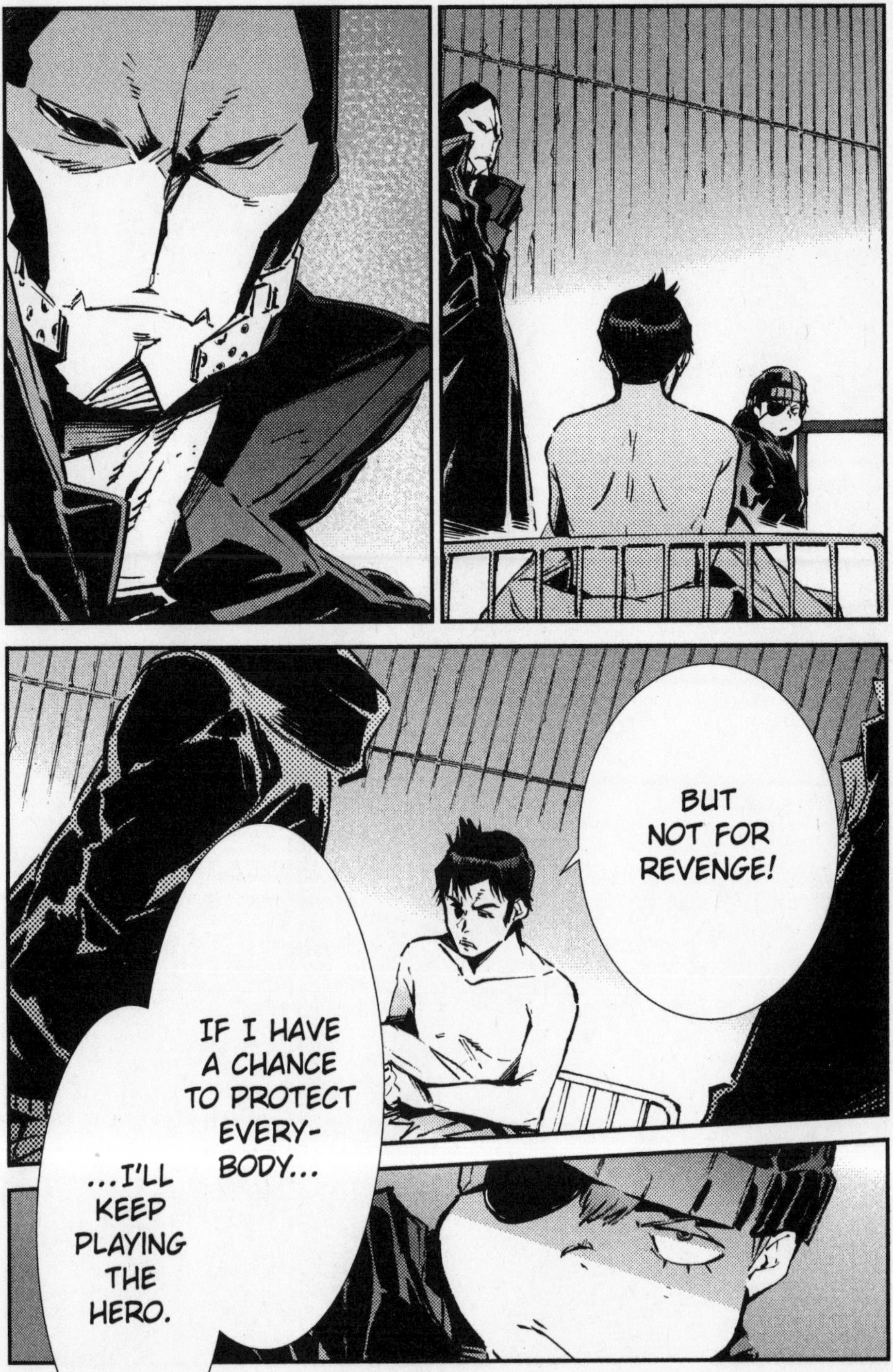
BUT NOT FOR REVENGE!
IF I HAVE A CHANCE TO PROTECT EVERY-BODY...
...I'LL KEEP PLAYING THE HERO.

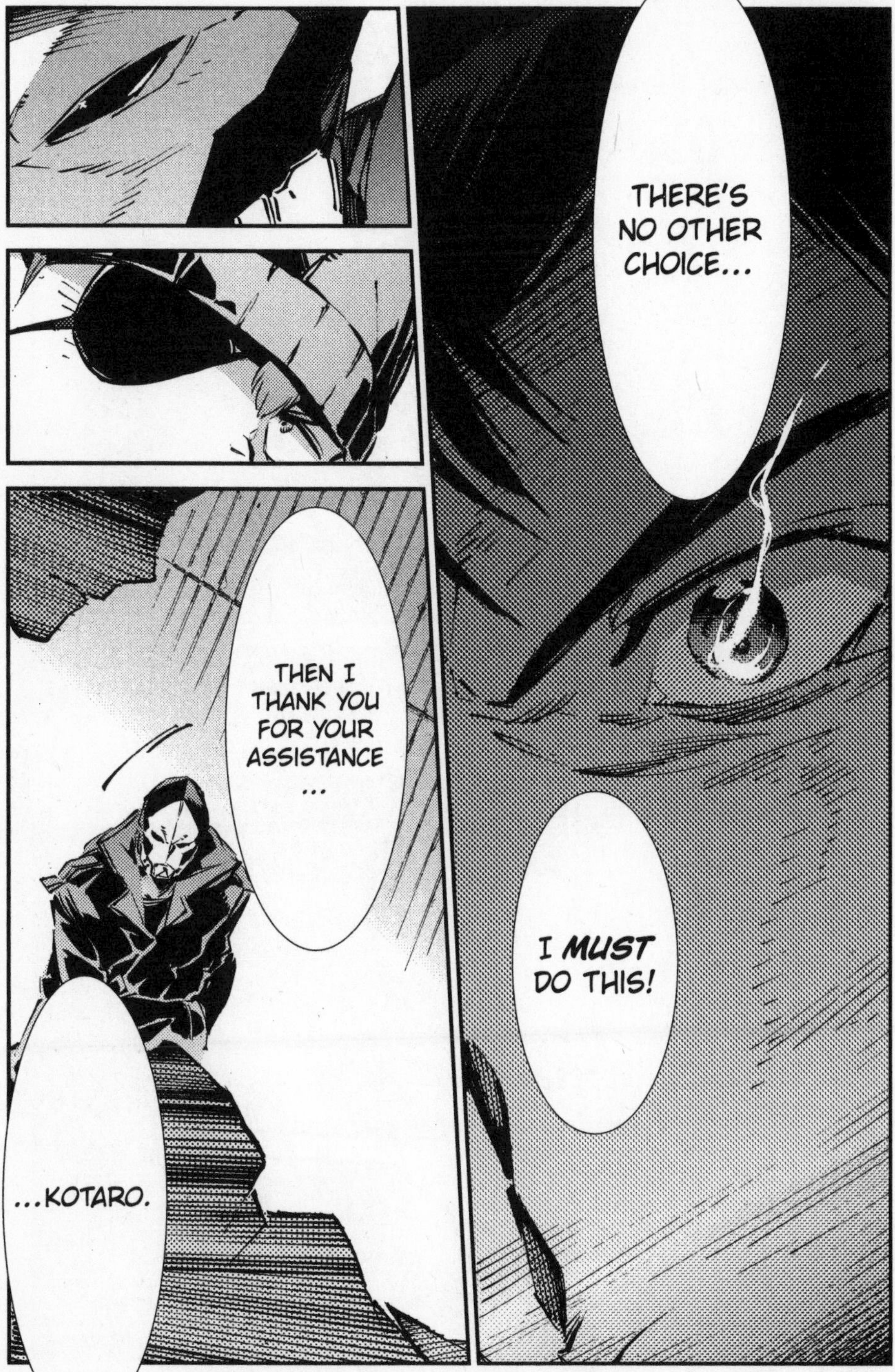
THERE'S NO OTHER CHOICE...
I *MUST* DO THIS!
THEN I THANK YOU FOR YOUR ASSISTANCE ...
...KOTARO.

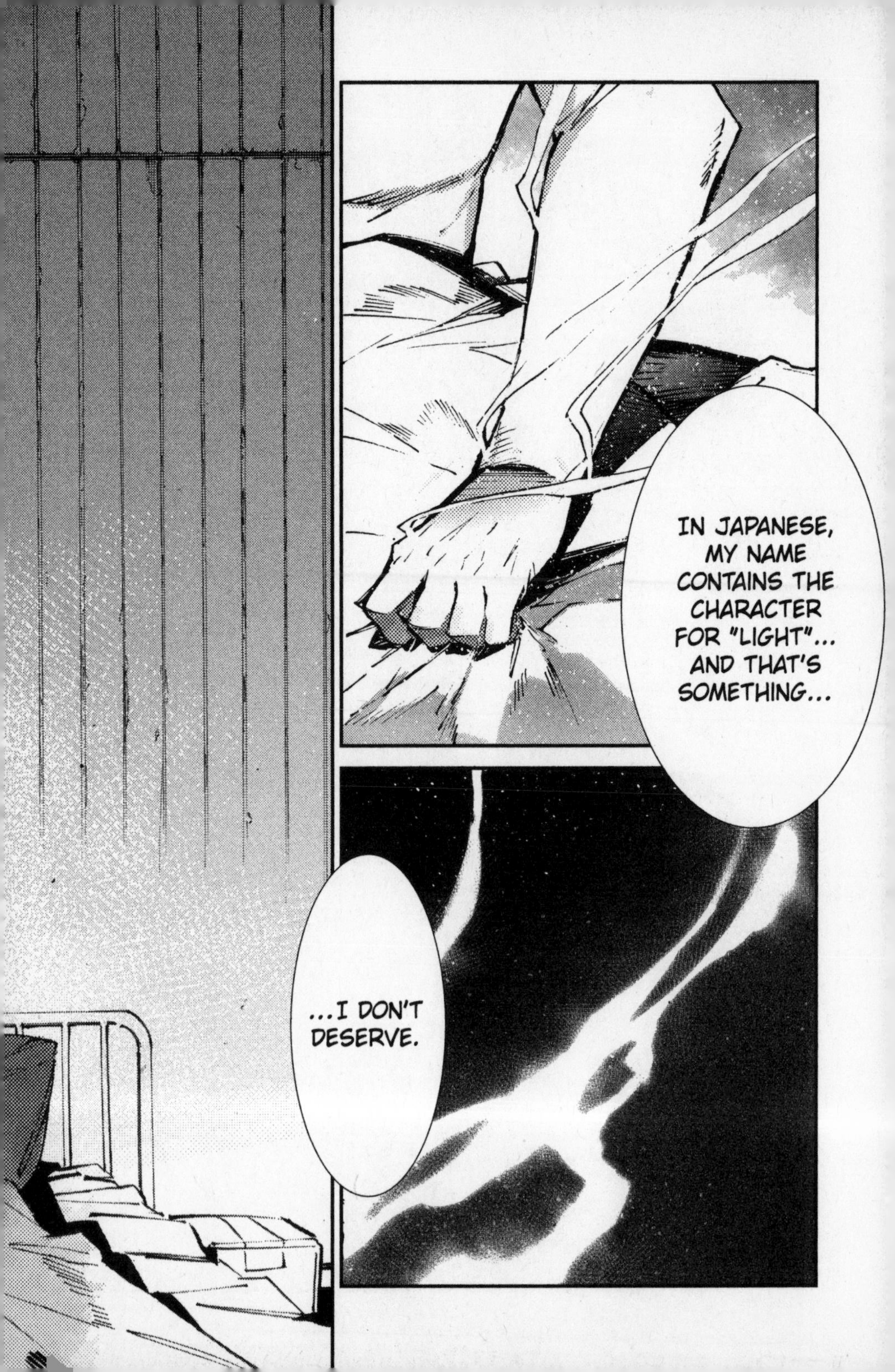
IN JAPANESE, MY NAME CONTAINS THE CHARACTER FOR "LIGHT"... AND THAT'S SOMETHING...
...I DON'T DESERVE.

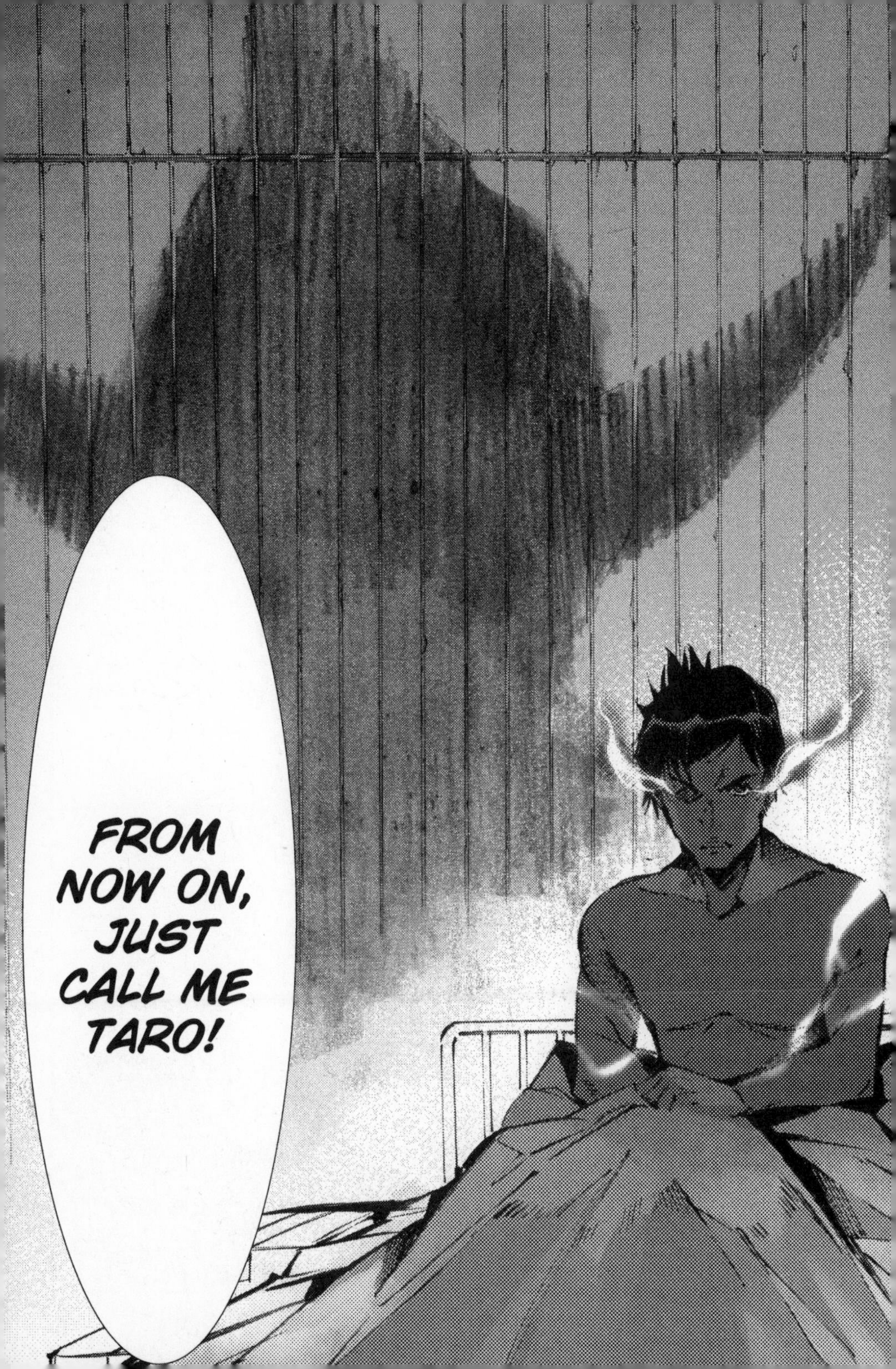
FROM NOW ON, JUST CALL ME TARO!

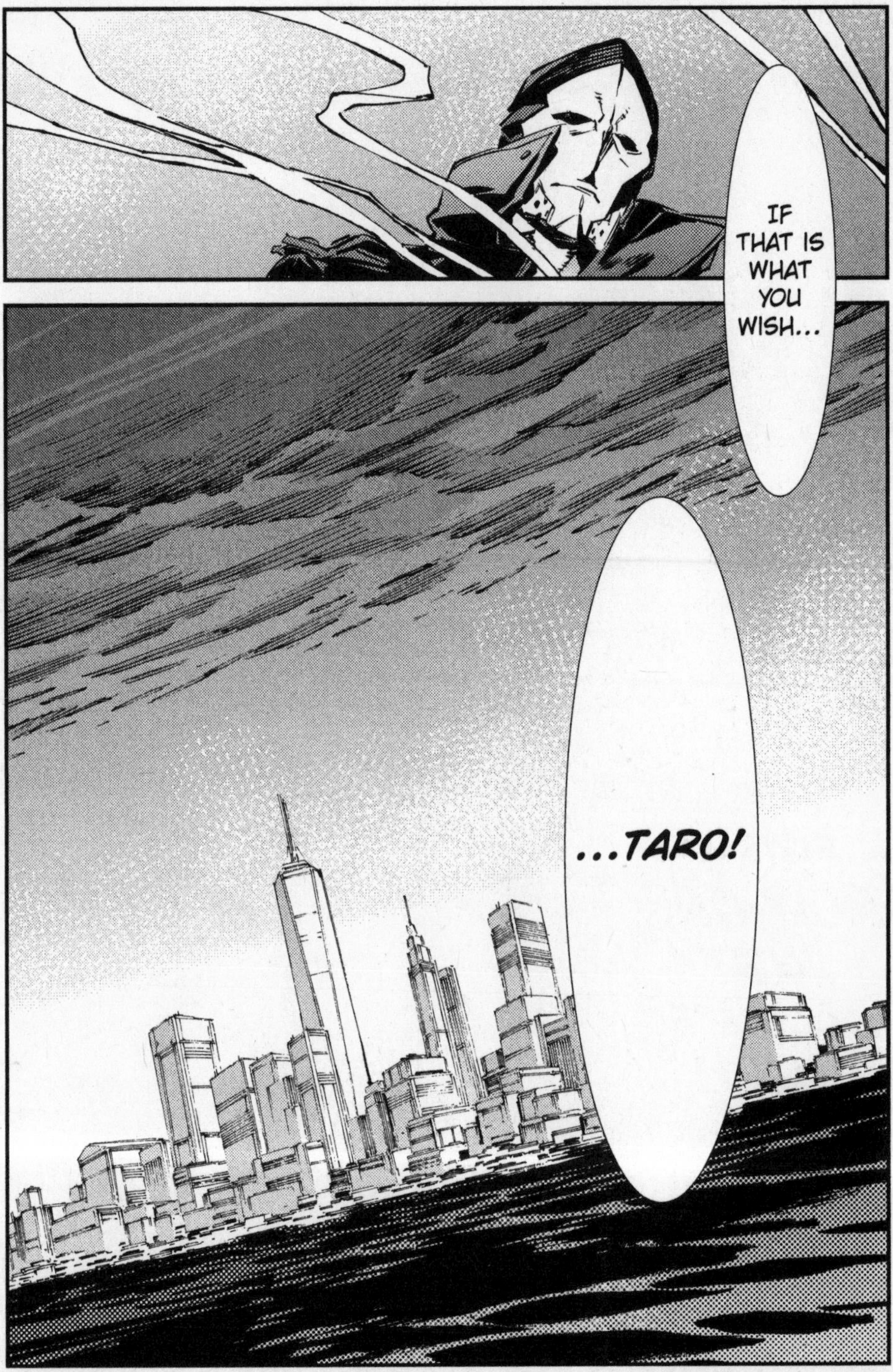
IF THAT IS WHAT YOU WISH...
...TARO!

ULTRAMAN 9 - END

THIS IS THE BEGINNING OF A NEW AGE

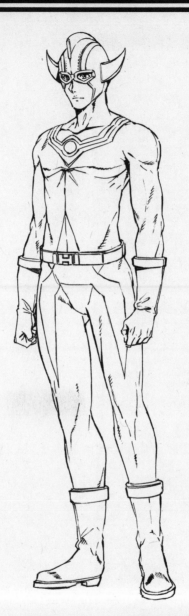

■ A suit designed to be reminiscent of Ultraman, handmade by Kotaro. The horns were added on either side to make him appear stronger. Reportedly, he considers this the highlight of the suit. Of course, the suit itself has no special functions. It is simply made to Kotaro's taste and to hide his identity. (People can still tell he is Asian, however.)

■ A member of an extremely brutal race that joined the Star of Darkness because it had plans of its own to conquer Earth. It can be said that the Star of Darkness is more dangerous than the mercenaries led by Ace Killer because it holds to a similar elitist philosophy.

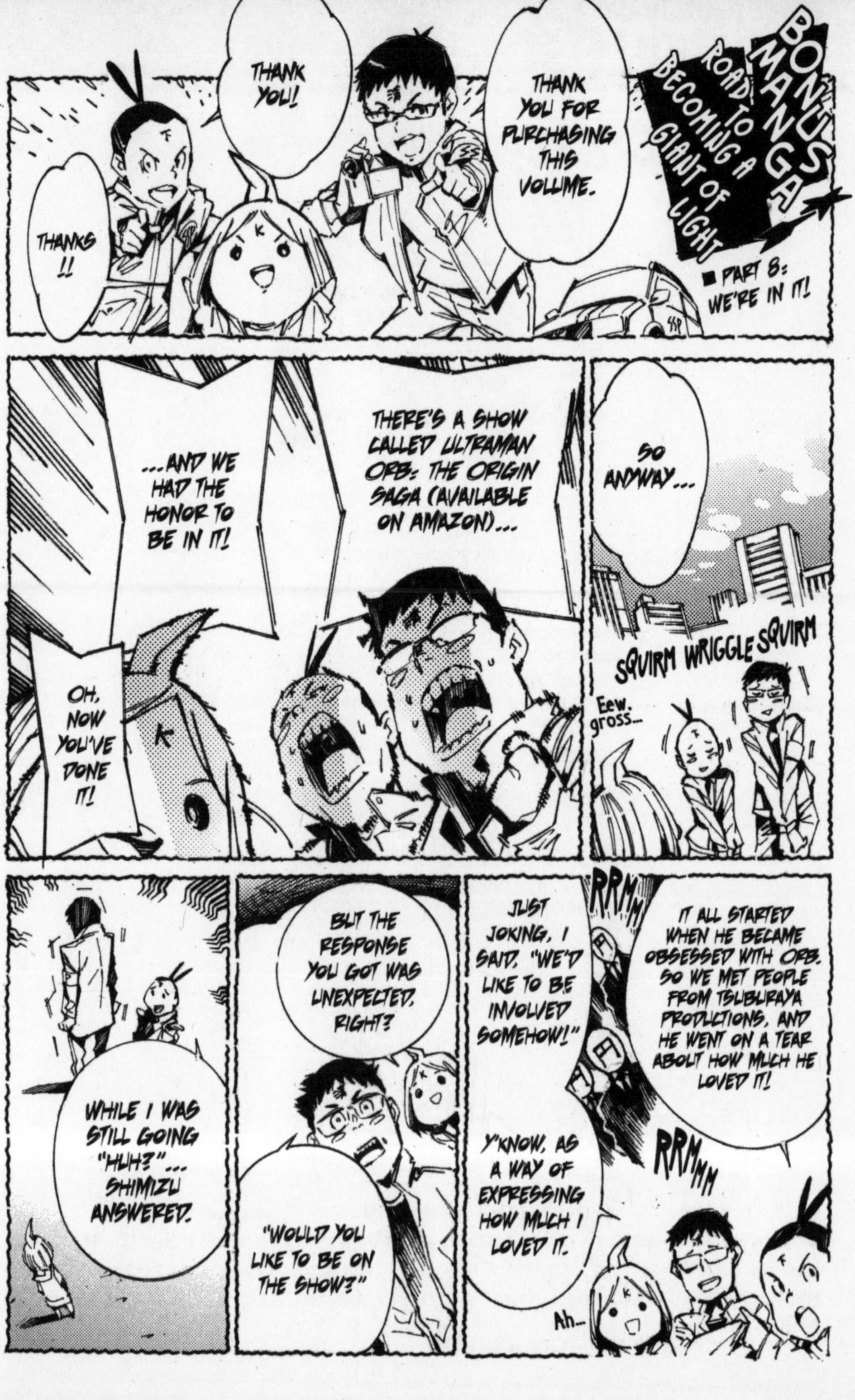
BONUS MANGA
ROAD TO BECOMING A GIANT OF LIGHT
■ PART 8: WE'RE IN IT!
THANK YOU FOR PURCHASING THIS VOLUME.
THANK YOU!
THANKS!!
SO ANYWAY...
SQUIRM WRIGGLE SQUIRM
Eew. gross...
THERE'S A SHOW CALLED ULTRAMAN ORB: THE ORIGIN SAGA (AVAILABLE ON AMAZON)...
...AND WE HAD THE HONOR TO BE IN IT!
OH, NOW YOU'VE DONE IT!
IT ALL STARTED WHEN HE BECAME OBSESSED WITH ORB. SO WE MET PEOPLE FROM TSUBURAYA PRODUCTIONS, AND HE WENT ON A TEAR ABOUT HOW MUCH HE LOVED IT!
RRMMM
JUST JOKING, I SAID, "WE'D LIKE TO BE INVOLVED SOMEHOW!"
Y'KNOW, AS A WAY OF EXPRESSING HOW MUCH I LOVED IT.
RRMMMM
Ah...
BUT THE RESPONSE YOU GOT WAS UNEXPECTED, RIGHT?
"WOULD YOU LIKE TO BE ON THE SHOW?"
WHILE I WAS STILL GOING "HUH?"... SHIMIZU ANSWERED.

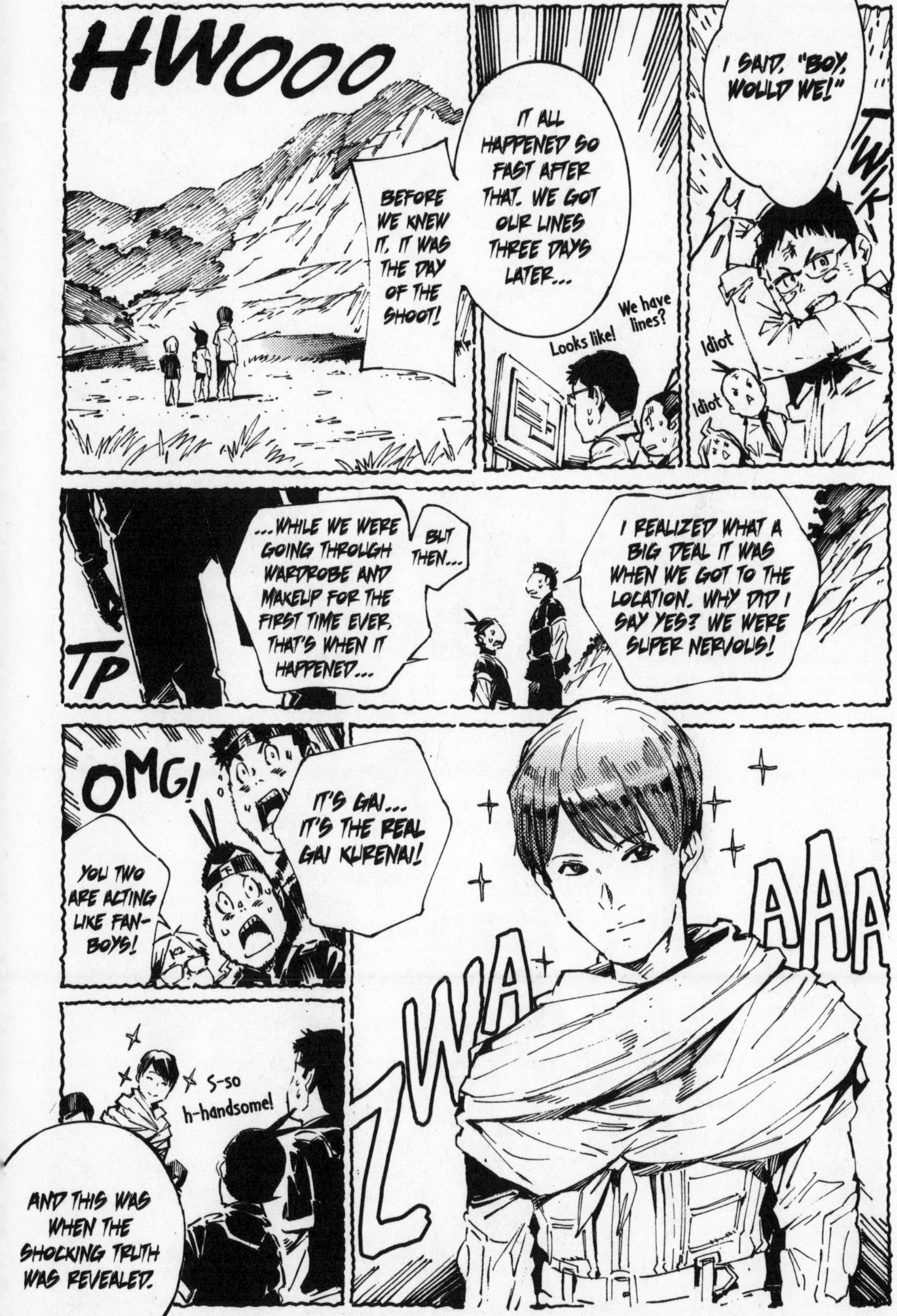
I SAID, "BOY, WOULD WE!"
TWIK
Idiot
Idiot
IT ALL HAPPENED SO FAST AFTER THAT. WE GOT OUR LINES THREE DAYS LATER...
We have lines?
Looks like!
BEFORE WE KNEW IT, IT WAS THE DAY OF THE SHOOT!
HWOOO
I REALIZED WHAT A BIG DEAL IT WAS WHEN WE GOT TO THE LOCATION. WHY DID I SAY YES? WE WERE SUPER NERVOUS!
BUT THEN...
...WHILE WE WERE GOING THROUGH WARDROBE AND MAKEUP FOR THE FIRST TIME EVER, THAT'S WHEN IT HAPPENED...
TP
ZWAAAA
OMG!
IT'S GAI... IT'S THE REAL GAI KURENAI!
YOU TWO ARE ACTING LIKE FAN-BOYS!
S-so h-handsome!
AND THIS WAS WHEN THE SHOCKING TRUTH WAS REVEALED.

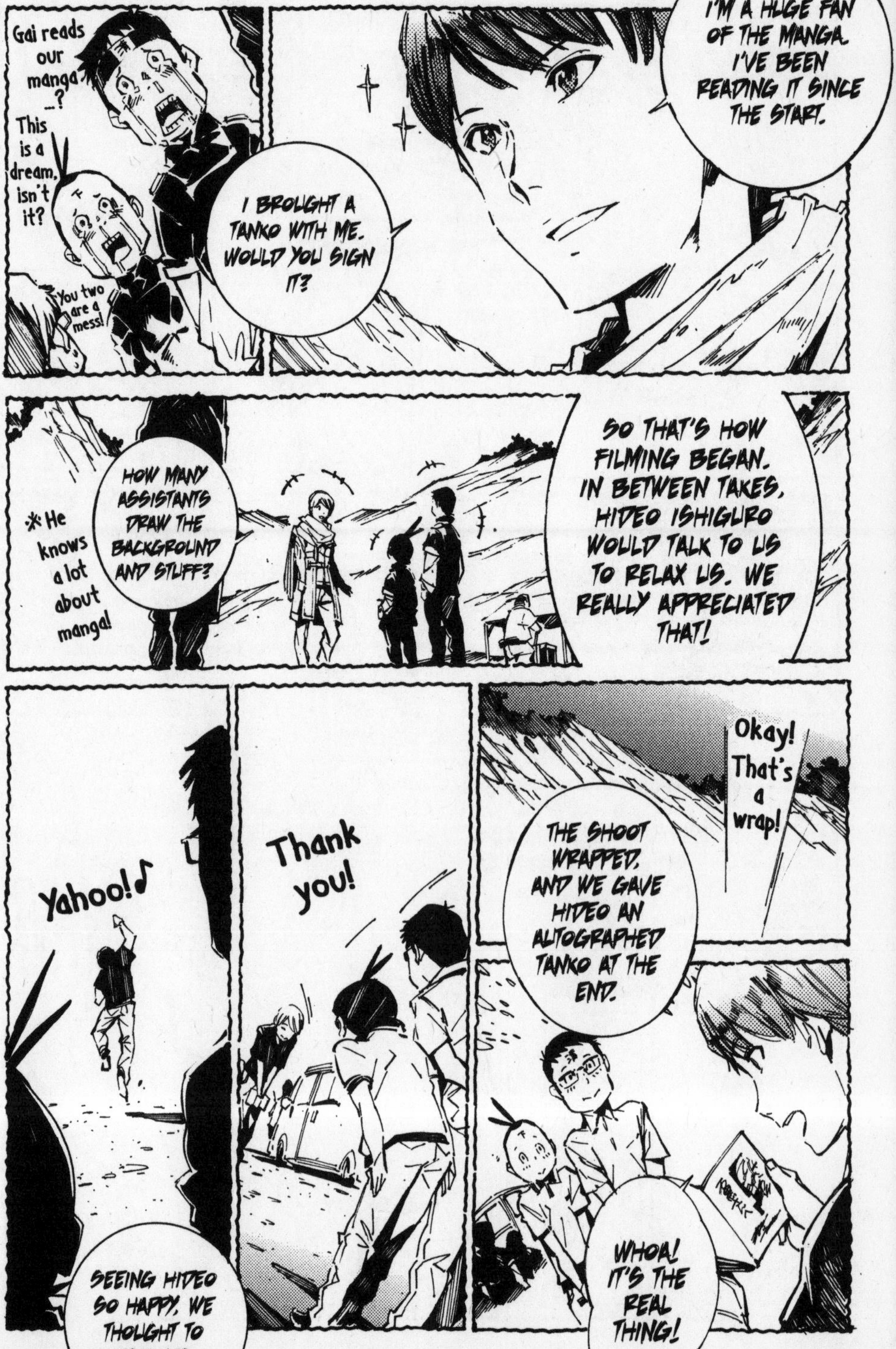
I'M A HUGE FAN OF THE MANGA. I'VE BEEN READING IT SINCE THE START.
I BROUGHT A TANKO WITH ME. WOULD YOU SIGN IT?
Gai reads our manga...?
This is a dream, isn't it?
You two are a mess!
SO THAT'S HOW FILMING BEGAN. IN BETWEEN TAKES, HIDEO ISHIGURO WOULD TALK TO US TO RELAX US. WE REALLY APPRECIATED THAT!
HOW MANY ASSISTANTS DRAW THE BACKGROUND AND STUFF?
※He knows a lot about manga!
Okay! That's a wrap!
THE SHOOT WRAPPED, AND WE GAVE HIDEO AN AUTOGRAPHED TANKO AT THE END.
WHOA! IT'S THE REAL THING!
Thank you!
Yahoo!♪
SEEING HIDEO SO HAPPY, WE THOUGHT TO OURSELVES...

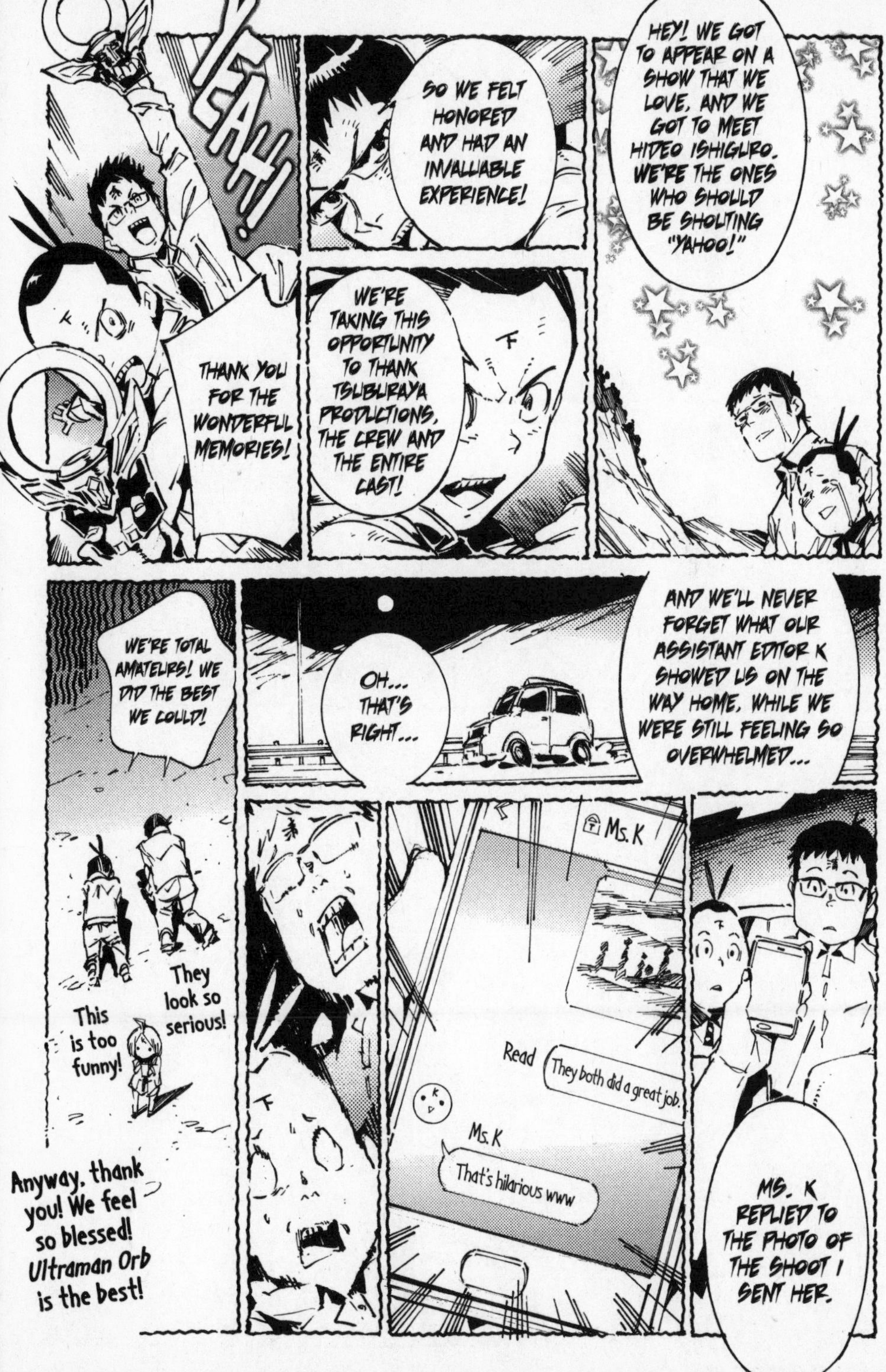
HEY! WE GOT TO APPEAR ON A SHOW THAT WE LOVE, AND WE GOT TO MEET HIDEO ISHIGURO. WE'RE THE ONES WHO SHOULD BE SHOUTING "YAHOO!"
SO WE FELT HONORED AND HAD AN INVALUABLE EXPERIENCE!
WE'RE TAKING THIS OPPORTUNITY TO THANK TSUBURAYA PRODUCTIONS, THE CREW AND THE ENTIRE CAST!
YEAH!
THANK YOU FOR THE WONDERFUL MEMORIES!
AND WE'LL NEVER FORGET WHAT OUR ASSISTANT EDITOR K SHOWED US ON THE WAY HOME, WHILE WE WERE STILL FEELING SO OVERWHELMED...
OH... THAT'S RIGHT...
MS. K REPLIED TO THE PHOTO OF THE SHOOT I SENT HER.
Ms. K
Read
They both did a great job.
Ms. K
That's hilarious www
WE'RE TOTAL AMATEURS! WE DID THE BEST WE COULD!
They look so serious!
This is too funny!
Anyway, thank you! We feel so blessed! Ultraman Orb is the best!

EIICHI SHIMIZU ✕ TOMOHIRO SHIMOGUCHI

You'll know after reading the bonus manga at
the end of the volume, but we did something
unspeakable. So we'd like to apologize in advance.
We're very sorry!!!
But it was so much fun!!
And even more nerve-racking!!

ULTRAMAN
VOLUME 9
VIZ SIGNATURE EDITION

STORY/ART BY EIICHI SHIMIZU AND TOMOHIRO SHIMOGUCHI

Originally published by HERO'S INC.

TRANSLATION JOE YAMAZAKI
ENGLISH ADAPTATION STAN!
TOUCH-UP ART & LETTERING EVAN WALDINGER
DESIGN KAM LI
EDITOR MIKE MONTESA

Printed in the U.S.A.

Published by VIZ Media, LLC
P.O. Box 77010
San Francisco, CA 94107

10 9 8 7 6 5 4 3 2 1
First printing, October 2017

VIZ SIGNATURE

www.viz.com

PARENTAL ADVISORY
ULTRAMAN is rated T for Teen and is recommended for ages 13 and up. This volume contains realistic and fantasy violence.

RATED T FOR TEEN

ratings.viz.com

HEY! YOU'RE READING IN THE WRONG DIRECTION!

This is the END of the graphic novel

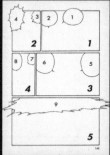

Follow the action this way.

To properly enjoy this VIZ graphic novel, please turn it around and begin reading from RIGHT TO LEFT. Unlike English, Japanese is read right to left, so Japanese comics are read in reverse order from the way English comics are typically read.

This book has been printed in the original Japanese format in order to preserve the orientation of the original artwork.

HAVE FUN WITH IT!